James H. McBurney, *Professor of Speech and Dean of the School of Speech, Northwestern University.*

Glen E. Mills, *Professor of Speech and Assistant Dean of the School of Speech, Northwestern University.*

Argumentation and Debate

TECHNIQUES OF A FREE SOCIETY

SECOND EDITION

The Macmillan Company

Collier-Macmillan Limited, London

Fifth Printing, 1969

Library of Congress catalog card number: 64-10584

THE MACMILLAN COMPANY

COLLIER-MACMILLAN CANADA, LTD., TORONTO, ONTARIO

Printed in the United States of America

Preface

THIS BOOK is an extensive revision of *Argumentation and Debate,* a work that has been in print for over half a century with several authors participating. Specifically, this is a revision of the 1951 edition written by the present authors in collaboration with Professor James M. O'Neill. Professor O'Neill, who has been associated with this enterprise for many years, has not participated in this revision. We acknowledge our indebtedness to him, and respectfully and affectionately dedicate this edition to him.

Our purpose here remains the same: to provide a sound, readable book for use in college and university courses in argumentation and debate and for all students interested in debating. Teachers and others familiar with earlier editions will note a few basic changes in emphasis and point of view, as well as many restatements of familiar doctrine designed to sharpen and clarify our analysis. We have tried to profit by the experiences of our own students in the classroom and in debating activities, and by the research in this field here and elsewhere over the past decade. In the degree that we have succeeded, we may be forgiven the hope that this edition will continue a long tradition of service to teachers and students alike.

Argumentation and debate are the modern descendants of studies in rhetoric and dialectic that have occupied students throughout the history of Western education. These studies have suffered various vicissitudes down through the years—there is an ebb and flow in many academic disciplines—but argumentation and debate have always shown a remarkable resilience. This is understandable, because so long as men encounter problems and differences of opinion, and so long as they remain free to discuss these problems, there will be a natural impulse to resolve their differences reasonably and amicably. Any democratic society will necessarily make wide use of argumentation and debate in private and public councils of all kinds. In America we have always done so. Most of our effective deliberative and adjudicative processes today are applications of these principles. There is now abundant evidence of mounting interest in this field among both scholars and practitioners.

We regard argumentation and debate as a liberal study of value to all students. These values will best be achieved when the principles and methods set forth here are applied to significant public questions of sufficient depth and breadth to merit serious study. The capacity to investigate, analyze, and represent such questions competently and responsibly is worthy of the best efforts of all students. Properly conducted, such a course of study is rigorous and demanding, but richly rewarding.

In this edition, Mr. McBurney is primarily responsible for Chapters 1 through 4, 6, and 8 through 10; Mr. Mills is primarily responsible for Chapters 5, 7, and 11 through 19.

James H. McBurney

Glen E. Mills

Contents

Chapter I

AN INTRODUCTION
TO ARGUMENTATION
AND DEBATE

Argumentation and debate are among the oldest disciplines in American education. Their antecedents reach back to the beginnings of Western education in ancient Greece and Rome. Many generations of American students have studied in these fields. And so long as we are a free society with democratic institutions, we may expect this interest to continue.

The purpose of this opening chapter is to lay down a few guidelines that will help direct this study and relate it to active participation in a free society.

SOME PRELIMINARY
DEFINITIONS

Argumentation defined.   Argumentation, we think, is best defined as *a method of analysis and reasoning designed to provide acceptable bases for belief and action.* As such, it provides an apparatus for testing propositions and representing them in reasoned discourse, written or oral.

As we shall see more fully in Chapter 3, argumentation typically begins with a proposition—an allegation, a claim, an appraisal, a recommendation, or a proposal. Any proposition can be affirmed or denied with or without qualifications. Most responsible people will wish to examine these claims on their credence and on their conduct carefully and critically before making commitments. Argumentation provides methods for examining and presenting such claims. At the risk of oversimplification, these methods consist essentially in discovering, arranging, and presenting cases (evidence and argument) for and against propositions in question. This process can be a valuable aid in reaching decisions on moot questions in situations varying from the privacy of one's own study to public debate.

Criticism and persuasion. In an earlier edition of this book, argumentation was defined as "the art or activity by which one person, through the use of reasoned discourse, seeks to get other persons to believe or to do what he wants them to believe or do." Our present view is that this definition neglects the critical function of argumentation and overemphasizes the personal involvement and desires of the advocate.

Let us say that you are considering the proposition that the legal voting age be lowered to eighteen in all national elections. The methods of argumentation explained in this book will tell you how to define, analyze, investigate, and argue the proposition pro and con. This process most certainly will help you reach an intelligent, informed opinion on the question, whether or not you choose to defend or oppose it in any public way. Moreover, it is quite possible for you to argue one side of this question in front of others without meaning to commit yourself irrevocably, and without "wanting" others to agree with your position except as your arguments recommend such endorsement. In short, such a proposition may be regarded as an hypothesis, and may be argued critically without personal involvement in the outcome. In this capacity, argumentation is essentially an instrument for judging and testing propositions, rather than an instrument for persuasion, as it is commonly understood.

In many—perhaps most—situations in which argument takes place, the speaker (or writer) deliberately seeks the acceptance of the proposition he is arguing. And whenever this is the case—whenever a speaker uses language to get other people to believe or do what he wants them to believe or do—he is attempting to persuade. The contribution of argumentation to this business of persuasion lies primarily in analysis and reasoned discourse. It is true, of course, that language may be used for purely emotional suggestion, without recourse to logical analysis or reasoning, in attempts to influence another person to believe or act. But this is *not* argumentation as we conceive it. Argumentative discourse always has a thread of reasoning running through it. This emphasis, however, by no means precludes the use of suggestion and motivation in arguments that give primary attention to analysis, evidence, and close reasoning.

Historically, the *critical* functions of argumentation have often been discussed as *dialectic,* and the *persuasive* functions of argumentation as *rhetoric.* Both should be recognized and understood by students of argumentation.

Belief and action. Belief and action as purposes of discourse should be distinguished from other possible objectives, such as informing or entertaining. Quite obviously, a speaker may be informative or entertaining (or both) without affecting belief or action and without intending to do so. Argumentative discourse, as we have seen, always attempts to provide acceptable bases for belief and action. If it proves to be informative and entertaining, so much the better, but the primary targets are belief and action. All others are (or should be) secondary.

When we say that argumentation may have as its purpose either belief or action, we may be challenged by some people who say that since either belief or action resulting from argument is a response to the stimuli of the arguer, and since all response necessarily involves action of some kind, either hidden or overt, it shows that we have one objective, namely action, instead of either belief or action. This position is arrived at through the failure to make a sufficient distinction between overt behavior and the hidden action which is involved, to greater or less degree, when the hearer simply agrees privately to himself that the speaker is right. In other words, simple intellectual agreement that is not carried out in overt action should be distinguished from the action that results when the hearer does what the speaker wants him to do (such as contributing money, signing a petition, voting in the affirmative). Regardless of the psychological similarity between the action that is intellectual assent and the action that is open public performance, it is clear that the rhetorical problem of the speaker or writer who is aiming at intellectual assent is very different from the rhetorical problem of the speaker or writer who is aiming at influencing conduct. For this reason it is held to be wise to distinguish in argumentation between belief and action as objectives.

Debate defined. Debate consists of opposing arguments on a given proposition between a supporting affirmative and an opposing negative. Each position, affirmative and negative, is represented by one or more debaters who may or may not collaborate in the stands they take and who may or may not appear in the presence of their opponents. Debate may be carried on either in writing or in speech. Face-to-face oral debate is probably typical, as in conversation when people disagree and defend their positions, or in any kind of a legislative assembly, board meeting, or committee where motions are argued pro and con. But the essence of debate is the confrontation of opposing views through reasoned discourse, no matter what the special circumstances, conditions, or conventions may be under which the debate takes place. As such, debate is one of the more important applications of argumentation. Debate, in fact, *is* argumentation in which advocates represent opposing positions on a specific proposition.

The purposes of debate, like those of argumentation, generally considered, range from the critical exploration of propositions approached as hypotheses to situations in which there is strong commitment and high personal involvement. The essence of debate, we repeat, lies in the juxtaposition and the confrontation of affirmative and negative positions on a given proposition. The audience to which the debate is addressed may be confined to those participating in the debate, or it may extend to any conceivable number of persons who have access to the debate. The debate may or may not be brought to a decision, and the debaters may or may not be participating in a situation in which they are under an obligation to accept a decision if it is given.

Some recent definitions of debate mistake the many accidental characteristics of debate for its essential characteristics. And often these definitions are slanted to make of debate what the authors want to make of it, or to give it what the authors regard as positive, acceptable sanctions. For example, to contend that debate is necessarily or essentially a critical, reflective, cooperative technique for solving problems is to make this kind of mistake. Debate may or may not be "critical" in the commonly accepted meaning of that term; the reasoning involved is typically "intentional" rather than "reflective"; and some of the best debates—many of the great debates in history—are no more "cooperative" than a boxing match presided over by a referee. Such naive distortions can only do the cause of debate a disservice. The fact that debate is often a competition between thoroughly committed advocates who are energetically seeking a favorable decision is an inescapable reality. And to suggest that this kind of debate is somehow or other depraved is to import a value judgment into the discussion that is completely gratuitous in objective definition.

As he reads this book, the student should keep in mind the differences between debating in actual life situations—such as legislature, court, or campaign—and the situations in school or contest debates. Obviously the basic principles of debating are identical in both situations. The debater in the legislature is trying to get a vote on the merits of the proposition, and the debater in the courtroom is trying to get a vote on the sufficiency or insufficiency of the plaintiff's or prosecution's (the affirmative's) case. In the school or contest debate, where the contestant is practicing and learning in order to achieve ability in debating, the debater, if the contest is judged, is trying to get an affirmative vote in regard to his ability as a debater as compared to that of his opponent. However, if the contest is competently judged, the judge will estimate the debater's ability on the basis of how well his debating exemplifies, uses, and observes the sound principles and techniques of debating in actual life.

In addition to these important differences between actual debates and contest debates, the student should bear in mind that there are certain procedural differences among other types of debate. In parliamentary or legislative debate, the debater is subject to the rules of the assembly and the laws under which the assembly is organized, and he has the advantages of any privileges which the laws or rules may give to him as a member of the assembly. For instance, under normal circumstances, a senator debating on the floor of the United States Senate can talk indefinitely and cannot be sued in court for any remarks he may make in the Senate debate. In many assemblies, however, he has limitations as to the frequency with which he can speak or the length of time for which he can hold the floor. The point is that in parliamentary debate the member of the assembly has all the limitations and all the privileges that are expressed in the rules.

In campaign debating, the debater is almost always on his own. He can probably talk for as long as he can hold the attention of the audience, or as long as the audience will stay and listen to him. However, such freedom may be interfered with by some aggressive chairman or other person or group of persons by demonstration, persuasion, or force. Almost any speaker, of course, is subject to the laws of slander, and may be sued if he violates the laws in remarks he makes on the public platform.

In courtroom debating, the lawyers are subject to rather rigid control by the presiding judge, and they are limited in regard to what they may or may not say by the laws of evidence and principles of sound courtroom procedure usually accepted in the courts.

In the informal debating of the street corner, the fireside, and the dinner table, debaters are obviously rather free except for the limitations of good taste, politeness, and the forbearance of their listeners. The debater preparing for a debate in any of these situations should be very careful to consider in advance what his probable privileges and limitations are, and to stay within them without breaking the laws, demanding improper privileges for himself, or violating the ordinary rules of acceptable behavior.

ARGUMENTATION AND
DEBATE IN A FREE SOCIETY

Social values. Controversies big and little arise inevitably and constantly among individuals, groups, and nations. Mankind throughout its history has known and used only two ultimate methods of settling the inevitable controversies which are a part of living. These two methods always and basically are either to *fight it out* and decide the controversy by force, giving the victory necessarily to the side with the stronger muscles, the heavier clubs, the abler armies, or the bigger bombs, or else to *talk it out* and decide it in private conversation, in court, in legislature, or in international conference, giving victory necessarily to the party with the more acceptable (either logically or emotionally) evidence, argument, appeal. In other words, the only ultimate choice is between bullets and arguments—force and reason.

Our American society is and always has been, from colonial times to the present, and probably will be throughout the foreseeable future, a society made up of an aggregation of minorities. We all belong to one or several American minorities. There is in America no homogeneous majority in racial background, religious affiliation, political philosophy, economic interests, or geographical loyalty. In such a society those who preach that we must avoid controversy are simply burying their timid heads in imaginary sand. Those who say we must live in peace and harmony and that therefore we must not engage in controversy and debate are saying substantially that we must cease to live an active, full, responsible life in a free society. Those who seek such peace and harmony as can be obtained only in the absence of differences of opinion and the controversies which inevitably arise from them are incapable of either the satisfactions or the responsibilities of freedom. Such people, of course, will profit little from studying argumentation and debate. In our society they can probably find complete freedom from responsibility, from thinking and acting, only in the shelter of some such social institution as the graveyard or the jail.

There are those who take the position that advocacy, argument, and debate are outmoded activities, no longer of value in a society that seeks to resolve its differences without controversy. This position we believe to be completely unrealistic! In the first place, conflict understood as difference or disagreement must be accepted as a given datum in any society. The question is not whether we are going to have differences of opinion, but rather how we are going to deal with them. In the second place, it is unrealistic to hope that all of these differences can be resolved on the basis of group consensus (agreement) without resort to argumentation and debate. Actually, we shall be very fortunate indeed if we can confine our controversies to the kind of intellectual and verbal differences that we meet in argumentation and debate. To deny people access to free private and public debate (and to deny them training in debate) is to invite the use of force and the denial of freedom in other areas of their lives.

Most important, it should be understood that the basic principles of argumentation—analysis, reasoning, evidence, and others—enter into all rational decision-making, whether "competitive" debate or "cooperative" discussion is the primary approach. These principles necessarily support any worthy consensus. The truth is that consensus per se has neither merit nor morality. Both the social wisdom and the ethical validity of any consensus depends, like any other human decisions, upon the nature of the consensus. If the consensus results from "the pooling of ignorance," or the sacrifice of moral or political principles, or other specious rewards, the consensus is always an evil thing. If, on the other hand, the consensus results from a distribution and understanding of accurate information, from sound reasoning, from an acceptance of valid principles and decent objectives, the consensus is a fine thing. Whether any discussion or debate ends by serving a decent and legitimate purpose depends inevitably upon the decency and legitimacy of the purpose and the validity of the process by which it is achieved. However, this is a long way from saying that in a world such as ours there is no place for advocacy and debate.

Personal values. If we are right in our analysis of the important role of argumentation and debate in a free society, it is hardly necessary to argue its importance in the lives of people who make up this society. Every person in a free society (except possibly the hermit and the recluse) will find it necessary and very much to his advantage to be able to represent his convictions competently in all sorts of private and public forums where ideas, values, and policies are being assessed. And whether or not we choose to participate as advocates, it is certain that we are all frequently on the receiving end of arguments aimed at us. It is almost impossible for any person who lives in a free society to avoid being in a position in which he has to react to argumentation. For his own protection, then, if nothing else, in order that he may evaluate with some degree of capability the written and spoken arguments to which we are all constantly exposed, every person should understand the technique of argument and be able to distinguish good argument from bad.

This book is prepared in the expectation that it will be helpful to those who are alive to the realities of the rewards and satisfactions, and the responsibilities, of a full and active life in a free society. It is prepared in the further conviction that unless our society can somehow develop citizens who are aware of, and able to promote and defend, the rewards and satisfactions of a free society through the effective use of argumentation and debate, we shall inevitably cease to be a free society.

EXERCISES

1. Discuss the following statement in relation to the point of view developed in this chapter: "The essential need is the improvement of the methods and conditions of debate, discussion, and persuasion. That is *the* need of the public." —John Dewey, *The Public and Its Problems*, p. 208.

2. Discuss the ways in which a speech designed to secure belief might be expected to differ from one designed to get action.

3. Write a two-hundred-word essay setting out what you believe to be proper objectives in the study of argumentation and debate. Read the Preface to this book and Chapter 1 before writing the paper. Compare these papers in class.

4. Discuss the relationships between the ideas in this chapter and one of the controversies that appear in the appendix.

Chapter 2

THE RESPONSIBILITIES
OF THE ADVOCATE

An advocate is one who attempts to provide acceptable bases for belief and action through analysis and reasoning. As we have seen, such advocacy embraces both the critical and persuasive functions of argumentation and debate. In this chapter we deal with the rights and responsibilities of the advocate in the performance of these tasks.

RESPONSIBILITY FOR THE
PROPOSITION

As we shall see in Chapter 3, the propositions with which advocates deal may be of their own choice (a result of their own inquiry and investigation), or they may be dictated by circumstances which limit this choice in very practical ways. Anyone who deliberately attempts to influence the belief and action of others in directions which he knows (or thinks he knows) to be false and unwise, if he has a completely free choice in the matter, is quite obviously in a difficult moral situation. Such advocacy is basically dishonest, and every effort consistent with the tenets of a free society should be made to expose such impostors. Fortunately, *free* public discussion and debate have within them the means of separating the true from the false and the honest from the dishonest in such ways as to protect society. Much of what is said in this book is written to explain how this can and should be accomplished.

We would be completely unrealistic, however, if we failed to recognize that the advocate does not always have a free choice in selecting the proposition. Many institutions in a free society that make use of argumentation and debate exist for the precise purpose of determining truth, wisdom, and justice. Our courts are such institutions, and they will serve as an example here. Lawyers appear before our courts as professional advocates. In this capacity their choice of propositions is limited by the circumstances of their clients. To be sure, they do not have to take a case, but our whole system of jurisprudence is based on the assumption that a man is innocent until he is proved guilty in a duly constituted court. He has a right to a trial and the right to expect that a competent advocate will undertake his defense. If we adjudge such an advocate morally reprehensible for taking the case, we are, in effect, judging the accused before the trial takes place.

Actually, there are many circumstances which may commit honest advocates to propositions—circumstances which at least *limit* freedom of choice. These may be circumstances of employment, as in the case of a salesman or public-relations counsel; circumstances of representation, as in the case of a man who represents a constituency; and circumstances of prior commitment, where promises have been made. These cases are illustrative of many factors which may limit the choice of an advocate in the propositions he elects to defend and attack, and they may or may not justify his decisions. It should be clear, however, that the decision to defend a proposition is in many circumstances a complex moral decision which one cannot consider morally reprehensible without knowing the factors which limit or dictate the choice.

RESPONSIBILITY FOR THE
CONDUCT OF THE ARGUMENT

Once a cause has been undertaken, the advocate has a responsibility to present *the best possible case for his proposition within the limits of the facts as he knows them or believes them to be.* He should not deliberately do less, nor does he have any moral right to attempt more. No man has a moral right to lie, cheat, or intentionally distort, much less a responsibility to do so. What is more, the practice of argumentation and debate in a free society is one of the better ways of exposing lying, cheating, and distortion by means that are not designed to make life pleasant for those who resort to such practices.

The primary purpose of the advocate is to secure belief (or action) through proof. By "belief" we mean conviction—the acceptance of a proposition on intellectual grounds or grounds which are thought to be logically adequate. It implies voluntary acceptance of a statement of fact, value, or policy on the assumption that this statement is true, just, or wise. The person who "believes" may or may not be correct in his conviction, but he thinks he is, and for reasons which appear to him to be adequate.

One way of influencing belief is through proof. By "proof" we mean a logical demonstration which establishes the truth, justice, or wisdom of a proposition or the *probability* that the proposition is true, just, and wise. Unfortunately, perhaps, the correlation between belief and proof is not a perfect one. In other words, people do not always believe what has been proved, and they most certainly believe many things which have not been proved. We are not unaware of the psychological factors that influence belief—emotions, desires, tastes, and the like; nor do we underestimate the powerful influence of faith. These factors can and often should be brought to the aid of proof in attempting to influence belief and action. Actually, they are inescapable in matters of human conduct.

The study and practice of argumentation and debate involve four basic assumptions which merit careful consideration.

Propositions can be proved. First, it is assumed that propositions *can* be proved, that evidence and argument can be adduced in support of a thesis to establish it as a true, just, or wise position. At least it is assumed that demonstrations can be presented which show that a proposition is more likely to be true than untrue, more likely to be just than unjust, and more likely to be wise than unwise. Only the confirmed skeptic would deny this assumption.

Truth, justice, and wisdom are more powerful than their opposites. It is further assumed that a proposition shown to embody truth, justice, or wisdom is more likely to prevail than one which is false, unjust, or unwise. Other things being equal, a sound proposition has a better chance for acceptance because it offers greater possibilities for support and defense. As Aristotle put it more than two thousand years ago, ". . . truth and justice are by nature more powerful than their opposites; so that, when decisions are not made as they should be, the speakers with the right on their side have only themselves to thank for the outcome." [1]

Rational decisions are preferred. Third, it is assumed that rational behavior is to be preferred to irrational behavior. In other words, it is desirable that men give their assent to propositions on rational grounds. Rational commitments are more likely to be sound, and they are pragmatically more significant because they are understandable. A man who believes something for good reason and knows *why* he believes it is in a better position than one who accepts blindly.

Emotional reactions are more easily enlisted in intellectually defensible causes. Finally, it is assumed that man's sympathies, tastes, faiths, desires, and intuitions are more natural allies of truth, justice, and wisdom than they are of the false, the unjust, and the unwise. The advocate who proves his point is in a better position to enlist the emotions of his listeners in his cause than one who does not. Rational behavior and emotional impulses are

---

[1] Aristotle's *Rhetoric* I. 1.

more likely to pull together than to pull apart. Even if more people can "feel" truly than can "think" accurately, there appears to be an inherent desire for truth, justice, and decency.

These basic assumptions not only lay the groundwork for what we believe to be a sound philosophy in argumentation and debate, but they also constitute a credo for the advocate—sound working principles for the speaker who seeks to influence the belief and action of others.

RESPONSIBILITIES TO
THE AUDIENCE

Arguments, written or oral, are aimed at audiences. The audience may be one person, or a hundred, or a hundred thousand, or more—any number. A listening audience may be in the speaker's presence, or removed, as in the case of radio or television. The audience may be known to the speaker, as in direct interpersonal communication, or largely unknown. In some cases, the speaker's only audience may be the person or persons with whom he is contending. In other cases, he (and his opponents, if any) may be primarily interested in a judge, jury, or some other third party. In any case, it is fairly obvious that a speaker's responsibilities to his audience will vary with time, place, and circumstances. It is possible, however, to lay down two guidelines that provide helpful directives in most situations.

Conduct yourself as though you had primary responsibility for the outcome of the argument. It is true that speakers will occasionally find themselves in situations where their interest in the proceedings is at most academic—situations in which the audience quite patently has much more at stake than they have. In such cases, an advocate can adopt a "take it or leave it" attitude if he chooses. Except in very rare cases indeed, we doubt the wisdom of this choice. If a proposition is worth representing at all, it is worth the best efforts of the speaker to carry conviction. This imposes a responsibility on the speaker to make himself understood and to accommodate his case to the predispositions of his audience within the limits of his logical responsibilities. The best advocacy is at once logically rigorous and persuasively designed. Adaptations that compromise sound analysis, evidence, and argument are not the best persuasion, and they may be dishonest.

Conduct yourself as though a competent, informed opponent were present. Of course, in many cases, competent, informed opponents *are* present and ready to point out weaknesses in your argument—poor evidence, fallacies, and cheap stratagems. Never underestimate your audience. If you always make the assumption that your case will be examined critically, you are less likely to do your audience a disservice, and you are on much safer ground yourself.

PROBABILITIES

From the standpoint of acceptance, a proposition may be regarded as *possible, plausible, probable,* or *certainly true.* These same terms may be used to characterize the support or the demonstration which the advocate offers in behalf of a proposition.

To show that a proposition is possible at best gives it the status of a hypothesis which one is willing to entertain as a possibility. When a man says, "That is possible," he does not mean to say that he accepts nor that he is disposed to accept. He says only, "That may be true."

Plausibility moves a step beyond possibility. The plausible proposition is one which appears likely. But discreet individuals will not ordinarily commit themselves on grounds of plausibility. They want more proof and are entitled to it. A quick, superficial analysis may lead one to give enough credence to a thesis to say it is plausible—"It appears to be true," or "It is worth looking into" —but it cannot as yet be depended upon as a basis for conviction or action.

When an advocate shows that a proposition is probable, he has shown that it is more likely to be true than untrue. He has shown it to be the most "likely" description, interpretation, or position among those available. It is the "best bet." It is true beyond a reasonable doubt. The establishment of such probabilities is the primary purpose of argumentation and debate. Under most circumstances a speaker cannot do more or be expected to do more. Sensible people govern their lives by probabilities. Indeed, in most areas in which argumentation and debate play any significant role, it cannot be otherwise.

It is a nice question to ask whether any proposition can be regarded as certainly true or whether any demonstration can achieve absolute and final certainty. Many modern scientists appear to support relativism in all areas of thought. Fortunately, this profound philosophical question does not have to be settled in order to clarify the role of argumentation and debate. No one will deny that the advocate should seek the best possible demonstration for his proposition. In some cases, such demonstrations will approach "practical" certainty. Propositions which lend themselves to such demonstrations are not the usual questions for public discussion and debate, however, because their very certainty removes them from the realm of debatable questions.

Classical writers in this field point out that argumentation and debate have their greatest usefulness in the fields of "ethics and politics." In more modern terminology, this is to say that questions amenable to argumentation and debate are usually those of value and of policy involving social, political, and economic issues. Actually, all personal and public questions of a controversial nature, about which people can and do differ in their opinions, lend themselves to debate. For many centuries debate has been the principal policy-determining method in such situations. As we shall see in the next chapter, many questions of fact must also be adjudicated by debate, as, for example, in a court of law.

In terms of this analysis, it may be said that argumentation and debate operate in the realm of probabilities. The purpose of the advocate is to present in support of a proposition a case which demonstrates the proposition to be true beyond reasonable doubt, or to demonstrate the proposition to be more probably true than false. In other words, he seeks to show that the probabilities are in favor of the proposition, cause, thesis, or position he is advocating.

PRESUMPTIONS

The best way to describe the logical responsibilities of the advocate is in terms of presumptions, burden of proof, and burden of rebuttal. Richard Whately presents one of the most competent treatments of this subject.

It is a point of great importance to decide in each case, at the outset, in your own mind, and clearly to point out to the hearer, as occasion may serve, on which side the *Presumption* lies, and to which belongs the (onus probandi) *Burden of Proof.* For though it may be expedient to bring forward more proofs than can be fairly *demanded* of you, it is always desirable, when this is the case, that it should be *known*, and that the strength of the cause should be estimated accordingly.

According to the most correct usage of the term, a "Presumption" in favour of any supposition means, not (as has been sometimes erroneously imagined) a preponderance of probability in its favour, but, such a *preoccupation* of the ground, as implies that it must stand good till some sufficient reason is adduced against it; in short, that the *Burden of Proof* lies on the side of him who would dispute it.[2]

The crux of Whately's explanation of presumptions is in the phrase "a preoccupation of the ground." The presumption is always with "things as they are." It may be defined as the *advantage* which lies with the party who is *defending* things as they are, or as they are commonly accepted or believed to be. As Whately very properly points out, this advantage does not mean that the position of the defense is any stronger or more probable than that of the party who opposes it. It is the function of the debate to assess the probabilities for purposes of decision. The "advantage" of the presumption is limited to such benefits as accrue to the party who is "in possession of the ground," who is defending the status quo or "an opinion commonly held." The nature of this advantage can be illustrated by the following example. A body

---

[2] Richard Whately, *Elements of Rhetoric*, Seventh Edition (London: John W. Parker, West Strand, 1846), p. 112.

of troops occupies a fortress which the opposing troops must take if they are to win their objective. The advantage has nothing to do with the merits of the cause for which the troops are fighting, and nothing to do with the relative strength of the opposing parties. The advantage is in the fact that one of the parties to the action is "in possession" and presumably will remain in possession until a decisive attack is made by the opposition.

Some of the more common presumptions encountered are the presumption in favor of existing institutions, the presumption of innocence, the presumption in favor of possession, and the presumptions in favor of traditions, customs, habits, mores, creeds, doctrines, and laws now in use or generally accepted.

With this explanation in mind, it is not difficult to see the great practical importance of knowing where the presumption lies in any situation which calls for argument. If the presumption is in your favor, you may fairly demand that your opponent show cause for reply before you advance any argument; and if you do choose to go forward with the argument even though the responsibility is not yours, it is decidedly in your interests to do so with full knowledge of this fact and with adequate explanation to all interested parties. On the other hand, if the presumption is against you, you have the obligation of initiating the argument and presenting a case for your position. If you fail to do this, your opponent may maintain his silence with impunity.

This whole doctrine of presumption is pretty much a matter of common sense. Let us say that you live in a community where divided opinion develops on the need for a new high-school building. If you oppose this project, quite obviously you are under no obligation to make a case against the new building until someone has made a case for it. After all, you are satisfied with the present building. If a campaign for the new building gathers sufficient momentum to challenge your position, then you had better organize a campaign against it. Should you choose to speak out against the new building before any case has been made for it, the risk you run of stirring up opposition that might not otherwise develop should be calculated, and the reasons for your apparent prematurity made clear to all concerned if it seems wise to do so.

THE BURDEN OF PROOF

The burden of proof is defined as "the risk of the proposition"—the burden upon that party to the controversy who will lose if nothing is done. It is the burden of making good his claim, and rests upon the one who starts an action, who demands a change from the existing situation. In terms of presumptions, the burden of proof may be defined as the responsibility which rests upon that party to the controversy who has the presumption against him. He is the dissatisfied party, the party who is opposing the status quo or an existing institution, custom, law, or creed. The responsibilities of the party with the burden of proof are identical with those of the party who has the presumption against him. He must present what we shall later explain as a "prima-facie case" (a case logically sufficient to raise a presumption in his favor) before he has any claim to a reply from the man who has the initial presumption in his favor in the argument.

As in the case of presumptions, it is a matter of considerable practical importance to understand the burden of proof and know where it lies in any controversy. The sides in an argument and their responsibilities are determined by the burden of proof. The *affirmative* should be understood as the party or side with the burden of proof, and the *negative* as the party or side with the presumption in its favor. Wherever there is debating which pays proper attention to logical sequence and economy of time, the case of the affirmative (opposing the present and advocating the new) is always advanced before the defense of the negative.

There are three vexing questions in argumentation concerning the burden of proof which need clarification: (1) How do changing situations and conditions affect the burden of proof? (2) How does a counterproposition affect the burden of proof? And (3) does the burden of proof ever shift in a debate? To illustrate the first of these problems, suppose it is proposed that Illinois adopt a state income tax. Since Illinois does not now have a state income tax, the burden of proof lies with the party who proposes it. If Illinois were to adopt an income tax at a later date, the burden of proof would then rest on the party who proposed its abolition. Changing conditions do affect the burden of proof in ways which are perfectly consistent with our definition of the burden of proof. This burden always rests with the party which opposes whatever may be the status quo at the time of the debate in the jurisdiction in which the change is proposed.

Whenever the answer of the negative takes the form of a counterproposition (in law an "affirmative defense"), it seeks to defeat the affirmative proposal by offering another proposal which counters that of the affirmative. In this case, the negative, of course, becomes essentially an affirmative, and has the burden of proof *on the new proposition*. For example, if in a first-degree murder case the answer of the defense is not that the accused did not kill the deceased, but that the accused was insane at the time, the defense has put forth a counterproposition. For the time being, the question at issue is not, "*Resolved,* That A is guilty of murder in the first degree," but, "*Resolved,* That A is (or was at the time in question) insane." On this proposition the original defense becomes the affirmative. The accused is presumed to be sane until the contrary is established. The original prosecution becomes the negative, and seeks to prevent the establishment of the fact of insanity. Here, clearly, there is no shifting of the original burden of proof. There is a new proposition with a burden of proof of its own, and this burden is on the new affirmative and never shifts.

It is frequently said that the burden of proof can shift from one side to the other in a debate. As we have defined the burden of proof here—and this is the only proper definition in general argumentation—the burden of proof *never* shifts. The man who has "the risk of the proposition" at the beginning of the argument holds it throughout the argument. To be sure, there devolves upon his opponent (the negative) a responsibility to reply when he (the affirmative) has presented a prima-facie case, but this does not mean that the burden of proof has shifted. The final adjudication of any argument will be made in the light of the original affirmative case, the rejoinder by the negative, and such replies and counterreplies as may be made by both sides. *All* of these arguments must be assessed in terms of the responsibilities imposed by the burden of proof—the success of the affirmative in discharging this burden in relation to the success of the negative in defending the presumption in its favor. To say that the burden of proof shifts after each reply serves only to confuse the final accounting.

THE BURDEN OF
REBUTTAL

The burden of proof (understood as "the risk of the proposition") does *not* shift, but the responsibility of "going forward with the argument" may, and usually does, change sides in a debate. As we have seen, the negative has a responsibility to reply after the affirmative has presented a prima-facie case, and the negative rejoinder may call for an answer from the affirmative. Unless there are prearranged agreements as to the number of replies and counterreplies, these may be limited only by the endurance of the protagonists or the settlement of the question. We shall refer to this responsibility of going forward with the argument as the "burden of rebuttal." Unlike the burden of proof, it may shift many times in a debate—just as many times as the parties to a controversy advance arguments of sufficient merit to demand a reply.

EXERCISES

1. Discuss the following statements. Are they true or false? Why?
   a. A lawyer has no moral right to defend a guilty man.
   b. Since you have not proved your proposition, it should not be accepted.
   c. A man who loses an argument has only himself to thank for the outcome.
   d. The man with the presumption on his side in an argument is defending a sound proposition.
2. Discuss the following statement: "Fortunately, *free* public discussion and debate have within them the means of separating the true

from the false and the honest from the dishonest in such ways as to protect society."

3. How are presumptions determined in argumentation and debate? Why is a man presumed to be innocent until he is proved guilty?

4. Where do the presumptions lie on the following propositions? Why?

    a. Honesty is the best policy.
    b. The President should be elected for a single six-year term.
    c. John Doe is a thief.
    d. Let's go to the movie tonight.
    e. The world is round.

5. Discuss the following statements. Are they true or false? Why?
    a. The burden of proof never shifts in debate.
    b. The burden of rebuttal never shifts in debate.
    c. The burden of proof rests with the party who has the presumption against him.
    d. The burden of proof shifts to the negative when the negative proposes a counterproposition.

6. How do the responsibilities discussed in this chapter apply to each writer and speaker in the appendix debates?

Chapter 3

THE PROPOSITION

THE NATURE OF
PROPOSITIONS

The proposition defined.   The word "proposition" is used in several fields of knowledge, as well as in colloquial speech, and its meanings are consequently varied. Linguistically, a proposition is a declarative sentence; psychologically, it is any judgment expressed in words; logically, it is a statement that is capable of being either true or false; rhetorically, as in argumentation, it is a judgment expressed in a declarative sentence which the listener or reader is asked to accept. The last meaning will be used in this book.

This judgment is stated in a declarative sentence consisting of two terms and a copula. The subject of the sentence is one term, the verb is the copula or connecting link, and the object of the verb or some other predicative expression is the other term. A judgment so stated is a proposition. The following propositions are divided into their three parts:

First Term	*Copula*	*Second Term*
Dictatorships	are	undemocratic.
Public utilities	should be	regulated.
Honesty	is	the best policy.

The proposition distinguished from other statements. A proposition is the indispensable basis of fruitful argumentation. It must be stated, or at least understood, as a complete sentence. The titles of discourses which are primarily narrative, descriptive, or expository need not be stated in sentence form, nor are they propositions: "My Experiences as a Football Player" suggests a narrative; "How to Play Guard" befits an exposition; and "Drama and Color in the Stadium" is appropriate for a description. A proposition for argumentative discourse must state, or be understood as, a sentence, such as, "Intercollegiate Football Should Be Abolished." These distinctions do not deny the frequent use of all four forms of discourse in a primarily argumentative composition.

Forms in which propositions are stated. Subjects for debate in parliamentary assemblies are expressed as motions, resolutions, or bills. In less formal situations the matter in dispute is often expressed as a statement of opinion, as a question, or as a single term. Lengthy propositions of educational debate may be shortened for publicity purposes into terse questions. It is erroneous to assume that there is no proposition simply because the subject is not formally phrased. However, all parties concerned in an argument should at least understand a complete sentence which poses the controversy.

The forms of statement are illustrated in the following table:

MOTION	Mr. Chairman, I move that the question be laid on the table.
RESOLUTION	*Resolved,* That capital punishment should be abolished.
BILL	Be it enacted by the Senate and House of Representatives of the United States of America in Congress assembled, That . . .
STATEMENT OF OPINION	Bridge is more fun than poker.
QUESTION	Should Railroads Be Publicly Owned?
SINGLE TERM	Public Ownership of Railroads.

THE FUNCTIONS OF
A PROPOSITION

To express a conclusion from study and reflection. A proposition is often (perhaps usually) a conclusion from study, reflection, inquiry, investigation, or discussion. In this capacity it should accurately express the conviction of the person or persons making the inquiry. It should represent their conclusion, their attitude toward the problem, the position on which they take their stand.

If an advocate discovers during the course of debate that the proposition he originally advanced no longer represents his convictions, he is at liberty to announce this change and to propose a new or revised proposition. This means, in effect, that he has conceded on his original contention and that the debate on the original proposition is over. The new proposition, if such is proposed, provides the basis for another debate should anyone choose to oppose this new position.

There are circumstances, of course, in which concession on the part of a debater during the course of debate would create an anomalous situation. In a school debate (contest debate), for example, where the convictions of the debaters may or may not be involved, it is expected that the debate will proceed on the original proposition under the agreed conditions.

To express the meaning and intent of an advocate. In all circumstances, the proposition should express the meaning and intent of the advocate. This is true irrespective of the source of the proposition and the speaker's convictions with respect to it. Any man who makes a motion or proposition has the *privilege* of phrasing the proposition, and the *responsibility* of making his meaning and intent clear. So long as he uses language accurately, he is within his rights in interpreting the proposition as he sees fit. A negative has no right to tell the affirmative what the affirmative means by its own proposition, so long as the affirmative interpretation is a reasonable and linguistically accurate one.

If the affirmative fails to make its meaning clear, or chooses to place strained and unreasonable interpretations on the terms of the proposition, the negative has a right to object. The discussion of the meaning of terms, which often occurs in a debate, should not be stigmatized as "quibbling" when a serious effort is being made to determine the intent of the affirmative and whether or not the affirmative interpretation is a legitimate interpretation of the proposition. "Quibbling" means a confusing or distorting misuse of words and ideas to evade the point or the truth. No intelligent debate can take place until the meaning of the advocate is clear.

Occasionally the discussion of meaning of terms will result in a situation in which debaters who *thought* they were opposed on the proposition will discover that they are, in fact, in agreement. Such agreement on the proposition, of course, means that the debate is over, unless the debaters are under some special obligation to continue. The clarification of terms, of meaning and intent, thus serves the very useful purpose of joining the debaters on a precise issue or else resolving the matter without further discussion.

To serve as the basis of the argument. Regardless of how formally or informally a proposition is stated, it should be the basis of every argument. An intelligent argumentative discourse cannot take place in the absence of such a statement. Thus a speaker or writer should phrase the proposition for his own use, even though he does not express it to his public.

When an individual is presenting one side of an argument, a well-phrased proposition is necessary if he is to analyze and organize his material adequately. Such a statement also assists listeners or readers in following the argument, because they are enabled to see the end in view and can relate individual arguments to that end or proposition. However, in dealing with a hostile audience, a speaker should determine whether it is wise to state his proposition at the outset.

When two or more persons speak and both sides are presented, a well-phrased proposition serves to keep the controversy within proper bounds. At times the statement of a proposition can even prevent pointless and futile argument. From the standpoint of the audience, it is a part of critical listening to attempt to identify the proposition, even if the disputants do not state it.

To name the affirmative and the negative. There are two sides to every argument—the affirmative, which favors the proposition, and the negative, which opposes it.

The fact that several positions may be taken on a proposition does not mean that there are more than two sides. One may affirm or deny for many different reasons. For instance, an advocate might oppose compulsory health insurance because it would allegedly undermine private medicine, or he might take the position that the extension of voluntary plans of health insurance is preferable. The taking of either of these positions would place one on the negative side.

To state the desired audience reaction. Since an advocate seeks to influence attitudes and actions, his proposition should state the desired reaction. It should tell the audience what they are being asked to buy, join, view with alarm, etc. One pragmatic test of the advocate's success is the willingness or unwillingness of the listeners to react as the proposition directs. Persuasive communication is unlikely if speakers and their audiences do not have a common notion of what is to be favored or opposed. Thus a proposition should not merely mention compulsory arbitration, for instance, but should call for its adoption or rejection in a definite context.

To place the presumption and the burden of proof. We have previously discussed the key concepts of presumption and burden of proof as they relate to matters of probability. One function of a correctly worded proposition is the placing of the burden of proof on the affirmative and the granting of the benefit of presumption to the negative. Thus the burden of proof falls upon the supporters of a well-worded motion—the state in a criminal trial, the plaintiff in a civil action, and the affirmative in a school debate on a properly worded proposition. The opposing side in each case has the initial benefit of presumption.

However, if the proposition is improperly worded, the side which nominally affirms it may escape the burden of proof. In order to understand this, it is necessary to distinguish between the nominal affirmative and the actual affirmative. The nominal (bearing the name of) affirmative is the side which affirms (says "yes" to) the proposition. The actual affirmative is always the side which has the burden of proof and thus remains unsatisfied if no action is taken.

Wrong: Congress should enact a federal income tax.
Right: Congress should reduce the federal income tax 10 per cent in all brackets.

Since we already have a federal income tax, the nominal affirmative (saying "yes") in the "wrong" proposition will be satisfied if no change is made, and is therefore the actual negative. On the same proposition the nominal negative (saying "no") is the actual affirmative, because it will be dissatisfied if nothing is done. The "right" proposition is worded so that the nominal and the actual affirmatives are the same, and the nominal and the actual negatives are also the same. Thus a properly phrased proposition always places the burden of proof on the affirmative and gives the benefit of presumption to the negative.

A CLASSIFICATION
OF PROPOSITIONS

The three types of propositions encountered in argumentation and debate are those of fact, value, and policy. The methods of analysis and proof discussed in later chapters are related to these propositional types.

Propositions of fact. These are statements alleging the existence of something—an object, an event, or relationship—at a point in time—past, present, or future. Such propositions purport to be accurate designations or descriptions of objects, events, or relationships that have existed in the past, exist now, or will exist in the future. Here are some examples:

John Doe is guilty of first-degree murder.
The election of the President by direct vote would impair states' rights.
Nuclear explosions affect weather conditions.

*We may expect the organization of a third major baseball
league in the near future.*

*Democracy, in the sense of social-political-economic equal-
ity of opportunity, does not exist in the United States.*

Propositions of value. These express evaluative judgments
concerning the goodness or badness, desirability or undesirability
of some person, institution, or conception without recommending
any policy or action. The following are examples:

*The strike is an ethically legitimate weapon of organized
labor.*

Military training is beneficial to most young men.

Chain stores are detrimental to the American public.

Propositions of policy. These propose a new policy or a
change of policy, and call for some specific action. A proposition
of policy raises the question, Should this be done? Here are some
examples:

Jurisdictional strikes should be outlawed by federal statute.

*The President of the United States should be elected for a
single six-year term.*

Intercollegiate football should be abolished.

The meaning of "should" in propositions of policy is often disputed in school debates. The consensus of experts is that "should"
implies "could" but obviously not "would." Assuming the establishment of a cause of action (need), we may say that a plan
"should" be adopted if it is sound, just, and in other ways the
best of the available remedies.

The foregoing sequence of fact, value, and policy propositions
is based upon developmental complexity. The first depends entirely upon the establishment of fact for proof. The second depends not only upon facts but also upon standards of judgment.
The third involves facts and values, but it extends into considerations of expediency, practicality, and action. In general, proposi-

tions of policy and value are better for debate than are those of fact, because factual matters such as dates of events, population data, authorship, and the like are more properly matters of investigation than of argument.

SELECTING THE
PROPOSITION

Generally speaking, there are three circumstances under which propositions become the subjects for argumentation and debate.

When a problem exists. When any group, however large or small, is confronted with a problem which must be resolved and in which disagreement persists, debate is the logical recourse. In such cases, motions are made and debated. These motions are propositions and are subject to all the requirements and conditions of propositions discussed in this chapter.

When the proposition is given to the advocate. The selection of a subject, or the proposition emerging from it, is often not a matter of independent choice. When an advertising agency or a lawyer is engaged by a client, the proposition and the side are imposed by circumstances. Similarly, when a student "goes out for debate," his proposition or propositions are seldom of his choice. Also, if one becomes a defendant in a legal action, the proposition and his side on it are determined without his being consulted. In case the general subject, but not the specific proposition, is imposed, one should carefully study the situation and phrase the proposition accordingly.

When a deliberate choice is made. There are many occasions on which the speaker is given the privilege of selecting what he is going to talk about. Under these circumstances, there are four general criteria which may help to direct his choice.

Can the proposition be argued profitably? It may be harmful as well as futile to argue propositions which cannot be handled rationally—that is, without emotional tirades. Furthermore, it is unwise to select trivial matters or those of sheer speculation, since they are not worthy of the best efforts of the participants. A substantial proposition of fact, value, or policy is preferable, either for purposes of instruction or policy formation.

Is the proposition adapted to the advocate? The speaker or writer ought to choose his subject and proposition from those fields in which his study and experience enable him to say something of interest and profit to others. He will then express himself with greater conviction, and his audience will be more likely to respect his judgment.

Is the proposition adaptable to the audience? The proposition should be of interest to the audience, or of such a nature that the speaker can make it so. Although one ought not to cater basely to an audience, he is obliged to select propositions (and treatments thereof) which have some potentialities in terms of interest, understanding, and conviction or persuasion.

Is the proposition adapted to the occasion? This criterion of appropriateness applies to the selection of subjects for all kinds of speeches and writings. There is no special doctrine for argumentative discourse. The suitability of subjects in terms of time and place is presumed to be common knowledge among readers of this book.

In case a deliberate choice is made by persons other than the advocate himself, additional criteria are sometimes used. Committee members who are asked to suggest subjects for use in the national referendum of the state high-school debate leagues are advised to bear these criteria in mind:

1. Is the subject of nationwide interest?
2. Is a discussion of the subject in the public interest?
3. Is the proposition to be worded from the subject likely to be removed from the realm of debate by being solved or exhausted during the debate season?
4. Are adequate research materials available, or can they be made available?
5. Is the subject interesting to young people?
6. Will audiences be interested in it?
7. Can a suitable proposition be phrased on this subject?

PHRASING THE
PROPOSITION

Importance of careful phrasing. Since all debate takes place on propositions, either expressed or implied, the phraseology of the proposition is a matter of importance. A resolution, bill, or motion that is poorly phrased is not only likely to result in confusion, but will also probably fail to serve the four functions that propositions should serve.

Some principles of phrasing. In the first place, the proposition should state specifically what the affirmative wants, never what the affirmative does not want. Thus, one widely used proposition calling for the abolition of the jury system is defective in that it fails to specify the scheme which the affirmative prefers. The possible substitutions include a single judge, a board of judges, a commission, etc. Equally objectionable propositions are those which call for the abolishment of the direct primary election or an unspecified change in our method of handling juvenile delinquents. These examples show what can happen if the wording of the resolution fails to state specifically what the affirmative wants.

In the second place, the language of the proposition should be simple and free of ambiguous and question-begging terms. By simple language we mean a degree of plainness that is consistent with accuracy of statement. An ambiguous term is one that may be legitimately interpreted as having two or more different meanings, while a question-begging term is one that slants the proposition in favor of one side. The difficulty which such terms may create is obvious. Consider this proposition, suggested by the Cambridge University team for the American tour in 1947: "In the opinion of this House the extreme emphasis on science and technology in modern education is destroying the foundations of Western Civilization." The word "extreme" is question-begging because it assumes what it should be the affirmative's burden to prove. To correct this fault, the word "present" was substituted for "extreme." An instance of ambiguity may be seen in the proposal, "The state should abolish child labor." What does "child labor" mean, and does "state" mean the federal government or one of the forty-eight states? A recent national proposition for college debates contained the expression "direct share," which was more than ambiguous; it was vague: "That labor should be given a direct share in the management of industry."

In the third place, the wording of the proposition must place the burden of proof on the affirmative. In discussing the functions of the proposition, we have defined burden of proof and presumption, and have shown why the nominal and actual affirmative must coincide. In propositions improperly worded with respect to this matter, there will be confusion as to the two sides and their responsibilities. In a school debate, for example, it is customary for the affirmative to open and close the debate. If the proposition is phrased in such a way as to place the burden of proof on the negative, the team opening the debate (nominal affirmative, but actual negative) will find itself in the position of having to defend the status quo, which has not yet been attacked, and the nominal negative (in this case, the actual affirmative) will be denied its right to close the debate.

The allocation of the burden of proof may be seen in two wordings of the proposal to take some action regarding capital punishment. In Michigan, which does not have the death penalty, we can debate the proposition that it be adopted; in Illinois, which does have it, we can debate the proposition that it be abolished. In both cases the burden of proof is properly placed, because the party saying "yes" to the proposition will be dissatisfied if no action is taken.

Special problems concerning the placing of the burden of proof on the affirmative often arise in phrasing propositions of fact and value. The matter is handled neatly in policy propositions by simply wording the statement so that the affirmative proposes a change. Actually, the same rule holds in questions of fact and value, but how are we to know what position represents a change? What is required here is an assessment of current beliefs and evaluations. Then the proposition should be phrased so that the affirmative is asked to oppose what appear to be widely accepted factual or evaluative judgments.

A fourth requirement is that the desired audience reaction should be stated in a single, declarative sentence. This should be a concise, accurate statement of the belief which the audience is asked to accept or the specific action called for.

A fifth possible requirement is that the proposition be single—that is, that it embody only one central idea. This is akin to the fourth requirement, but it goes further to stipulate that the single sentence must have only one main idea. Otherwise, one might resolve that the term of office of Congressmen be extended to four years and that the Congressional districts be remapped.

Some critics of current practices in the wording of propositions for nationwide use suggest a sixth requirement: that a statement of context be framed to supplement the announced proposition. It is argued that this would reduce uncertainty or argument about the interpretation. Such a statement should, whenever possible, be avoided by exercising great care in phrasing the proposition or by making reference to a specific bill, book, or other document.

Finally, it is argued that the interest of contest debaters and their audiences would be enhanced by modifying the proposition during the season in order to adapt to local conditions or to fit new circumstances. A familiar parallel can be drawn between this procedure and that of amending a motion, bill, or resolution during the process of deliberation. This may well be done whenever agreements can be reached easily in regard to changes.

DEFINING TERMS

So far as possible, propositions should be phrased in terms that are clear and unmistakable without protracted definition. Definitions can be tedious and laborious, especially if the debater appears to be pressing the obvious. But if questions about meaning remain after every effort has been made to state the proposition clearly, simply, and accurately, then the definition of terms is essential.

Definition by Classification. Classification provides the basic method of definition. Understanding of the assumptions underlying such definition is important to the student of argumentation and debate. This matter is related to the process of analyzing the proposition (Chapter 4) and to the nature and structure of argument (Chapter 9).

Meanings are assigned to terms on the basis of their relations to other terms. By placing the term in question in the class or category in which it falls and then differentiating it from other members of this class, it is possible to identify the term. Most dictionary definitions employ this method. A few of these definitions, selected at random, will serve as simple examples:

> *a door* is a movable barrier of wood or other material, commonly turning on hinges or sliding in a groove, for closing and opening a passage into a building, room, cupboard, etc.
> *a doorbell* is a bell at a door or connected with a door, rung by persons outside seeking admittance.
> *a doorknob* is the handle for opening a door.

The following definition of "the humanities" is a much more sophisticated example of the same method.

When we search for the common element among the various types of work usually regarded as humanistic, as well as among the various approaches to a definition of the term, the humanities will be seen to include those forms of art or learning which are directly concerned with human responses to all forms of experience, and therefore primarily with those aspects of human experience "that cannot be resolved into either natural processes common to men and animals or into impersonal forces affecting all members of a given society." Inseparably involved in them are questions of human uses and goals, of the ends toward which men direct themselves and the means they use to gain them. Accordingly, they are drawn to such issues as beauty and ugliness, happiness and misery, right and wrong, good and evil, and the like. They reveal the potentialities of men as human beings, and reflect on the possibility of the full realization of these through feeling, thought, and action.[1]

---

[1] Moody E. Prior, *Science and the Humanities* (Evanston, Ill.: Northwestern University Press, 1962), p. 11.

Definition by classification makes the assumption that human knowledge is classifiable, that all phenomena can be reduced to categories. Thus, any term is given meaning by locating it in the proper class and by pointing out similarities, differences, and unique characteristics that distinguish it from other members of this same class. By noting that a doorknob is a handle, we classify it as a handle; by noting that it is used to open doors, we differentiate it from other handles.

Any definition of this kind has rigor and general negotiability to the degree that the class into which it is placed is discrete and the differentiating characteristics are unique and invariably present. Tight definitions of this kind are always desirable in closely reasoned argument. And, so far as possible, propositions entering into argument should be phrased in terms amenable to such definition.

It is important to point out, however, that not all the matters with which we deal in argumentation are reducible to these tight classifications. Variability is often more characteristic than discreteness. In such cases, accuracy in definition is served by caution in recognizing *degrees* of difference and similiarity. And if a definition appears arbitrary, it should be made clear that this definition is being employed for a precise purpose in a precise context.

Aids in Defining. Useful supplementary methods of definition include: (1) negation, or defining by pointing out what is *not* meant; (2) illustration or example, which means the citing of a specific case; (3) context, or the placing of the term in meaningful surroundings which show the verbal or nonverbal (real-life) situation or thing to which the term refers; (4) quotation of synonyms found in dictionaries and other reference works; (5) etymology, or reference to origin or derivation of the term.

EXERCISES

1. On each of the following subjects, phrase a proposition of fact, a proposition of value, and a proposition of policy:
   a. Labor-management relations
   b. Capital punishment

    c. College athletics

    d. Military training

2. State the propositions involved in three selected samples of argument, such as editorials, articles, speeches, or advertisements. Classify each as fact, value, or policy.

3. Criticize these propositions:

    a. The paving on Main Street should be improved.

    b. The jury system should be abolished and a judge or board of judges substituted for the jury in all trial courts.

    c. One term of office of the President should be four years.

    d. Our unjust immigration quotas should be revised.

    e. The powers of state governors should be extended.

    f. The welfare state is detrimental to the best interests of the American people.

    g. Labor unions deserve the confidence of the American people.

4. Prepare a short expository talk or paper in which you explain how you chose a controversial subject, phrased a proposition about it, tested it according to functions and the first five rules of phrasing, classified it, and prepared a context for it, or avoided the necessity for doing so.

5. Phrase four propositions of policy which you would like to use for short argumentative speeches in class. Be prepared to submit these propositions to the class for criticism and suggestions.

6. Prepare and present a five-minute affirmative or negative speech on the proposition you choose from the list of four submitted in Exercise 5.

7. What are the propositions in the appendix debates?

Chapter 4

ANALYZING THE PROPOSITION:
THE ISSUES

Competence in argumentation and debate requires skill in analysis —the ability to get to the heart of a matter, to separate the important from the unimportant, to get at the critical issues involved in a proposition. Not only does the advocate need these analytical powers, but the study and practice of argumentation and debate are among the best means of acquiring such skill. The ability to analyze carefully and accurately is one of the highest marks of statesmanship in most areas of endeavor, both private and public.

ISSUES DEFINED

The issues are the inherently vital points, contentions, or subpropositions, affirmed by the affirmative and denied by the negative, upon the establishment of which depends the establishment of the main proposition. They are the ultimate, irreducible, essential matters of fact or of principle upon which the conclusion of the question hinges. They are not simply "important main points" or "points on which there is a clash of opinion." They are the crucial points, each one of which the affirmative must establish (unless it is admitted by the negative) in order to establish the proposition.

Issues are inherent in the proposition. The issues in any proposition are inherent in the essential meaning of the proposition itself. Many English sentences, even some which can be used as propositions in argumentation or debate, are capable of more than one legitimate meaning. It is the first duty of every advocate (whether he is writing an individual speech or editorial, or engaging in an oral debate with an opponent) to decide early in his preparation what the proposition means to him. He should then plan to make that meaning clear to readers or hearers near the start of his writing or his speech.

It should be realized that this problem of meaning frequently has different implications for the affirmative and the negative. For instance, when in a debate a proposition is capable of two *legitimate* interpretations, it is clearly the privilege of the affirmative to choose which is the meaning to be debated. It is the affirmative that speaks in the proposition. The proposition belongs to it, expresses its position. The negative may not tell the affirmative what the affirmative means by any legitimate use of language. As soon as possible, of course, this meaning should be made known to the negative. The negative ought to have an opportunity to prepare its argument against the actual position which it is going to have to oppose, which, of course, is the affirmative position.

Having determined an inherent and legitimate meaning of the proposition, the next thing the parties must realize is that *the issues are to be discovered in the meaning of the proposition.* Finding the issues in a proposition is essentially parallel to finding the elements in a chemical compound. If one has a chemical compound to analyze, he cannot very well decide in advance that he is going to find three elements or six elements or two elements. If he is a competent chemist, he will so analyze the compound as to find the number of elements that are there. And if he is dealing with a chemical element instead of a compound, he won't attempt to break the element into separate elements for convenience. In other words, we must realize that if we work competently in analysis, we find the number of issues that are inherent in the proposition, whether this be one or half a dozen.

Frequently the issues in a proposition are evident as soon as one finds an authoritative definition of a key word in the proposition. The elements of the charge of burglary (to be explained later) are a good example. The same would be true of any criminal charge. In a charge of first-degree murder, trespass, or grand larceny, there are just as many issues as there are *essential* elements in the criminal charge specified. Especially in propositions of fact which lie clearly within the limits of highly specialized fields such as law, medicine, government, or engineering, one should realize that there are many terms which will be found to have highly specialized, professional meanings. In all such cases the burden of analysis is pretty well carried when one learns the exact meaning of the words used.

When an understanding of the words used and a bit of preliminary research give the exact meaning that one has to attack or defend in argument, one ought to be able to state the issues *tentatively* and then proceed with his investigation on the basis of the tentative list of issues. As the work of investigation brings more understanding, the phrasing of the issues may be improved. This possibility should be held in mind until all of the work of investigation and organization has been completed.

Issues are vital matters. Not only are issues *inherent* in the proposition; they are *vital* to the "life" of the proposition. Just as an animal is killed by the destruction of one vital organ, so a proposition is lost by negating any one issue. Examples from law and general argument will help to make clear the exact nature of the issues.

In law. Let us say, for example, that A is accused of the crime of burglary at common law. This crime has five essential elements: (1) breaking and (2) entering (3) a dwelling (4) at night (5) with felonious intent. There are five possible or "potential" issues here. The state (affirmative) must prove all that are not admitted. They are all *vital.* If the defense (negative) prevents the affirmative from establishing any single one beyond reasonable doubt, the case of the affirmative fails. Then the defendant is not guilty of burglary. He may be guilty of a number of other things, but that is another story. The defendant may admit that he broke and entered a dwelling at night, but may deny that it was done with felonious intent—may say he did it to put out a fire. Even if the affirmative has established (or gained an admission of) four of the five necessary points, the whole case falls. No affirmative case can stand after the loss of a single issue. Any point which the affirmative can fail on and still establish the case *cannot be an issue,* though it may be very important. Importance is not enough; each issue is *vital* in the strictest sense of that word, in the sense in which every *vital* organ is necessary to the life of a dog. When only one vital organ is destroyed, the dog is dead.

In general discussion. Here the situation is essentially the same. Consider as an example the proposition: *"Resolved, That the town of A should adopt a new water system taking water from Lake B."* What are the issues?

Obviously the first issue is, "Is the present well-water system unsatisfactory?" It is a very common type of proposition, in which the affirmative first has to demonstrate (or gain an admission of its contention) that the present system is vitally unsatisfactory. Having established (or received the admission) that the well-water system is indefensible and must be abandoned, does it follow that the city must use the water of Lake B? Clearly not. First, the people of city A ought to know whether if they go to the expense of a new water system from Lake B, they will (1) have water enough, (2) that the water they get will be fit to use, and (3) that they will get it at a price they can afford to pay. In other words, after the affirmative has established the position that the well-water system must be abandoned, it still has to establish three vital contentions concerning the water in Lake B, that is, that it is satisfactory in *quantity, quality,* and *price* or *accessibility.*

In the above example there are four essential issues involved. If the negative can show that the present well-water system is satisfactory, they win. Similarly, even if they concede the disadvantages of the well-water system, if they can demonstrate the Lake-water system will not yield enough water, or that the water

is contaminated, or that the cost of the proposed system is prohibitive (any one or all of these), quite obviously the affirmative
proposal fails.

The Lake-water proposition is typical of many, if not most,
propositions encountered in general argumentation. Occasionally,
however, propositions are debated in which there may appear to
be several issues involved when in fact there is only one issue.
The following proposition is a good example: *"Resolved, That
the X Manufacturing Company should adopt the Y system of
production and distribution."* Let us assume that the X Manufacturing Company exists for the purpose of making money for
its stockholders, and that there is no question of the legality, labor
problems, or public morality involved. It follows that the only
real question at issue is whether or not it will be profitable to
change to the Y system. Let us assume further that the proponents
of the Y system are ready to argue that under this system the X
Company will (1) buy cheaper raw material, (2) save a great
deal of money in advertising, (3) save further large sums in the
payment for royalties and patents, and (4) greatly increase sales.
Let us suppose that the affirmative inevitably goes into the debate
with argument and evidence on each of these four points, and
that the negative goes into the debate with argument and evidence against each of these four points. Do we have four issues?
The answer is no. There is only one issue. And that issue will
ultimately be resolved by striking a balance and adding up probable profits and probable losses and seeing whether, on the whole,
financial advantage or disadvantage is indicated by the change.
If the affirmative succeeds in carrying three of these points and
the negative carries one, it does not mean that the affirmative
wins the debate. Suppose the affirmative convinces the board of
directors that they will have additional profits of a million dollars
a year on raw material, another million on advertising, and another million on sales, but the negative succeeds in convincing
the board of directors that they will have a loss of six million a
year on royalties and patents. The balance is in favor of the negative by three million dollars.

The issues in any proposition are the mutually exclusive, all
inclusive points upon which the truth or falsity of the proposition

hinges. Each is different in kind. If several points are merely aspects of the same matter, they constitute one issue rather than several. Where a balance can be struck between several points, as in the case above, the issue is the single matter to which these several points are related. The test of any issue is a relatively simple one: Can the proposition stand if this point is negated successfully? If the answer to this question is "no," the point is an issue. If the answer is "yes," the point, whether it be relevant or irrelevant, important or unimportant, is not in and of itself an issue.

THE ISSUES AND KINDS
OF PROPOSITIONS

Before one attempts to analyze any proposition, he should have in mind clearly the kind of proposition with which he is dealing—whether it is a proposition of fact, or value, or policy. The issues in all cases must meet the specifications we have discussed, but there are different methods of discovering the issues involved in questions of fact, value, and policy.

The issues in propositions of fact. As we have seen, a proposition of fact alleges the existence of an object, event, or relationship in the past, present, or future, without evaluation or appraisal and without any suggestion of action with respect to the matter. The issues are best revealed by establishing criteria that can be used to test the judgment in question. Very often these criteria or tests can be discovered by careful definition of the key terms in the proposition.

In analyzing a proposition of fact, always raise the question, How can this statement be tested? In other words, what conditions, specifications, or circumstances have to be met in order to qualify the proposition as a true statement. If these tests are established as mutually exclusive items, including all the relevant criteria, with each item critical in its own right, such tests may be taken as the issues (or a close approximation of them).

In defending a proposition of fact, the affirmative always faces two responsibilities: it must first present and defend (or be prepared to present and defend) the tests or criteria it proposes to use as a measuring stick in assessing the proposition; and second, it must show that the proposition as stated satisfies these criteria.

A few examples may help to clarify this method of analysis. If it is alleged that "a whale is a mammal," then it must be shown that the whale possesses the essential characteristics of the mammal. Is it a vertebrate? Is it viviparous (bringing forth living young rather than eggs)? Does it suckle its young?

If it is asserted that "speech, as commonly taught in American colleges and universities, is a humanistic study," it is necessary first to specify the nature of humanistic study, and second to show that "speech, as commonly taught," meets these specifications.

If it is asserted that "labor unions seek to control American industry," the first question is what "control of American industry" means, and the second question is whether or not the policies and practices of labor unions indicate that they are seeking such control. The issues might be these: (1) Do restraint and direction of policy (with or without ownership) constitute control? (2) Are the unions seeking to restrain American business and direct its policies?

The issues in propositions of value. A proposition of value expresses an evaluative judgment. This may be a moral judgment or an esthetic judgment—any kind of judgment that makes an assessment or appraisal. The issues may be discovered here by the same kind of analytical process we suggested for propositions of fact, with one important difference: the standards, criteria, or tests by which the judgment is to be measured can seldom be defined as objectively as they can be in factual propositions. Values are peculiarly personal things. "One man's meat may be another man's poison." Your preferences, likes, and dislikes may be very different from mine, and very different from those held by most people, but you still have a right to them within reasonable limits.

In arguing a question of value, then, the special and unique problem is that of establishing the standards (the values) to be applied in the case in question. There are several ways of doing this: (1) use your own personal values as standards; (2) ascertain as best you can the values held by your judges or audience, and apply these as standards; (3) adopt what appear to be values held by the majority of people (public opinion); (4) adopt the values held by experts or persons of recognized competence in the area under discussion. Unfortunately, perhaps, no one of these approaches is satisfactory in all cases.

Quite obviously, in making a personal decision on a question of value, your personal values will provide the standard. If you are trying to persuade a specific audience or certain judges, you will have to satisfy the standards of those who are to judge; if you are concerned with the decision of a larger public, then public opinion on the values brought into question need to be considered. Decisions on propositions of value will always be made on the basis of the values held by those who are to judge. If you do not like these standards, then your only alternative is to convert the judges to standards that you think are sound. Actually, much of the deliberation on propositions of value is concerned with these standards of judgment.

We are concerned here with the analysis of propositions of value for the purpose of determining the issues. If issues are the vital, inherent matters we have held them to be, then the vagaries of personal and public opinion are hardly relevant in their determination. We suggest, therefore, that the most reliable guides in analyzing propositions of value are the standards held by persons of recognized competence and expertness in the area under discussion. An example will help us to see how this works out.

Let us say that you are analyzing the proposition, "Carl Sandburg is a great poet." Here you need to know first what great poetry is, and second how well Mr. Sandburg's poetry meets these standards. Literary scholars have concerned themselves for centuries with the criticism of poetry, and have evolved standards of judgment that are generally accepted. In other words, there is something approaching a consensus among literary critics concerning poetic greatness. The issues in the case of Mr. Sandburg's greatness as a poet will be vital, inherent considerations necessary in the application of these standards to his poetry. You may not agree with these standards, and your judges may not agree with them, but they are nonetheless the issues. You and the judges can defy the critics if you wish—at your own peril, we might add— but in any case, you ought to know what the real issues are.

There can be no judgment on whether a certain act, program, or practice is morally justifiable, economically sound, or esthetically good in the absence of moral, economic, or esthetic standards. If a moral judgment is involved, then you had better look to the moral code generally held in our Judaic-Christian culture, and consult those who have the greatest competence in interpreting this code; if economic standards are involved, there will be a presumption in favor of the standards generally held by the most competent persons in the economic community; if esthetic standards are relevant, then you will be well advised to consult the estheticians.

We are fully aware that this position is open to the criticism that you are being advised to defer to "the experts" in matters that are often peculiarly personal. In answer, we suggest that you try to determine the issues in these questions of value as objectively and impersonally as possible. This kind of objective determination of issues need not dictate your position (affirmative or negative) on the proposition, and it most certainly is not the final answer in deciding how you are going to approach an audience in arguing whatever position you choose to take.

The whole field of contests and competitions provides examples of value judgments and the methods of their analysis and determination. Anyone who judges competitions of any kind, whether it be beauty contests, dog shows, flower exhibits, livestock competitions, dramatic production, debates, or any other competition, necessarily has to make value judgments. And often such a judge is called upon to defend his decision, or at least to explain it to interested parties. In each such case (presumably, at least) the judge has made his decision on the basis of certain standards. Sometimes, in fact, the rules of the competition define these standards carefully. The decision of the judge has the status of a proposition of value when he undertakes to defend it, and the issues are to be found in the standards of judgment he has used in reaching his decision. If two or more judges disagree in their decisions, it means either that they are employing different standards of judgment or that they are applying these standards differently.

One more example may be helpful: Let us say that you are

considering an apartment house as an investment. The question may be stated, "Is this property a good investment?" or, stated as a proposition of value, "Property A is a good investment." The issues appear to be these: Is the property fairly priced on the present market? Will it yield a satisfactory return on the investment (maintenance, rentals, and other such factors considered)? And third, is it likely to offer advantageous opportunities for resale?

The issues in propositions of policy. A proposition of policy always proposes action of some kind—that something be done that is not now being done, or that something that is now being done be stopped. Any policy judgment necessarily involves both factual and evaluative judgments. Rational policy decisions are based on the facts as we know them and on what we believe to be the proper standards of value.

An analysis of any proposition of policy will show that there are four responsibilities the affirmative must be prepared to discharge: (1) show that evils or problems exist, (2) show that these evils are produced by causes that can be remedied, (3) show that the action or policy proposed provides a remedy, and (4) show that this remedy is practicable in terms of cost, new problems it might create, and other possible remedies. For quick reference, these may be referred to as "ill," "blame," "cure," and "cost." [1]

We do not suggest that "ill," "blame," "cure," and "cost" are the issues in propositions of policy. Rather, we propose them as areas or "hunting grounds" in which the real issues may be discovered. The following outline is a rough breakdown of these four areas into questions that may profitably be explored in searching for the issues. It can be seen that both factual and evaluative judgments are involved in answering these questions.

---

[1] We borrow these terms from Lee S. Hultzen's essay, "Status in Deliberative Analysis," included in *The Rhetorical Idiom* (Ithaca, New York: Cornell University Press, 1958), pp. 97–123. In our opinion, Mr. Hultzen's essay is one of the most competent and penetrating analyses in the literature. However, we have preferred not to follow his guidelines in all cases.

We also acknowledge our indebtedness to Warren Choate Shaw, *The Art of Debate* (New York: Allyn and Bacon, 1922), pp. 150–184.

I. *Ill*
   a. Do conditions exist that appear to be evils?   (Fact)
   b. Are these alleged evils real evils?   (Value)
II. *Blame*
   a. Can these evils be attributed to specified causes?   (Fact)
   b. Are these causes remediable?   (Fact)
III. *Cure*
   a. Will the proposed remedy remove the causes of the evils? (Fact)
   b. Will the proposed remedy produce alleged benefits?   (Fact)
   c. Are these alleged benefits real benefits?   (Value)
IV. *Cost*
   a. Will the proposed remedy produce alleged new evils?   (Fact)
   b. Are these alleged new evils real evils?   (Value)
   c. Does the proposed remedy pre-empt the possibility of a better remedy?   (Fact and Value)

A statement on "Fiscal and Monetary Policy for High Employment," by the Research and Policy Committee of the Committee for Economic Development, provides a good example of the analysis of a proposition of policy.[2] The specific recommendation is presented as a proposition of policy: "It should be the policy of the government to set its expenditure programs and tax rates so that they would yield a constant, moderate surplus under conditions of high employment and price stability."

The analysis begins with careful definitions of *fiscal policy* and *monetary policy,* and proceeds to consider the potential contribution of federal fiscal and monetary policy to employment. Since the proposition is concerned primarily with fiscal policy, the next step in analysis develops "two main deficiencies that should be corrected in order to increase the contribution of fiscal policy to maintaining high employment." Then the analysis sets out "the main characteristics of a desirable budget policy from the standpoint not only of economic stability but also of economic growth and efficiency." Five such characteristics are specified. The next step in analysis considers the proposed policy as a means of meeting these five requirements for a desirable budget policy. Each

[2] T. O. Yntema, Chairman, Research and Policy Committee, December, 1961. 59 pages. Library of Congress Catalogue Card Number: 62-11839.

of these standards is applied to the proposed policy. Finally, it is suggested that the general policy proposed "would be furthered by two changes in budget presentation and procedure." These "two changes" are specified and considered as means for "implementation of the policy."

The following issues are derived from this analysis:

1. Can the wise exercise of our fiscal and monetary policies contribute significantly to steadier, higher employment?
2. Do deficiencies now exist in our fiscal policy that limit significantly its contribution to maintaining high employment?
3. Is it possible to devise a federal budget policy that will contribute more effectively to economic stability and economic growth and efficiency?
4. Would a budget policy designed to set expenditures and tax rates so that they would yield a constant, moderate surplus under conditions of high employment and price stability best realize those potentialities?
5. Can such a budget policy be implemented by appropriate changes in budget presentation and procedure?

In another statement on national policy, the Research and Policy Committee of the Committee for Economic Development analyzes "A New Trade Policy for the United States." [3] The policy proposed is stated as follows: "A general decision to reduce tariff barriers should be agreed to by the United States and other industrial countries apart from and prior to the decision about tariff rates on particular commodities."

The analysis begins with a consideration of "the basic elements in the present situation." Nine such elements are considered, all dealing with needs and problems growing out of our present international trade situation. The analysis concludes with eleven recommendations designed to meet present needs and to implement the proposed policy. Throughout the analysis, care is taken

---

[3] *Ibid.*, April, 1962. 35 pages. Library of Congress Catalogue Card Number: 62-16627.

to interpret the proposition to mean that "the fundamental goal is reduction of all obstacles to trade and payments [and that] insistence on a particular approach in tariff negotiations should not be allowed to prevent progress toward this goal."

The issues derived from this analysis may be stated as follows:

1. Do existing barriers to international trade (our own and those of our trading partners) significantly limit international trade?
2. Does this limitation reduce the economic efficiency and growth of the Western world, including the United States?
3. Would a general decision to reduce tariff barriers increase international trade in advantageous ways?
4. Should such a decision be made apart from, and prior to, the decision about tariff rates on particular commodities?
5. Are the specification and negotiation of such a general agreement feasible at this time?

KINDS OF ISSUES

Since various kinds of issues are frequently mentioned in argument, it is helpful to consider the uses of the word with its appropriate modifiers.

Potential issues. These are the issues that are inherent in the proposition—the possible issues, each one of which the affirmative must either prove affirmatively or gain an admission of from the negative (or the judge, jury, or audience) in order to establish its case. These are the issues we have been discussing up to this point. They may be described as "potential" in the sense that they inhere in the proposition and are there to be discovered by anyone who searches for them; and they are further "potential" in the fact that they may or may not become points of clash in a debate, depending upon the acuity of the debaters and the direction of the negative's attack.

The potential issues are always the same in the same proposition; they exist independently of the wills of the debaters. They are to be discovered, not invented or chosen. They are always the same for the affirmative and the negative—always the same for every affirmative and every negative on any given proposition. Of course, if propositions vary in any way, the issues may also vary. *"Resolved,* That the commission form of government should be adopted in Chicago" is not *necessarily* the same proposition you would have if you substituted Dayton or New Orleans for Chicago.

Admitted issues. Any "potential issues" that the negative chooses to admit may, for convenience, be called "admitted issues." These, of course, drop out of the controversy. It is often wise for the affirmative to note such admissions so that the fact of the admission and the significance of it will be clear to all concerned. But, quite obviously, nothing is gained and time and energy are wasted if points already conceded are belabored.

An admission of one or more issues by the negative is not, in and of itself, a sign of weakness in the negative, so long as the negative presents a convincing case against at least one vital issue. The affirmative occasionally tries to interpret such admissions as a weakness, but the negative may actually be in a stronger position by presenting a massive attack on what it regards as the most vulnerable point in the armor of the affirmative.

Actual issues. These are simply the issues that are left after the admitted issues are subtracted from the potential issues. These "actual issues" are sometimes called "ultimate issues." They are "actual" or "ultimate" in the sense that they become the points of clash in a given debate. They are the inherently vital points that are controverted by the negative, and are thus the centers of controversy in the debate.

It should be borne in mind that the affirmative has the burden of proving all the potential issues which the negative declines to admit. The affirmative has no authority to demand the admission of any particular issues. The negative may admit whatever it wishes to admit, and the affirmative must be prepared to prove the rest. It is well for an affirmative, in preparing to meet a negative whose detailed proof is not known in advance, to make a tentative guess as to what the negative probably will admit and to try to find out as early as possible whether the guess is right. The well-prepared affirmative, however, will go into the debate with the necessary evidence and argument to do whatever it can to substantiate the affirmative side of any potential issue on which the negative offers an effective challenge.

Stock issues. These are points or questions designed to apply to all propositions of a given kind. They are not the real issues in any particular proposition, but rather a formulation of questions that may prove helpful in finding the real issues.

We have already considered the stock issues applicable to propositions of policy, and have labeled them conveniently as "ill," "blame," "cure," and "cost." These may be variously phrased, but the meaning is essentially the same.

Often *two* stock issues, phrased in various ways, are suggested for propositions of policy:

> 1. Is the present unsatisfactory? Are there fatal evils in the existing situation? Is there a cause for action? Is there a disease? Do we need a change?
> 2. Is the proposed action an improvement? Will it cure the evils? Is this the action we should take? Is this the proper remedy? Is the proposed change the right one?

New systems will not be adopted while the present is satisfactory, and the proposed scheme must look like a satisfactory remedy or improvement. So the man with a new scheme for doing something must always show somehow or other (or get it admitted) that there is something wrong and that his scheme will make it right.

Why, then, are these not really the exact issues in all such cases? For two reasons it is unsafe to accept them as such: first, because analysis may show a *more specific wording* for these general questions, and this will aid in many ways; second, and principally, because on accurate analysis it may be found that one of these questions will break up into, say, three questions, *each of which* must be proved by the affirmative.

We have tried many times to formulate sets of stock issues applicable to propositions of fact and value. We have been unable to invent any system of practical value, and those we have met in the literature are either faulty or limited to theoretical interests.

THE ROLE OF ISSUES
IN DEBATE

The necessity of knowing the issues. The importance of know-ing the issues cannot be overestimated. Argument on any question implies some difference of opinion; it means that there are certain ideas affirmed by one side and denied by the other. The proposi-tion is merely an expression of this clash of opinion, and an under-standing of its meaning depends entirely upon a comprehension of the points of conflict. If the writer or speaker would prove his proposition, he must prove these critical points. Moreover, the value of his materials depends upon their relation to these points; any evidence that gives a direct and substantial support to these vital contentions is valuable, and whatever does not bear directly on these basic positions is, at best, of secondary importance. If an advocate makes a mistake in his search for these critical points, he may well waste his time in proving some point that will not help him after it is proved, or he may be surprised in debate by attack on some vital point which he is not ready to defend. This danger is realized and guarded against in the courts of law. The rules of legal procedure demand that the issues shall be clearly stated in the pleadings before a trial begins, and that every piece of evidence, whether of fact or of law, shall have a direct and evident bearing on some one of these issues; anything that cannot conform to this test is declared irrelevent and is excluded from consideration. Then again, a speaker or writer who does not know the issues will probably confuse his readers or hearers by giving them a false, distorted view of his case. If a debater does not com-prehend just what are the few vital points of his case, around which all the lesser facts must be grouped, his proof will almost certainly lack the unity and coherence that are indispensable for clearness and force in presentation.

Proposition and issues. We have seen in the preceding chapter that in order to have intelligent argumentation, we must first have a proposition. The proper formulating of the proposition insures that we have one single question that can be argued pro and con directly, and so brought to a definite conclusion. This proposition thus makes clear the general position which the advocate must argue for or against. But he is not yet ready to select the evidence or the arguments with which to support his contention. He has merely found the field of battle. Before he can open the fight or even arrange his forces, he must examine the ground he has chosen and find out its points of vantage and of weakness. The proposition discloses the task that must in the end be accomplished, but it does not show the steps necessary for the accomplishment, or just what method may be most effective. The proposition gives a single question for discussion, but even in any such single question there are innumerable arguments, points, and masses of evidence that may be brought forward. All these arguments and all this evidence cannot be used; it is not all of equal value. Some of it will have such a direct and powerful bearing on the question that it must have great weight, but much of it will have such an indefinite and remote bearing that to use it at all would be a waste of time. Clearly, then, the next thing for the debater to do is to get some standards to which he can refer in order to determine the value of these materials. A century and a half ago, John Ward, in his *Systems of Oratory*, said: "But in all disputes it is of the greatest consequence to observe where the stress of the controversy lies. For, without attending to this, persons may cavil about different matters, without understanding each other or deciding anything." In any discussion the "stress of the controversy" inevitably falls upon the proving or disproving of a few points, which are the center and soul of the question. Only if those who have the burden of proof win in the struggle over these points can they win the whole contest. In order, therefore, to know what evidence to use, the advocate on either side must first find out just what are the points that the affirmative must establish by the evidence and the argument based on it, in order to establish *the proposition*. These points are the issues.

Issues and burden of proof. It is well to consider the relation of the theory of issues to various aspects of the theory of burden of proof, in order that their complete harmony may be clear and all misunderstanding avoided.

The issues, and the affirmative and negative. The affirmative has no *choice* in regard to issues. Every "potential issue" which the negative chooses to fight on must be established. The negative, on the other hand, may choose among the potential issues which ones to admit and which to oppose. In law this choice must be made known to the affirmative in the course of the pleading, so that a suit never starts unless all parties know the issues and agree on what the issues are. In general discussion this situation should be approximated as closely as possible. Before a debate starts, or early in the debate, a direct clash should be brought about on vital points that are left after all admissions have been made. The affirmative, of course, has the burden of proof on *each* issue. Establishing usually means "beyond a reasonable doubt" or "by preponderating evidence," so the negative, in trying to block a case, seeks to raise reasonable doubts on as many issues as possible, and usually does not risk everything on fewer issues than are absolutely necessary. One man may doubt on one issue and one on another, so it is well to fight on as many as offer a good chance, unless one can be absolutely sure of winning on fewer. Suppose the waterworks case mentioned above was to be decided by a city council of twenty men. If the negative were ready to grant that the present system was indefensible, that would be "an admitted issue." Then it might oppose the affirmative on each of the other three potential issues. If the negative persuaded four men to believe that the proposed lake water was not good enough, but failed to convince them on the other two issues, and then persuaded four others to agree that the lake water would be too expensive to use, and four others that there would not be enough of it, it would win its case by a wote of 12 to 8. If it had limited its efforts to two issues, it would have lost by a vote of 12 to 8, and if it had limited its argument to any one issue, it would have lost by a vote of 16 to 4. A competent negative opposes the affirmative on every issue on which it sees a good chance to get votes in court, legislature, or on the public platform.

Issues and counterpropositions. Sometimes the negative sets up a substitute or counterplan or -proposition. When this is the case, the negative, of course, has the burden of proof *on its plan.* The issues of the case are not changed by this plan of defense. If the substitute does not offer an obstacle to the establishing of the affirmative side of the issues, it is a waste of time to talk about it. If the substitute can be so presented that it blocks one or more of the *vital* points of the affirmative, the case fails—the negative wins. But the substitute may not have won, as explained below.

Suppose, in the burglary case already referred to, that instead of confining its case to proving unfounded one or more of the five accusations, the defense simply denies them all and offers evidence that proves conclusively that not A, the accused, but X committed the crime in question. When it accuses X, it necessarily takes the burden of proving that X did these things. But its only purpose is to show thereby that A is innocent. And note that X is not declared guilty as the result of this trial. The proposition is that A is guilty. The affirmative has failed to establish its case either by having been blocked on one or more of the issues, or by the negative's offering a substitute. But the substitute did not *win*—not in this trial. It is advanced only enough to show that the claims of the affirmative are unfounded. In such a situation the indictment and trial of X might well follow, but that is another story.

The issues, and winning or losing. In what we have just said concerning issues, burden of proof, and "winning" and "losing," we have had in mind actual cases in real life, not contest or school debates before judges who are to say who "won" the debate. Everything that has been said about issues, however, applies in these contest debates exactly as it does in a law court or political campaign, except for the remarks on winning or losing. In a law court, in a political campaign, in business, in science, it is *the case* that is being passed on. The decision is on the "merits of the question," not on *the way* in which certain advocates handle the case. But in an intercollegiate debate, for instance, the decision should be determined *always* by the skill of the debaters, *never* on the strength of the case (except in so far as this is indicative of the skill of the debaters). The decision, to mean anything at all, must be based on the ability shown in debating, not on the strength of the evidence or the merits of the case. A debate should, of course, be worked out and presented *as though the decision were to be made by the audience,* or jury, or judge, on the merits of the case, for only in this way can the contestants show their real ability as debaters. But the judges should know enough about *debating* to render a decision on debating alone.

The issues, and conviction and persuasion. The issues are the points that will have to be established by the affirmative in order to *convince* competent judges that their plan should be adopted. The issues have to do primarily with conviction rather than persuasion. They are the basis of the appeal to the intellect. The work of persuasion may be done in connection with proving the issues. In selecting evidence, illustration, and phraseology, the emotional side of each audience (sentiments, taste, prejudices) should always be kept in mind as one of the guides in all that we do. But in discovering the issues in any case, we must consider only the intellectual side of our case—the facts and the justifiable inferences from the facts. The analysis of the proposition in order to find the issues should be impersonal—not done with particular audiences or judges in mind. After the impersonal case is discovered, then the adjusting of it to any particular tribunal should be carefully undertaken. This, of course, means paying a good deal of attention to persuasion.

Number and form of issues. The number of issues varies necessarily in different propositions. There are usually not more than three or four (in some technical or legal proposition there may be a large number). In a great many propositions there is but one issue. The issues are to be discovered. Careful analysis will reveal them. We cannot decide in advance to "pick out" three or four issues. We may find three or four, and we may find but one. When we have found the number of points that may be issues from the nature of the case, our next step is to find out if any of them are admitted. If so, we place them in the introduction as admitted matter. The others are our actual issues for this controversy.

When found, the issues should be expressed in such *question* form that the affirmative will answer "Yes" and the negative "No." They should be always so stated in a brief, and usually so stated in a speech or written argument. Do not say, "The issue is that this plan will be financially advantageous." Do not say, "The issue is, 'What will be the financial effect?'" The proper form is, "The issue is, 'Will this plan be financially advantageous?'" This represents the clean-cut question that must be answered—the exact point which the affirmative affirms and the negative denies.

Issues and partition. The partition consists of a statement of the main points to be taken up in the discussion. It is an enumeration of the steps to be taken in presenting the case. It is a plan of campaign, determined (and usually announced) in advance. *The partition must not be confused with the issues.* The points in partition may, it is true, be substantially identical with the issues, but they may differ widely. There may be one issue and four points in partition, or three points which cover the three issues. The issues must all be *vital* points. The points in partition must all be *important*, but not necessarily vital. If a single issue is lost, the case fails. But a team may lose one or more points in partition without losing the case.

Suppose a table is hanging suspended from the ceiling by a chain of three links. If one link is destroyed the table falls. The table represents the case, the contention of the affirmative; the links of chain represent the issues. Suppose the table is standing on five legs. One, two, or three legs *may* be removed, and still the table may be left standing. It might be that four legs could be removed, and if the fifth were big enough, and placed directly in the center of the table, it might hold up the table, especially if the attack on it were very weak. Here the table again represents the case, and the legs represent the points in partition. Or suppose two armies are contending for the possession of a given territory, the control of which both armies understand must depend upon the occupation of two particular points (the issues): a pass and a certain height of ground. There are various positions which the two opposing forces may seize and hold, and various lines of attack which they may adopt, depending upon the peculiar habits and methods of the respective generals; but these positions and this strategy (the partition) are valuable only as they serve to give the command of these two critical points. A partition, then, is a statement of the points that the arguer intends to prove; the issues are the points that the affirmative *must prove* in order to prove its case. If the points of the partition are well chosen, they will frequently correspond closely to the issues; but they may be entirely different, and they are not in any case necessarily identical.

FINDING THE ISSUES

The problem of finding the issue or the issues may be simple or complex. In many propositions the issues are obvious. They are there in sight; we have only to recognize them. In other propositions the problem of analysis is a long and difficult one. For such cases it is useful to have a method or plan of action. It should be understood, however, that there is no one method that should necessarily always be applied in all its details to any case that is to be analyzed. The five steps suggested below provide a plan for analysis that may be applied in whole or in part, as necessary. Some of these suggestions will be clear from what had already been said.

Know what you are looking for. Be certain you know what issues are before you start looking for them. Everything we have said in this chapter is designed to be helpful at this point.

Interpret the proposition. Be certain you recognize *the kind* of proposition you are analyzing, and then determine exactly what the proposition means: What does it say? What does it allege? What does it propose? Define the terms carefully. If the proposition is at all complex, note carefully any syntactical or grammatical constructions that may shed light on meaning.

In looking for the issues, you are looking for the crucial points upon which the truth of the proposition hinges. Quite obviously, you cannot be sure of these points until you know precisely what the proposition means. If the proposition does not express accurately what you want to propose, then by all means revise it *if you are at liberty to do so.* If you are committed to the proposition as worded, then be sure you know the precise nature and meaning of this commitment.

Study both sides of the question. In many cases the issues are not apparent by a simple examination of the terms and syntax of the proposition. Careful study of the evidence and argument bearing on the proposition is required. And in most cases, such investigation will serve to sharpen and refine any tentative analysis you may have made. This study should examine both sides of the question critically and impartially. At this point you are looking for the issues, rather than a case to defend or attack. Suggestions for investigating the proposition through reading and discussion are given in Chapters 5 and 6.

Array the arguments pro and con. Written lists of the arguments for and against the proposition arranged in roughly parallel columns are often helpful in discovering the issues. After these lists have been prepared, go as far as you can in consolidating the arguments in each list under main headings. Then compare the affirmative and negative lists. Note where the main affirmative and negative arguments clash. These points of clash are likely to be the issues—or, at least, a close approximation of the issues.

Test the points believed to be issues. Phrase the issue or issues tentatively, and then apply these tests: (1) Is *each* proposed issue vital to the proposition? (2) Do the proposed issues include *all* the vital points necessary to establish the proposition? (3) Are the issues as proposed *mutually exclusive?* Does each issue operate as a single, independent factor or variable? (4) Are the issues so phrased that the affirmative answers "yes" to each issue and the negative answers "no"?

EXERCISES

1. Phrase a proposition of fact, a proposition of value, and a proposition of policy. Refer to Chapter 3. List the potential issues for each proposition.

2. Examine the printed debate in the appendix. State what you believe to be the potential issues, the admitted issues (if any), and the actual issue or issues.

3. Write an expository essay in which you explain how you found the issues in an assigned proposition or a proposition of your own choice.

4. State the issues in one proposition of fact, one of value, and one of policy. Indicate the circumstances in which one or more issues might be admitted.

5. Plan an affirmative argumentative speech on a proposition of policy. Present a four-minute introduction which would be appropriate

for this speech. State the proposition, define terms, give background of proposition, exclude irrelevant matter, state the issues, and partition your case. Criticize these introductions from the standpoint of adequacy of analysis.

6. Select a proposition for class analysis. Prepare individual analyses before class, and come prepared to participate in class discussion for the purpose of working out an analysis acceptable to the group.

Chapter 5

INVESTIGATING
THE PROPOSITION

INVESTIGATION DEFINED

Investigation is the process of acquiring information about the proposition. It may properly be called research if it is done in a scholarly manner. Investigative procedures include, first of all, surveying one's own thoughts, and then reading, discussing, observing, conversing, listening to informed speakers, corresponding with knowledgeable people, conducting experiments, and recording the results of these activities. Any reasonably thorough investigation is undertaken for the purpose of accumulating a general background of information, finding the available evidence, and discovering the specific lines of argument to support an answer to the issues which analysis has revealed.

Many of these kinds of inquiry are likely to be unoriginal, which means that the advocate uses the reports of others' investigations. Original investigation, on the other hand, means firsthand inquiry. For instance, in order to obtain evidence on the civic competence of persons between the ages of eighteen and twenty-one, some debaters who advocated lowering the voting age to eighteen administered current-affairs tests to young persons in that age group. Speeches and essays which contain this sort of material are more likely to avoid the dullness and the lack of personal authority which characterize many communications which are based only upon reading. But original investigation requires much time, if well done. Therefore, it should be attempted only if the desired data are not available in print.

The purposes of investigation may be served by direct and indirect preparation. Direct preparation is the study and thought which are undertaken in terms of a specific problem for a specific occasion. The work which an advocate does on a proposition after it has been stated is direct preparation. Indirect preparation is that which takes place over a period of time and without reference to a particular occasion. It involves general knowledge and experience. An advocate who is well read and otherwise informed on public questions has an advantage over one who "starts from scratch" with direct preparation. Obviously, both kinds of preparation are useful in that they complement each other.

IMPORTANCE OF
INVESTIGATION

The importance of investigation should be obvious to most persons. We expect an advocate to know what he is talking or writing about. Regardless of its outcome—whether victory or defeat—the practice of shoddy preparation is censurable. It reveals the lack of a scholarly attitude and implies contempt for the audience. For this reason we say, "Knowledge first, and techniques later."

LIBRARY RESOURCES

Encyclopedias. These general references provide background information on various branches of knowledge or topics of interest. Being composed of articles rather than book-length discourses, they can be wide and comprehensive in scope. Often this is the best place to get a first acquaintance with a subject. The better-known general encyclopedias are the *Britannica, Americana, New International,* and *Colliers'*. Specialized encyclopedias are available, for example, in social sciences, education, American government, and social reform.

General guides to reference works. These sources are designed to help the investigator to locate the more specific reference works: *Basic Reference Sources,* by Louis Shores; *Guide to Reference Books,* by Constance Winchell; *How and Where to Look It Up,* by Robert W. Murphey; *How to Locate Educational Information and Data,* by Alexander and Burke; *Subject Guide to Reference Books,* by Herbert Hirshberg.

Bibliographies. A bibliography is a list of source materials on a subject. The name suggests that only books are included, but such is often not the case. Periodicals, papers, documents, recordings, and other materials are frequently listed. Scholars who wish to consult bibliographies on a variety of subjects locate these references through a bibliography of bibliographies. The two major works of this kind are Besterman's *World Bibliography of Bibliographies* and the *Bibliographic Index.* National bibliographies include the *Cumulative Book Index* and the *British National Bibliography.*

Specialized subject bibliographies are numerous. The Library of Congress, state-university extension divisions, and special-interest groups issue lists on subjects of current interest. These are a few of the specialized lists: *Cambridge Bibliography of English Literature,* "American Bibliography" in *PMLA, International Bibliography of Political Science,* and *State Government.*

Sometimes a list is annotated, which means that an entry includes a brief statement on the nature of the material in the book, article, or other such source.

Card catalogue (alphabetically arranged) for books:

Author cards. Authors are usually individual persons, but organizations such as societies, institutions, and government departments which issue annual reports, year books, and series of bulletins, etc., are considered authors of their publications. Author cards often carry more information than subject or title cards.

Subject cards. For each book on a particular subject, there will be a card with the subject word or phrase on the top line underlined in red. Be as specific as possible when looking up a subject. For instance, look under *Oak,* not *Trees,* and under *Normandy, History,* not *History,* or *France, History.*

Sometimes you will be referred from terms not used by the library to synonymous terms which seem more helpful—for example, *Animal Kingdom,* see *Zoology.* Under some subject headings the last card will suggest related topics which you may wish to explore—for example, *Ethics,* see also *Altruism, Ascetism, Business ethic, Conduct of life, Good and evil, Utilitarianism.*

Title cards. Books with distinctive titles have title cards. In general, do not use this approach for books which have titles such as *Principles of . . . , History of . . . ,* or *Biography of. . . .* If you don't know the author of such a book, look under the subject.

Serial catalog for bound periodicals and society publications. Magazines are generally found under their titles—for example, *Atlantic Monthly* or *Journal of Higher Education.* Many serials, however, can be found only by looking under the name of the issuing organization. For instance, the *Proceedings* of the National Education Association will be found under National Education Association, not under Proceedings.

The cards in this catalog show which volumes of a particular serial are owned by the library. However, the recent issues of many periodicals are shelved in the periodical room, and these recent issues are not recorded in the serial catalog. Where this is the case, the cards will refer you to the periodical room for current issues. The cards will also indicate which journals are located in the various special reading rooms and special libraries. There are no subject cards in the serial catalog.

Indexes to periodicals. To look up magazine articles on a particular subject, one would most likely turn first to the *Readers' Guide to Periodical Literature.* There are, however, several more specialized indexes which will be merely listed, because their titles are indicative of the contents: *Art Index; Bibliographie der Deutschen Zeitschriften-literatur* (a German index to German periodicals); *Bibliographie der Fremdsprachigen Zeitschriften-literatur* (a German index to non-German periodicals); *Biography*

Index (biographical material in books and magazines); *Book Review Digest* (an index to book reviews); *Canadian Index* (an index to Canadian periodicals); *Education Index, Essay and General Literature Index* (indexes essays in collections, chapters in books, and other miscellaneous writings); *The International Index* (Humanities and Social Science); *Magazine Subject Index and Dramatic Index* (American & British); *PAIS* (Economics, Political Science, Public Administration); *Poole's Index* (general); *Subject Index to Periodicals* (British); *Russkaia Periodicheskia Pechat* (Russian, arranged by year, periodical, and author); *Willing's Press Guide* (address, phone, price, and frequency of British and Commonwealth periodicals and newspapers).

Newspaper indexes. The best way to locate newspaper stories on specific topics is to look up those items in the New York *Times Index* or the *Index to the Times* (London). Other papers of the same or approximate dates can then be checked for the same items.

Yearbooks. Information on recent events, as well as on some older records, can be found in *Statesman's Yearbook, World Almanac, Information Please Almanac, New International Yearbook, American Yearbook, Statistical Abstract of the United States, Commerce Yearbook,* and the *Reference Shelf* series.

Dictionaries. General dictionaries, both unabridged and abridged, contain information on pronunciation, usage, and derivation. Some of them include place geography, postal information, foreign exchange rates, tables of weights and measures, holidays, colleges, and other miscellaneous items. Some of the familiar general dictionaries are *Webster's, Funk and Wagnalls, Oxford,* and *American College Dictionary.* There are specialized dictionaries in fields such as law and politics.

Biographies. Personal data concerning the qualifications of authors whom we may wish to quote may be found in biographical reference works. These are the general ones: *Allgemeine Deutsche Biographie* (Germans no longer living); *Biographie Universelle* (universal); *Current Biographies* (universal); *Dictionary of American Biography* (Americans no longer living); *Dictionnaire de Biographie Française* (Frenchmen no longer living); *The Dictionary of National Biography* (Englishmen no longer living); *Neue Deutsche Biographie* (Germans no longer living); *Nouvelle Biographie Generale* (universal); *Who's Who* (living Englishmen); *Who Was Who* (Englishmen no longer living); *Who Was Who in America* (Americans no longer living); *Who's Who in America* (living Americans). There are biographical reference works which are specialized in terms of region, field of endeavor, and the like. Among these are *Who's Who in the Midwest, Who's Who in American Education, Directory of American Scholars, American Men of Science,* and *Who Knows—and What.*

Current periodicals and newspapers on public affairs. Students who wish to keep abreast of public affairs read with some regularity at least a few papers and magazines. In this category are the New York *Times, Wall Street Journal, Christian Science Monitor, Time, Newsweek, U.S. News and World Report, Congressional Record, Vital Speeches, Reporter, Business Week, Atlantic, Harper's, New Republic, Nation, Fortune, Monthly Labor Review, Congressional Digest, American Economic Review, Foreign Affairs,* and *Annals of the American Academy of Political and Social Sciences.*

Book reviews. Keeping up with the new books, particularly in the fields of popular interest, is a difficult task at best. It can be facilitated by skimming the reviews in publications such as these: New York *Times,* New York *Herald-Tribune, Saturday Review, Book Review Digest,* and *Index to Book Reviews in the Humanities.*

Government documents. These represent important source material on many subjects. They are not usually listed in card catalogues, but they can be located in guides such as *United States Government Publications* and *Manual of Government Publications.* There are also official publications of the United Nations, League of Nations, International Labor Office, states and municipalities, and others. The U.S. Government Printing Office offers a *Documents Catalogue* and *United States Government Publications: Monthly Catalogue.*

Directories and Miscellaneous. Directories of local telephone subscribers and of organization membership lists are generally well known, but there are others which a researcher may have occasion to consult. A few examples will suggest the variety of available references: United States Department of Commerce, *Directory of National Trade Associations; Directory of American Psychological Services; College Entrance Guide;* and Historical Manuscripts Commission (Great Britain), *List of Accessions to Repositories.*

Pamphlets on seemingly countless subjects are collected by large libraries. Some have upwards of fifty thousand items. *Public Affairs Pamphlets,* a bulletin of the United States Office of Education, indexes this kind of material.

Until recently, a scholar who wished to examine an item which was held by a distant library had either to travel there or pay for an interlibrary loan. Now, thanks to new devices and closer cooperation among libraries, one can obtain microcards, microfilm, microprint, and other reproductions of the original materials. The borrower must have access to machines which magnify and illuminate the miniaturized material.

A few titles will suggest the great variety of miscellaneous reference works which many libraries have: *World Wide Money Converter and Tipping Guide, B.B.C. Handbook, American Counties,* and *Facts About the Presidents.*

HINTS ON READING

When to read. In case the advocate has an opportunity to phrase his own proposition, part of the reading should precede the act of phrasing. An informed person is better qualified to state accurately a proposition which will express the essence of the controversy.

Similarly, if worthwhile discussion is to precede the wording of a proposition and the subsequent debate upon it, systematic reading is usually indispensable. If five uninformed persons pool their ignorance in a discussion, we may say that five times zero is still zero.

In the instances of school debaters and professional advocates, such as lawyers, whose propositions are imposed by circumstances, the reading which is direct preparation necessarily occurs *after* the proposition has been worded. In case the proposition can be altered, it may be that the results of his reading will lead the advocate to revise the original wording. Thus there is something to be said for beginning one's study with a tentative statement and then revising the proposition as the study progresses. In actual practice, however, the advocate whose proposition is given to him is not at liberty to alter the wording of it. His reading is simply a matter of discovering the materials pro and con on the proposition as phrased.

Whether the reading takes place before or after the proposition is phrased, the reading may profitably alternate with analysis. In other words, the first step of direct preparation should be a preliminary discovery of issues, the second step should be the reading as directed by these tentative issues, the third step should be a refinement of the issues, and the fourth step should be further reading in terms of the specific issues.

Try a study guide. Some sort of preliminary outline usually serves to guide one's reading. For instance, on a proposition of policy, the following simple outline is suggestive:

1. What does the question or the proposition mean?
   a. Define the terms.
   b. Identify the class in which the problem belongs—for example, social security, international politics, medical economics, labor economics, etc.
   c. Isolate the assumptions involved—for example, the relationship between national sovereignty and world peace in a debate on world organization.
2. How has the problem developed?
   a. Explore briefly its origin and history.
   b. Appraise its present timeliness.
   c. Discover evidence of the existence and the extent of the problem.
3. By what criteria should any solution be evaluated?
4. How does the status quo measure up to these criteria?

5. What are the other possible solutions?
6. How does each proposal measure up to the criteria?

Read selectively. One way to do this is to seek primary sources whenever feasible. For instance, it is better to quote from the original source, such as the *Bulletin of Atomic Scientists*, than to use a secondhand comment on it from the *Reader's Digest*. Experienced researchers realize the possibility of errors in condensing or in reporting original or primary materials.

Since we can seldom read everything on a proposition, we should try to read the best. This involves our applying the tests of the credibility of sources, which are explained in Chapter 7. Perhaps the most familiar enemy of credibility is bias or "slant" for or against some ideas, persons, countries, institutions, and so on.

Adapt your speed of reading. Material that is not relevant to the issues can be skimmed, while sentences, pages, or chapters that bear upon the essential points may properly be read thoroughly with the view to taking notes. In general, read rapidly, but not at the expense of comprehension. Avoid the tendency to dismiss lightly the ideas or sources that disagree with your preconceived notions. Apply the tests of evidence as objectively as possible.

Read from general to specific. It is obviously better to read general background articles before going to sources that present specific details. This order of reading will reduce the amount of useless note-taking in the early stages of the investigation. General reference works, histories, or other textbooks should take chronological precedence over periodicals and newspapers of recent dates. One who is preparing to discuss or debate some current scheme of world organization may need, first of all, a background knowledge of mankind's attempts in that direction in the past.

Assimilate the raw materials. The mere accumulation of quotations and facts is not the real purpose of reading. These items are the raw materials of proof. They should be weighed and related to other similar materials and to the reader's attitudes. Think while you read. Understand not only what was said, but also why it was said. Unassimilated reading notes mean little to the speaker or his audience. The best results are obtained when the product of one's reading is an indivisible composite of the writers' ideas and the reader's reactions.

RECORDING MATERIAL

Why it is necessary. Even though it is easier at the moment to avoid this bane of preparation by relying on makeshift notes, the advantage is short-lived. The positive advantages of systematic recording make the practice worthwhile; it assembles in an orderly fashion the materials for discussion outlines, case outlines, and rebuttals; it permits the exchange of notes among persons; it prevents the forgetting of ideas and sources.

What to record. How much should be recorded? The nature of the subject, the investigator's prior knowledge of it, the time involved, and the number, length, and importance of the papers or speeches in which the material is to be used are determining factors. The general tendency is to record too little. Thus it is wise to record, briefly at least, all the apparently significant evidence and argument which the study uncovers.

Enough should be written about each item so that it will be meaningful to the investigator or his colleagues at the moment or even months later. The topic involved, the authority and his qualifications (if opinion evidence), the quotation or précis, and documentation are minimum essentials. Each note or card should have on it the materials necessary for its defense against the charge that it fails to meet one or more of the tests of evidence.

Methods of recording. One should distinguish between the recording of bibliography and that of evidence and argument. If the bibliography is to be listed on sheets of paper, it should bear a title and be divided into sections on the basis of different types of publications, such as books, periodicals, government documents, etc. For details of form, see one of several recently published writer's guides and manuals of style. Usage in the matter of punctuation and the placing of authors' initials and given names varies among editors.

Student debaters are more likely to prepare annotated bibliographies with one item on each card. When debate squad members practice division of labor, they divide the bibiliography, make these cards, and exchange them or keep them in a common file. Bibliography cards are 3 × 5 or 4 × 6 inches, but they must be uniform in size and arrangement of data. The following information should be on each bibliographical card: identification of reference, including author's name, title of article and magazine or book, date of publication, and pagination; where the publication is kept, such as closed reserve, open reserve, stacks, general library, law library, etc.; summary of contents and notation of special-interest items; appraisal of its usefulness to one or both sides. The identification of the reference should be placed at the top of the card.

Students of debate use several methods of recording evidence and rebuttal ideas. Some use loose-leaf notebooks, but that method is cumbersome, even if only one item is put on a page. The preferred method is the use of a file box containing 3 × 5 or 4 × 6 cards, alphabetized dividers, and a table of contents in the lid. If cards on one topic are grouped in a section, and if key words and documentation appear at the top of each card, a specific reference can be found quickly. The topics in the detailed study outline, or some variation of them, may be used as a basis for grouping the cards, placing the dividers, and itemizing the table of contents. Of the following samples, the first is factual and the second is an expression of expert opinion, according to the classification in Chapter 7.

EXERCISES

1. Investigate a proposition, preferably the one analyzed for an exercise in Chapter 4.
   a. Record the material on cards as shown in this chapter.
   b. The assigned number of cards may be divided among a stated number of points in the study outline.
   c. Prepare a classified bibliography or a set of annotated bibliography cards.

Union figures seniority from date of membership, not employment	107 N. L. R. B. 837 (1954), at 840, N. 3.
In the case of the Pacific Intermountain Express Company and the Teamsters' Union, the latter "established the seniority dates of employees who were not members of the union when hired as of the date upon which they became members of the union rather than as of the date of their employment."	

Teamsters' policy aids union but harms man	Professor Sylvester Petro, School of Law, New York University	The Labor Policy of The Free Society 1957, p. 219
"For there is nothing beneficial to the employee as such in the Teamsters' conception of seniority. That conception essentially promotes the union, and in fact amounts to a kind of economic coercion to immediate union membership."		

2. Class committees may be assigned to prepare sections of a study outline on a proposition.

3. If a division of labor, as suggested in this chapter, has been practiced, the teacher might designate a period in which questions from the study outline will be asked, and students will be called upon to read cards of material which provide answers.

4. Or, following Exercise 3, the teacher might call for the reading of file cards which pertain to specific issues or sub-issues which were found in the preceding lesson on analyzing this proposition.

5. Exercises 3 and 4 may be modified to direct the attention of specific students to separate sections (A to M) under "Library Resources."

6. On the first page of this chapter we recommended that investigation should begin with a survey of the investigator's own thoughts on the matter. Why so?

7. Ask a scholar who has published some research how he proceeded. Compare this with what a school debater reports on his procedure.

Chapter 6

DISCUSSION AS

PREPARATION FOR DEBATE

The usual methods of preparing for debate are *reading* and *discussion*. In Chapter 5 we were primarily concerned with investigation through reading. Our interests here are the relations of discussion and debate and the role of discussion in preparing for debate.

THE RATIONALE OF
DISCUSSION AND DEBATE

Discussion is often a forerunner of debate in two ways: (1) the propositions that people choose to defend as advocates and debaters are very often the *outcomes* of discussion; and (2) the planning of the debater's case, *after the proposition has been formulated,* can often benefit by discussion.

The nature and purpose of discussion. Discussion may be defined as "the cooperative deliberation of problems by persons thinking and conversing together in face-to-face or coacting groups under the direction of a leader for purposes of understanding and action." [1] A brief analysis of this definition will provide an adequate understanding of discussion for our purposes here.

Discussion begins with a problem (rather than a proposition) and seeks a solution to this problem (which can be phrased as a proposition) through cooperative (rather than competitive) thinking; this thinking is reflective (rather than intentional) in character and proceeds through the steps usual in such thinking —problem, analysis, suggested solutions or hypotheses, reasoned development of these hypotheses, and acceptance or rejection of the hypotheses (rather than an organized structure of evidence and argument offered as proof). As a group undertaking, discussion is normally under the direction of a leader who seeks to provide guidance and direction. The purposes may be a better understanding of the problem under consideration, or the determination of policy as a basis for action, or both. The typical situation for discussion is the small face-to-face group so arranged that everyone can be seen and heard in normal conversation. With some adaptations, discussion can also be conducted in coacting groups where a speaker-audience situation obtains—for example, the panel discussion or symposium.

The relations of discussion and debate. These relations can best be seen by comparing *inquiry and advocacy, reflective thinking and intentional reasoning,* and *cooperation and competition.*

Inquiry and advocacy. Richard Whately made this distinction over a century ago in these words:

Reasoning may be considered as applicable to two purposes . . . the *ascertainment* of the truth by investigation (inquiry) and the *establishment* of it to the satisfaction of *another* (proof). . . . The process of *investigation* must be supposed completed, and certain conclusions arrived at by that process, before the advocate undertakes to *prove* the justness of those conclusions. And in doing this, the advocate will not always find it expedient to adhere to the same course of reasoning by which his own discoveries were originally made; other arguments may occur to him afterwards, more clear, or more concise, or better adapted to the understanding of those he addresses.

[1] James H. McBurney and Kenneth G. Hance, *Discussion in Human Affairs* (New York: Harper and Brothers, 1950), p. 10.

If a man begins (as is too plainly a frequent mode of proceeding) by hastily adopting, or strongly leaning to, some opinion which suits his inclination, or which is sanctioned by some authority that he blindly venerates, and then studies with the utmost diligence, not as an Investigator of Truth, but as an Advocate labouring to prove his point, his talents and his researches, whatever effect they may produce in making converts to his notions, will avail nothing in enlightening his own judgment, and securing him from error.[2]

Discussion may be understood as a method of inquiry in which two or more people "reason together" in an attempt to "ascertain the truth" by a kind of "reflective exploration." Debate, on the other hand, is advocacy in which reason is employed "to establish truth to the satisfaction of another." To continue our paraphrase of Whately, "the discussion must be supposed completed, and certain conclusions arrived at, before the advocate (the debater) undertakes to prove the justness of those conclusions."

Reflective thinking and intentional reasoning. Mr. Whately says that "reasoning may be considered as applicable to two purposes—*inquiry* (or investigation) and *proof* (or advocacy). The reasoning serving these two purposes is often described as two kinds of reasoning: constructive reasoning (or reflective thinking) and intentional reasoning. Eugenio Rignano puts it this way:

In constructive reasoning it is the object of the reasoner to discover truths yet unknown, that is to say, new derivations of one group of phenomena from another. . . .

In such reasoning, the reasoner has at the outset no intention or desire to maintain certain points at the expense of certain others. He wishes only to discover *the truth,* whatever it may be. The "intentional" reasoner, on the other hand, starts reasoning in order to try to demonstrate the accuracy of definite assertions in which he has a particular interest. In one case the reasoner does not know in advance the final result of the new series of imagined experiments any more than the experimentalist knows the result of certain experiments which he sets out to perform for the first time. The second, on the other hand, always knows the results of his reasoning *because he desires it.*

[2] Richard Whately, *Elements of Rhetoric,* 7th ed. (London: John W. Parker, West Strand, 1846), pp. 5–6.

. . . It is clear that such "intentional" reasoning must, on account of this very different function, present aspects and peculiarities very different from "constructive" reasoning.[3]

At the risk of some oversimplification, then, discussion attempts to bring the constructive reasoning (or reflective thinking) of two or more persons to bear on a question or problem for the purpose of discovering an answer to the question or a solution to the problem. The debater or the advocate, on the other hand, begins with a conclusion phrased as a proposition and attempts through intentional reasoning to prove this proposition to be a sound conclusion.

Cooperation and competition. Discussion, by its very nature, is a cooperative undertaking of two or more persons with a common goal—better understanding and resolution of the problem under consideration. The participants in a true discussion do not know the answer to the problem, and they join their efforts to discover that answer. There is no basis for competition as there is in a debate where sides are taken on a specific proposition. In debate there is necessarily a built-in competition that pits the affirmative against the negative. This competition may be friendly and may be directed toward a critical examination of the proposition, or it may be spirited contention directed toward a favorable decision. In either case, however, it is competition.

If a discussion turns into a "proposition-centered" competition with committed spokesmen for and against this proposition, it has turned into a debate. And if the participants in a debate lose their identity as protagonists for or against a given proposition and deliberate without commitments to any proposition, the debate has become a discussion.

THE ROLE OF
ARGUMENTATION IN DISCUSSION AND DEBATE

We have defined argumentation as "a method of analysis and reasoning designed to provide acceptable bases for belief and

---

[3] Eugenio Rignano, *The Psychology of Reasoning* (New York: Harcourt, Brace and Company, 1927), pp. 209–210.

action." As such, the basic principles of argumentation have a wide application in both discussion and debate. The *propositions* of fact, value, and policy phrased as conclusions for the debater to defend or oppose may be phrased as *questions* of fact, value, or policy for people to discuss. Both debaters and discussers must necessarily be interested in discovering the issues through analysis. And the kinds of evidence and reasoning used in discussion and debate are ultimately reducible to the same types and subject to the same tests.

Both discussion and debate apply the basic principles of argumentation in their own unique contexts to serve their own special purposes. These different applications do require different methods, however, to achieve the best results. We set out below some suggestions for the conduct of discussion that we have found helpful.

DISCUSSION METHODS

Structuring the discussion. It is probably true that most of the discussions in which we participate have no consciously directed organization or structure. Since discussion normally arises out of problems or "felt difficulties" of one kind or another, it is to be expected that the discussion will take a course at least approximating the *steps in reflective thinking*. Over half a century ago, the American philosopher, John Dewey, analyzed reflective thinking in this way.

Upon examination, each instance [of reflective thought] reveals, more or less clearly, five logically distinct steps: (1) a felt difficulty; (2) its location and definition; (3) suggestion of possible solution; (4) development by reasoning of the bearings of the suggestion; (5) further observation and experiment leading to its acceptance or rejection; that is, the conclusion of belief or disbelief.[4]

A quarter of a century later, the American psychologist J. F. Dashiell concluded from an examination of experimental studies

[4] John Dewey, *How We Think* (Boston: D. C. Heath and Company, 1910), p. 72.

that "qualitatively, group discussion seems to be adequately characterized by the traditional analyses of individual thinking, as, e.g., stated by Dewey. . . ." [5]

Our own studies confirm Professor Dashiell's conclusion. Problem-solving discussion almost always exhibits these steps in reflective thinking more or less clearly. Since this is the case, they provide a helpful guide in exploring a problem in preparation for discussion and a logical pattern to follow during the discussion. This developmental plan is outlined below:

1. *Locate, define, and delimit the problem.*
2. *Analyze the problem.* What causes are operating to produce the problem?
3. *Suggest possible solutions to the problem.* Phrase these as hypotheses for consideration.
4. *Compare the merits of these hypotheses.* Weigh the evidence and argument bearing on each.
5. *Select the best hypothesis and reconsider it as a solution to the problem.* This solution or answer may be phrased as a proposition.

Pedantic insistence on this pattern in conducting discussion is a mistake. Good discussion is "thought in process," a kind of creative conversation that gives rise to new ideas and clearer insights. It is better to let a discussion that is going well take its own course, even if it is a bit random and discursive. But if it appears that it can profit by more order and direction, these steps in reflective thinking provide useful guidelines.

Contributing in discussion. Any discussion necessarily proceeds through the individual contributions of the participants. These are the sources of the ideas and the evidence and thinking bearing on these speculations. Although we have all had the experience of flashes of insight while speaking, for the most part our contributions in discussion, however tentative, are reasoned

[5] J. F. Dashiell, "Experimental Studies of the Influence of Social Situations on the Behavior of Individual Human Adults," *Handbook of Social Psychology,* edited by Carl Murchison (Worcester, Massachusetts: Clark University Press, 1935), p. 1131.

formulations thought out before we begin to speak—seconds before, minutes before, or hours before. If these trains of thought are presented for the inspection and criticism of others without premature insistence on conclusions, the participants will come as close as they are likely to come to thinking together cooperatively. This has been called the empirical method of contributing.

The empirical method points out when and where and how things of a designated description have been arrived at. It places before others a map of the road that has been travelled; they may accordingly, if they will, retravel the road to inspect the landscape for themselves. The scientific investigator convinces others not by the plausibility of his definitions and the cogency of his dialectic, but by placing before them the specified course of experiences, searchings, doings, and findings in consequence of which certain things have been found. . . . Dialectic thereby itself receives a designated status and office. . . . All the wit and subtlety of reflection and of dialectic find scope in the elaboration and conveying of directions that intelligibly point out a course to be followed.[6]

This method of exposing your own thinking to the scrutiny of others is simple enough to describe, but it does make heavy demands on the objectivity and integrity of the speaker. Anyone who holds an opinion of any kind presumably has arrived at this conclusion by some kind of process. The empirical method simply calls for a frank explanation of why and how this conclusion was reached. Such an explanation will bring out into the open the *real* factors entering into this conclusion—your reasons, the evidence as you see it, your hunches, your intuitions, and your motives. In the final analysis, this is the only way that others can share in your reactions (reasoned or otherwise) and reply to you in terms that get at your real position.

If your *real* reasons and your *real* motives for taking a certain position will not stand public inspection, *and you know it,* the obvious advice is to abandon this position in favor of one you will be glad to have examined. But human nature being what it is,

[6] John Dewey, *Experience and Nature* (Chicago, London: Open Court Publishing Company, 1925), p. 11.

the temptation is often present to cling to what we *want* and to argue for it in terms that have little or nothing to do with our *real* reasons. A reply to this kind of case, of course, may provide an interesting dialectical exercise, but it does not deal with the realities affecting mutual understanding and cooperative decision.

Without meaning to be cynical, we have long since abandoned the hope that the readers of this book (or the authors) will achieve the kind of selfless objectivity that banishes from human deliberation all the hidden motives and the specious rationalizations that provide a false front for what is really going on in our heads. Be that as it may, what we have described here as the empirical method of contributing is close to the essence of "thinking together." And we know by long experience that people can grow in their capacity to discuss issues in terms of the realities as they see them. At the very least, we may be forgiven the hope that this analysis will provide the basis for a more sophisticated evaluation of what passes as "reflective deliberation."

It is a fair question to ask whether the affirmative and the negative in a debate might not present their cases "empirically" and thus achieve through debate the kind of reflective deliberation we suggest for discussion. If they treat the proposition they are arguing as an hypothesis to which they have no commitments and for which they have no responsibilities, such a debate, of course, will serve much the same purposes as discussion. And, by the same token, if people engaged in discussion find themselves committed to a given position and responsible for it, the discussion is likely to take on most of the characteristics of debate. This fact, we feel certain, should disturb no one. Anyone who has had much experience with discussion and debate in the workaday world, apart from college classrooms and textbook models, will soon learn that the fine distinctions between discussion and debate are seldom respected even if they are understood.

Discovering purposes and attitudes in discusson. The purposes and the attitudes of the participants in discussion (or debate) are important determinants of the character of the deliberation. If the *real* purpose of the discussion (or debate) is the critical examination of a problem (or a proposition), the attitudes of the speakers must necessarily approach those of the scientific investigator. These have been described by a distinguished psychologist, the late Professor Robert H. Seashore:

Attitudes may be thought of as a general orientation or proneness to adopt certain approaches to various situations. The present list is presented as a tentative description of scientific attitudes.

1. Open-minded willingness to investigate any problem by the objective (impersonal) method wherever necessary. Likewise, a corresponding willingness to change a point of view if further data warrant reconsideration.
2. The recognition of many alternative explanations and the corresponding necessity for suspension of judgment until all critical factors have been investigated.
3. Intellectual curiosity: wide-spread use of careful observation in in search for *significant* interrelations with other phenomena, and interest in knowledge for its own sake, which in later stages becomes relatively independent of outside motivations.
4. Recognition of the value of the long range point of view as the basic program for the advancement of knowledge. Scientific method is equally applicable to immediate, practical situations, but success in these is usually dependent upon the existence of a large body of general knowledge from the pure fields.
5. A clear recognition and labelling as such of assumptions, hypotheses, and theories, as distinguished from established facts or principles.
6. A critical, analytical approach, demanding proof for assertions. Speculation as to basic explanation usually leads to an experimental investigation and checking of hypotheses, rather than continued deductive reasoning. A fertile imagination in forming hypotheses, but great caution in drawing conclusions.
7. Systematic procedures, implying logic and statistics, as well as the experimental method in seeking to reduce everything to a quantitative basis. (Does not neglect simple descriptions, but endeavors to keep all descriptions on a translatable basis, referable to fundamental descriptions of other sciences.)
8. Straightforward approach, analyzing problems carefully so as to avoid confusing side-issues or other matters of superficial interest.
9. Care in drawing conclusions: (a) Limiting conclusions to data at hand; (b) Recognizing the possibility of and guarding against sources of error, such as: prejudice, insufficient evidence, neglect of negative instances, selected or unrepresentative examples,

effects of chance, forgetting, unreliability of testimony, gaps in reasoning, parallel but non-causal relationships, etc; (c) Recognizing the probability of partial relationships in multi-causal situations, and of degrees of relationships, rather than all-or-none cases; (d) Avoidance of spurious appearance of accuracy, such as many decimal places on figures where other factors in the situation render such accuracy unimportant.

10. Emphasis upon integrity of work as a guarantee of accuracy.
11. A recognition of the appropriateness of scientific attitudes in certain situations, and other attitudes (for instance, social, esthetic, etc.) as more important in other situations. The various types of attitudes should theoretically form parts of a consistent philosophy.
12. A recognition of one's fallibility outside of his own special field of study, and a consequent evaluation of statements according to the competence of persons to speak on various topics." [7]

There can be no question but that belligerent, dogmatic attitudes, unless somehow or other contained or diverted, will largely defeat any deliberative effort. Other things being equal, any discussion will be effective in approximately the degree that the participants work together cooperatively in a common cause.

Leading discussion. The principal functions of leadership in discussion are *stimulation, guidance,* and *integration.* These functions may be served by a single individual or by several individuals—indeed, by anyone participating in the discussion. The important thing is that someone, or many, or all assume responsibility for the conduct of the discussion. Any discussion will be better if people are stimulated to contribute their best thinking, if some attention is given to a sequential development that begins someplace, goes someplace, and ends someplace, and if a serious effort is made to "pull together" the ideas contributed so that differences and agreements on focal points are clear to all concerned.

EXERCISES

1. Define discussion, and distinguish between discussion and debate. In what ways is discussion a precursor of debate? A preparation for debate?

[7] Robert H. Seashore, *Experimental Methods in Psychology* (Evanston, Illinois: mimeographed for class use, 1948), pp. 8–10.

2. Select a problem for class discussion. Phrase the subject for discussion as a question. Appoint a leader and conduct a discussion organized in terms of these steps in reflective thinking:

    a. Definition and delimitation of the problem
    b. Analysis of the problem
    c. Possible solutions to the problem
    d. Comparison of advantages and disadvantages of solutions
    e. Selection of best solution and consideration of ways and means of putting it into operation.

3. Phrase the solutions in Step C, above, as propositions for debate.

4. Divide the class into affirmatives and negatives on a proposition of policy. Convene the affirmatives and the negatives as separate discussion groups for the purpose of planning affirmative and negative cases.

Chapter 7

EVIDENCE

INTRODUCTION TO EVIDENCE

Definitions of evidence. Evidence consists of facts, opinions (ordinary and expert), and material things that are used in generating proof. It is the raw material from which the finished product, proof, is made by the process of reasoning. Evidence differs from reasoning, which is the other ingredient of proof, in that evidence is independent of and external to the advocate. In other words, the advocate finds evidence, but develops the reasoning.

Whether we are dealing with evidence in general argumentation or in specialized contexts such as courtroom debating or school debating, we need to recognize its several forms. Empirical or factual evidence consists of presumably verifiable statements, including those which are expressed statistically. Facts appear in reports of occurrences, the existence of something, classification of material, and the character of phenomena. Ordinary opinion is the testimony of a lay witness—that is, a person who does not qualify as an expert. Expert opinion is, as the name indicates, authoritative material. It is a statement of opinion by a person whose training and practice qualify him as an authority. Material things, known as real evidence in law, include many items, a few of which are burglar tools, a murder weapon, and an object that someone made.

Before discussing the kinds and tests of evidence, we should have clearly in mind what legal evidence means as distinct from evidence used in other contexts. First, the definition is narrower. Textbooks on the law of evidence define evidence as the material used to satisfy the court of the truth or untruth of disputed allegations of fact made by the parties in their pleadings. Second, the law of evidence is designed to facilitate the rendering of *judicial* decisions on specific matters. Legal disputes are not academic, hypothetical, or abstract. Third, the law of evidence is based upon *exclusion,* which means that certain kinds of relevant evidence are not admissible. There is no list of the kinds of evidence which are admissible in courts of law.

There is no law of evidence for nonlegal situations. In general argumentation we may have good evidence that would not be admitted in court. However, it is sometimes helpful to check our evidence against the rules of exclusion to determine whether one of the courtroom disqualifications also applies to our nonlegal evidence. For instance, an ordinary witness in court may report what he perceived, not what he thought. Sometimes this rule could be applied profitably to nonlegal argumentation.

Are facts and opinions as easily distinguished as the preceding discussion implies? Not unless most ultimate truths are presently available and widely understood. An experienced journalist has said that one cannot always isolate opinion from fact; opinion sometimes *is* fact, and interpretation may be news. In *Science Is a Sacred Cow,* Anthony Standen charges that scientists' findings are not truths but a body of well-supported probable opinions only, and that these may be exploded at any time.

Importance of evidence. It has been asserted that believing without evidence is the worst sin against the human mind. However, the source of that opinion did not define "evidence" as he meant it. Bernard Baruch's view of evidence is clearer: "Every man has a right to his opinion, but no man has a right to be wrong in his facts."

The exacting standard expressed above applies particularly to situations in which cogent or closely reasoned discourse is expected, but we recognize that evidence is less essential to the success of popular persuasion. Needless to say, the principles of argumentation are more carefully applied in the former context than the latter. Two instances will serve to suggest the practical importance of evidence in these settings. Judicial proceedings, especially in murder trials, tend to be rather demanding in terms of evidence, but despite this care, some innocent persons have been imprisoned for murder because untrained officials bungled the medical investigations. Popular persuaders are under no established rules of evidence, so their readers and listeners must exercise their own critical faculties.

This is not to say that every advocate must prove everything down to the last subpoint. To do so would be an endless task. Consequently, in general argumentation, we can profit from the legal experience with judicial notice. The doctrine of judicial notice holds that there are certain facts and judgments which are so well known or so easily verified that to require evidence of them would be a waste of time. Thus, it would not be necessary for a nonlegal advocate to adduce evidence to prove that the Wagner Act provided for the recognition of labor unions as bargaining agents.

Admissions are another exception to the principle that assertions should be evidenced. Inexperienced debaters tend to behave as if any admission would be disastrous. Their mistake wastes time and makes them look ridiculous. In summary, we can say that controversial points should be evidenced unless the information is generally known or the point can be admitted safely.

Sources of evidence. Evidence which seems on its face to be credible, consistent, and convincing may be rendered of no account by an exposure of weakness in its source. For this reason a consideration of sources is in order. The sources of evidence are three: *persons, documents,* and *things.* Persons, of course, are the most important source. The testimony of persons may be written as well as spoken. Not all written evidence is documentary. Books, magazine articles, etc., used in general argumentation should be used as the personal testimony of their authors. When a writer states in a book that a certain thing is true, this is personal testimony that the thing is true and documentary evidence that he stated that it is true. The person behind all personal testimony should be tested alike in written and oral evidence. So it is always necessary, in selecting one's own proof or in attacking the proof of an opponent, to know what kinds of witnesses give good evidence and what kinds give bad evidence.

Our classification of sources in terms of persons, documents, and things may be clearer to many if the familiar constituents of these categories are listed. Personal evidence may appear in public records (minutes, committee records, the *Congressional Record*), public written material (books, newspapers, magazines), private written material (diaries, letters, company books), and personal testimony (under oath or in informal reports). Documentary evidence, which overlaps personal evidence at some points, may appear in public records (statutes, ordinances, vital statistics, etc.) and private written material (wills, contracts, ledgers, etc.). Things, or real evidence, are submitted to be seen; thus the source is sometimes classified as "inspection."

KINDS OF EVIDENCE

No doubt there are many of us who use evidence without classifying it or even knowing that there are several kinds, but among those who use evidence professionally there are some accepted divisions. These are more or less arbitrary, and there is some variety in nomenclature. Nevertheless, it is well to be aware of the kinds of evidence, because each one has its characteristic strengths and weaknesses.

In some books on legal evidence we observe that evidence is usually classified in a series of pairs of labels. More often than not, an item of evidence will bear one label from each pair. That is, an item is likely to be admissible or inadmissible, primary or secondary, etc. Categories like these are less important in general argumentation, but they are worthy of notice because of their relevance to the testing of evidence.

Admissible or inadmissible. This classification is rarely mentioned outside of judicial proceedings, with the possible exception of some school debate associations which permit the use of only printed evidence. In general argumentation, excluding legal proceedings and some school debates, there are no rules of evidence; therefore, the parties (affirmative, negative, and audience) are supposed to protect themselves by applying the *tests* of evidence which appear in the next section of this chapter.

Primary (original) or secondary (hearsay). Primary evidence is reported by the person who perceived it at its source. This kind affords the greatest assurance of accuracy, because it is based on the original document or the first observation. In the process of authenticating it, only one source has to be tested. Primary evidence of Dean Smith's opinion of deferred rushing would be his own words. If John says that he saw Bill at the ball game on July 4, he is the primary or original source.

Secondary evidence is a lesser method of proof. Hearsay has a stigma attached to it, but often it is the best evidence available, and sometimes it is all we have. Authentication is complicated by the necessity of testing the primary source and all subsequent ones. An unsigned copy of a document or an oral statement of its contents would be secondary evidence. Someone else's report of Dean Smith's views is hearsay or secondary evidence. In general usage, this kind of evidence is worthless only if it comes from ignorant, careless, or vicious persons. But hearsay from accurate, honest, trained minds is acceptable in most situations.

Care must be taken not to confuse direct and original evidence. If A testifies that B said that he saw X kill Y, this is direct but hearsay. If A testifies that he saw X running away from the scene of the murder of Y at about the time Y must have been killed, this is original but circumstantial evidence that X murdered Y.

Direct or circumstantial. Direct evidence refers to the precise point at issue; that is, it establishes *directly* the truth of the contention. One cannot classify evidence as direct or circumstantial until he knows the point to which the evidence applies. "Direct" and "circumstantial" are only labels of the *relation of the evidence* *to the issue.* If the question is, "Did A shoot B?" the testimony of an eyewitness that he saw A shoot B is direct. In general argumentation, evidence is cited to support points or subpoints, not the whole proposition.

Circumstantial evidence relates to a series of facts, other than those at issue, which *inferentially* tend to establish the fact or point at issue. The alleged relationship between excessive smoking and the incidence of heart disease and lung cancer is based upon circumstantial evidence. In the following account there is circumstantial evidence of gambling: Police raided an apartment and found, in addition to the furnishings, three pairs of dice, twelve decks of cards, a bottle of gin, and twenty-three men who explained that they had gathered to discuss current events.

The most effective proof is gained by the use of these two kinds of evidence *in combination.* Direct evidence may be untrustworthy because of mistakes in the observation of the witness, inaccuracy in reporting, or because of prejudice. Circumstantial evidence may be inconclusive because of a possible ambiguity in the inferences to be drawn from it. But when the two kinds are used together, each confirming the other, the evidence becomes of the highest possible efficacy.

Ordinary or expert. Looked at from the point of view of its source, evidence is classifiable as ordinary or expert. An ordinary source is one who has no special training or experience in the subject at hand. In court an ordinary witness may report an observation and possibly an impression, but he may not state an inference. This distinction may seem simple enough, but observation and inference are frequently confused. A laborer may testify as to his being forced (or not) to join a union, but his imputation of a motive would probably be ruled out.

Ordinary evidence is supposed to be on factual matters in court, but in general argumentation it is used for both fact and opinion. Most evidence is of this kind. In general argumentation the distinction between ordinary and expert evidence is less important than whether a quotation is reporting a fact or expressing an opinion. If it is the latter, we should ask whether the opinion is ordinary or expert. For instance, many politicians' remarks actually are ordinary opinion, but the voters and the news media often expect expert-opinion pronouncements on all public questions. How often does a politician say, "I don't know"? Ordinary-opinion evidence often appears in commercial testimonials, too.

Expert evidence, which usually involves opinion, is used in court to help in finding "facts," as they are called there. However, in general argumentation we use quotations from experts to corroborate a judgment. Raw data could be reported by an ordinary witness, but the statistical interpretation of those data would call for an expert. This source must have special training or experience in the subject at hand. His qualifications are ascertained in court before he is permitted to testify. The same principle of qualifying before quoting should apply in general argumentation. Disagreement among experts will be considered under "tests of sources." A career officer in the United States Forest Service would be an expert witness on the subject of lumbering practices, for example.

Written or unwritten. With respect to its form, we may classify evidence as written and unwritten. In courts of law a considerable part of the evidence is unwritten. It consists of the spoken testimony of witnesses present before the judge or jury. In formal debate elsewhere, however, most evidence is from written (printed) sources.

Real or personal. Real evidence is evidence of which any *object* is the source. It is not hearsay, because it is presented directly (without interpretation) to the senses of those who are to judge. Weapons, blood tests, and viewing of the scene are familiar examples. Sometimes real evidence is demonstrative; that is, it is "acted out," as in the case of a city claims adjustor who had a bus door close on his neck three times to show that no injury was caused.

Personal evidence is evidence afforded by a human agent, either in the way of discourse or by voluntary signs made for the purpose of communicating thoughts. Whenever a witness communicates thought to a judge or jury either by spoken language or by signs, he is giving personal evidence; but if he *shows* the jury a wound, or shows that he can raise his arm by raising it for them to see, he is giving real evidence.

A bacteriologist gave both kinds of evidence in a soft-drink case. He testified that a dead mouse in the bottle would not cause stomach spasms, and then he drank Exhibit One to demonstrate his conviction.

Preappointed or casual. Wherever the creation or preservation of an article of evidence has been, either to public or private minds, an object of solicitude, that is, in the view of its serving to give effect to a right, or enforce an obligation, on some future contingent occasion), the evidence so created and preserved comes under the heading of "preappointed" evidence. Deeds, notes, written contracts, etc., are forms of written, preappointed evidence. When a man arranges to have certain persons witness his words or actions in order that they may testify to what he said or did, we have unwritten, preappointed evidence. Any evidence not coming under the head of preappointed evidence is "casual" or "undesigned" evidence. This is evidence that has been neither created nor preserved for the purpose of using it as evidence of the fact now being substantiated by it. This kind of evidence consists of testimony given by persons who, when they obtained it, had no thought that it would ever be used as evidence in the case in question. Speaking for another purpose, a person often lets fall a statement that is merely incidental. The value of such evidence lies in its freedom from the suspicion of any hidden motive. It is ingenuous and presumably honest. But it has very serious weaknesses; the testimony may well have been careless. The witness, thinking the assertion of slight importance, may have been indifferent as to its accuracy.

A similar distinction is sometimes made between the willing and the unwilling, or the eager and the reluctant, witness. This is more nearly a test (of moral qualification) than a kind of evidence, because the motivation of the source may have a great deal to do with the credibility of his testimony. An eager source may be self-serving, whereas a reluctant source may be testifying against his own interest.

Negative. This category is markedly different from the preceding ones in that it has no opposite and is not evidence in the usual sense. It means a significant absence of evidence, or testimony of silence. It is said to be particularly valuable because, like casual evidence, it is difficult to contrive. "If it were true, we would have heard of it," expresses the widespread faith in negative evidence. The failure of an investigation to find evidence of graft in an office would be negative evidence of wrong-doing. To put the idea differently, we should conclude that a certain college did not offer a credit-bearing course in speech in 1930 if the bulletins and other records for that year made no mention of such a course.

THE TESTS OF EVIDENCE

Very important for our purposes are the tests to be applied to determine the value of evidence. To know whether a piece of evidence is strong or weak is essential to the intelligent conduct of a case. We can frequently use only a limited amount of all that is available. We must have the power to discriminate. Then, too, we must know what is strong enough to be put in the forefront of the proof, and what is so weak as to be valuable only for the purpose of "filling in" and reinforcing the more important parts. For these purposes we have two vital tests of evidence: the test of the *substance* of the evidence itself, and the test of the *sources* from whence it comes. There are two additional, lesser tests—those of reporting and those of documentation—both of which are often associated with the tests of sources.

Tests of substance. These relate to the quality of the evidence itself. For this reason they are more crucial than the tests of sources, because dependable evidence *can* come from a questionable source. In a judicial context these tests are at times complex, but most of them have obvious applications to general argumentation.

Recency, or what a difference the date makes, is sometimes an important test. We know that many a "fact" of yesteryear has been proved wrong, and we have heard of authorities who have changed their minds. During the 1960 campaign for the office of State's Attorney of Cook County, Illinois, a group of Democratic lawyers published a booklet of editorials from Chicago newspapers under the title, "What the Press Says About the State's Attorney." The collection was designed to prove that the city dailies, including the *Daily News,* were opposed to the incumbent, Mr.

Adamowski. These headlines from the *Daily News* were quoted: "Adamowski Might Do More If He Talked Less" (June 16, 1959), and "Adamowski's Mouthing Hampers Police Reform" (March 8, 1960). However, on the following November 1, shortly before the election, the *Daily News* lead editorial was titled, "Daily News Recommends Re-election of Adamowski."

Relevancy, which is not easily determined in some situations, is an important test nevertheless. In general argumentation we have the common-sense principle of *logical* relevancy, which holds that evidence should pertain to the point in connection with which it is used. A breach of logical relevancy is also an instance of fallacious reasoning, as in a television commercial which purported to demonstrate that A's cigarette filter would absorb and retain more tar and nicotine than B's filter. This was evidenced by pouring water into two glass tubes, one containing A's filter and the other B's. How does the ability to soak up water relate to the claimed ability to remove tar and nicotine from cigarette smoke?

Internal consistency of evidence can be tested by asking whether the evidence is consistent with itself. Evidence that contradicts itself is of course the worst possible kind. Some answer may be made, some explanation given, to save the situation when one's evidence is shown to be inconsistent with human experience or known facts. But when our evidence has an inconsistency within itself, we cannot escape without suffering some disadvantage. We cannot go outside and show the error is on the other side. There is something wrong with our own evidence, and when this is exposed by our opponent, or detected by readers or hearers, our cause has suffered more than would have been the case had we failed to meet any other test. Inconsistency in the disputant himself is unpardonable. So, when Oppius was charged with defrauding the soldiers of their pensions, Cicero refuted the charge by proving that the *same persons* charged Oppius with a design to corrupt the army with his extravagant gifts and liberality. We speak of internal inconsistency when we charge that someone's story doesn't "hang together."

External consistency of evidence is judged by comparing the testimony with similar data outside itself. Is the evidence consistent with human nature and experience? Is it consistent with known facts? Is it verifiable in some other way?

Any man properly hesitates to accept as a fact anything that runs contrary to his own past experience or the experience of his fellowmen. To make him believe in any evidence that contradicts the beliefs of his life and his habits of thinking requires explanation, enforcement, and substantiation that soon become an argument in themselves, and even then the unqualified acceptance of the proof may be a matter of doubt. If the evidence is in this way contrary to ordinary human experience, one must never neglect to maintain its truthfulness by explaining just why it is credible and valuable. Applying this test, an editorial writer on the *Wall Street Journal* questioned the testimony of a retail druggist (that consumers paid as much in non –"fair trade" areas as they did in "fair trade" areas), saying, "This was mystifying because, first, it ran counter to the experience of many people. . . ."

It is clearly advisable to avoid contradiction between evidence presented and some well-known facts. Discovery of this inconsistency by an opponent or by the audience will undermine any confidence in the offending person. The mistake of adducing evidence that is contradicted by commonly known or easily proved facts can be seen in the testimony of a physician before a Seattle council committee which was studying the proposed fluoridation of the local water supply. Despite the findings of medical societies, the United States Public Health Service, and the experiences of several other cities, this witness said there was no evidence that fluoridated water reduces tooth decay.

A skeptical businessman who doubted the dependability of sales forecasts based upon sampling interviews decided to test the evidence against outside criteria. He sought to verify the findings of the first survey by conducting another on a different basis. Instead of asking the interviewees what books they liked, he offered a free book of each interviewee's choice. In the second survey, fewer persons selected Shakespeare and the *Bible,* and more persons than before selected *Murder of a Burlesque Queen,* for example.

Sufficiency of evidence may be a test of either the quantity of the evidence or the quality of the generalizing therefrom. Some points are acceptable without proof, as we noted under "judicial notice." Others require a great deal of support. Some advertising claims for contact lenses were questioned by the Federal Trade Commission for lacking evidence—"continual comfortable wear," "provide better vision than other eyeglasses," "protect the eyes in all active sports." Other advertisers have been disciplined for basing their claims on "preliminary data which are still experimental, incomplete, and contradictory." This was the view of the Food and Drug Administration in relation to the claims that certain oils and margarines containing unsaturated fats would help prevent heart disease by reducing the cholesterol content of the blood. But who would require "all the facts," even on a simple event such as a traffic accident? Volumes might be required to contain the policeman's report, the traffic engineer's report, the insurance adjustor's report, the oculist's report, psychologist's report, the weather man's report, and the testimony of witnesses.

Comparative quality of one kind of evidence in relation to the others is known as the "best evidence" principle in law. Whether one is working in a legal situation or not, he should put forward the best available evidence. To do less is to invite censure on ethical grounds. For example, primary evidence is better than secondary, but secondary evidence is acceptable if it is all that a diligent search can produce. The intent of this principle is that the evidence used shall have the greatest probative force that the advocate can muster.

A few examples of the kinds of evidence that are exceptionally valuable will further explain the meaning of comparative quality. An admission or a declaration against one's own interest is highly valued if the witness is aware of the implications of his statement. This would be true of a "protected" manufacturer's testimony that the tariff on his foreign competitors' products is too high. Casual or undersigned evidence, which has been discussed, is especially valuable because of its freedom from suspicion. Negative evidence is likewise valuable because, as has been explained, it cannot be easily contrived. Finally, real evidence, or the object itself, is better evidence than someone's oral description of it.

Special tests of statistical evidence may be stated as principles to be observed. They do not include the inferences drawn from statistics; those matters belong under a discussion of reasoning or fallacies.

Sets of data which are to be compared should be based upon identical definitions of terms and values of units. A government economist who tries to prove that the country is in better financial condition now than it was five years ago is likely to cite figures on the gross national product. A higher G.N.P. means better times, he would say, but does he adjust his figures for any difference in the buying power of the dollar?

Computation of changes in terms of percentages should proceed upon a constant base. The story is told of a teacher who was hired by a school at a salary of $6,000 for the first year. For his second year he received a raise of 10 per cent. But for the third year, because of financial reverses, the college reduced salaries 10 per cent. "Oh, well," said he, "I'm only back where I started." The base of calculation shifted from $6,000 to $6,600, thereby making his third-year salary $60 below his starting salary.

Material which is to be treated statistically should be quantifiable—that is, amenable to being counted by numbers. This problem would confront anyone who would attempt to prove that college students are 5 per cent happier this year than they were last year.

Sampling error should be avoided by determining that the sample is representative of the universe to be generalized about. Let us take an extreme example of a self-biasing sample. Imagine what would happen if you sent to a random sample of our citizens a questionnaire that included this item: "Do you enjoy answering questionnaires?" The fact that the "yes" people would be much more likely to return the forms is a biasing factor.

Pertinent factors in the situation should not be altered during extrapolation. This principle applies to the making of predictions by extending a trend line or a curve from known data on indefinitely in the direction in which it was headed. The projection of past percentages into the future may not reliably indicate probabilities.

All variables which might affect the result should be taken into account. In our desire for simplification of the complex, we sometimes attribute an event or a condition to only one factor, as in the case of arguing that X was elected because he was handsome. In national elections there are so many elusive variables that accurate predicting is difficult to achieve. What is the effect of age, appearance, voice, religion, marital status, wealth, etc., upon political success? Or which personal attributes of a corporation executive account for his status?

The nature of any average should be specified, lest it misrepresent the situation. Perhaps a median would be more suitable. Terms like "average man" and "average income" are so widely used that many persons are misled into thinking that those words mean something precise. The word "average" covers median, mean, mode, and possibly other situations without some persons' knowing it. In many cases an average should not be used as evidence. When reporting wage or salary data, for instance, a median will give a reasonably good picture of conditions, and a mean will make the figures look better than they are, but an unspecified average may be little better than a lie.

When a correlation is used, it is essential to distinguish among simple, multiple, and partial correlations. The relationship between temperature and consumption of heating oil can be treated as a simple correlation. A multiple correlation would be involved in a study of the factors contributing to a decline in stock-market quotations. Partial correlations are trickiest of all. For instance, one might argue a partial correlation between low income and juvenile deliquency, even though other factors are known to be operating.

When applicable, the level of statistical significance should be given. This is a way of saying how much better than chance our result is. In some contexts a change of 3 per cent would be significant, while in others a figure of 30 per cent might not be. A result may be statistically significant but not socially or psychologically important. For instance, a sex difference of .10 I.Q. points might be statistically significant but actually trivial.

Tests of sources. The *quality* of the evidence is the most vital consideration in terms of the tests of evidence, but the source becomes important when one is unable definitively to test the truth or wisdom of the evidence itself. Information on a source may provide fallible signs of its reliability. This is especially true if we consider the audience acceptability of evidence, as we must when we use argumentation in persuasion.

Tests of ordinary witnesses. In judicial situations, ordinary witnesses or laymen usually testify as to an observed fact, but in general argumentation their opinions are also used. An ordinary witness is one who lacks the experience, training, or education to qualify him as an expert on the matter in question.

Tests are obviously important when one is confronted with conflicting testimony. A choice must be made, because not all of the accounts can be right. What should we believe about a burglary suspect after hearing these five reports from as many witnesses: He was caught inside a garage; he was pounced upon in an alley twenty feet from the garage; he was empty-handed; he had three hundred dollars in his hand; he held a screwdriver in his hand?

Moral qualification is the most frequently used test of ordinary witnesses in court. Actually, in many nonlegal situations, too, the credibility of a witness is dependent upon his impartiality and his reputation for veracity. We want to know whether the one giving evidence has a selfish interest in the disputed matter, has a prejudice or bias for or against one side, or has previously given conflicting or false testimony. The report of a fact-finding committee of a legislative body becomes vulnerable on this count when we note that the division of the members over the findings coincides with their partisan affiliation.

These criteria of moral qualification express ideals which cannot always be insisted upon in practice. There are times when rather good sources of evidence have that widespread human frailty, prejudice. Hence it is unwise to make the sweeping declaration that a biased source must never be used. When or how to use such evidence will be explained later in this chapter.

Opportunity to get the truth or to form a competent opinion is an obvious and an important test. If the situation or experience of the witness has been such that he has not had a chance to observe the facts to which he testifies, and to observe them closely and carefully, his statements are clearly untrustworthy. It is a common method of impeaching testimony to show that a witness was too far from the scene to see clearly, or that he did not have time to observe carefully. Innumerable writers are ready to venture the most positive statements on the foundation of a few weeks' investigation, or to make bold assertions of some general truth when they have observed only a few phenomena and when those they have observed are exceptional or sporadic in nature. It is not uncommon for a traveler to visit a foreign country for a few months or a year and, on his return, to write articles or a book on the society, political methods, or economic prospects of the unfamiliar land. Such a man is not to be criticized for writing in the magazines or publishing a book; his narrative may well be interesting. But *as evidence*, his statements and prophecies generally amount to little. The opportunities for observation are insufficient to make good evidence.

Mental qualifications of a person who gives evidence can be taken to include intelligence, education, perceptiveness, memory, and accuracy of expression. In general argumentation this test of an ordinary witness is broader and compartively more important than it seems to be in the courtroom context. The reason, which has been stated before, is that in nonlegal situations we often use the opinions as well as the observations of ordinary witnesses.

The test of the memory of a witness is applicable everywhere. In the courts, it is a part of the "stock in trade" of a cross-examiner. A defective memory is damaging, because it raises a strong presumption of error in the statement of testimony. If the witness cannot remember things in general, it is probable that he cannot clearly remember about the particular fact in question. His impressions will probably be vague and indistinct, and so his statements will be unreliable.

Accuracy in the use of language is not by any means universal. We have previously described different kinds of "liars," but many mistakes of verbal expression are wholly undesigned. Provincial phrases, personal peculiarities in speech, or a tendency toward exaggeration may often lead a witness to say what he does not really mean. In getting written evidence, to avoid the mistake of misunderstanding the witness, the real import of the testimony should be gathered from the evidence as a whole rather than from the exact words of any particular sentences. Witnesses who are habitually inaccurate must, of course, be treated with suspicion. There are many writers whose practice it is to deal in generalities and bold overstatements. If a man has a reputation for that style of writing, his testimony should be discounted in proportion to the relevancy of his style to the type of evidence he is giving. Accidental or thoughtless exaggeration is very common in oral testimony, and arises from habits of mind in the witness. Some men have an irresistible impulse to "make things big," like Falstaff, with his "eleven men in buckram." Intentional exaggeration is simply one kind of deliberate lying. A witness who exaggerates can best be exposed by investigating his accuracy in other instances.

Education as a mental qualification of an ordinary witness in a community controversy was aptly expressed in an editorial by a local newspaper on the dispute over the United States history textbooks used in the high school: ". . . those who talk loudest and most violently will be those who have never read any of the history texts in question and who haven't any standards for judging them if they did."

Physical qualifications of an ordinary witness relate to the acuity of his senses of sight, hearing, smell, taste, and touch. Most human knowledge comes through the avenues of the senses, and it is from the information so received that we get evidence. Clearly, then, the perceptive powers of a witness may have great influence upon his reliability. If a witness is color-blind, his testimony that green signal lights were displayed at the time and place of a railroad accident must be ignored. However, this test is not very common outside of the courtroom. The writers that furnish the materials of student debate and of ordinary argument everywhere are usually beyond the reach of such examination, and their testimony is not commonly of such a nature that it makes much difference whether they are blind, deaf, or otherwise physically handicapped. But whenever physical weakness may have any important effect on the testimony, the test should be rigorously applied. It is one of the most effective of all possible tests, for such a defect in a witness is conclusive against his testimony.

Tests of expert witnesses. Statements of opinion from "authorities" or "experts" are widely used in support of contentions. In general argumentative discourse we cite this kind of evidence to corroborate our own views. In effect, the advocate says his point is valid because it is supported by "someone who should know." But before this evidence is either used or believed, at least two tests should be applied.

Are expert opinions relevant and needed here?   Do not offend your audience by giving the *opinions* of alleged authorities on questions on which the facts are available and understandable to any intelligent man. Do not ask A to believe a thing *because* B believes it, when A's opinion is just as good as B's. No authorities, no matter how good, should be used to settle questions where opinion evidence is not *needed*.

Does the witness qualify as an expert?   This is often difficult to establish objectively. Someone has defined an expert as one who can take something we already know and make it sound confusing. Another defined him as an ordinary fellow a long way from home. We can recall that the "experts" told Charles Kettering in 1911 that his invention, the self-starter, wouldn't work. Other innovators whose qualifications were later acknowledged were at one time denied expert status by their peers. Copernicus was ridiculed by the eminent astronomer, Brache; Hemholtz was shunned because he was not a physicist; Pasteur, a chemist, met resistance from physicians.

Now suppose there are two or more accredited experts whose views are in conflict. Whose opinion should we accept? When the Interstate Commerce Commission and the Illinois Commerce Commision were holding hearings on the petition to allow the abandonment of the North Shore Line, a University of Chicago sociologist and authority on population trends testified that rail service was needed, while a Northwestern University professor of transportation favored abandonment. The choice is not as easy as a *Saturday Review* writer alleged: "But one does not have to be an expert in order to judge the handiwork of experts." How about choosing between the opinions of Linus Pauling and Edward Teller on the effects of nuclear-weapons tests, or aren't these "handiwork"?

Tests of reporting, including context.   Often these tests are discussed as tests of sources, but they are treated separately here because the communication media and the quality of the reporting are often beyond the control of the human source of the evidence. Three questions will be suggested: Is the medium credible? Is the reporting clear? Is the reporting fair?

Is the medium credible? Some persons, newspapers, and magazines have better reputations than others for reliable communication. Studies in the credibility of communicators (Hovland studies at Yale) show that the credibility of an advertisement or of a controversial essay is related to the reputation of the publication in which it appears. Some persons might assume that a death certificate, being an official document dealing with a serious matter, is a highly credible medium. Such was not the case, according to the *New England Journal of Medicine,* when a sampling of more than nine hundred death certificates was found to be from 27 to 63 per cent in error on the number of deaths attributable to coronary disease.

Is the reporting clear? Even though the substance of the evidence and reliability of its source are above reproach, someone may fail to report clearly what was said. A financial reporter once wondered in print why a western railroad's earnings were off 50 per cent when its carloadings were down only 6 per cent. What he failed to make clear was that the long-haul business, which makes the more money, was down forty per cent.

Is the reporting fair? It should be reasonably free of exaggeration or a biased selection of details, and it should present the proper context. A case of exaggeration occurred when a national news magazine gave the impression that a multitude of television viewers had "incessantly" complained "across the nation" because the networks had canceled or interrupted some entertaining shows in order to report a crisis in the United Nations. Actually, the letters and calls were comparatively few, and most were favorable to the network policy (*Saturday Review,* August 30, 1958). Using a biased selection of specifics, a writer or speaker with modest talent as a propagandist could present a distinctly unpleasant picture of a country. He could recite figures on poverty, slum housing, juvenile delinquency, corruption, racial friction, and the like. The items might be true, but the omission of favorable material would distort the effect. Quoting a statement out of context is a similar device. This occurred when a reporter chose one sentence from a twenty-page convention paper on the future of audio-visual instruction. The speaker was quoted as saying that machines should replace teachers and schools, when what he really said was that technology in the wrong hands would threaten basic human values.

Tests of documentation. When evidence is important, it should be authenticated. Listeners and readers have a right to know enough about the evidence to enable them to check it if they so desire. There is great potential mischief in undocumented evidence. For instance, in legislative hearings, documents are sometimes referred to when there is no opportunity to determine whether they even exist or whether they contain what a witness says they contain. Much damage may result, even though the evidence may have been ruled inadmissible *after* it was given. In a lighter vein, there was a national advertisement for electric toy trains which asserted, among other claims: "Psychologists say, 'If he controls a ——— train today, he'll control his life tomorrow! . . . contributes significantly to the child's appreciation of real values, . . . starts your youngster on the way to maturity.'" The challenge to document this claim came from *The American Psychologist* (January, 1959, page 57) which asked, ". . . if any reader can advise us as to the identity of the psychologists who speak so strongly for the predictive value of electric train control."

Tests of audience acceptability. One who tries to persuade others risks failure if he ignores this test. However, the intellectually rigorous proof of a contention may require the use of evidence which many persons would not accept. At times this choice between "what is right" and "what works" poses an ethical dilemma, but for a sophist the choice is simple: he takes the latter. According to this sophistic "results" criterion, a bit of evidence can be called proof only when the given readers or listeners believe it. In our view, proof is not always to be equated with belief.

Audience acceptance of evidence can be understood in three ways: that the content is believed, that the content is understood, and that the source is approved. One difficulty is that legends and traditional symbols often seem to be more durable than facts.

Many of us would hesitate to accept evidence which would discredit some of our notions concerning Washington's wisdom, Lincoln's idealism, and the eagle's nobility. In the case of opinion evidence, the problem of audience acceptance is potentially greater than in the case of factual evidence. However great the knowledge or skill of an expert, if his greatness is unknown to the hearer or reader, the effect of quoting him will be of little benefit and may do harm. The audience or reader will see in the pretended "authority" nothing more than a meaningless name, and so may ignore or resent his statement. The advocate must always be sure that the worth of his expert is accepted; and if there be any doubt, his first duty is to establish, for his expert, a satisfactory reputation.

HOW TO USE EVIDENCE

Much of the advice which could be offered under this topic would be a restatement of what has been said about the kinds and the tests of evidence. Those principles are applicable whether one is acting as an advocate, or is reading or listening to someone else's case. Ethically speaking, one should give his evidence the weight it deserves—no more and no less.

When quoting evidence, it is well to distinguish fact from opinion in so far as possible. This can be expressed by saying, "Facts as reported by . . ." or "In the opinion of . . ."

Citations of expert opinion should be used to corroborate the advocate's reasoning, not to substitute for it. When possible, one should give the factual basis, if any, for the opinion evidence. Finally, the expert should be carefully qualified, because cross-examination is often not possible.

Hearsay evidence is acceptable for general use if it is reliable and the best that is available. It is, of course, better if it was first stated before the dispute arose. Books and documents, being open to public inspection, are comparable to sources which can be cross-examined.

Circumstantial evidence should be used cumulatively—that is, in quantity for the purpose of showing a trend or a tendency. Exceptions should be sought and, if found, allowed for in the drawing of an inference from the evidence.

Theoretically, evidence should be completely documented, but in popular or nonscholarly discourse the stylistic considerations render such advice unwise. An experimental study in which the amount of documentation and the qualifications of authorities were the tested variables showed that there was little difference in persuasive effect between the undocumented and the partly documented evidence. A significant difference appeared only after the documentation included a considerable "build-up" of the source.[1] A seminar study of a final debate in a national tournament revealed that one side gave complete documentation for 50 per cent of its evidence, while the opposition's percentage was 16. The latter team gave absolutely no documentation for 55 per cent of its evidence. How can we judge whether the evidence is the best available when so few clues are given? The answer is that we cannot, and the situation will not improve until readers and listeners learn to demand better use of evidence.

Not every point requires evidence. Only the important ones that are neither admitted nor of common knowledge call for evidential support. Speaking of admissions, we should add that an able advocate knows when an admission is safe, and he has the good sense to use it to save time.

EXERCISES

1. Prepare and deliver a five-minute argumentative speech in which more than one kind of evidence is used to support the point or points in partition. Quote the evidence from cards such as those you made for the lesson on research.

2. Apply the appropriate tests of evidence to a stated number of specimens which you select from a printed debate such as Appendix A or B.

[1] Robert Cathcart, "An Experimental Study of the Relative Effectiveness of Selected Means of Handling Evidence in Speeches of Advocacy." (Unpublished Dissertation, Northwestern University, 1953.)

3. Quote an argumentative editorial, and analyze it in terms of the kinds and tests of evidence.

4. Perform the operation in Question 3 with an advertisement or a "letter to the editor," provided that it contains argumentative discourse.

5. Cite a specimen of evidence, and classify it in terms of as many categories (A to H) as you can.

6. A cumulative lesson in report form. Prepare it in outline form suitable for handing in. Use the proposition on which you have done the preceding chapter exercises. Take the position of a speaker or a writer, rather than a listener or a reader, and follow these steps:
   a. State your proposition.
   b. State your side (affirmative or negative).
   c. State *one* issue which you choose to affirm or deny.
   d. State the point or points in partition which you would use in answer to that issue. These are identified with Roman numerals in a logical outline.
   e. Subordinate the supporting reasons (A-B-C, etc.) for each point in partition.
   f. Under each supporting reason you will subordinate its supporting evidence in the form of Arabic-numeral items (1-2-3). Evidence may be facts, expert-opinion quotations, etc.
   g. In parentheses after each item of evidence you will document and qualify the source.
   h. Be prepared to meet the tests of evidence if an item is challenged. This will not appear on your outline.

[Illustration of items "d" to "g" above:

I. World government is the best framework for international relations, because
   A. Federal-type government has the best record in resolving intergroup conflicts, because
      1. In the United States, the faults of government under Articles of Confederation were remedied by the adoption of federal powers by the National government (Commager & Morrison, eminent American historians, in *Growth of the American Republic,* Vol. I, pp. 350–370.]

Chapter 8

KINDS OF ARGUMENT

The term "argument" has at least two meanings, which should be distinguished. When one refers to a debate or a controversy or a dispute as an "argument," he is using the term in its broader sense. In a more limited sense, argument may be defined as *the process of reasoning by which conclusions are inferred from premises*. In this chapter we are using the term in the second, more restricted sense. Thus, an argument is a line of reasoning, or an inference from premises, offered to support a conclusion, and the kinds of argument reported here are the several types of reasoning which can be so employed.

Proof is a result of evidence *and* argument; evidence and argument are the two essential elements of proof. In proving a proposition, then, evidence and argument are presented for the purpose of establishing the "truth," justice, or wisdom of this proposition. The sounder the evidence and the more conclusive the argument, the greater is the probability of the conclusion.

THE NATURE OF
ARGUMENT

In studying this chapter, the student should remember that an argument is simply a reason presented in support of a proposition. In other words, it is one proposition offered to support another. The supporting proposition is called a *premise,* and the proposition thus supported is the *conclusion.* In argumentative discourse, several premises may be given to support a single conclusion, and these premises may themselves become the conclusions drawn from subpremises. The structure of reasoned discourse may thus be a fabric of interrelated premises and conclusions, but the unit of such discourse is always a reason given to support a conclusion. In composing or in analyzing such discourse, then, it is important to be able to identify the individual arguments involved and to test them separately.

Correlation and causation. Argument typically involves two basic relations: *correlation* (sign relations) and *causation* (causal relations). In other words, the essential functions of argument are *identification* and *explanation.* "Is it?" and "Why is it?" are the fundamental questions to which argument is addressed. An unsupported proposition stands as a simple assertion until reasons are advanced to show that it *is* true or *why* it is true, or both.

For example, in a recent report it is argued that there is a shortage of qualified teachers for our colleges and universities.[1] Two lines of reasoning are advanced to prove this claim: First, to show that a shortage actually *does* exist, it is argued (a) that there is a strong, persistent demand for new (additional) teachers, (b) that many teaching positions remain unfilled, and (c) that colleges and universities have been forced to accept many candidates with severely limited preparation; second to explain *why* this condition exists, it is argued (a) that there is a rapid increase in the number of students entering our colleges and universities because of the increased birth rate and the higher percentage of students from the high schools seeking admission, and (b) that

[1] *Teacher Supply and Demand in Universities, Colleges and Junior Colleges, 1959–60 and 1960–61,* Research Division, National Education Association, Higher Education Series 1961–R12.

our graduate schools are failing to turn out a sufficient number of qualified teachers.

Induction and deduction. The sign relations (correlations) and the causal relations (causation) relevant in any given case are discovered by a process known as induction. These inductively given premises are then interpreted and related to the proposition by a process known as deduction.

Inductive arguments draw direct conclusions from the evidence. These conclusions purport to be accurate formulations of the relations (correlation and causation) observed in the phenomenon examined. Deductive argument, on the other hand, works with the conclusions yielded by induction; these conclusions are entered as premises (signs and causes) to support the proposition under consideration. In other words, inductive arguments start with the facts—raw data—and yield verbal statements about these data; deductive arguments start with verbal statements and yield additional statements expressing new insights and meaning.

In the example above, all of the arguments advanced to support the claim of a shortage of college and university teachers are *deductive* arguments. No evidence whatsoever is presented. Three indications, or signs, are given to show that a shortage of teachers does exist, and two explanations or causes of this shortage are advanced. All of these arguments call for *inductive* support. Let's see how this might be accomplished.

Take, for example, the premise "that many teaching positions remain unfilled." A survey reveals these facts:

. . . a substantial number of teaching positions (for which budgetary provision was made) were permitted to remain vacant during at least one of the past two years through lack of acceptable candidates. The impressive number of 1275 such vacancies was reported by 519 universities and colleges. All of the principal fields of instruction were included.[2]

These data, in effect, present 1275 *examples* from which it can be inferred that many unfilled teaching positions exist. The 1275

[2] *Ibid.,* p. 21.

cases constitute evidence, and the inference they permit is an inductive argument.

As a second example of inductive argument, take the premise "that colleges and universities have been forced to accept many candidates (teachers) with severely limited preparation." This is inferred from the fact that many new teachers come from "the bachelor's degree class" without graduate study.

Cause for sober consideration is the substantial number of new full-time teachers who entered classroom service in universities and colleges directly from the preceding bachelor's degree class. During the past two years new teachers at this limited level of preparation comprised 4.3 per cent of the total. The high was 6.1 per cent of those employed by small nonpublic colleges, then 5.9 in land-grant colleges. The low was 3.1 in state colleges, then 3.5 per cent in nonpublic universities and teachers colleges.[3]

One of the *causes* alleged to explain the shortage of college and university teachers was the failure of our graduate schools to turn out a sufficient number of qualified teachers. Inductive support for this allegation is provided by the following facts:

Consider these facts: the present national output of earned doctorates in the United States runs to about 9,600 a year. Of these, only approximately 60 per cent can be counted on for careers in higher education: they are either already employed in higher education, or will take positions in higher education. The present output of some 5,800 earned doctorates for higher education each year, if only maintained during the coming decade, would produce 58,000 to meet the employment need of 336,000 estimated earlier in this article. . . .

Herein lies the true problem: the need to accelerate the rate at which our graduate schools are expected to grow, and to increase the immediate annual productivity of these schools.[4]

In investigating a problem, the inductive processes normally precede the deductive inferences. Conclusions are drawn from

---

[3] *Ibid.*, p. 19.
[4] Homer D. Babbidge, Jr., "Staffing the Nation's Colleges and Universities: Some Perspectives," *AAUP Bulletin,* Vol. 7, No. 3, p. 213.

an examination of the facts, and these conclusions are used as premises to deduce other conclusions. In presenting argument, however, the deductive arguments supporting the proposition are often stated first, with the inductive support following.

The classification of argument. It is possible to classify the kinds of argument in various different ways. The literature of the subject provides ample evidence of this and, we might add, considerable evidence of confusion. The classification we believe to be most acceptable and most useful reduces all argument to two kinds of deductive argument—sign and cause—and two kinds of inductive argument—example and analogy. The rest of this chapter is devoted to an explanation of these four kinds of argument and the tests that may be applied to them.

THE FOUR BASIC
KINDS OF ARGUMENT

For purposes of convenience, we begin with the deductive arguments (sign and cause) and follow with a discussion of the two inductive types (example and analogy).

Argument from sign. An argument from sign is one which gives an indication that the proposition is true without attempting to explain why it is true. It is a *ratio cognoscendi*, or reason for acknowledging or recognizing the truth of a proposition, as distinguished from a *ratio essendi*, or reason why the proposition is true. A few simple examples will explain the nature of signs.

We may offer as signs of the coming of spring such indications as the northern flight of migratory birds, longer days, the breaking up of ice on lakes and streams, the budding of trees, the appearance of farmers in their fields, etc. All of these are familiar signs of spring which in no sense explain *why* spring is coming. Similarly, the presence of picket lines might be offered to prove that a plant is on strike, boarded-up windows and an unkempt lawn as signs that a property is vacant, applause as an indication of approval, or rusty rails as an argument that a railroad track is used infrequently.

All arguments from sign are based on the assumption (stated or implied) that two or more variables are related in such a way that the presence or absence of one may be taken as an indication of the presence or absence of the other. Such relationships are *reciprocal* when either variable may be taken as the sign of the other. Thus, a thermometer showing freezing temperature may be taken as a sign of ice on the pond, and ice on the pond may be taken as a sign that the thermometer will register a freezing temperature. Sign relationships are *nonreciprocal* when one variable serves as a sign of the second, but this second *cannot* be reliably deduced from the first. For example, it might be inferred that a book is good because it bears the Macmillan imprint, but it cannot be concluded with equal force that a good book is a sign of the Macmillan imprint.

All signs are either *natural* or *conventional*. Natural signs inhere in correlative relations observed in nature, such as smoke taken as a sign of fire, reduced tread as a sign of wear on an automobile tire, or gray hair as a sign of age. Conventional signs are based on customary relations established by habit and general usage or arbitrary association. A red-and-white barber pole signifies a barber shop; a campaign button indicates political preferences; the Cadillac car is sometimes taken as a sign of wealth and status.

Some signs may be helpfully understood as *substance-attribute* relations. Since every substance (object, thing, person, concept, event, item, etc.) has certain distinguishing attributes or characteristics (size, shape, color, speed, number, etc.), the attributes may be taken as signs of the substance, or the substance as a sign of the attributes. Such signs will be *natural* if the substance has a real, physical existence, and *conventional* if the substance is a construct or concept resulting from a synthesis by the mind. In most cases, the attributes of a substance (natural or conventional) will constitute a reliable sign only where they are presented collectively. In other words, it is seldom safe to infer from only one attribute where several attributes are characteristic.

All deductive arguments, including those from sign, are based on generalizations either stated or implied. In arguments from sign, this generalization is always a stated or implied correlation. Earlier we defined an argument as a reason offered in support of a proposition. It is now necessary to point out that every such supporting reason or premise necessarily demands a second premise (stated or implied) to complete the argument. As we shall see in the next chapter, these two premises, one stating the reason (the minor premise) and the other the generalization upon which the reason is based (the major premise), together with the conclusion drawn from these premises, constitute what is known as a syllogism (or enthymeme). Such a syllogism (or enthymeme) is a *single* argument and may be regarded as the working unit in argument for purposes of analysis and composition.

In the arguments from sign given below, the assumed generalizations upon which the arguments are based are stated in parentheses.

CONCLUSION	The temperature is below 32 degrees because
PREMISE	I. It is snowing.
ASSUMED GENERALIZATION	(I'. It never snows unless the temperature is below 32 degrees.)

CONCLUSION	This penal institution is failing to rehabilitate criminals, because
PREMISE	I. Persons released usually return to a life of crime.
ASSUMED GENERALIZATION	(I'. If released prisoners return to crime, the prison has failed to rehabilitate them.)

If we may return to our earlier example about the shortage of college and university teachers, you will recall that three signs were presented to establish this shortage: the strong demand for new teachers, unfilled teaching positions, and the acceptance of teachers with limited preparation. Quite obviously, the assumptions underlying these arguments are the implied correlations between these signs and the alleged shortages. Thus a speaker might say, "If I can show that there is a strong demand for new teachers, that many teaching positions remain unfilled, and that the colleges and universities are having to employ poorly qualified teachers, we must conclude that a shortage of college and university teachers exists." This states the generalization upon which his thinking is based. If challenged, he should be prepared to defend it. Then, of course, he must go on to establish the three signs he has alleged.

The tests of any argument from sign lie in the soundness of the generalization upon which it is based and in the application of this generalization to the matter about which a conclusion is sought. The following questions may be applied as tests in constructing and appraising such arguments.

Is the sign relationship accidental or coincidental? Quite obviously, an accidental or coincidental association between certain phenomena cannot be regarded as a reliable basis for argument from sign. Many unfair attitudes toward people of different races and creeds are based upon such accidental associations. If a man has been unfortunate enough to meet a few Catholics or a few Methodists or a few Jews with undesirable characteristics, he must be exceedingly careful about imputing these characteristics to others of the same faith.

Is the sign relationship reciprocal? As we have already seen, X may be a reliable sign of Y without Y being an equally reliable sign of X. Even though we may be able to argue that pablum is nourishing because the baby grows fat on it, we cannot with equal propriety take plumpness in the baby as a sign that he eats pablum.

Have special factors intervened which alter normal relations? Time and space affect many sign relationships. Things that are related at one time may not be similarly related at a later time, and things which are related in one context may not be related in another. A crowd in Wrigley Field may be taken as a fairly reliable sign that a baseball game is scheduled, *if it is during the baseball season;* later in the year, such a crowd would probably mean a football game. High temperatures in one city are usually a reliable sign of high temperatures in a neighboring city, but if a high mountain range separates the two locations, this may not be the case.

Is the sign reliable without the collaboration or concurrence of other signs? The probative force of argument from sign is usually greater as additional signs are presented to support the same conclusion. A quite inconclusive sign may become significant when offered in concert with others. Thus, the presence of a man at the scene of a crime might not establish his guilt, but if it could be shown that he attempted to flee and that he possessed a weapon of the type that was used to commit the crime, the inference would be much more compelling.

Causal argument. A causal argument is one which serves to *account for* the truth of a proposition, or *explain why* the proposition is true. Such an argument does not attempt to establish the proposition as being true, but, assuming its truth, attempts to show what causes it to be true. Typically, causal arguments follow arguments from sign in a rhetorical demonstration. The speaker first presents signs to show that the proposition *is* true, and then goes on to present arguments which show *why* it is true.

It is often difficult to distinguish between sign and causal arguments, because the English connectives commonly used in argumentative discourse are ambiguous with respect to this distinction. Such words as "because," "for," "hence," and "therefore" may be used to express the relation of either cause *or* sign between premise and conclusion with equal acceptability. The word "because," for example, does not necessarily imply causation. Whately's advice on the point is helpful:

The only decisive test by which to distinguish the Arguments which belong to the one, and to the other of these classes, is to ask the question, "Supposing the proposition in question to be admitted, would this statement here used as an Argument, serve to *account* for and explain the truth, or not?" It will then be readily referred to the former or to the latter class, according as the answer is in the affirmative or the negative; as *e.g.* if a murder were imputed to anyone on the grounds of his "having a hatred to the deceased, and an interest in his death," the Argument would belong to the former class; because, *supposing* his guilt to be admitted, and an inquiry to be made how he could have committed the murder, the circumstances just mentioned would serve to *account* for it; but not so, with respect to such an Argument as his "having blood on his clothes"; which would therefore be referred to the other class.[5]

[5] Richard Whately, *Elements of Rhetoric* (London: John W. Parker, West Strand, 1846), pp. 46–47.

Another problem in distinguishing between sign and causal argument is in the fact that causal connections often underlie the relations between variables in a correlation. All natural signs are, of course, causally related to the matter they signify. Typically in such cases, the *effects* of a given cause are employed as signs that this cause has operated or is operating. Conventional signs, on the other hand, are usually based on convenient or habitual associations that may be altogether arbitrary so far as a causal explanation is concerned. In either case, however, an argument from sign is always used to identify, rather than to explain or account for.

Causal arguments are analytical in nature and usually require more insight and discernment than inferences from signs. In other words, it is usually easier to identify than to explain. It might not be difficult to convince a person that the atomic bomb is capable of vast destructive power (Hiroshima and Nagasaki provide ample signs), but it is exceedingly difficult to explain *why* this bomb works as it does. We "know" many things on the basis of signs which we do not understand *causally*. I know *what* to expect when I push certain buttons and work certain pedals in my car, but I do not know why they operate as they do; a garage mechanic knows more of the explanation than I do, and the automotive enginer can provide a more basic explanation than the mechanic. As this example suggests, even a causal argument may be relatively superficial, or it may be fundamental and basic. The speaker's purpose (to say nothing of his capacities) and the demands of the occasion will usually dictate the extent to which causation should be pursued.

A recent analysis of our national agricultural problem presents some good examples of causal reasoning.[6] After giving several indications or signs that establish the economic plight of our farmers, the report proceeds to a discussion of the causes of this problem. In summary it is argued that "the roots of the American farm problem are to be found in a combination of five conditions [causes], no one of which, alone, would have caused it." The five causes presented are (1) swiftly rising productivity, (2) declining

[6] "An Adaptive Program for Agriculture," A Statement on National Policy by the Research and Policy Committee of the Committee for Economic Development, Library of Congress catalog card no. 62-19145, July, 1962, pp. 15–19.

use of labor relative to capital, (3) the slow growth of demand for farm goods, (4) the slow responsiveness of demand to price changes, and (5) the inadequate flow of resources out of farming.

The gist of this causal analysis is that we are producing more agricultural commodities than the market will absorb at prices high enough to give the farmer an adequate return. This over-production has been accomplished largely by the increased use of better farm machinery and fertilizers. Fewer farmers are required to produce for the market, but they are not moving out of agriculture at the rate necessary to avoid falling incomes.

Another example of causal reasoning appears when the question is raised, Why hasn't labor moved out of agriculture? The report suggests two causes that have operated:

Although the exodus from agriculture in the past decade or longer has been large by almost any standards, it has not been large enough. Two important special factors, in addition to the large scale of the movement required, should be mentioned in explanation. *First,* the need for movement has been disguised by temporary upsurges of demand for agricultural products, during World War II and the Korean War, and by the price-supporting programs of the government. *Second,* the excessively high level of urban unemployment in the four years 1958–61 tended to keep the movement of labor out of agriculture less than it should have been.[7]

All causal arguments (as is true of signs) are based on generalizations either stated or implied. In the examples cited below, these generalizations are given in parentheses.

CONCLUSION The temperature is below 32 degrees, because
PREMISE I. A cold mass of air is blowing in from the north.
ASSUMED
GENERALIZATION (I'. North winds often bring in freezing temperatures.)

CONCLUSION This penal institution is failing to rehabilitate criminals, because
PREMISE I. The warden is not a trained criminologist.
ASSUMED (I'. We can seldom expect competent rehabilitative meas-
GENERALIZATION ures from wardens with little or no training in criminol-
ogy.)

[7] *Ibid.,* p. 19.

The basic tests of any causal argument lie in the reliability or universality of the generalization upon which it is based and in the application of this generalization to the case in point. The following questions may be applied as tests in constructing and appraising such arguments.

Is the connection between the cause and effect broken or incomplete? In causal argument the cause and effect are often separated by several intermediate steps. In other words, the cause is often *mediate* rather than *immediate*. The pull on the trigger will fire the shot if, and only if, the catch, the spring, the hammer, the cap, and so on, all act in the expected manner. The closer the causal connection, the surer the argument, and any argument can be destroyed by showing that some of the intermediate links are lacking. It might be proved that A was inspired with a most malevolent hatred of B, that he would welcome any favorable opportunity of attacking him, even that he had actually sought to do him injury; but in order to connect this motive with the murder of B, it must be shown that none of the necessary intermediate steps was lacking. It must be proved that A was present at the time, that he had the necessary weapon, and that he was physically strong enough to do the deed. The destruction of one of these links of the chain destroys the argument.

C——————————————   ——————————————E

(CAUSAL CONNECTION IS INCOMPLETE)

Have other causes operated (or will they operate) to prevent or alter the cause under discussion? The normal progress between the cause and the effect is often stopped or turned from its course by the intervention of some other cause which destroys or alters the natural result of the first cause. If a man takes a dose of deadly poison, the chances are that it will cause his death; but it may be shown that this effect will not actually follow in this case by showing that the man took an antidote. The antidote prevents the occurrence of the natural effect. One may argue that capital punishment will serve as a deterrent to crime because of the sever-

ity of the penalty; but this reasoning may be questioned by showing that the very severity of the punishment is such that juries
will not convict where the penalty is mandatory and that judges
are reluctant to impose it for the same reason.

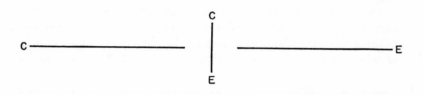

(OTHER CAUSES MAY PREVENT EXPECTED EFFECT)

To what extent is the effect the result of the cause? In other
words, is the cause adequate to produce the effect? One of the
most common mistakes in causal argument arises when a speaker
offers an explanation which is inadequate, or anticipates results
greater than can be reasonably expected. This gives rise to the
fallacy of *part cause.* To argue that college athletes are healthier
than nonathletes because they participate in sports neglects the
probability that they were selected to be athletes because of their
superior health; even if it is conceded that athletic participation
is a contributing cause, this additional factor must be recognized.
Similarly, to contend that a tax will yield certain required revenue
without considering the cost of collection is to suggest an inadequate cause; additional sources will have to be tapped to raise the
required amount.

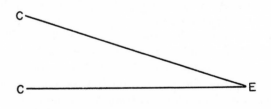

(OTHER CAUSES CONTRIBUTE)

Does the cause produce other effects? If it can be shown that a cause may be expected to produce effects other than those in question, the absence of these side effects will throw doubt on the analysis. Thus, an argument that death was caused by drowning would be seriously questioned if it were shown that the lungs of the victim were not filled with water. Or a contention that a short supply of wheat caused a certain brand of flour to increase in price would be doubtful if it could be shown that other brands of wheat flour had not been similarly affected. The same ques-

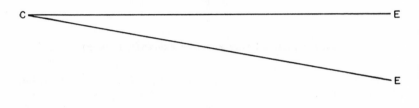

(OTHER EFFECTS MAY BE PRODUCED)

tion should be considered in discussing future effects. Where it is argued that a cause *will* operate to produce certain effects, it is important to ask whether the effects anticipated are *all* the effects. The negative argument that the affirmative plan will produce "new and greater evils" is a familiar one in debate.

It is helpful to note that a speaker may consider causation in relation to *past fact, present fact,* or *future fact.* While this has been implied throughout our discussion of causal argument, we make it explicit here. If an event has already occurred, we necessarily discuss its cause in retrospect. If it is occurring now, we examine the cause while it is operating. If the cause has not yet operated, we then anticipate effects on the basis of past experience. The tests of causal reasoning apply in all cases.

Argument by example. In most argumentative discourse, the speaker begins with his proposition and then presents argument from sign to prove the proposition *is* true, and presents causal arguments to explain *why* it is true. All of these arguments may have to be supported by examples to make them convincing. An example is a case or instance in point, and argument from example is the process of inference by which a conclusion is drawn from one or more such cases or instances in point. Examples or cases offered in argument constitute evidence. The immediate inference from such evidence is argument from example. As we shall see in the next chapter, the kinds of propositions argued in public debate can rarely be supported *directly* by examples. The arguments from example are ordinarily connected with the speaker's proposition through the mediation of arguments from sign and cause. Thus, the premises of these arguments (sign and cause) become the conclusions of arguments from example in connected discourse.

Argument from example is sometimes called "generalization" or "argument by generalization." These labels are appropriate because such a generalization—a general law or principle—is the object in view in argument from example. This kind of argument involves an examination of the real, phenomenal, existential world for the purpose of making accurate statements about it.

The case cited below shows the use of examples to support a generalization. In this instance the argument is advanced that the primary cause of economically depressed areas in our country is "the decline of one or more major local industries as a source of employment." Among the major causes of decline of major local industries are: "competition from other firms or other products; changes in production technology; changes in locational advantages; competition from abroad; and exhaustion of local natural resources that were being mined or harvested." The following examples are given to support this analysis:

Quite a few depressed areas have been dependent on coal mining as a major employment source. Most of the areas in West Virginia and Eastern Kentucky, several in Pennsylvania and Illinois, as well as scattered communities in other Eastern and Southern states are involved. Anthracite and bituminous have been losing out to gas and oil in home heating and extensive technological improvements have at the same time increased productivity in the coal mines, thus reducing employment needs. Expansion of output and the use of protectionist measures in Europe have also reduced the export market for bituminous coal. There is little hope for an early expansion in employment in coal mining communities. A second group of communities has suffered heavy losses of employment in cotton and wool textile manufacturing. The major centers of textile manufacture have shifted from New England and the Middle Atlantic States to North Carolina, South Carolina and Georgia, leaving large unemployed labor forces behind. Production of textiles from synthetic products also has cut into the market for wool and cotton and almost eliminated the market for silk products. There is also a threat of increasing foreign competition in textiles. Centers of railway equipment manufacture and railway car repair are also among the distressed group. These include Altoona and Berwick, Pennsylvania; and Centralia, Illinois. The shift from steam to diesel locomotives, the decline of passenger traffic and the loss of some freight traffic to truck transportation, have all played a part in reducing employment here. A decline in employment in defense-oriented jobs coupled with a declining share of employment in the national motor vehicle industry left Detroit and several smaller Michigan communities with a substantial and persistent labor surplus in the latter part of the 1950's. Defense employment rose sharply in the early years, and declined almost as sharply. In the Detroit labor market area there were 100,000 fewer defense jobs at the end of the decade than in the peak year, 1953. Competitive forces within the industry were a major factor in reducing Detroit's share of motor vehicle employment from 40 per cent of the national total in 1950 to less than 30 per cent in 1960.[8]

The crux of argument from example consists in presenting one or more individual objects or instances, of a certain class, as fair specimens in respect of some point or other, and drawing an inference from them respecting the whole class. The following questions may be applied as tests of such argument.

Are the specimens fair in respect to the point in issue? The failure to meet this test is very common in dishonest and partisan controversy. The statement, "One hundred students were asked if they wanted the ———— system introduced, and only three said 'Yes,'" has no valid force whatever if the hundred students were all unfair specimens of the general student body of five thousand in regard to the particular point in issue. Choosing unfair speci-

[8] "Depressed Areas in a Growing Economy," a Statement on National Policy by the Research and Policy Committee of the Committee for Economic Development, Library of Congress catalogue card no. 61-14416, June, 1961, pp. 24–25.

mens and making out a plausible but dishonest and worthless generalization is a favorite trick of partisan investigators and advocates who have to make out a preconceived case regardless of truth.

Has a large-enough part of the class been observed to justify an inference regarding the whole class? To apply this test, as in applying the first one, it is necessary to know the exact nature of the question at issue. In questions which concern the working-out of natural laws, as in chemistry, physics, biology, etc., a very small number of specimens are needed to determine the rule. If a certain treatment of a dozen rabbits causes the same results in each case, it is reasonably safe to formulate a rule for all of the millions of rabbits, or for other animals as well. In chemistry or physics, one very carefully performed experiment may well settle some question for all time. A rule can be formulated and followed with confidence in every case. This is *generalization from a single instance*. It is usually allowable when dealing with the working of natural laws on inanimate materials and sometimes on plants and animals. Of course, many questions, such as questions in chemistry or physics, plants and animals, even human beings, are to be tested in the same manner as inanimate materials. It is as we get further from this type of question and nearer to questions involving personal taste, ability, prejudice, opinion, and belief, that we must increasingly enlarge the proportion of observed instances. The greater the possible variations in answer to our question, the wider must be the field of observation, in order to justify a generalization. And, of course, the very nature of many questions precludes the possibility of getting a rule that will work without exceptions. In practically all questions affecting human conduct, a high degree of probability is all that we can hope to get for any general rule.

There is another circumstance under which generalizations can be drawn from a single example: in those cases in which the example used is demonstrably least favorable to the generalization. Some years ago the colleges debated the proposition that the several states should derive at least 50 per cent of their tax revenue from sources other than tangible property. One affirmative team undertook to show that this tax program would be at its worst in North Dakota because the wealth of this state, more than any other, lay in tangible property. Having established this, they went on to show that the proposed distribution of taxes would be wise even in North Dakota, and concluded that if the program was advisable in the state least favorable to it, then surely it should be adopted in the others.

What is sought, of course, in making a generalization is a fair sample of the phenomena about which a generalization is being made. An ideal sample will represent all the significant variables entering into the generalization, with proper regard to the weight or frequency of each. If the cross section is carefully chosen, a relatively small sample will often permit a sound generalization.

Are negative instances accounted for? Whenever a generalization is drawn in which there are negative instances—that is, cases in which the relationship alleged is not borne out—it is advisable to account for these cases. Failure to do this paves the way for an opponent to produce these cases and thereby throw doubt on the entire matter. In the first place, every generalization should be qualified as accurately as possible in terms of the available data; and in the second place, instances which do not conform to the rule should be shown to be exceptional cases, or cases which are not significant for other reasons.

Is the relationship generalized apparent in the examples adduced? Examples are presented to support a generalization. These generalizations asert sign relations (mallard drakes have green heads) or causal relations (loud noises cause ducks to alert). To be effective, such examples should clearly exhibit the relation which is being generalized. Unless this is the case, the examples themselves become subjects for argument. Suppose it is contended that city X should adopt the city-manager form of government because it has succeeded in cities A, B, and C. If A, B, and C exhibit this success without further argument, they may be regarded as examples. If not, they must in this case be taken as signs, and arguments must be offered to prove the allegation with respect to A, B, and C. These arguments must, in turn, be supported by further arguments. This process is refined until premises are reached which can be supported by examples—examples in which the relationship generalized is apparent. In any chain of argument which begins with the proposition, the arguments from example, if such appear at all, are the last arguments in this chain.

Analogy. In argument from analogy, the ground of inference is the resemblance between two individual objects or kinds of objects in a certain number of points, and the inference is that they resemble one another in some other point, known to belong to the one but not known to belong to the other. Whereas argument from example generalizes from one or more cases, analogy infers a conclusion about one case by comparing it with another. "Two things go together in many cases, therefore in all, including this one" is the argument in extending a generalization; "two things agree in many respects, therefore in this other" is the argument from analogy—"If two cases are alike in all essential repects, they will (in all probability) be alike in the respect under question." The classic example of argument from analogy is that given by Thomas Reid in his *Intellectual Powers:*

We may observe a very great similitude between this earth which we inhabit, and the other planets, Saturn, Jupiter, Mars, Venus, and Mercury. They all revolve around the sun, as the earth does, although at different distances and in different periods. They borrow all their light from the sun, as the earth does. Several of them are known to revolve around their visible axis like the earth, and by that means have like succession of day and night. Some of them have moons, that serve to give them light in the absence of the sun, as our moon does to us. They are all, in their motions, subject to the same law of gravitation as the earth is. From all this similitude it is not unreasonable to think that these planets may, like our earth, be the habitations of various orders of living creatures. There is some probability in this conclusion from analogy.

There are two kinds of analogies: *literal* and *figurative*. The analogy is literal when the cases, objects, or things compared are in the same general class—for example, two dwellings, two farms, two cities, two planets, etc. The analogy is figurative when the cases, objects, or things compared are in different classes, as in the following example: "You should not change horses in the middle of a stream; you should not, therefore, change generals in the middle of a campaign." Figurative analogies are useful for illustrative purposes only; they have no probative force. Literal analogies, on the other hand, may be used to prove a point in argument if they are carefully constituted. The questions which follow may be used as tests.

Are the compared cases alike in all essential respects? This is the vital test in analogical reasoning. And the important word in this question is "essential." If I reason that a fireplace is adequate in my neighbor's cottage and therefore should be adequate in mine, the fact that my cottage is white and his green is completely immaterial. It is not an essential difference for purposes of this analogy. Essential factors would certainly include the size and construction of the two buildings. In order to give grounds for any analogical argument, it is important not that the resemblances are many, but that they are such as bear directly on the argument. "Caesar had his Brutus, Charles I his Cromwell, and George III may profit by their example." Caesar was unlike Charles I in most of his personal qualities; he ruled a different country in a different age. George III was the very opposite of the Roman in temper and character; his people, his advisers, and his century were not similar to those of either of the men with whom he was compared. But the three cases were similar in the essential element: Caesar, Charles I, and George III all represented the pressure of tyranny upon a spirited, liberty-loving people. In each case, oppression was the cause of the effect—rebellion. And whatever other differences there were in the circumstances, the *causes* were similar in nature.

Are differences in the compared cases accounted for? Any differences which *appear* to be essential should be shown to be nonessential, nonexistent, or disposed of in some other manner.

Is the argument from analogy cumulative? Analogical reasoning becomes cumulative when more than one comparison is adduced to support the conclusion. For instance, if we argued that a certain project would be successful in Michigan, it might be possible to draw analogies with several other states in which this project was in operation. Cumulative analogy is not identical with generalization, as it is sometimes claimed, because a particular conclusion regarding some specific case is always drawn in analogical reasoning, while a general conclusion pertaining to all cases is the result of generalization. From a series of analogies showing the success of a certain project we argue that it will be successful in a particular case. From a series of cases in generalization we conclude that the project will be successful in all cases. Reasoning from analogy becomes increasingly strong as the number of comparisons is increased or, in other words, as the analogies are cumulated.

SPECIAL APPLICATIONS

As we have seen, the four basic kinds of argument are sign, cause, example, and analogy. There are several special applications of these basic types that merit attention because of their frequent use and because they are often misunderstood.

Argument from authority. The so-called argument from authority is the citation of an opinion (expert or otherwise) in support of a proposition. Such opinions are usually cited in support of propositions presented as premises or subpremises in a chain of reasoning. Actually, the use of authority is not a separate kind of reasoning. We have already seen that competent opinions, properly introduced and used, constitute evidence. And in our chapter on evidence, we have set out in some detail the tests applicable to opinion evidence. The question here concerns the nature of the inference from such opinion evidence to the proposition that it is offered to support. This will be determined by *what it is that the opinion alleges.* In terms of our analysis, the possible allegations are signs, causal explanations, examples, or analogies. If this be the case, then the tests appropriate to these kinds of argument are applicable. If the opinion cited merely reasserts what is alleged by the proposition that it is offered to support, it may have good rhetorical effect, but it is purely tautological so far as the inferential process is concerned.

Argument from definition. The so-called argument from definition can be explained in much the same way we discussed argument from authority. In the first place, most definitions are offered to clarify the terms used in a proposition. As we have seen earlier, such clarifications can serve very useful purposes and often are essential to understanding. But this clarification is exposition preliminary to argument, rather than argument itself. Definition in this role is not properly regarded as argument. No inference is involved.

If a definition is used as a premise in argument, then the definition must make one or more allegations that can be classified as sign, cause, example, or analogy, and be tested accordingly. Definitions that merely repeat in other words what is said in the proposition are redundant if they do not add clarification, and, in any case, they are tautological so far as the argument is concerned.

Disjunctive reasoning. A disjunctive proposition is an "either-or" statement. It expresses one or more alternatives or possibilities. For example, it might be asserted that there are three possible sources of water supply for a certain village: private wells, a central municipal well, or utilization of water from a nearby river. To begin with, this kind of analysis has validity if the disjunction is complete (all possibilities considered) and if the several members of the disjunction are mutually exclusive. Given a valid disjunction, each alternative can then be argued on its own merits. The methods of argument are, of course, the kinds we have already discussed.

A disjunctive proposition provides the basis for dilemmatic reasoning. A *dilemma* is a form of argument in which two or more alternatives are presented, each of which is shown to have undesirable consequences for the one who must choose. *The method of residues* proceeds much as in dilemmatic reasoning, except that all the alternatives *save one* are shown to be undesirable. This remaining alternative is then defended as the logical choice.

Hypothetical reasoning. Hypothetical propositions are conditional statements containing two members, one the *antecedent* and the other the *consequent*. Here are some examples: "If the weather is good, we will go." "If he has studied this book, he understands argumentation." "If a student has a good high-school record, good test scores, and good recommendations, he should be admitted to the college." The "if" clause in each of these statements is the *antecedent,* or the conditional clause; the second member is the result that follows if the condition is satisfied, or the *consequent.* Such hypothetical propositions may express or imply either correlative or causal relations.

In arguing a hypothetical proposition, the speaker must be prepared, first, to show that his hypothesis is sound—that the condition or conditions set out in the antecedent do warrant the consequent—and second, to show that these conditions are met in the case in question. Both of these responsibilities will be discharged by citing relevant signs, causes, examples, and analogies.

This kind of hypothetical reasoning is often used in representing propositions of value. Here the relevant standards of value are set up as criteria for judgment and expressed as the necessary conditions in the antecedent. It remains then to show that the subject in question meets these conditions or these standards or criteria.

EXERCISES

1. Bring in five original examples of each of the four kinds of argument discussed in this chapter. Criticize these examples in class. Apply the appropriate tests to them.

2. Present an affirmative or negative argumentative speech which will illustrate the four kinds of argument. Hand in an outline of this speech in which the kinds of argument are identified marginally.

3. Identify and criticize the kinds of argument in an article selected from a contemporary journal of opinion.

4. Select a proposition of policy for class debate. Divide the class into an affirmative group and a negative group. Alternate affirmative and negative speeches with attention to the kinds of argument used and refutation which points out weakness in argument.

5. Conduct class debates on the following plan: affirmative constructive case, six minutes; negative rejoinder, nine minutes; affirmative rebuttal, three minutes.

Chapter 9

THE STRUCTURE OF ARGUMENT

In Chapter 7 we discussed evidence—the kinds of evidence and the tests that can be applied to it. In Chapter 8 we explained the four basic kinds of argument: example, analogy, cause, and sign. In this chapter we point out the forms which these proofs take in argumentative discourse, and how they are related to the brief or the outline of argumentative discourse. The problem is one of giving the evidence and argument (reasoning) of the speaker a context and structure which will recommend his proposition to the listener; it is a matter of expressing in language the grounds from which another can reason to the conclusion upheld by the advocate.

DEDUCTIVE REASONING
IN ARGUMENT

In preparing his brief and presenting his case, the advocate usually begins with his proposition. He then sets forth the primary argument (main points) in support of this proposition. These primary arguments must usually be supported by secondary arguments (subpoints), and the secondary arguments may need to be supported by tertiary arguments, etc. This process of refinement results in chains of argument in which the primary arguments play an important role because they determine the principal division of the matter of the entire discourse.

Structurally the whole argument is dominated by the arguments that stand logically next to the original proposition . . . for it is on the basis of these arguments that the first division of the matter is made. And these primary arguments must be deductive in the case of, literally, quite ninety-nine of every hundred subjects of public discussion or of academic debate. . . . In ninety-nine arguments out of a hundred, then, of the class we are considering, it is only after the primary arguments have divided the material that inductive arguments may appear. And even then, though often they are by no means less important than deductive arguments, they are in most debates less frequent. In nearly every discourse on a question of public discussion, then, the arguments that determine the main structural lines and most of those that determine subordinate structural lines are deductive.[1]

The "arguments that stand logically next to the original proposition" are almost always deductive for the very simple and practical reason that the questions which people ordinarily debate cannot be supported directly by inductive arguments. An inductive argument is one which draws its conclusion immediately from the facts. Suppose the proposition that capital punishment be abolished is under consideration. This proposition cannot possibly be inferred directly from the facts. It is necessary first to adduce reasons which can be inductively supported. One such reason might be the argument that capital punishment is not an effective deterrent to crime; another might be the argument that the lives of innocent people may be taken. The first argument might be supported inductively by citing statistics (examples) to show that capital crimes are increasing in states which employ the death penalty; the second might be given inductive support by citing

---

[1] C. G. Hoag, "The Logic of Argument," *Haverford Essays* (Haverford, Pa.: 1909), p. 30.

examples of persons who suffered capital punishment and later were found to have been innocent.

In the illustration we are using, the two primary arguments cited are *deductive*. They may be stated in full as follows:

> Capital punishment should be abolished, because
> I. Legal penalties which fail as a deterrent to crime should be abolished, and
> I'. Capital punishment fails as a deterrent to crime.
> II. Any legal penalty which takes the lives of innocent people should be abolished, and
> II'. Capital punishment takes the lives of innocent people.

A deductive argument is typically one which applies a generalization to a specific case (Chapter 8). Points I and II in the foregoing illustration are generalizations, and points I' and II' are the cases to which the generalizations are applied.

Every deductive argument contains two premises and a conclusion. The premise that states the generalization is called the *major premise*, and the premise that relates a specific case to the generalization is calld the *minor premise*. In most cases the major premises are not expressed in general argumentation on the assumption that listeners will make the desired inferences without them. If the major premise is one which the listener has already formulated or one which patently comports with general experience, its omission in argument is a wise economy of time and energy. If there is question about it, however, the speaker will do well to state it explicitly, and he is under obligation to defend it if challenged by an opponent. It is always a vital part of the structure of argument. It can be assumed only tentatively. If questioned, it must be proved.

The syllogism. The form in which deductive arguments are expressed has been called a syllogism for many centuries. "When two propositions are so formulated and laid down that a third proposition necessarily follows from these two propositions, we have a syllogism." [2]

---

[2] Aristotle *Prior Analytics,* 1.

The relationships involved in the syllogism are those between generalizations and cases (as explained above) or, stated differently, those between classes and members of these classes (class inclusion). Both of the arguments cited above to prove that capital punishment should be abolished may be taken as examples of syllogisms. Structurally, they are identical with the classical example of the syllogism:

> All men are mortal (major premise).
> Socrates is a man (minor premise).
> Therefore, Socrates is mortal (conclusion).

Here again, the major premise expresses a generalization, and the minor premise relates a particular case to the generalization, or, stated differently, the major premise places *all* men in the class of *mortal beings,* and the minor premise classifies Socrates as a man. Since all A's are B's, and since C is an A, it follows that C is a B. When deductive arguments are explained as syllogisms, it is possible to examine the logical grounds upon which these arguments rest with considerably more precision than is otherwise possible. Students of argumentation and debate can profit greatly from a careful study of logic, wherein the forms and regulations of the syllogism are examined in greater detail than is possible here.

The theory of the syllogism. If it is possible to formulate the premises necessary to the establishment of a proposition in such a way that this proposition follows from these premises with certainty, quite obviously we have an instrument of considerable value in argumentation. The syllogism attempts to provide such an instrument. Here is how it works.

a. *Formal Validity and Material Truth.* By "formal validity" we mean simply that a given conclusion follows certainly from given premises. By "material truth" we mean "true to life"; a statement that is materially true is an accurate description or representation of the phenomenon with which it is concerned. Both of these factors enter into every argument. Formal validity is determined *deductively.* Material truth is determined *induc-*

tively. The following examples will help to clarify these distinctions.

All normal dogs have four legs (materially true).
My neighbor's pet is a normal dog (materially true).
Therefore, this pet has four legs (materially true and formally valid).

All normal dogs have five legs (materially false).
My neighbor's pet is a normal dog (materially true).
Therefore, this pet has five legs (materially false, but formally valid).

All normal dogs have four legs (materially true).
My neighbor's pet is a normal cat (materially true).
Therefore, this pet has four legs (materially true, but formally invalid).

It should be clear from these examples that the formal validity of an argument has nothing to do with its material truth. False premises properly related can yield formally valid conclusions just as readily as true premises similarly related. The point, of course, is that both of these factors enter into the process of drawing useful conclusions. We rely on *induction* (on the examination of cases and examples) to give us "true" premises, and we rely on deduction (on the syllogism) to interpret these premises correctly. Any argument may be vulnerable on either or both counts. As we have seen, a formally valid argument is one in which care has been taken to relate the premises in such a way that the conclusion follows. The conclusion of such a formally valid argument will be materially true if the premises are inductively derived (existentially sound).

b. The Laws of Thought. The concept of formal validity in logic rests upon what have been called the laws of thought: the law of identity ($A = A$), the law of contradiction (every A has its non-A), and the law of excluded middle (B is either A or non-A). These laws make the assumption that it is possible to define terms categorically, thereby setting up classes which include or do not include other terms. Thus one may define "horse" with sufficient accuracy to make it possible to say of any animal (or any conceivable thing) that either it is a horse or it is not a horse. Similarly, one may define "sanity" with sufficient accuracy to be able to say of any man that he is either sane or not sane.

Precise definitions are essential to formal validity. Each term in each premise entering into an argument must be identified, and this identity must be maintained without change or equivocation throughout the argument. These definitions may or may not be arbitrary, but they must be tight and rigorous if valid conclusions are to be drawn.

When all the terms in a given argument have been defined, we are then concerned with *the relations* between and among these terms. The premises in the argument assert these relations. Since each definition establishes a discrete class of things, it is possible to say that some other term either does or does not belong in this class. If these relations among terms are strictly observed, it is then possible to draw formally valid conclusions from premises. Syllogistic logic sets forth the various ways in which premises can be combined to yield valid conclusions. But careful definition and careful relating of one term (or class) to another underlies the entire process.

c. The Middle Term Distributed. Every syllogism contains three, and only three, terms: the middle term, the major term, and the minor term. These are normally arranged as follows:

MAJOR PREMISE:	Middle term—Major term
MINOR PREMISE:	Minor term—Middle term
CONCLUSION:	Minor term—Major term

The most critical rule governing the syllogism is that the middle term must be "distributed" in at least one of the premises. By a distributed term is meant one that refers to a class of things in its entirety, such as "all men" or "every law." A term is distributed when it includes all the members of any category or all the parts of a whole; and it is undistributed when it is not universal or all-inclusive, such as "some men," "a part of the group," or "many animals."

The fallacy in reasoning occasioned by the failure to distribute the middle term in at least one of the premises is illustrated in the following syllogism:

Some college men belong to fraternities.
John Smith is a college man.
Therefore, John Smith belongs to a fraternity.

Even though the premises in this syllogism are true and the conclusion *may* be true, the conclusion lacks formal validity because it does not necessarily follow from the premises.

The syllogism in argumentation and debate. We have already explained how syllogisms enter into argumentative discourse. Each argument offered in support of the proposition can be expressed in full syllogistic form if so desired. While such fully stated syllogisms rarely occur in argumentative speaking or writing, the structure of this discourse is none the less syllogistic in character, even if major premises are omitted and assumed, or if conclusions are stated first and premises follow. The essential rhetorical problem in the syllogism is the fact that its rules and regulations contemplate a degree of certainty which can rarely be achieved in a rhetorical demonstration. As we have seen, the crucial test of the syllogism is that the middle term be distributed in at least one of the premises. The point here is that the middle terms in rhetorical syllogisms can rarely be distributed perfectly and completely. The things we talk about in most public and private debates are variable rather than discrete and categorical. The best we can say in most cases is "most," "the great majority," "the trend is in this direction," "in 60 per cent of the cases," "usually," "frequently," etc. A series of syllogisms whose middle terms are qualified in such manner might very well establish an exceedingly high degree of probability; and yet, logically, strictly speaking, they amount to exactly zero, because the middle terms are not distributed. This anomalous situation was recognized by none other than the Greek philosopher, Aristotle, the man who first described the syllogism over two thousand years ago. In order, then, to accommodate his syllogistic doctrine to the kinds of proof which speakers and writers must ordinarily use, he invented the "rhetorical syllogism," or the enthymeme.

The enthymeme. The enthymeme (as conceived by Aristotle) is a concept of great theoretical importance and practical utility to the practitioner of argumentation and debate.[3] It is almost universally defined today by rhetoricians and logicians alike as an elided or truncated syllogism—that is, as a syllogism with one of its premises or the conclusion omitted. Such an omission (usually the major premise) is characteristic of rhetorical discourse, as we have seen, but it is *not* the essential difference between the syllogism and the enthymeme as originally conceived and *as it should be conceived of today*. The real difference is in the certainty of the matter and the form. The logical syllogism is built on premises which are "materially" true, it is tested by the rules of formal validity, the middle term *must* be distributed in at least one of the premises, and the conclusion either follows *certainly* from the premises or it does not follow at all. The rhetorical syllogism, or the enthymeme, is built on "probable" premises, admits middle terms which are only "partially distributed," and limits its conclusions to probabilities. This accords with the nature of rhetorical discourse as we know it to be and as we have discussed it throughout this book (See Chapter 2).

Although the enthymeme deals with probabilities, it always seeks (or should seek) the highest possible degree of probability. If complete certainty can be achieved, so much the better. In this sense, the logical rigor of the syllogism is the goal of every argument. Every speaker or writer wishes (or should wish) to make his case as tight and irrefutable as possible. The syllogism provides standards that enthymemes approximate as closely as possible. The better our choice of premises, the tighter our definitions, and the more completely distributed our middle terms, the closer we approximate the conditions imposed by the syllogism. This is as it should be, but the position that an argument has no stature, that it is inadmissible and unacceptable because it falls short of a certain demonstration, is either a serious misunderstanding of the nature of rhetorical argument or a deliberate sophism in and of itself.[4]

[3] See James H. McBurney, "The Place of the Enthymeme in Rhetorical Theory," *Speech Monographs*, Vol. III (1936), pp. 49–74; *ibid.*, "Some Recent Interpretations of the Aristotelian Enthymeme," *Papers of the Michigan Academy of Science, Arts, and Letters*, Vol. XXI (1935), pp. 489–500.
[4] See *The Rhetoric of Aristotle*, 1.2 and 2.25.

Kinds of enthymemes. Enthymemes can be classified in three ways: (1) on the basis of the omission of one or more parts of a complete argument, (2) on the basis of the character of the major premise, and (3) on the basis of the relation which the minor premise bears to the conclusion.

A fully expressed enthymeme, likely a fully expressed syllogism, has two premises and a conclusion. If the major premise is omitted, the argument is an enthymeme of the "first order"; if the minor premise is omitted, it is one of the "second order"; and if the conclusion is omitted, it is one of the "third order." The full enthymeme is infrequent; the first order is typical; the second order is rare; and the third order is used occasionally for "rhetorical effect."

Enthymemes, like syllogisms, may also be classified as *categorical, disjunctive,* or *hypothetical.* These labels derive from the character of the major premise. A categorical statement classifies without qualification, a disjunctive statement poses alternatives, and a hypothetical statement invokes a condition, or "if" clause. "All men are mortal" is a categorical statement; "The trees are either coniferous or deciduous" is a disjunctive statement; "If cars are parked at the ball park, a game is probably in progress" is a hypothetical statement. Since the major premises of syllogisms or enthymemes may be categorical, disjunctive, or hypothetical generalizations, the arguments applying such generalizations to particular cases may with some propriety be similarly labeled.

Thirdly, enthymemes may be classified on the basis of the relation which the minor premise bears to the conclusion. So classified, there are four types of enthymemes or four kinds of argument: cause, sign, example, and analogy. This we believe to be the most useful classification. It is explained in detail in Chapter 8. In presenting arguments to support a proposition, as we have seen, we can present a reason which explains *why* the proposition is true (cause), or a reason which provides a basis for believing that it *is true* (sign), or examples, or analogies. All arguments are reducible to these types.

The careful reader of this book will ask at this point, Can you properly list *example* and *analogy* as types of enthymemes, since example and analogy are inductive arguments and the enthymeme

is a deductive instrument? Historically, this is a moot question.[5]
We raise the question here to avoid the appearance of an inconsistency, and also because consideration of the question will help
clarify our analysis. Arguments from cause and sign are clearly
deductive as we have explained them. The following illustrations
will help to make this clear.

(CONCLUSION)	Antihistaminic drugs in proper dosages relieve the symptoms of allergic colds, because
(MINOR PREMISE)	I. These drugs contain chemicals which combat the histamine generated by the body in allergic reaction, and
(MAJOR PREMISE)	I'. If we can combat the histamine generated by the body in allergic reaction, we can expect relief from colds caused by allergy.
(MINOR PREMISE)	II. Clinical evidence indicates that such relief may be expected in most allergic colds where proper dosages are administered, and
(MAJOR PREMISE)	II'. If clinical evidence shows such results, we may conclude that the antihistaminics are helpful in the symptomatic relief of allergic colds.

We have here two fully expressed enthymemes (arguments)
adduced to support the same conclusion. The first enthymeme is
a causal argument, because it attempts to explain why the anti-
histaminic drugs relieve allergic colds. The second enthymeme is
an argument from sign, because it attempts to show that anti-
histamines *actually do* relieve allergic colds. Both are "hypothetical" enthymemes as here expressed. All of the premises in these
two arguments, with the exception of II', would need to be expressed and proved inductively to make the case convincing to
most people. Such inductive support would call for examples or
analogies.

The major premise of the first enthymeme in the foregoing illustration expresses, of course, a causal generalization (in hypothetical form). In substance, it alleges that any drug which com-
bats the histamine generated by the body in allergic reaction will
usually *cause* the symptoms of the allergic cold to be so reduced

---

[5] Compare Aristotle's *Rhetoric* i.2 and ii.25. See also *Prior Analytics*
ii.27.

as to give relief. This is the theory or hypothesis upon which anti-histaminic medication rests. To prove it inductively, one would need to cite convincing experimental evidence. Such evidence might consist in, let us say, ten controlled experiments in ten different laboratories by ten different experimenters, each example supporting this causal relationship. Actually, in this kind of case, any one experiment might involve hundreds of subjects and thus hundreds of examples. In terms of our analysis here, the cases reported are the evidence, and the inference from the cases, which permits the generalization, is argument from example.

We still have the question, Can an *inductive* argument from example be cast in syllogistic or enthymematic form? The answer is yes, but not in such a way as to add anything to the force of the argument. The assumed major premise in all inductive enthymemes is this: "If the examples cited are acceptable, the conclusion follows"; or "If examples 1, 2, 3, 4, etc., are reliable and representative, the relationship they exhibit may be generalized." Since such a major premise patently adds nothing to the argument, these inductive arguments are rarely thrown into syllogistic form.

The use of enthymemes in argumentative discourse. The syllogism and the enthymeme explain the structure of argument as it is exhibited in a properly drawn brief or logical outline, and provide the structural basis, through such outlines, for the composition of the finished discourse. They also make it clear that all (deductive) reasoning proceeds by relating generalizations to particular cases through the mediation of middle terms which are common to both and which provide tests that can be used to check the validity of deductive inferences.

John Quincy Adams discusses the rhetorical applications of the syllogism in these words:

A syllogism, as you well know, consists of three propositions, denominated the major and minor propositions, and the conclusion. From the two former, which are the premises, the latter is a necessary inference; because in them the subject and predicate of the conclusion, called by logicians the major and minor terms, or the extremes, are distinctly compared with a middle term, or particular common to them both. These propositions in the simple syllogism are all categorical or positive affirmations. And these propositions all belong alike to the *enthymeme*. The difference is that, as the domain of rhetorical argument is not certainty but probability, the propositions are not absolute but always in some degree problematical. The logician lays down his propositions as incontestable truths; and uses no words other than those which clothe the propositions themselves, to obtain the assent of his auditor to them. And as they must either be true or false, they can be opposed only in the same categorical manner in which they are asserted. The opposition admits of no degrees or modifications; it must either be received with implicit acquiescence, or express denial.

But the propositions of the orator are only given as probabilities. They do not exact unhesitating belief. The major or the minor proposition, from which he purposes to draw his conclusion, or both of them, may require reasons for their own support. . . .[6]

Mr. Adams, in a later passage, explains how the enthymeme usually appears in discourse.

It is to be remembered that uniformity is the favorite character of logic, and variety is equally essential to rhetoric. The syllogism is confined to a very few modifications, and rejects every irregularity of arrangement. It has but one process, from which it inflexibly refuses to depart. Whether proceeding in affirmation or in negation, whether evolving particular or general conclusions, the order of march is eternally the same. The propositions are always categorical. The major advances in the van; the minor settles in the center; the middle term is common to them both; and the conclusion closes in the rear. In rhetoric, the syllogism, by sliding into the enthymeme or spreading into the epichirema, seems to change its nature. It retains all its powers, but is emancipated from all its restrictions. It reverses at pleasure the order of its propositions. It gives alternate precedency to either of the premises, or posts the conclusion in front of both. It is not always arrayed in the dogmatism of unqualified assertion. Is it uncertain, it states its proposition in the diffidence of the potential mood. Is it emphatically certain, it bids defiance to the opponent by challenging denial in the shape of interrogation. Is it humble, it may convey its

[6] John Quincy Adams, *Lectures on Rhetoric and Oratory*, Vol. II (Cambridge: Hilliard and Metcalf, 1810), pp. 38–39. The term "enthymeme" has been substituted for "epichirema" in this quotation, and italics supplied.

idea in the form of conjecture. Is it conscious of authority, it may assume the language of command. It adapts itself to every gradation of intellect. It suits itself to every variety of disposition. But under all its metamorphoses the primary matter of the syllogism, the major, minor, and middle terms, must substantially remain, or the reasoning will be imperfect.[7]

Aristotle has this advice to offer on the use of enthymemes:

We have already stated that the Enthymeme is a syllogism, and in what sense it is so. And we have noted how enthymemes differ from the syllogisms of Dialectic: [when you wish to persuade], you must not begin the chain of reasoning too far back, or its length will render the argument obscure; and you must not put in every single link, or the statement of what is obvious will render it prolix. . . . Our speaker, accordingly, must start out, not from any and every premise that may be regarded as true, but from opinions of a definite sort—the [actual] opinions of the judges [audience], or else the opinions of persons whose authority they accept. And the speaker must make sure that his premises do appear in this light to most, if not all, of his audience. And he must argue not only from necessary truths, but from probable truths as well.[8]

INDUCTIVE REASONING
IN ARGUMENT

Inductive reasoning consists in drawing inferences from the facts, from experience, from evidence. It is the means by which we attempt to make true statements about the phenomena with which we are concerned. "Inductively given" statements are statements which presumably meet the tests of "material" validity; they are true to life, true to the existential world. Whereas deductive inferences deal with the relationships among *given* propositions for the purpose of interpreting these propositions and deriving new propositions from *given* propositions, induction is the logical process by which we "get" the propositions in the first place.

[7] *Ibid.*, pp. 42–43.
[8] *Rhetoric* ii.22.

As we have seen, inductive arguments usually appear as the *last* arguments in the chains of reasoning supporting the proposition. If the proposition can be supported directly by inductive arguments, so much the better, but this is rarely possible. More frequently, the primary arguments are deductive. Each primary argument (if deductive) potentially involves two premises which must be supported. If these premises can be supported inductively, so much the better. If not, they become the conclusions of secondary arguments, each of which potentially involves two premises. The premises of the secondary arguments become the conclusions of tertiary arguments, etc. In other words, each chain of reasoning is refined to a point where the "last" premises can be supported inductively. The evidence always lies next to the inductive argument, hence "below" (in a written brief) or "in support of" the last premises.

When we say that the inductive arguments appear "last" in a chain of reasoning, we of course make the assumption that the advocate begins with his proposition, as is usually the case. To be entirely correct in this matter, we should say that the deductive argument (if any) lies *between* the proposition and the inductive arguments. Actually, the speaker may begin with his evidence and inductive arguments, and then proceed to his proposition via such deductive arguments as may be required. This approach withholds the proposition until the groundwork in evidence and argument has been laid. It simply reverses the usual sequence in presenting a case, and the outline, of course, is inverted. Changing the sequence of arguments, however, does *not* change the arguments. Since some writers refer to this inverted sequence as the "inductive approach," and the sequence which begins with the proposition as the "deductive approach," it should be emphasized that the terms "inductive" and "deductive" in this context are used differently from the way we have used them. If labels are necessary, we prefer to avoid this confusion by referring to the so-called "inductive approach" as the indirect approach, and the so-called "deductive approach" as the direct approach. Aristotle has an interesting comment on this matter:

In the absence of Enthymemes, the speaker must make Examples serve the ends of logical proofs, since it is proofs that carry conviction in the audience. If, however, he has Enthymemes, he must use Examples for the ends of confirmation, subsequent and complementary to the Enthymemes. The Examples should not precede, for then the argument will seem like an induction; but [anything like a scientific] induction is not appropriate in Rhetoric, save in rare cases only. When they follow the Enthymemes, Examples function like witnesses—and there is always a tendency to believe a witness. Accordingly, when the speaker puts the Examples before, he must use a good many of them; if he puts them after, one may suffice—on the principle that a single witness, if you have a good one, will serve the purpose.[9]

It might be inferred from what has been said in this chapter that all "basic" or final premises must be supported inductively. *This is the logical responsibility of the speaker* wherever such support is demanded and can be given. Actually, many of the premises entering into an argument will be accepted without proof because the listener already believes them; in such cases, for rhetorical purposes, the inductive proof is redundant. In other cases, where speculative or philosophical matters are involved, inductive proof may be impossible; here the speaker can do no better than rest his argument on deductive interpretations. And in many practical situations in which conclusions have to be drawn quickly and action taken immediately, in which time and circumstances do not permit careful inductive investigation, we can do no better than make the best guesses we can and enter our premises into the argument as postulates, assumptions, or hypotheses.

EXERCISES

1. Outline the constructive speeches in the oral debate in the Appendix of this book. Having made this outline, use it to assist you in identifying the kinds of argument employed. State all the deductive arguments in full syllogistic form.

2. Prepare a careful outline in support of a proposition. Identify marginally the kinds of argument used, and be prepared to state these arguments in syllogistic and enthymematic form.

3. Prepare four good examples of argument from sign and four of

[9] *Rhetoric* ii.20.

causal argument. State these in syllogistic form, and present one or more inductive arguments in support of the premises involved.

4. Present six-minute argumentative speeches in class in which special attention is given to the organization of the speech and the structure of the argument.

Chapter 10

EXPLANATION AS ARGUMENT

The four principal forms of discourse are description, narration, exposition, and argumentation. In Chapters 8 and 9, we discussed the kinds of argument and the structure of argument in speaking and writing. This is the doctrine of argumentation in the traditional and restricted meaning of the term. Actually, however, there are many circumstances under which description, narration, and exposition may be used to serve the ends of argumentation— to influence belief and action. This is what we mean by explanation as argument.

THE NATURE OF
EXPLANATION

The point has been made previously that "a clear explanation of a subject will often constitute a wholly persuasive treatment of it." [1] This is precisely the thesis we develop here. In other

---

[1] J. M. O'Neill and A. T. Weaver, *The Elements of Speech* (Boston: Longmans, Green and Company, 1926), p. 434.

words, it is possible to provide acceptable bases for belief and action by explaining a proposition. This fact comports with commonplace experiences that we have all had. We want someone to read a novel that we think is good, so we tell him enough of the story to get him interested. We want someone to visit Yellowstone National Park, so we describe the natural beauty of the park and the facilities available to visitors. We want support for a community project, so we explain the purposes of this project and our plans for it.

Explanation defined. Explanation is a form of analysis and reasoning in which description, narration, and exposition are used to provide acceptable bases for belief and action by placing a proposition in a context that implies its truth. The method has been described as follows:

Its plan [that of support by explanation] is simply to portray a situation which gradually, of itself, without compulsion or contention on the part of the speaker, through the compelling power of a developing situation, makes evident to the mind of the hearer the necessity of one certain solution. The method is not in the orthodox and generally accepted sense argumentative; rather it is that of exposition with a goodly dash of narration and description. It does not appear to argue; it merely sets forth—yet slowly, definitely, as it proceeds, the lines of descriptive development begin to converge and it becomes compellingly evident to each thinking mind that such a set of conditions implies, necessitates, one thing, the conclusion toward which an approach has been made from the beginning. It is argument in a very true sense, its aim is to convince and persuade, yet it is argument of which exposition, narration, and description are handmaidens.[2]

The explanatory approach in argument seeks to involve the proposition in question as a necessary circumstance of the data presented. The key to this is *implication*. The proposition is implied or suggested as naturally to be inferred, often without being expressly stated.

Implication has been defined as "the connection between terms or sets of terms in virtue of a common nature which binds them into parts within a continuous system such that you can tell from

[2] Gladys Murphy Graham, "The Natural Procedure in Argument," *The Quarterly Journal of Speech*, Vol. XI, No. 4, p. 321.

one or more parts of it what the other parts of it, or some of them, are and how they are behaving."[3] This is the nature of the inference in argument by explanation. It consists in a juxtaposition of the original data connected with the proposition, and out of the necessities which impose themselves when these data are thus arranged and exhibited arises a datum—a premise which partakes of the nature of a conclusion and is accepted as such.[4] Bosanquet, who speaks of this as "the natural procedure in argument," states, "I believe that the natural method of opening the case descriptively, and placing the reader or hearer within the system which is the development of our subject, not merely follows an instinct of common sense, but is a well grounded logical procedure and ultimately fundamental."[5]

Implication and linear inference. A fair question to ask is whether this explanatory or implicative approach in argument is in fact "a well grounded logical procedure" that differs essentially from the traditional syllogistic-enthymematic approach discussed earlier. This is a theoretical question that need not concern us here in any final way. In the work cited above, *Implication and Linear Inference*, Bosanquet argues that the difference is basic. He refers to "the syllogism and generalization from recurrent particulars" as the linear conception of inference, and distinguishes this, as we have here, from "implication" as a theory of inference.[6] But whatever the ultimate theoretical differences, there can be no serious question that the two approaches are quite different methodologically. And this is the matter with which we are immediately concerned.

THE METHOD OF
EXPLANATION

There are examples of the explanatory approach in argument all around us. In attempting to influence attitudes and be-

[3] Bernard Bosanquet, *Implication and Linear Inference* (London: Macmillan and Company, 1920), p. 14.
[4] *Ibid.*, p. 116.
[5] *Ibid.*, p. 113.
[6] *Ibid.* See Chapter II, "The Linear Conception of Inference," especially pp. 21–30.

liefs in areas where the relevant data lend themselves to description, narration, or exposition, there does appear to be a "natural"
impulse to use this approach. Travel brochures, posters, bill-
boards, radio and television commercials—indeed, the whole field
of advertising and selling—attest the confidence that entrepre-
neurs of all kinds place in the persuasive power of description,
narration, and exposition. And most people, in trying to justify
their behavior, recommend a course of action, or make a questionable proposition believable, will often resort to explanation. In a
quite different area, the reports of scholarly investigations are
frequently expositions serving the normal purposes of argument.
Scientists, for example, typically support their conclusions by explaining the processes they went through in arriving at these
conclusions.

In an essay, "Science and the Non-Scientist," Moody Prior develops the thesis that American education has failed to provide
adequate knowledge and understanding of science for the non-
scientist.[7] The reasons for this failure and the consequences of it
are explained and possible answers suggested. The development
is essentially expository rather than argumentative in the traditional sense, but the conclusion is clearly implied before it is
drawn.

. . . the assimilation of science into the whole of our culture cannot
take place without the help of the scientists in promoting an understanding of the human relevance and meaning of their work. . . . We
cannot close the enormous gap between science and those who do not
practice science by providing sufficient conventional instruction in
science to make the non-scientist proficient in science. The only hope
lies in trying to introduce a scholarly, interpretative approach to the
teaching of science such as is now available in other departments of a
university where the works of man are the subject of instruction. . . .
Such a step in the direction of general scientific literacy may in the
long run prove to be at least as important as the training of more scientists.[8]

Description, narration, and exposition are *not* argument unless
they are organized and presented in ways that serve the purposes

[7] *Science and the Humanities* (Evanston, Illinois: Northwestern University Press, 1962), Chapter V, "Science for the Non-Scientist," pp. 92–117.
[8] *Ibid.,* pp. 109 and 117 with adaptations.

of argument. This is accomplished by putting together an *implicative system* that directs an inference to a predetermined conclusion to the exclusion of other possible conclusions.

The implicative system. Such a system may be defined as a logical thought-whole consisting of a set of propositions so related (by implication) that the truth of one is implied by the truth of the others. A proposition may be looked upon as a part of this whole or system. In argument by explanation, the proposition for discussion is always one of the propositions of an implicative system. It is the task of the speaker to present the other related propositions in such a way that the truth of the proposition under discussion will be implied. The accompanying figure illustrates the point we are making.

Let us say that the larger square represents an implicative system, and each of the smaller squares a proposition. If we let the square marked by the X indicate the proposition for argument, we suggest that its truth may be implied as we explain the propositions or data represented by the other squares. The more of these related propositions we explain, the more evident will become the proposition under discussion. The whole process is comparable to a picture puzzle which is unintelligible until its various parts are assembled. As the fragments are pieced together, the place of each remaining part becomes increasingly evident from the nature of the picture which is beginning to take form. Propositions, like the pieces of the puzzle, are not intelligible as isolated entities. Their identity as true or false statements, so far as any individual is concerned, is determined by many relationships. It is the task of the speaker to bring these relationships to light. If the proposition under discussion can be identified with a group of other propositions which cannot be logically denied and thus are accepted by the audience, the truth of the proposition is thereby implied. A proposition is thus related to a system as a part is related to the whole. It is the speaker's task to make it clear that the proposition he is defending is a part of a system which the listener cannot safely or logically deny. When that system has been explained, the truth or falsity of the proposition can be implied by it. In most cases the implication is perfectly obvious if the speaker's work has been well done. The conclusion simply rushes ahead of the argument.

The this-or-nothing disjunction. Needless to say, it is a matter of considerable importance that the conclusion drawn by the audience be the conclusion which the speaker intends to be drawn. In other words, the explanation developed should be sufficiently under the control and guidance of the speaker to give reasonable assurance that his purpose will be accomplished. This can best be done by developing the argument so that the only alternative to the acceptance of the suggested proposition is the rejection of all the data presented. As Bosanquet puts it, "The Essence of the Inference in Implication, then, would be in showing of any suggested proposition, that unless we accepted it, our province of truth would as a whole be taken from us." [9]

In a tightly drawn argument by explanation, the speaker builds an implicative system that confronts his audience with a this-or-nothing disjunction in which his proposition is the "this" in the disjunction and the rejection of the related propositions implying its truth is the "nothing." This nothing means the absence of all logical grounds—the denial of truth as we know it and commonly accept it.

All of this is simply a way of saying, helpfully we hope, that explanation satisfies the conditions of argument when it implies a given proposition on the basis of descriptive, narrative, and ex-

[9] *Op. cit.,* p. 3.

pository data acceptable to reasonable people. Explanation fails as argument if no proposition is implied, if the proposition is rejected, or if a different proposition is implied.

Topical organization. The outline of explanatory argument is topical rather than enthymematic. In other words, the main points and the subpoints are usually key words or phrases rather than premises. The implicative system may be regarded as a thought whole that is divided into its parts by the main points, and these main points, in turn, divided into their parts by the subpoints. In this organization each coordinate list of points is a descriptive, narrative, or expository breakdown of the point they are intended to explain. The composition (oral or written) developing this outline, then, will be description, narration, exposition, or some combination of these designed to place the suggested proposition in a context that warrants its implication.

Explanatory development. It is hardly necessary here to analyze the nature and methods of description, narration, and exposition in any detail. Suffice it to say that description paints a picture—"exhibits the properties, attributes, and relations of *spacial* objects in their proper order." [10] Narration tells a story— "presents a matter in its *time* relations . . . , exhibits events in their proper order." [11] Exposition exhibits a proposition as "a logical thought whole independent of time or space relations." [12]

From these definitions it can be seen that exposition deals largely with abstract and general conceptions, while pure description and narration are generally occupied with concrete things. Whereas description and narration deal with things seen, heard, depicted (matters of observation), exposition is concerned with things conceived, identified, classified (matters of penetrative and systematic thinking). Description and narration consider traits and acts that distinguish objects as individuals; exposition looks for the traits and acts that unite individuals into classes. Assume, for instance, that you have occasion to explain some controversial religious doctrine or scientific principle. Neither narration nor

[10] James H. Hyslop, *Logic and Argument* (New York: Charles Scribner's Sons, 1899), p. 66.
[11] *Ibid.*, p. 68.
[12] *Ibid.*, p. 69.

description would suffice, because such a subject cannot usually be exhibited in relations of time or space. It is an abstract concept which can be adequately explained only by an exposition of its logical relations to other known concepts.

In practice, it is rarely possible to support a proposition of any complexity with simple description or narration without first dividing the matter by main points or topics. This primary division will ordinarily be an expository breakdown designed to yield topics (subtopics) that are amenable to description or narration. This is roughly comparable to the enthymematic approach, in which deductive arguments are used as primary premises, as main points supporting the proposition, and inductive arguments are employed as secondary or tertiary subpoints confirming these main points.

Concrete helps in explanation. Charts, diagrams, maps, pictures, models, samples, and demonstrations are often valuable aids in argument of any kind, and they can be especially helpful in argument by explanation. However, these devices have dubious value in and of themselves, and unless they add significantly to the clarity and force of the presentation, a speaker is better off without them. In other words, be careful of using visual aids as a crutch in cases where verbal development will serve the same purpose as well or better. And in any case, be certain that these devices can be seen or heard easily and that they are introduced at the point in the argument where attention to them is desired.

THE PERSUASIVE VALUES
OF EXPLANATION

The differences between enthymematic and explanatory argument are probably relative rather than absolute; the same may be said of the differences between explanation for purposes of clarity and explanation designed as argument. Complete objectivity in reporting is rarely achieved. But distortion of the facts in any kind of speaking or writing is reprehensible, and deliberate slanting of an explanation for persuasive purposes can be a pretty shoddy business. The persuasive values of explanation can be realized without resorting to dishonest or devious tactics. We suggest the values outlined below.

It dispels unfamiliarity. Support by explanation has special value as a means of persuading an audience which is inadequately informed on the proposition. What argument could be more persuasive to a person who is indifferent, or opposed to a proposition because he is not informed regarding it, than one which supplies him with this information? Almost invariably, when the opposition has its basis in unfamiliarity, the speaker has only to explain the proposition in order to dispel this opposition and secure the desired action.

The audience is prepared for the conclusion by its own thinking. That you cannot pour conclusions into the heads of people as you would pour water into a receptacle is a matter of common knowledge. Only as the listener is stirred to "purposeful activity" can you expect to influence his thinking or overt conduct. Conclusions arrived at by one's own thinking are thus infinitely stronger than those imposed by others, so far as the individual is concerned. In the explanatory method the persuader does not simply recite his own conclusions before the audience; rather, he sets forth those facts and opinions which led him to conclude as he did in such a way that the hearers will be prodded to go through the same reasoning process.

It avoids the "contrarient idea." This method also avoids what some writers have called the "contrarient idea." When a speaker starts his presentation with certain conclusions, the very announcement of these conclusions invariably sets off inhibitions which might never otherwise occur. Some people seem to resist other people's conclusions. They question at the slightest opportunity. They immediately begin a mental argument with the speaker and fight him from the first word to the last. In many situations these obstacles can be avoided, or at least greatly minimized, by the method of explanation.

EXERCISES

1. Write a 300-word explanation on one of the following subjects. Have a definite proposition in mind, and make your treatment as persuasive as possible.

    a. A book to read
    b. A place to go for a vacation
    c. An athletic event to attend
    d. A play or movie to see

2. Prepare a five-minute argumentative speech on some proposition of local, state, or national policy in which you use the explanatory method. Hand in an outline of this speech and an explanation of the implicative system that you have tried to construct.

3. Present a five-minute explanatory argument in which you make use of charts, diagrams, maps, models, samples, or demonstrations.

4. Divide the class into groups of two, and assign a proposition to each group. Let one member of each group support the assigned proposition with a confirmatory argument and the other member support the same proposition with an explanatory argument. Compare methods and results.

PERSUASION

IN RELATION TO
ARGUMENTATION

It will be recalled that we have treated argumentation mainly in terms of the logical attack on, and the defense of, propositions. It will also be recalled that argumentation may serve analytical and critical functions as well as persuasive ones. In this chapter, however, we are concerned with only the persuasive applications of argumentation. But in order to provide a meaningful context for this treatment, we are sketching the broader field of persuasion.

On this subject, as on that of discussion, there are specialized textbooks which present much more of the theory than we intend to offer here. Actually, the emphasis of this chapter is upon the role of experimental research in the development of the principles of persuasion.

We mean by persuasion either the *process* of influencing human behavior (attitudes, opinions, overt acts, etc.) through the use of oral and written communication, or the *academic disci-*

pline in which applied rhetoric and psychology are studied.

Persuasion is a broader term than argumentation. In argumentation we study propositions, analysis, evidence, reasoning, attack and defense, etc. In persuasion we may study some of the same topics, but in addition we are likely to be concerned with the ethos of the source, motive appeals, the suggestive impact of style and delivery, and other nonlogical factors in the communicative process.

Although we distinguish between motivation and reasoning, we do not regard these categories as mutually exclusive or discrete. The reason-emotion dichotomy, for example, is considered unsound as a psychological classification. The ways of reacting which we call thoughtful and emotional are not distinct units motivating particular instances of behavior, but exist in varying proportions in the different situations. We know that emotional behavior comes increasingly into play when goals are sought with unusual tenacity and vigor. In fact, it is obvious that all behavior has its motives, be they strong or weak. Thus an argument may have logical validity *and* emotional appeal. In other words, a case which is adapted to the interests, wants, values, and understanding of the listeners or readers is not necessarily less cogent intellectually.

Should every effective argument enlist the desires of the audience in the cause for which the appeal is being advanced? This question brings up the dual problem of logical adequacy and audience acceptability. In the first place, we feel that there are occasions when the speaker's first concern should be with logical unity, continuity, and completeness, irrespective of the desires of the audience. In the second place, we feel that it is possible at times (even when audience acceptability is taken as the primary test) to premise the argument on existing beliefs of the audience and to reason both persuasively and convincingly without giving special attention to the desires of the listeners. It is also possible at times to influence persons to respond to interests, wants, or values other than those which would otherwise have determined their behavior. For instance, the desire to save money has accounted for the failure of some schools to have a science program, but the substituted desire to "keep up with Russia" has in many cases proved to be sufficient to correct that deficiency.

Finally, with respect to the relative emphasis upon the logical and the psychological ingredients in persuasive communication, it should be noted that the ratio varies with circumstances, and that a persuasive message is not simply a "logical" one with some "emotional appeals" added like frosting to a cake. The fact that the ratio between these types of supporting material varies is observable in a comparison of jury pleas with pleas to judges, and of speeches to laymen with those to experts.

PREDISPOSING FACTORS

Students of persuasion have long wondered why some stimuli influence persons to modify their attitudes, beliefs, and decisions, while others fail to win the desired response. The explanation is not always to be found in the message itself; we know that the same message may lead to different reactions when the communicator or the receiver is changed. Obviously, some persons respond more readily to one kind of stimulus, while others are influenced by different kinds. This observation has led to the search for predisposing factors which may account for individual differences in receptiveness to persuasion. Some of these factors, which are described below, affect the tasks of audience analysis and adaptation.[1]

Subject matter. There are experimental data and experiential testimony to indicate that the subject of the communication may be a predisposing factor. Sometimes it is a specific subject, and in some cases it is a general one. In either case the explanation is that one's motives, values, affiliations, or ideological commitments predispose him toward an affirmative or a negative posture on certain propositions, such as those dealing with race relations, religious differences, partisan politics, foreign aid, the treatment of

[1] The most extensive compilation of summaries of such studies is the five-volume *Yale Studies in Attitude and Communication,* edited by Carl I. Hovland and published by Yale University Press, 1953–1961.

social deviants, and many others. Some listeners and readers are so "allergic" to certain ideas that any advocate who incidentally alludes to one of them while discussing something else will almost surely fail to influence those persons in the direction of his purpose.

Appeals. There are persons who respond more readily to certain emotional appeals than to other potential sources of influence. Comparative responsiveness to social approval or disapproval is a case in point. Also, we know that there are differing degrees of sensitivity to fear, shame, envy, remorse, revenge, and other emotional states. Let us consider fear-arousing appeals for a moment. There is a lack of precise evidence on the relationships between motivation and the changing of opinions, but it is thought that an intensely disturbing emotional state may act as a drive to behavior. However, unless the threat is thought to be familiar, real, and imminent, we tend to minimize or ignore it. On the other hand, if the threat seems too strong, we may refuse to pay attention, or we may reject the source, or we may defensively avoid the situation.

Logical relations. While considering this predisposing factor, we can notice the closest connection between argumentation and persuasion: that is, the former is a part of the latter in this setting. The arrangement and the logical consistency of the topics in a discourse make more difference to some persons than to others, as the following references to research will show.

Should an advocate state his proposition explicitly, or should he leave it implicit and expect readers or listeners to draw the intended conclusion? Explicit statement was found to be the more effective, but not invariably so. Factors which made a difference included the personal traits of the speaker, the pre-speech audience attitude, and the nature of the subject involved. The theory is that an implicative order is more effective with an opposed audience.

When speaking to a doubtful or an opposed audience, should an advocate state his proposition at the outset, or delay it until the conclusion? There is some advantage in favor of the delayed disclosure, but only under certain conditions. Factors other than position may be the determinants of opinion change.

Is it better to state only your own side, or to present both sides, if you are the only speaker? Both-sides presentations proved to be more persuasive with men who were initially opposed to the speaker's own opinion and with the better-educated men in the group. It was also more effective in terms of resistance to subsequent counterpropaganda. One-sided presentation was superior when the listeners were initially favorable, provided that no counterpropaganda followed.

Which is more persuasive, the climax order or the anticlimax order, in a one-sided speech? Some advantage for the climax order was found when the issue was salient—that is, when it mattered a good deal to the listeners. Conversely, the anticlimax order fared somewhat better when listeners were unfamiliar with, or not interested in, the issue.

When both sides are given, does the first position have an advantage? If it did, we could affirm a principle of primacy. Actually, there is more support for the principle of recency, which means that there is a tendency to remember the more recent message more accurately. Thus the last position has an advantage.

What if some event occurs between the affirmative and the negative presentations? If the audience were asked to perform some act, or if someone inserted a warning against a possible error in either message, the result would differ from that described immediately above. It has also been found that if a listener expresses a public commitment after hearing the first side, he will be less influenced by the opposite side's following statement. Giving an anonymous, paper-and-pencil response to an opinion questionnaire after hearing the first side does not have such a prejudicial effect.

Is the need–satisfaction order more effective than its inverse order? If the audience is not already concerned and motivated with respect to the problem at hand, the need should be stated first. Otherwise, they require only to be reminded of the need which they believe exists.

If a speaker has some points which are in agreement with his listeners' desires and some which are not, which should be stated first? There is some evidence which suggests that it is more persuasive to open with arguments which are more nearly in agree-

ment with the listeners' desires. The avoidance of initial antagonism or indifference seems to be the explanation.

Suppose we have an authoritative communicator who plans to
give some points favorable to his own view plus some points from
the opposition. Would the pro-con or the con-pro order be preferable? If the con points are not salient with his audience, he should
begin with his own side, but if a con point is salient, it should be
acknowledged early.

These are only a few of the limited generalizations which may
be drawn from the published studies. Many of the questions concerning persuasion are as yet unanswered.

Style and delivery. Apparently there are social and educational bases for preferences among the levels of usage, the stylistic
features, and the characteristics of delivery. Some persons, for
example, prefer informal English, earthy metaphors, and bom-
bastic physical delivery; others are repelled by these characteristics. The importance of audience analysis and adaptation by the
speaker cannot be overemphasized here.

Can we judge the effectiveness of a style of presentation by its
popularity? Straight talk, dramatization, and the two combined
were tested for impact and preference. The combined form was
voted the most popular, but it was not the most effective in
achieving a stated purpose. Apparently, preference and impact do
not coincide.

Will a "readability yardstick" predict listenability of mass communication? The well-publicized Flesch formula for readability
has not been shown to be a reliable predictor of listenability as
measured by the retention of materials given in informational
broadcasts.

Which elements of oral style can increase the intelligibility of a
speech? The use of the following devices increases by at least 10
per cent the amount of information imparted to an audience: precise terms, suggestive words, direct quotations, emotional words,
questions, illustrations, simple words, figures of speech, and simple
sentence structures.

How much effect does speaking rate have upon a listener's
comprehension and his opinion of the delivery? If the rates are
not perceived as being either unusually slow or unusually fast,

there is not much difference. Rates from 126 to 172 words per minute were used in the research.

An advocate's choice of strategy, whether it be suggestion, rationalization, or forthright statement, seems to be an important factor. Suggestion involves the offering of a stimulus in such a way as to produce a response unchecked by critical thought. When it is intentionally used, this technique of indirect influence is a process in which the advocate's main idea works in the fringes of the listener's attention while a related idea occupies the center of attention. Thus a defense attorney might focus the facts of the case in narrative form upon each juror's center of attention, but his selection of facts, his choice of language, and his delivery might lodge in the fringes of the jurors' attention a strong emotional reaction of pity for the accused.

A rationalization is an emotionally aroused conclusion that is rendered plausible on pseudological grounds. Even though we react nonrationally at times, we prefer to believe that we behave rationally. Rationalizing occurs when we do what we want to do and then seek an acceptable reason to justify the impulsive act. This pseudological thinking has several characteristics: it centers attention on materials that *seem* to be relevant; its apparently definite ideas are vaguely outlined; it masks suggestion as deliberation; "good" reasons are presented as "real" ones; subjective ideas are disguised as objective ones; it thwarts careful scrutiny while seeming to encourage it; it often involves certain fallacies and stratagems (to be described in a separate chapter).

Forthright statement involves a frank and open explanation or demonstration. Rather than using suggestion or rationalization, the arguer proceeds directly to establish the connection between certain desires and his proposition. He may explain how the acceptance of his proposition will lead to certain satisfactions, he may demonstrate or give a sample, or he may do both. This doctrine is consistent with that principle of learning which states that the proffered motive should be logically relevant to the goal.

Communicator. The personality of the communicator has for more than twenty centuries been identified as a predisposing factor in persuasion. *Who* says something often makes a great difference in the impact. Students of this phenomenon have known it in terms of ethos, prestige suggestion, credibility of the communicator, and the like. Expertness, which is one dimension of this factor, is often attributed to persons who seem to be intelligent, well informed, of an age or in a job which suggests an opportunity to know about the matter in question, and who seem to have interests similar to those of the evaluator.

The advocate is usually identified with his subject in a more personal way than are other speakers. This factor, more than anything else, distinguishes the speaking of the advocate. He always recommends a position, point of view, or course of action to others, and in this capacity he stands as a sponsor of a cause. Indifference or detachment on his part is usually interpreted to mean a lack of conviction. He is asking his listeners to accept the proposition which *he* represents. Unless his presentation is such as to convey personal enthusiasm, interest, and conviction, his proposition may suffer an undeserved fate. By the same token, we must confess, a weak position may often be given an acceptance which it does not merit because of the force of the personality supporting it. Psychologically, the advocate and his cause are one, at least while he is speaking. They are likely to stand or fall together.

This phenomenon is peculiarly associated with advocacy. It applies in all speaking, but speakers who seek primarily to entertain or inform are much less intimately associated with their ideas. The speaking advocate, more than any other speaker, must concern himself with those personal qualities which recommend him *and* his cause to his listeners.

It would be a mistake, though, to assume that credibility in the communicator will uniformly make his remarks acceptable. This factor will increase the impact of his material only if the ideas are not highly acceptable by themselves. When the source is respected but the message is unacceptable, there is a tendency of listeners and readers to dissociate the person and his remark. If the message is extremely unacceptable, we tend to turn against the source, and he loses his high-credibility status.

When a person is attracted more by the source of a controversial assertion than by its intrinsic merit, does the effect persist for long? This effect wears off in time, generally within three weeks, possibly because the subject forgets how he acquired the opinion.

Are observers likely to be influenced more by their impressions of the communicator's personality than by the content of his message? Not invariably so, as indicated above, but when other factors were held as nearly constant as possible, the impressions of expertness, past behavior, and bias accounted for significant amounts of change in opinions.

Does the phenomenon of credibility of source extend to magazines and professions? Research in advertising points to a positive correlation between the credibility of an advertisement and the reputation of the magazine in which it appears. When statements about economic and fiscal problems were attributed to persons in several professions, the quotations were most often approved when attributed to educators and businessmen, and least often when attributed to ministers. Perhaps the opinions did not relate primarily to the *ethical* aspect of the economic and fiscal problems.

What effect does a speaker's social status have upon listeners' ratings of his character? He will, as a rule, get higher ratings from listeners who think he is one of them in terms of social class. The rating of character tends to go down as the perceived social distance between the speaker and his listeners increases.

In introducing a speaker to an audience, how important is prestige suggestion? When favorable information on experience, education, or honors is given, the listeners are more likely to accept his views than if unfavorable information or no information were given. Thus the advance publicity and the speech of introduction can help a speaker if they are not spoiled by fulsome praise.

Does this principle apply to the use of opinion testimony in a speech of advocacy? Apparently so. Evidenced contentions were found to be more persuasive than unsupported assertions, and those citations which included a "build-up" for the qualifications of the sources were the most persuasive.

How important is a listener's impression of the speaker's sincerity, even when the intent to persuade is known? Listeners' impressions of a speaker's expertness, trustworthiness, and sincerity modify the impact very much. A popular entertainer who sold war bonds in a radio marathon was perceived as "really meaning it," rather than as "just another salesman." Patriotic rather than selfish motives were attributed to the source.

When a communicator is perceived as meaning to persuade, will his impact be less than that of a seemingly casual persuader? Except in cases analogous to the preceding one, there is some mistrust of intentional persuaders; they seem to be out for their own gain. Seemingly casual or overheard remarks are often more persuasive, probably because the receivers do not have a critical or a suspicious mental set in that situation.

Medium. There is some experimental evidence to support the view that the medium of communication is a predisposing factor. Some persons seem to be more influenced by face-to-face communication, while others respond better to television, movies, print, or some other medium. The possession of more reliable knowledge about this problem than we now have would be of untold value to educators, political campaigners, and other communicators. Some experiments have estimated the effectiveness of the auditory medium alone, the visual alone, and a combination of the two. Often the audio-visual combination has been superior, but there have been times when the so-called visual aid was a handicap. Perhaps the quality or the appropriateness of the auditory or the visual aid is the critical factor. It is known, however, that education and intelligence correlate with some preferences for specific media of communication.

Situation. The general setting in which one receives persuasive communication is a variable, predisposing factor. A few studies imply that there are personality traits which are signs of greater or less sensitivity to extraneous factors such as crowd reaction, music, decoration, and pleasantness of the experience. Somewhat more evidence is available on the persuasive impact of the situational factors such as the known majority opinion, active participation, and affiliations. These three will now be explained.

How much does a person's affiliation with a group affect his responsiveness to "counternorm persuasion" (that which runs counter to the prevailing opinion of that group)? Here we are dealing with the influence of a group upon its membership. As we might expect, a member's conformity to group norms is related to his popularity with the group and the value he places upon his membership. The goal of a counternorm persuader is the reduction of the incentive value of group conformity and an increase in the incentive value of deviant (nonconforming) behavior. Cross pressures such as this account for the inconsistent public and private expressions of opinion that individuals sometimes make.

Does indulgence in relevant overt behavior help to persuade persons? Convictions have been acquired or modified through active participation, as in role-playing, debating both sides, giving speeches, and writing letters in experimental situations. The influence of role-playing has been explained by the fact that overt verbal responses increase learning. When debaters change their minds after practicing on a second side, they may be responding to increased understanding more than to autosuggestion. Finally, the experiments with letter writers and extemporaneous speakers have shown that an appreciable number of subjects shifted in the direction of their assigned letters or speeches. However, the more intelligent, the better-educated, and the more stable individuals were less influenced by participation. The shifts, when they occurred, were attributed to focused attention upon the ideas.

Are persons influenced by an awareness of majority opinion on the proposition? Several aspects of the effects of majority opinion have been investigated. In one experiment the persons who were persuaded by a case changed their estimate of majority opinion in the direction advocated by that case. They tended to interpret their individual shifts as parts of a shift by the majority. Another study showed the majority opinion to be most influential with individuals who valued their group membership and who were reminded of group loyalty during the communication. Each person's estimate of his self-interest seems to have been a strong factor. This phenomenon was found to be related to maturity; that is, high-school seniors showed the most shifts of opinion after learning the majority view, college seniors shifted less, and the adults shifted the least.

Personality correlates. How much do personality traits have to do with a person's reactions to discourse that is intended to persuade? A general theory based upon correlating personality traits would be enormously useful, but research has thus far failed to achieve that result. In fact, the personality traits have more often proved to be only minor determinants of persuadability. This largely negative result may not be definitive; it may merely reflect inadequate measurement. Even so, there are four questions which can be answered tentatively.

Are there sex differences in persuadability? An affirmative answer is indicated by the findings of several studies in discussion, public speaking, and psychology. Some writers hypothesize that the observed differences stem from the stereotyped roles which our culture imposes upon each sex. Among males there is more correlation between high persuadability and low self-esteem and indulgence in fantasy. Girls tend to be more persuadable if in childhood they have been dominated by parents, but boys appear to react differently to such conditioning.

Is there a way to predict gullibility? In other words, are there any personality correlates of high persuadability? Those who run confidence games must have found some. The psychologists who have worked on this have pointed to these signs: low self-esteem, low or inhibited aggressiveness, low hostility feelings, depressive effects, inadequate perception, high group conformity or adaptation (proneness to anticipate social rewards), inability to evaluate argument, and lack of interest in critical thinking. The fact that some of these conditions are remediable through instruction and counseling should give us some hope.

Does the opposite condition, low persuadability, correlate with any specific traits of personality? Once again, the limited amount of evidence permits only a few modest generalizations. The following traits have been associated with resistance to persuasion: persistent aggressiveness, social withdrawal, indifference to social rewards, acute neurotic conflicts, motivated critical evaluation, low interest in perceiving or understanding, and low ability in attention and verbalization.

Does general intelligence have much bearing upon persuadability? These did not correlate as highly as the investigators anticipated, but there is some evidence to suggest that intelligent persons are more often influenced by logical arguments, while the less intelligent ones are more likely to accept fallacious reasoning.

STAGES OF THE PROCESS

Let it be understood at the outset of this discussion that we regard persuasion as a complex process that is configurational rather than unitary. However, for pedagogical purposes, we divide the process of persuasion into stages which can be treated separately, even though they function as a whole. Within these stages any or all of the determinants of behavior may be used. The three main stages are termed attention, comprehension, and acceptance. What will be learned from the persuasive communication is determined in the first two, while acceptance or rejection is determined in the third.

Attention. Readiness to respond to the stimulus situation is what this stage is concerned with. It is of crucial importance, because without attention there can be no influence exerted. No doubt this is why the gaining of attention is so often given as the first function of a speaker's introductory remarks. In fact, probably most communicators often have to be concerned with getting their intended audiences to look or listen. One reason is that there are competing stimuli, including private thoughts, in the perceptual fields of the listeners, readers, or viewers. Another is the shortness of the span of attention—the problem of keeping the focus of attention upon one source of stimuli for a sufficiently long time.

Two classes of factors, extrinsic and intrinsic, have much to do with attention. Extrinsic factors, meaning those outside the message itself, include seating, music, visual symbols, group activity, control of distractions, tricks of print, delivery, and other facets of showmanship. We know that thousands of persons standing shoulder to shoulder in a public square make a more easily polarized audience than a seated group, and that a closely seated group is more easily managed than a scattered audience. Some of the more successful rallies for political, religious, and athletic purposes afford ample evidence of the extrinsic factors at work.

Intrinsic factors of attention, meaning those within the communication itself, tend to encourage voluntary attention. This is the kind of attention we give because we want to; the message seems to have something which interests us. The message itself may attract our attention because it ties the proposition to our motives and goals, because it promises to relieve some tension or difficulty, because it arouses our curiosity, or because in some other way it relates to self-interest.

Comprehension. Between perception and acceptance there must be some sort of comprehension, because one cannot respond to a message if he does not understand what he is supposed to respond to. He must understand the tension or perceive the condition which the persuader offers to relieve, and he must comprehend the linkage between the proffered remedy and some goal. This sort of interpretation requires a modicum of intelligence.

Sometimes, however, a persuader will strive to stimulate in his readers or listeners a kind of understanding which is more accurately termed *mis*understanding. *He* has a clear goal, to be sure, but he wants his audience to react to a vague, or at least ambiguous, message as if it were clear and precise. Thus, a multimillion-dollar business in a proprietary medicine was built upon the slogan, "For a better tomorrow." Occasional instances of this sort should not obscure the fact that straightforward advocates try to achieve clarity rather than obscurity.

In order to do this, they must at times counteract the perceptual habits of their listeners or readers. These barriers to efficient comprehension include polar concepts, selective perception, confusion of perception and inference, the habit of ignoring details, and the like. Polar concepts are those based upon the extremes of a continuum, such as good-bad and radical-reactionary, and they are discussed by some semanticists under "two-valued orientation." Selective perception obviously means seeing or hearing what one wishes to notice, while the confusion of perception and inference involves the embellishment of a factual report by the addition of opinion or interpretation.

With reference to the comprehension step, it is pertinent to ask whether or not information can change an attitude. Some research has found a high correlation between the amount of information concerning an ethnic group and a favorable attitude toward the group. However, when controlled analytical experiments were conducted, the results cast some doubt upon the causal link between the reception of information and the changing of attitudes. It seems clear that attitudes which are of long standing, of great intensity, and which are emotionally involved are not likely to be changed by exposure to information. But one who is doubtful or slightly opposed because of unfamiliarity with a proposition can occasionally be influenced by explication.

Acceptance. This third stage in the process of persuasion will be treated under four substages in chronological order: belief; association of message with wants, values, and goals; motivation to surmount obstacles; the retention of change. Matters of audience analysis and adaptation will not be discussed under each step, but it is understood that those processes may go on before, during, and after the presentation of the message.

Belief. Acceptance or rejection of a proposition as a result of critical thinking, which means the exercise of evaluative ability, is the principal concern here. Mere compliance or pretense does not count; there must be a change in the verbalized attitude or value judgment. In case there is a belief dilemma, which means a difficult choice between conclusions, there is a preference for the one which involves the less effort.

This points up the difficulty in trying to define belief as an uncompromisingly intellectual activity. As we stated in our discussion of "emotional" and "rational" proofs, the two are not discrete. In support of this view we can cite several experiments during the past thirty years which have indicated that there is no clearcut distinction between emotional and intellectual appeals in terms of the ability of readers and listeners to identify them. The most we can say is that belief should be more often based upon critical thinking than it now is.

Association of message with wants, values, and goals. As we have stated earlier, it is quite possible to make a forthright, intellectually cogent linkage between a proposition and the wants, values, and goals of the readers or listeners. In actual practice, though, this association is often characterized by emotional overtones. This step is so important because motives for action stem from needs and wants; that is, we tend to like that which furthers our ends and values. It seems clear that our values influence our choices among the needs which we choose to meet, and that obstacles modify those choices.

One generalization which has been rather well supported is that, despite the motivating force of desire, it does not necessarily determine acceptance. Desire can determine acceptance if a claim is vague or if the means of establishing the credibility of the claim are ambiguous, but desire is often unable to make an extreme argument credible. Research evidence shows that arguments which increase consistency are in general more persuasive. It also demonstrates the variability in the influence of desire, both within one person and among persons. Finally, if a statement is important to us, we tend to seek evidence pro or con on it, and our decision tends to be influenced by knowledge of what the majority view is.

Motivation to surmount obstacles. We have seen that obstacles as well as values may affect a person's choice of a need to meet or a way to meet it. Suppose one wants to mingle with others in some activity, and that he is about to choose between skiing and dancing as a means of meeting his social need. In terms of his values, skiing is more exciting and is more in vogue at the moment, while dancing is acceptable but not very exciting. His choice would favor dancing if the obstacles were equal, but they are not; he can dance nearby in comfort and with no thought of physical injury, while skiing involves travel, exposure to cold, and some risk of injury. Thus, anyone who tries to persuade him to choose skiing must motivate him enough to surmount the obstacles.

How much motivation is enough? Experimenters have observed that it can be too intense or too weak, and that the optimum point is the threshold of frustration tolerance. In general, this is reached by arousing a sense of inconsistency or disparity between what one wants and what he has. Enough mental ability to imagine consequences is, of course, usually required.

The retention of change. Unless an advocate is interested in only a single, immediate reaction, he must be concerned with retention. In other words, he wants his audience to remain persuaded for some time. We know that the retention of a change depends upon the retention of some of the content of the message as well as the incentive for acceptance. Thus, intelligence is not the only consequential factor in the retention of the induced change.

Published research, particularly in the Yale studies, points to a few important generalizations concerning retention: a conclusion tends to be retained better than its supporting materials; that which interests a person or is pleasant to him is retained better; strong agreement or disagreement aids retention; a commitment, such as an overt act of acceptance, facilitates retention and inhibits the impact of counterpersuasion; some devices of emphasis in style and delivery improve retention. In this last category are occasional reminders of the importance of specific statements, judicious use of repetition, the use of a slower rate or a pause immediately preceding the key phrase, gesturing for emphasis, and placing the key item last to capitalize upon recency.

ETHICAL CONSIDERATIONS

Unless one believes that "anything goes," he must be concerned with the ethics of persuasion. Our view is that an academic study of persuasion must deal with the application of moral standards to the process. These should be applied to the ends sought and the means used. We shall proceed at once to a discussion of means, because the unethical ends are too well known to require explication here. In short, the controversy in this field turns upon the *techniques* of persuasion.

The position of this book on the legitimacy of the several forms of support for a proposition has been stated in part under a number of topics, including the responsibilities of the advocate, the definition of persuasion, analysis, and fallacies. From these pronouncements one can conclude that we regard as ethically defensible those extralogical materials and techniques which supplement but do not subvert the rational process of decision-making.

PRACTICAL APPLICATIONS

In our view, the first responsibility of a persuader is to make sense, and this is where the principles of argumentation have practical applications to the persuasive process. Although many of the principles are relevant, the most important ones are likely to be those relating to investigation, analysis, evidence, and reasoning.

Then, in connection with audience analysis and the consequent adaptations, one needs to consider the potential predisposing factors which may account for individual differences in persuadability: the subject matter of the communication, the appeals used, the logical relations within the case, stylistic and delivery traits, the ethos or image of the persuader himself, the situation or setting in which the persuasive communication takes place, and some less definite factors such as the medium of communication (face-to-face, film, television, etc.) and the personality traits of the listeners or readers.

Next, the stages in the process of persuasion need to be taken into account. These are indicated by the questions which a persuader might ask at this point: How can I gain attention? How can I achieve comprehension in my audience? How can I secure acceptance of my view?

Finally, after these matters have been taken into account, there remains the problem of maintaining an ethically defensible position. This and the other practical applications of the doctrine of persuasion have been treated in the preceding four sections of this chapter.

EXERCISES

1. In her highly successful radio marathon to sell U.S. war bonds, Kate Smith's points included servicemen's sacrifices, civilians' sacrifices, satisfaction from participating in a mass action, intercity competition, family ties, ease of telephoning a pledge, and her own sacrifice. No

economic argument was developed. Was this persuasion ethical? Expound your view.

2. Prepare and deliver a persuasive speech of a specified length in which you use at least two of the strategic procedures (suggestion, rationalization, and forthright statement) and the three stages of persuasion (attention, comprehension, and acceptance). Label these items parenthetically in the outline or the manuscript.

3. Analyze a persuasive essay or printed speech in terms of your own response to it. Try to identify and explain the influence of the eight predisposing factors upon your reaction to the message.

4. Using the first three substages of acceptance (belief, association, and motivation) as your critical apparatus, make an analysis of selected advertisements, editorials, or speeches.

5. Study the introductory paragraphs of a selected sample of persuasive speeches for the purpose of identifying the techniques of gaining favorable attention.

6. Point out some differences, in terms of this chapter, between a speech that you would give on free trade before judges in a tournament debate and one that you would give to a local Rotary Club, for example.

7. Study a persuasive message, and point out the comparative emphasis upon belief, wants-values-goals, and motivation to surmount obstacles.

Chapter 12

THE CASE

THE CASE DEFINED

General meaning. The word "case" is used to designate the total position or stand which either an affirmative or a negative advocate or a team takes on the proposition. It may appear as a complete speech or essay, or it may take the form of a case outline or a précis. In any of its forms, a case is the approach which an advocate or a team of advocates presents to the listeners or readers. This statement embodies the evidence, reasoning, exposition, narration, description, and motivation upon which one side chooses to rest its cause and upon which it must win or lose. It is, or should be, the best presentation that a side can make in terms of its logical and ethical responsibilities (discussed in Chapter 2).

The concept of a prima-facie case. A case is said to be prima facie when it is logically adequate to establish a reasonably high degree of probable truth in its favor. In other words, "on its face" it has probative force. In fact, the presentation of a logically adequate case is the only way to prove a given side of a proposition. For this reason we urge the advocate to present a case which logically supports his position. The degree in which it does so can be determined in relation to the presumption and the burden of proof, the issues, and the burden of rebuttal. These relationships, which are discussed below, require that a prima-facie case be more than merely a "good" case.

RELATIONSHIPS IN A
PRIMA-FACIE CASE

Prima-facie case, presumption, and burden of proof. The theory of argument is that the affirmative, upon whom the burden of proof always rests in a correctly phrased proposition, can discharge this burden only by presenting a prima-facie case—one that answers the issues affirmatively. At the outset, as we have said, the affirmative is under obligation to present proof of the proposition before the negative should be expected to reply. The presumption favors the negative at the outset of the debate, and this advantage can be overcome only by the presentation of a prima-facie affirmative case. If such a case is presented, the negative must make a rejoinder which will block it and thereby overcome the presumption which has been raised against the negative case. Thus it is imperative that the affirmative present a prima-facie constructive or opening case and that the negative present a prima-facie rejoinder; otherwise a good debate cannot ensue.

Prima-facie case and the issues. In Chapter 4 we defined issues as the inherently vital points or subpropositions, stated in question form, all of which are usually to be affirmed by the affirmative and some or which must be denied by the negative, upon the establishment of which depends the establishment of the main proposition. Thus, any affirmative case which is used in an attempt to prove the proposition must contain evidence and reasoning which will logically support affirmative answers to all potential issues except those which were expressly waived or admitted at the outset. In other words, the affirmative must (except as noted later in the chapter) prepare as if the negative were going to contest every issue. Likewise, any negative case which is used in an attempt to disprove the proposition must contain evidence and reasoning which will logically support a negative answer to *one or more* of the issues. Thus, if the case treats the issues in the manner explained here, it meets the proof requirement which was stated in the preceding paragraph. At this point one should recall that each of the three kinds of propositions (fact, value, policy) has its characteristic type of issues which should be sought in the process of analysis. Chapter 4 treats this matter in detail.

In stressing the vital importance of issues to a prima-facie case, we do not mean to say that the stock expressions such as "Are there serious, inherent evils in the status quo?" should be spoken or written. It is preferable to ask, "Are local and state resources in some places inadequate to support a desirable quality of public education?" Issues are more meaningfully worded in terms of the subject matter of the proposition and the kind of argumentative situation (legislative, judicial, etc.)

In this process of building a case which answers the issues, one is concerned with points in partition, or "talking points." The main points of a case, which are labeled with Roman numerals in a case outline, are known as points in partition. They are not necessarily issues. The wording and the grouping of these points may differ somewhat from the statement of the issues. The considerations of effective composition sometimes require this distinction. For instance, an issue might be expressed in this fashion: "Are the financial conditions of Lilliput in a serious plight?" An affirmative point in partition might say, "Lilliput is broke."

From the standpoint of critical thinking, the requirements for a prima-facie case serve to test the adequacy of an advocate's analysis as well as the completeness and the consistency of his case. Our point is raised by this question: Is he covering all that he should, and does his case "hang together"?

In nonlegal situations the term "prima facie" does not normally apply to specific items of evidence in the exacting way that it does in court. In general argumentation the principle is that if the submitted evidence appears, before further examination, to support its point, it is prima facie. It may even be easily refuted and still be called prima facie.

Prima-facie case and the burden of rebuttal. When we pointed out the obligation of the negative to reply to the prima-facie case of the affirmative, we were dealing with the burden of rebuttal which the negative had at that stage in the proceedings. When the negative makes a prima-facie rejoinder, the burden of rebuttal is shifted to the affirmative. Following this, a successful affirmative counterrejoinder shifts the burden of rebuttal back to the negative. Thus it is that the burden of rebuttal, not the burden of proof, can and often does shift from one side to the other in a debate. The presentation of a prima-facie case for one side places the burden of rebuttal on the opposing side.

When a case is not prima facie, an opponent should not say that it requires no rebuttal; instead, he should point out this flaw, explain why it is one, and spell out its significance. In judicial proceedings this is occasionally accomplished with one sentence: "Your Honor, I move that the charge be dismissed for want of a prima-facie case."

PRIMA-FACIE CASE NOT ALWAYS REQUIRED

There are relatively few situations in which the presentation of a prima-facie case is not required or at least expected. For instance, in the arguments in which only one side is represented, some advocates present cases which fall short of prima-facie proof of their propositions. A time limit may be the guiding factor in some cases. It is certainly more effective to treat thoroughly a limited aspect of the proposition in the alloted time than to attempt a complete prima-facie case which cannot be developed adequately. Furthermore, there are situations in which only certain phases of the proposition are important. For instance, in the case of an argument for a new building on the campus, one audience might be primarily interested in the financing of the project, while another might be concerned with the uses to which the structure was to be put.

In class speeches or other similar situations with respect to time limits, it is advisable to partition the whole case in the introduction and then state the point or points which are to be developed in the speech. This enables the audience to get a perspective of the whole case, even though it is argued only in part. Closely related to this method of saving time is the expedient of narrowing the proposition. Instead of establishing the whole proposition, the advocate substitutes a subproposition or issue for the original proposition. His points in partition will then answer only one issue instead of all of them.

Quite apart from these situations, however, there are occasions on which persuasive discourses are given without proving the proposition. We see evidence of this in political campaign speeches, sermons, sales talks, and argumentative conversations, especially those in which only one side is represented—or at least only one side is represented by an advocate who is prepared to meet the situation. The effectiveness of these logically inadequate cases can be attributed to the failure of listeners and readers to think critically, because such cases are easily refuted.

For this reason we repeatedly point out that the presentation of a logically adequate case is the only way to prove the proposition, and in many situations it is the best way to secure belief. Certainly there are circumstances in which this is the only legitimate method. Thus, we urge the advocate to present a case which logically supports his position on the proposition, at least in so far as the circumstances make it feasible.

It is important that both sides present prima-facie cases in debates that are regulated with respect to the division of time and the order of speeches. In fact, the presence of an opponent should serve to warn an advocate that his case must be prima facie, regardless of its persuasiveness, or else the logical shortcomings will be pointed out. Theoretically, the negative is not called upon to reply until the affirmative has set out a prima-facie case. If such an affirmative case is made out, the affirmative may rest until the negative submits a prima-facie rejoinder. In actual practice, particularly in school debates and argumentative conversation, both sides attempt to break down the opposing case before it is com-completed, and the argument becomes a give-and-take affair throughout. In short, it is safer to present a prima-facie case in arguments in which both sides are represented. One exception to this rule is the affirmative case which omits a vital point because the negative has admitted it before the affirmative brought it up.

STEPS IN DEVELOPING A
CASE

For a proposition of policy. The following array of statements is designed to illustrate the steps which an advocate might take in the process of building the framework of his case for the affirmative on a proposition of policy. Several items would be worded negatively for the opposite side. The number of issues, contentions, and points in partition varies among propositions.

1. State the general problem:
   What should be done concerning child labor?
2. Phrase one of the possible propositions which will express the controversial solution the advocate desires to promote or attack:
   Resolved, That the proposed amendment to the Constitution in reference to child labor should be adopted.
3. Identify the potential issues:
   a. Is child labor a national menace?
   b. Does this require a national remedy?
   c. Would the proposed amendment most effectively resolve the problem?
4. List the contentions or specific points which the affirmative will use in answering the issues:
   a. Child labor is more than a local problem.
   b. It is increasing in amount.
   c. It is a menace to our future citizenry.
   d. States have failed to remedy the matter.
   e. A national remedy would be most effective.
   f. This proposal would give Congress effective power.
5. Compose a few points in partition (often two or three) which will cover the several specific contentions:
   a. A national program for dealing with child labor is needed.

b. The proposed amendment is the best answer to the
child-labor problem.
6. Finally, set down the main lines of argument for the case
outline. This is done by rearranging the items under 4
and 5 above:
I. A national program for dealing with child labor is
needed, because
A. Child labor is more than a local problem, and
B. It is increasing in amount, and
C. It is a menace to our future citizenry, and
D. States have failed to remedy the matter.
II. The proposed amendment is the best solution to the
child-labor problem, because
A. A national remedy would be most effective,
and
B. This proposal would give Congress effective
power.

For a proposition of fact. In this category there are propositions of past fact, of present fact, and of future fact. We shall
comment on only the propositions of future fact—otherwise
known as controversial predictions—because they are more complex in the sense that they are less likely to be resolved through
investigation alone. Obviously they offer the most opportunities
for argument.

There is an additional step in the process of building the framework of a case on a proposition of fact or one of value. It is the
inclusion of questions which lead to the finding of criteria or standards which are of crucial importance to these two kinds of propositions. An illustration of the case-building steps follows.

1. State the general problem:
How well will Small Wonder common stock do in the
short term?
2. Phrase one of several possible propositions:
Resolved, That Small Wonder common stock will out-
perform the market average next quarter.
3. Ask questions to determine the criteria or standards:

What characteristics must a common stock have if it is
to perform unusually well over the short term?
Does Small Wonder have enough of these characteristics?
4. Identify the potential issues stemming from Item 3 above:
   a. Are improved-earnings prospects likely to result in
      price appreciation?
   b. Would this appreciation occur within three months?
   c. Does Small Wonder have improved-earnings pros-
      pects?
5. List the contentions or specific points which the affirmative will use in answering the isues:
   a. Improved-earnings prospects normally result in a
      price appreciation of the company's stock.
   b. This appreciation typically occurs within three
      months.
   c. Small Wonder has improved-earnings prospects.
6. The points in partition and their principal subpoints are
   not given here, because they are to be derived as in "For
   a proposition of policy."

For a proposition of value. In philosophical argument there
are generally fewer standard definitions and predictable interpretations than we observe in the other kinds. For this reason each
item after the third in the procedure suggested below is to be
taken as only one of many possible responses to the analytical
questions on criteria and their application.

1. State the general problem:
   Can we accept the seemingly prevailing view that
   social approval is a worthy human goal?
2. Phrase one of several possible propositions:
   Resolved, That social approval is an unworthy goal of
   human behavior.
3. Ask questions to determine the criteria and their applicability:
   a. What are the criteria for making the value judgment

expressed here? Specifically, by what standards may a goal of human behavior be judged unworthy?
   b. Does the subject qualify in terms of the criteria? Specifically, does social approval qualify as unworthy in terms of the aforesaid criteria?
4. Identify the potential issues stemming from Item 3 above:
   a. Is a goal of human behavior unworthy if it supersedes any fundamental ethical tenets?
   b. Does the social-approval goal supersede any fundamental ethical tenets?
5. The remaining steps are developed in the same manner as in the illustrations of propositions of policy and fact.

DIVISIONS OF THE CASE

As we shall explain in the next chapter, there are three divisions of a case outline. Consequently, the case itself is likewise divided into introduction, body, and conclusion. Since the processes of outlining, composing, and presenting these divisions of the case are treated in detail in other chapters, we shall briefly mention the divisions of the case at this time.

The introduction. This has some elements in common with the introductions of other types of speeches and essays. In general, it appears at the beginning of the argument and prepares the audience for the development which is to follow in the body. The material in the introduction is more likely to be noncontroversial. It is intended to gain attention, arouse interest, provide a setting for the present argument, define terms, set out the issues, partition the case, and provide a smooth transition to the body.

The body. This is the part of the case which presents the argument proper. It constitutes the main support of the proposition. The materials which are noted in the body of the case outline are fully developed in the body of the case. In other words, the points in partition for one side are fully supported and developed in this section. The materials for this purpose are discussed at length in Chapters 7, 8, 10, 11, and 14.

The conclusion. The final portion of the case is relatively short. It strives for a lasting, favorable impression of the case and its proponent. Like the introduction, it does not develop an argument which belongs in the body. As Aristotle pointed out many centuries ago, the functions of an advocate's conclusion are (1) to render the audience well disposed to his side and otherwise to the other side, (2) to magnify his points and depreciate those of the other side, (3) to put the audience in a favorable emotional state toward his case, (4) to refresh memories by recapitulating the major clashes of argument. In effect, the advocate says, "I have done; you all have heard; you have the facts; give your judgment."

TYPES OF CASES

Affirmative cases. Except in those special situations noted earlier in this chapter, the affirmative case is required to discharge the burden of proof by affirming the issues in a logically adequate fashion. The case thus made should be of sufficient merit to win, if not refuted. Any case which is intended to have such probative force should be based upon a sound interpretation of the proposition and should be organized as simply and clearly as is feasible. In this connection it is well to realize that an affirmative case should not assume more burden of proof than the proposition requires. If the proposition calls for the installation of parking meters in specified city blocks, the affirmative case does not urge such installation throughout the city. In general, it is better to limit the affirmative case to a firm support of the objective as stated in the proposition, and to concentrate the support of that position upon as few arguments as will constitute an adequate case for the purpose. Extreme affirmative cases—those based upon freakish or strained interpretations, or those whose support is scattered over a wide variety of points—are seldom effective.

One type of affirmative case—the traditional—for a proposition of policy (child labor) was sketched earlier in this chapter under "Steps In Developing A Case." In the traditional affirmative case for a proposition of policy, the speaker or writer points to signs of serious trouble, relates them causally to the aspect of the present situation which he proposes to change, explains his reform, alleges that it will remedy the troubles which he complained of, and probably argues that it will do so better than any other plan could. By means of these points he expects to meet his logical responsibility to present a prima-facie case.

In connection with this kind of case, there has arisen, particularly in school debating circles, a dispute over the necessity of an affirmative plan. In our view, the affirmative on a proposition of policy is under obligation to *explain how* the problem is to be met, unless the wording of the proposition divulges all that is necessary (as in the instances of lowering the voting age to eighteen, recognizing Red China, or, as in Congress, enacting a numbered or titled bill) or unless the proposition is clearly one of principle. This latter situation, which usually arises in philosophical debates, will be discussed next.

Many philosophical debates have taken place on voluntarism *vs.* compulsion (as in medical-care plans), states' rights *vs.* federal power, local autonomy *vs.* state or federal control (as in education), the legal responsibility of parents for juvenile delinquency, and a single standard (admissions, grants-in-aid, and academic) for athletes and nonathletes. But affirmatives have been known to stand exclusively on principle because they had no practicable plan. Then too, some advocates have offered propositions of policy which have been worded so as to focus upon a principle, instead of stating a proposition of value which would more sharply have expressed the basis of the controversy.

Assuming that a "principles" case is used legitimately, we advise the affirmative at the beginning to declare its intention to stand on such a case, to stipulate the principle or principles, and to define it or them. Then, in its first opportunity, the negative should respond to these three points. Strictly speaking, a "principles" case makes more sense when the proposition is changed to one of value, as we shall see at the end of this section.

A third type of affirmative case on a proposition of policy is called "comparative advantages," because it compares the present plan with the affirmative proposal on the basis of results. The cause-for-action or "need" argument is given much less importance

and is handled indirectly. For example, one who urges that a college which is on the quarter plan should adopt the semester plan will sound ridiculous if he alleges that the quarter calendar is ruining the institution. The most he can safely assert is that the semester plan would show some advantages which would justify the trouble involved in making the change. Thus he would be showing, by implication, a need for a change.

Affirmative cases on propositions of fact and value are likewise built by affirming with proof those issues which were discovered during the process of analysis (discussed in Chapter 4). For propositions of past, present, or future (predicted) fact, the affirmative is under obligation to defend his criteria for the determination of fact and to show that the matter in question satisfies those criteria. Likewise, for a proposition of value as in a philosophical dispute, the affirmative is logically responsible for setting out and defending the criteria for that value judgment and for showing that the matter in question meets those criteria. Thus, in defending the proposition that compulsion by government in matters of health insurance is unwise public policy, the affirmative must show what constitutes unwise public policy in this area and how this exercise of compulsion qualifies under those criteria.

Negative cases. Any case for this side must constitute a vital objection to the acceptance of the proposition. As in the case of the affirmative, it is usually better to take a fundamentally sound position and to concentrate upon a few decisive arguments. For instance, some negatives on propositions of policy have stood on one point: "It won't work." In terms of the *logical* aspect of the situation, as we have explained several times, the negative case needs only to block the affirmative on *one issue*. However, this may require the refutation of more than a single affirmative point in partition. The strategic options which may be available to the negative side will now be explained.

Pure refutation. This is one of five kinds of negative cases. Its basic strategy involves the logically adequate denial of one or more issues without the presentation of a preconceived constructive case. Since the burden of proof is on the affirmative, the negative can win by successfully refuting the vital arguments of the affirmative, in so far as the logic of the situation is concerned. In other words, this is one way to prevent the affirmative from establishing and maintaining a prima-facie case.

However, there are logical and psychological weaknesses in this strategy. Pure refutation is likely to be safe only when the affirmative case is weak. In addition, a purely destructive negative approach may give the affirmation a psychological advantage with the audience. The negative in a legal situation, with a judge presiding, can win by pointing out that the affirmative (plaintiff or prosecution) has not proved its case, but public audiences generally prefer that an advocate stand *for* something. For these reasons we conclude that pure refutation alone is not usually the best strategy. It works better in combination with others.

One point in its favor, though, is its adaptability to all kinds of propositions. On a proposition of fact, the negative may charge that the affirmative has not correctly identified the elements needed to establish the alleged fact, and/or it may deny that the elements are present. On a proposition of value, it may attack the criteria and/or their applicability to the subject. On a proposition of policy, the negative may deny one or more of these points: assumptions behind the case, alleged defects in the present situation, causes of these defects, ability of the proposal to remedy the problem, practicability of administration, and so on. More will be said of refutation in a separate chapter.

Defense of the present, at least in principle. This is a strong negative stand if the present situation is defensible. The presentation of this preconceived case, plus the adaptation of it to the affirmative case, results in the refutation of the affirmative. The difference between this strategy and pure refutation is that a defense of the present is not only *against* the affirmative, but it stands *for* something. Even if the present situation (status quo) is not entirely defensible, the negative is usually well advised to minimize the grievances as stated by the affirmative. This removes much of the force of the affirmative case.

As its name suggests, this strategic pattern is best suited to propositions of policy, although it does have interesting possibilities for some propositions of value. It has the merit of giving the negative side a constructive position. In a controversy on policy, the negative points to the accomplishments of the status quo and denies a need for a change, but it tends to assume a static society. After an affirmative case called for the enactment of a certain bill to regulate labor-management relations, the negative argued that existing laws were sufficient. In reply to the value judgment that the Modern Jazz Quartet was unworthy of critical acclaim, the negative countered with a seven-point defense, including the claims that it does swing, it improvises authentically, its arrangements change, etc.

Adjustment or repair of the present situation. This involves an admission by the negative that the present situation has some faults, however small, plus the recommendation of certain reforms, changes, or repairs which are intended to remedy these admitted faults without going so far as the affirmative does in departing from the status quo. This is a popular kind of negative case, and it is usually strong. It concedes the existence of shortcomings in the present state of affairs, argues that these faults are not inherent, and contends that they can be corrected by changes that are easier, less expensive, more expedient, etc., than the "drastic" change supported by the affirmative.

A "repairs" case is used mainly for propositions of policy and infrequently for value judgments. Some refutation, of course, is used to minimize the "need" argument before the minor reforms are offered. If the affirmative contends for the construction of a new building, the negative might urge instead the remodeling of an existing structure. "Instead of outlawing installment buying, as the affirmative proposes, let's regulate consumer credit so as to prevent abuses," a negative might say. When a disputed value judgment closely resembles a proposition of policy, there is some use for a "repairs" case, particularly in response to the affirmative point which applies the criteria to the subject in question. For instance, in response to the previously mentioned issue, "Does the social-approval goal supersede any fundamental ethical tenets?" a negative might stress certain modifications in the social-approval goal so that the criteria of unworthiness would not apply very well.

A counterproposition. This is usually the most radical kind of negative case on a proposition of policy. It admits the affirmative indictment of the present situation, but it offers a solution which is vitally inconsistent with the affirmative remedy. As we have explained earlier, each side must prove its own case in this strategic situation. The contest is between Plan A and Plan B as rival solutions to an admitted need for *some* solution which is essentially unlike the present situation. For example, if the affirmative case demands statehood for Puerto Rico, a negative proposal of independence as a nation is a counterproposition. This alternative must be shown to be better than the present situation and at least as good as the affirmative plan. The theory is that the affirmative has the burden to show that its plan is the best solution.

There are two principles which must be observed in the use of this kind of negative case. In the first place, the counterproposition must be stated with the utmost clearness. Since the negative must assume responsibility for its alternative, it is imperative in terms of safety and clearness that the counterproposition be carefully conceived and phrased. In the second place, the counterproposition must be truly counter to the affirmative proposal. It is not enough that the counterproposition be different; it must be vitally inconsistent with the affirmative plan. If an affirmative case demands the nationalization of *several* industries, and if the negative counters with a proposal to nationalize only *one* industry, the affirmative may adopt the negative plan as a means to its own end. Thus, the negative loses. But suppose an affirmative case calls for the construction of a memorial shaft in the public square of a city. A negative proposal calling for a similar investment in scholarships for the children of the commemorated heroes could be a legitimate counterproposition. In other words, a negative case of whatever type must *clash* with the affirmative case on some vital issue; otherwise the negative loses.

While it is true that the counterproposition as defined here is used only with propositions of policy, it is not true that this negative approach is limited to school debating. It can be used in legislative and political contexts, but there are some differences which are worth noting. If the debate is parliamentary, regardless of the legislative, political, or school setting, a counterproposition is offered as an amendment or a substitute motion. If either is accepted for debate, the original proposition ceases to exist, and the negative on it becomes the affirmative on the new proposition. In school and political debates which are not regulated by parliamentary rules, it is possible to have the proposition and the counterproposition before the audience at the same time. Frequently a counterproposition is offered merely to block the affirmative; it is not seriously intended for adoption.

Combined approach. This is a fifth kind of negative case only in the sense that it combines elements of two or more of the four distinct kinds. A familiar instance combines a minimization of the cause for action, an adjustment of the present plan, and a refutation of the affirmative plan. The following points appeared in a large newspaper advertisement sponsored by the American Medical Association in opposition to compulsory health insurance in 1960: the need is exaggerated; Title VI of the Mills Bill will best serve the nation; a compulsory scheme through Social Security threatens serious hazards.

EXERCISES

1. Read a printed debate of sufficient length for this sort of analysis. See the *University Debater's Annual, Intercollegiate Debates,* or Appendix A or B. On the basis of the selected debate, prepare a diagram and a list of items such as you read in the section on "Steps in the Development of a Case."

2. In preparation for your own argumentative speech on a proposition of value, prepare a chart and a list of items as explained above, using the ideas which you will employ in that speech.

3. Phrase a policy proposition of current interest, state the issues, and sketch briefly the major points which a negative advocate might make in terms of each of the five kinds of negative cases.

4. Phrase a proposition, state the issues, and sketch briefly the main lines of argument which would be needed in a prima-facie affirmative case.

5. Analyze a debate printed in an appendix of this book. State the proposition, set out the actual issue or issues, list the main ideas which are developed by each side, and identify the type of negative case used. List separately the ideas from the introduction and the conclusion.

6. Conduct class debates using the following plan: affirmative con-

structive case, 6 minutes; negative rejoinder, 9 minutes; affirmative rebuttal, 3 minutes. Pay particular attention to the types of affirmative and negative cases used.

7. Critical observers of printed or oral debates such as those in the appendixes will judge whether or not prima-facie cases were offered. In so doing, they will consider the relationships among prima-facie case, presumption, burden of proof, issues, and burden of rebuttal. Did each situation require a prima-facie case?

8. Oral assignments on types of cases:
   a. Prima-facie affirmative case on a proposition of fact *vs* pure refutation negative;
   b. Prima-facie affirmative case on a proposition of value *vs* negative defense of status quo in principle;
   c. Prima-facie affirmative case on a proposition of policy *vs* negative case of adjustment and repairs;
   d. Prima-facie affirmative case on a proposition of policy *vs* counterproposition negative (or a combined type if a counterproposition is not appropriate).

BRIEFING AND OUTLINING

THE PURPOSES OF
OUTLINING ARGUMENT

To aid in preparing the case. Making an outline is an indispensable step in the preparation of a case. This process typically consists of listing the points which one might make. An outline differs from a simple list in these respects: (1) it deals with only those points which seem most useful; (2) it is divided into an introduction, body, and conclusion; (3) it is supported by evidence; and (4) the points in the outline are organized in a systematic manner.

A preparation outline is useful in that it organizes the evidence and argument in an orderly fashion. It becomes a storehouse of information. When it is carefully drawn, the speaker can observe in perspective the main lines of argument, the relation of the several parts, the adequacy of his evidence, and the logical adequacy of the whole.

To aid in presenting the case. An outline is equally necessary as an aid in presenting the case to listeners or readers. Its orderly arrangement assists the advocate in maintaining his line of thought, and it likewise enables others to follow the argument. Clear organization is basic to effective communication.

KINDS OF OUTLINING

Logical outlining. In a logical outline, there is a necessary relationship among the ideas. Each subpoint must stand as a reason for the validity of the point to which it is immediately subordinated. The following sequence of ideas illustrates this principle:

I. The regulation of child labor by the Federal Government is impractical, for
  A. The states are the proper agencies to cope with the problem, for
    1. The child-labor problems differ widely among states, and
    2. Existing state laws evidence the competence of the states to deal with the problem.

The relationships which obtain in this type of outlining should always be indicated by the preposition "for" or "because." In fact, the logical adequacy of the outline can be tested by reading it from top to bottom and stressing the connectives. Then the points can be read in inverse order, substituting "therefore" in place of "for" or "because." If both readings make sense, the outline is probably sound. The reliability of this test depends upon the use of complete sentences in all points and subpoints.

The chain of reasoning in a logical outline is well adapted to the inferences used in confirmation or proof. Such an outline usually consists of a series of enthymemes whose premises are supported by one or more of the four modes of reasoning. This may be seen in the specimen brief and case outlines which appear later in this chapter. The student should work with logical outlining until he can readily reduce all confirmatory inferences to such a framework, and until he can readily discern in a logical outline the confirmatory inferences involved.

Topical outlining. Topical outlining is peculiarly adapted to expository, descriptive, or narrative speaking and writing. In the topical outline each subtopic stands as an *explanation* or *illustration* of the point to which it is immediately subordinated. The relation between any given topic and the subtopics listed under it is that of whole to part. Depending upon the nature of the composition, the subpoints, then, may be nonargumentative parts of the idea expressed in the main heading.

It is possible, but not essential, to use complete sentences; words or phrases will often suffice. Then, too, the connectives, if any are used, differ from those of logical outlining. Some common expository connectives are "as follows," "namely," "for instance," and "in that." The following samples illustrate the use of description, narration, and exposition in topical outlining:

DESCRIPTION OF MR. X

I. His discipline
    A. Reasonably firm
    B. Gives students benefit of doubt
        1. Assumes the best until a student proves himself untrustworthy
II. His humanness
    A. Attends games and parties
    B. Appreciates jokes on himself
III. His appearance
    A. Height
    B. Weight
    C. Dress, etc.

NARRATION OF AN INCIDENT

I. Tourist arrives in strange city
    A. Alights from train
    B. Looks for a taxi
    C. Finds and enters one
II. Takes short ride to hotel
    A. Observes new sights
    B. Wonders what the fare will be

III. Incident at end of trip
  A. Driver announces the charge
  B. Passenger believes it excessive
  C. Indignantly refuses to pay
  D. Driver threatens to call policeman
  E. The compromise

EXPOSITION OF A WRITING TECHNIQUE

I. Typical characteristics to incorporate in familiar essay
  A. Use free and easy style
  B. Make it plausible
  C. Employ specificity
  D. Choose from wide range of subjects
  E. Achieve freshness
  F. Avoid conclusiveness

GENERAL PRINCIPLES OF
ALL OUTLINING

Coordination. There are five fundamental principles which must be observed in both types of outlining, either logical or topical. The first of these is coordination. This means a series of generically related points, all of which have one or more important elements in common. This principle is violated when foreign or unrelated ideas are placed in an otherwise homogeneous list. Note the error in Point C:

I. Political parties in national politics
  A. Democratic
  B. Republican
  C. Norman Thomas
  D. Prohibition

Subordination. This means that topics or reasons should be subordinated or placed in inferior order to others on the basis of some significant relation which obtains between or among them.

This rule is violated when subtopics are introduced which bear no significant relation to the topic to which they are subordinated. Note that Point C does not prove, explain, or illustrate I:

I. Values of the gyropilot
   A. Increased comfort for passengers
   B. Relieves pilot of physical burden
   C. First used in planes in 1909

Discreteness. Each point in the outline should represent a separate and distinct idea in its own right. This principle is violated when points overlap, merge, or are otherwise indistinct and confused, one with another. Note that Point C overlaps A and B:

I. How to choose a camp site
   A. Locate near a source of drinking water
   B. Be sure of proper drainage in case of rain
   C. Avoid a swamp

Sequence. Effort should be made to arrange the points in each coordinate list in some kind of significant order or progression. The common sequences are those of time, place, magnitude, or such order as may be dictated by the proof requirements of a thesis. In the following specimen, Point C deviates from the time order:

I. Development of football
   A. Rugby developed in English boys' schools
   B. First college game in U.S. in 1869
   C. Early Spartans and Romans played harpaston

Symbolization. Every point in the outline should be marked by a symbol which at once designates the degree of subordination and also its place in a coordinate list. Moreover, it is wise for a speaker to adopt some set of symbols and to use them consistently in all of his outlines. The common practice is to use Roman numerals for main points, capital letters for the first series of subpoints, and then Arabic numerals and lower-case letters. The following arrangement of symbols illustrates this practice:

I. First main talking point
   A. First support of I
      1. Proves, explains, or illustrates A
         a. Supports 1

The careful observance of these principles will improve the unity, coherence, and emphasis of one's composition. In fact, unity, coherence, and emphasis are very largely functions of these principles.

THE BRIEF

What it is. The brief of a nonlegal case is a complete, logical outline which organizes and records all the usable material on one side of a proposition. It is not intended to serve as a case outline or a speaker's outline; it is strictly a preparation outline. Some consequences of this distinction will be elaborated in the discussion of "The Case Outline" later in this chapter. As we have said above, a brief is a storehouse of material. In addition, it serves as a device to test the logical adequacy of one's potential proof.

Briefing, as we know it in general argumentation, is an offspring of the legal brief. Although there are points of similarity, there are also some noteworthy differences in purpose and structure. Both kinds of briefs are finished, logical arrangements of the evidence and argument on one side of a proposition. They are impersonal; neither is designed to persuade a popular audience. The legal brief is not a preliminary outline for a speech or an essay. It may be presented to judges without additional comment of any kind, or it may be presented preliminary to oral argument. The general argumentative brief is a complete, logical statement of one side so that the debaters will understand the whole argument. It may be used as the basis of a number of case outlines, and it serves to record and test the results of preparation. In terms of form, the general argumentative brief is a detailed outline including quotations and the like, while the legal brief is likely to have some solid paragraphs and to appear unlike an outline as we know it.

Is it indispensable?   In general, probably not, but the affirmative answer is that the brief should constitute a step in the preparation of every *comprehensive argument*. It is designed to compel the speaker to think the proposition through logically and completely, carefully scrutinizing the evidence and argument needed to confirm the proposition.

Briefing is sometimes criticized on literary and logical grounds, but these objections do not invalidate the foregoing argument in defense of briefing. Strict adherence to the brief in composing a speech will probably produce a wooden style. It is a mistake, therefore, to think that the language, or even the specific order of ideas, of the brief must appear in the finished speech. It is also true that a brief is not well adapted to explanation or (to some extent) motivation. However, there is a useful logical discipline involved in reducing arguments to a linear statement, as in a brief, even though the subsequent presentation outline assumes a quite different form.

Let us apply a pragmatic test. Do debaters and their directors find briefing to be an indispensable preparatory step? Most of them do not, and some of these have been consistently successful in terms of critics' decisions, shift-of-opinion ballots, and other measuring devices. They do, however, prepare case outlines with great care. The extra steps involved in briefing are probably done informally and are not committed to writing.

Rules governing the brief.   There are numerous rules or principles governing the brief. Some of them are specific applications of the five general principles of all outlining which we have discussed previously.

General rules:

1. The brief should bear a title. See the specimen brief for the application of this and other rules.

2. There should be three main parts, the introduction, the discussion, and the conclusion. Each of these three parts should be labeled with its name and should be treated as a separate unit. The various steps in each part should be numbered independently. That is, if there are four main divi-

sions in the introduction, they should be labeled I, II, III and IV, respectively. The main points of the discussion start with I again.

3. Complete sentences are used in the major portion of the brief, which is a logical outline. The possible exceptions are the introduction, in which topical outlining is often used, and the statement of statistics or similar lists of data in the discussion. These statistics or lists should appear in the lowest-order subpoints under a major point which they support.

4. A definite set of symbols should be used consistently. Refer to the explanation of this rule under "Symbolization" earlier in this chapter.

5. Use only one symbol per heading or subheading. Symbols and indentions indicate the relation of ideas. Each statement is either a heading or a subheading. A person is likely to err in using two symbols for one statement when he cannot invent a heading which will cover the subheadings. Note this example of the error:

I. A. Free trade will result in national economic dependence.
   B. Existing international relations make such dependence dangerous.
   C. A protective tariff is sound in principle.

One of two actions must be taken in this case. Either a main point must be found to include the three subpoints, or the list must be reorganized under headings which will stand as conclusions. In this example, Point *C* is the disturbing item. Discard it or use it elsewhere, and brief the remainder as follows:

I. The removal of the protective tariff is dangerous under existing international political conditions, for
   A. Free trade will result in national economic dependence, and
   B. Existing international relations make such a condition dangerous.

6. All subpoints should be given a wider left-hand margin than the points to which they are subordinated. We have seen that symbols and indentions indicate the relative rank of ideas.

7. All coordinate lists of points should be indented uniformly. All Roman numerals should be equidistant from the left edge of the paper, and all capitals should be uniformly indented but farther from the edge than the Roman numerals, and so on.

8. Each heading and subheading should contain only a single idea. It may be necessary at times to use more than one sentence per point in the introduction, in quotations of opinion evidence, or in the development of a complex idea. Even so, a single sentence should be used in most cases.

9. If the statement of any point requires more than one line, indent all of those lines equally. This prevents the obscuring of the symbols.

10. The brief should be an impersonal statement of evidence and inference. It should not include the personal touches of the speaker's notes or the final persuasive composition. Expressions such as "Let me read to you," "We contend," etc., are to be avoided.

Rules governing the introduction

1. Include *only* as many of the following eight items as are essential to an understanding of the discussion or body of the brief: a statement of the proposition, the origin and history of the problem, the immediate cause for discussion (present timeliness), a definition of terms, a statement of irrelevant matter, a statement of admitted or waived matter, a statement of issues, and a statement of the points in partition. Make a separate heading for each item used.

There is a distinction between issues and points in partition which beginning students of argumentation frequently find troublesome. The points in partition are the main points in the discussion section of the brief and the case outline. Their symbols are Roman numerals. They *may* correspond with the issues only when the outline encompasses all of one side of a proposition. An important difference is that issues are stated as questions, while points in partition are stated as declarative sentences. The issues are the logically complete and irreducible questions upon which the truth or falsity of the proposition turns, but the partition simply states the topics which will be developed as answers to the selected issues. For instance, an arguer who is preparing to speak in favor of establishing a federal world government might begin with the stock issue, "Is there a need for a change?" In his introduction he might phrase the issue, "Can any confederation-type of world government succeed?" His point in partition might become, "The United Nations is bound to fail," or he might use two or three points in partition as answers to one issue.

2. Present only noncontroversial material in the introduction. Do not argue; merely explain or illustrate. The introduction is designed to make way for the support of one's stand on the proposition, and not to set forth that support.

3. Finally, use topical outlining. Complete sentences need not be used. The subpoints explain or illustrate their superior points. Refer to our treatment of topical outlining in section II of this chapter.

Rules governing the discussion

1. As we stated above, the points in partition should appear as the main points in the discussion or body of the brief. Each point in partition should be supported by evidence and reasoning.

2. Logical outlining must be used throughout the discussion. This kind of outlining was explained earlier in this chapter.

3. The outlining should begin with an accurate statement of the proposition, and be refined through the level of evidence. The question "Why?" is answered by developing all the evidence and arguments on one side of the proposition. Therefore, in order to test each point in the discussion sec-

tion of the brief, ask that question and see whether the evidence is sufficient to answer it.

4. Carefully document each item of evidence. Adopt one of three methods and use it consistently. The exact source may be stated in one of three places: (1) in a footnote, (2) in the margin at the left of the evidence being documented, or (3) in parentheses at the end of the citation. The third place is used in our specimen brief.

5. The points in each coordinate series of topics should be mutually exclusive. As we stated under "Discreteness," there must be no overlapping of points. It is well to avoid broad terms such as "undesirable" and "unnecessary."

6. The points in each coordinate series of topics should be all-inclusive. The subpoints should constitute a logically adequate support for the point to which they are subordinated. As we stated in discussing subordination as a general principle of outlining, the Arabic numerals support the capital letters, and the latter support the Roman numerals. If every series of subpoints is to constitute logically adequate support for its superior point, the brief must include all the significant evidence and argument on one side of the proposition.

7. Objections to be refuted should be dealt with as they arise. While drawing a brief, one may have occasion to include refutation of opposing points. Such refutation should not be segregated; it should be inserted wherever the point naturally arises.

8. In phrasing refutation, the heading should state clearly the argument to be answered and the character of that answer. Refutation should be clearly indicated in a brief. In order to make refutation effective, it is necessary that the attention of the audience be first directed toward the exact point in controversy, in order that they may see the contrast between the sides and so feel the destructive force of the answer. State the point and answer it as in this illustration:

A. The charge that a world federation would cause more and worse wars is false, because

1. ...., because
2. ...., and
    a. ...., and
    b. ....

9. Finally, whenever a concession (admitted matter) is to be stated in connection with a point, it should be written as a subordinate clause attached to that heading or subheading. Note this example: "Although it is true that confederations have a record of failures in national and international governments, yet that system is not inherently unsound."

Rules governing the conclusion:

1. The conclusion should be a summary of the essential points of the discussion. Usually it is a list of the points in partition.

2. Close with a statement of the proposition to be established. We suggest the following form, which exemplifies the two preceding principles:

Therefore, since:
    I. Any international confederation cannot succeed, and
   II. There is a workable plan for world federation, and
  III. This federation will best further international peace and progress.

It is to be concluded that a federal world government should be established.

For an illustration of these rules or principles of briefing, see the specimen brief in Appendix C.

THE CASE OUTLINE

Distinguished from the brief. The case has been defined as the argument which the speaker plans to take before a specific audience. Hence, the case outline is an outline of that argument. Doubtless we can define the case outline more clearly by distinguishing it from the brief.

First, let us consider the general differences. After the impersonal brief is finished, a case outline should be drawn up for the speech or speeches to be presented. The case outline and the speaker's outline based upon it should be drawn with the considerations of audience adaptation and persuasion in mind. Thus the arrangement of ideas and the rhetorical style of their statement in a presentation outline should differ from those in a brief.

There are four specific differences between the brief and the case outline. One is that the case outline is for presentation, whereas the brief is a preparation outline. The audience is not considered in brief-drawing. The writer is solely concerned with completeness and logical adequacy. A second difference is that the discussion section of the case outline may include either logical or topical outlining or some combination of the two, depending upon the type of support used. The presentation outline tempers logical adequacy with audience psychology. Third, the case outline is more selective in coverage than the brief in that only the materials required by a given occasion are presented. The scope of the brief is not required by most audiences, and there is seldom enough time anyway. Finally, the sequence and arrangement of materials in a case outline are adjusted to persuade a particular audience. The brief would be less persuasive than the case because it proceeds from genus to species, from conclusion to premise, and from main points to supporting materials. The brief would be tiresome to listen to, and its form is not in the typical mode of thought. The sequence of ideas in a brief is particularly unsuited to a doubtful or a hostile audience.

In summary of these four points of difference, we see that the case outline is adapted to take cognizance of the reaction tendencies of an audience, whereas the brief is a complete, logical survey of proof which takes no account of specific reactors. The case outline is a psychological variable; the brief, a logical constant.

Drawing the case outline from the brief. We have said that the case outline is drawn from the brief. This process necessitates two steps: selection and arrangement. The persuader selects from the brief the materials of proof which a specific audience seems to require. He then arranges his materials in a psychological order and determines the proportion or amplification of each minor point. His decisions in these matters should be governed by considerations of time, audience attitude and information, and presence or absence of other speakers.

The divisions of a case outline. The case outline, like the brief, has three divisions: the introduction, the discussion, and the conclusion. However, each serves a somewhat different function here from that which it serves in the brief. This matter will be treated at length in the next chapter, "The Composition of Argument." Suffice it to say here that the purely expository introduction, the strictly linear development, and the formal summary, which characterize the brief, are rarely the best rhetorical forms in which to state a finished argument. The case outline and the speech or essay based upon it are more likely to provide for the problems of attention, interest, desire, and the like.

Thus, a case outline includes evidence, reasoning, and possibly narration, description, exposition, and motive appeals. These may be arranged to develop a linear argument as in a brief, or they may be organized so that the argument seems to unfold into this-or-nothing logic by the implicative process. The case outline, then, must be a form which is capable of expressing any or all of these forms of support.

Specimen case outlines.[1] In order to illustrate current practice, we have included an affirmative and a negative case outline on a recent proposition for school debates.

AFFIRMATIVE CASE OUTLINE

on

Resolved, That the United States should promote a common market for the Western Hemisphere.

INTRODUCTION

(Use a few introductory items similar to those in the brief, but adapt them to the proposition at hand.)

[1] Adapted by Bernard L. Brock from the 1962 *Syllabus* of the National High School Institute in Speech at Northwestern University.

DISCUSSION

I. Present trade arrangements are detrimental to the nations of the Western Hemisphere, because

    A. Latin American economies are being harmed, because
        1. Trade restrictions curb their economic development, because
           a. Tariffs and quotas seriously restrict U.S.–Latin American trade, because
              1) "(Lead) The hardest hit has been Peru; its annual quota of 58,080 tons compares with actual 1957 exports to the U.S. of 81,994 tons. For Bolivia the reduction was from 16,442 tons in 1957 to 10,080 tons." (*United States–Latin American Relations,* Study of the Committee on Foreign Relations, United States Senate, by The National Planning Association, No. 5, Jan. 31, 1960, p. 36), and
              2) "Import restrictions, particularly section 22, have been quite stringent. The result has been an impediment to trade with the Latin American countries that has limited their dollar earnings and in turn, their ability to import from the United States." (*ibid.,* p. 57)
           b. Tariffs and quotas curtail industrialization, because
              1) "High U.S. tariffs on processed and semiprocessed metal products are responsible for preventing the development of industries based on the area's rich mineral resources." (*ibid.,* p. 39,) and
              2) "Many countries of Latin America are smaller than most of our states. It is difficult, if not impossible, for a steel mill, or an aluminum or cement plant, to be successfully operated in one of them, with its market severely restricted; in such circumstances, an industry cannot develop the efficiency which would permit it to sell products in competition with those produced by U.S., Canadian, and European industries." ("U.S.–Latin American Relations," *U.S. Dept. of State Bulletin,* Jan. 19, 1959, Vol. XL, No. 1021, p. 98)
        2. Latin American economies are not stable, because

a. They depend upon too few items for export, because
   1) "Most of the less developed countries depend for 70 to 80% of export earnings upon two or three primary products. In some cases this dependence is as high as 90% or more as in the case of Chile's dependence on copper and nitrates and Columbia's dependence on coffee." (United States Congress, Joint Economic Committee, *Economic Policies Toward Less Developed Countries,* Studies, 1961, 87th Congress, first session, Committee print, p. 70), and
   2) "Of the many maladies that afflict Latin American nations, one of the most worrisome is their dependence on one or two fragile commodities for the bulk of their export income. Of the 20 Latin American nations 14 depend on one commodity for at least 50% of their export income." (*Time,* Vol. 78, July 21, 1961, p. 27)
b. They quickly feel effects of world market price fluctuations, because
   1) "Instability in world markets for primary commodities causes sharp fluctuation in the exchange earnings of less developed countries. Recurrent disruption of import flows and balance-of-payment crises in less developed countries deter economic development and induce fluctuation in export of industrial countries. Present policies are inadequate either to halt the fluctuations in exchange earnings or to prevent their harmful impact." (*Economic Policies Toward Less Developed Countries,* p. 67)
3. Latin America is losing markets to Europe, because
   a. "West European tariffs and quotas are even more damaging to primary commodity trade. Nearly all agricultural products are subjected to quotas and tariffs. On some products including coffee, cocoa, and bananas, European countries levy excise taxes for revenue purposes. In addition, some European countries give trade preferences to countries with which they have historical ties." (*Prospect for America,* Rockefeller Panel Report, "Promoting Hemisphere Economic Growth," 1961, p. 79)
B. The United States is adversely affected, because

1. High tariffs and quotas encourage unfavorable balance of payments, because
   a. "The increasing gap between imports and exports in the postwar period for less developed countries has been financed by liquidation of foreign exchange reserves, and by loans and grants from the industrial countries . . . at the end of 1955 the foreign public debt of less developed countries was $6.9 billion. Brazil was the most important debtor with Argentina, Chile, Colombia, Peru, . . ." (*Economic Policies Toward Less Developed Countries,* p. 83)
2. Present trade restrictions hinder expansion of U.S. markets in Latin America, because
   a. "There is hardly a country in Latin America today that does not levy severe and often prohibitive import duties or quotas on all imports. Moreover, the vast majority of them exact exorbitant export taxes on the products they ship to this country, even those that come into the United States duty-free." (Edward Tominson, *Look Southward Uncle,* N.Y., Deven-Adair Co., 1959, p. 204), and
   b. "The Latin Americans themselves further hamper things by placing restrictive measures on exports in the misguided notion that they are encouraging local processors and manufactures." (*Time,* July 21, 1961, p. 27)
C. Canada is feeling the economic pinch, because
   1. It is losing in foreign exchange, because
      a. "The recent announcement by Prime Minister John Diefenbaker that Canada has been forced to arrange for over $1 billion worth of loans and credit to bolster its economy came, no doubt, as a surprise to most Americans."
      "In the last few months the drain on the supply of foreign exchange has been particularly heavy, exceeding, comparatively, even that of the United States. (Speaking about John Diefenbaker's necessary actions . . .)" (*The Commonweal,* July 6, 1962, p. 364)
   2. Capital inflow to Canada is shrinking, because
      a. "Few Canadians paid much attention to these threats. But numbers of American investors did. Last year U.S. capital inflow to Canada began to shrink, and recently there have been steady withdrawals. Canada used to

attract more than $1.1 billion of investment capital a year, but, on balance, none at all flowed in during the first four months of 1962. To offset the $363 million deficit, Canada had to dip into its exchange reserves." (*Newsweek*, July 9, 1962, p. 36)

II. A common market would be the best solution to these problems, because

A. There is a method of implementation, because
  1. Tariffs and other trade barriers among the nations of the Western Hemisphere would be lowered gradually within a specified time period, and
  2. Common external trade restrictions would be established between the common market and the rest of the world, and
  3. A commission would be established to work toward a common currency.

B. It would meet the economic needs of Latin America, because
  1. Trade between U.S. and Latin America would increase, because
    a. "Latin American countries could expand their exports of some agricultural products quite substantially if U.S. import quotas were relaxed or suspended." (*United States–Latin American Relations*, p. 39)
  2. Production in Latin America would increase, because
    a. ". . . a recent study published by the National Planning Association has indicated that the elimination of United States import restrictions would result in increased sales of $850 million to $1.7 billion annually by Latin America alone." (*Economic Policies Toward Less Developed Countries*, p. 78)
  3. Economic diversification will be encouraged, because
    a. "The prospect of larger markets resulting from the creation of free-trade areas of customs unions among groups of underdeveloped countries might make it possible for existing resources to be fully utilized. Above all, economic integration may act as an incentive to entrepreneurs to invest in the creation of types of industrial capacity which could operate only at low efficiency in small markets. This is the case particularly in some heavy industries—steels, chemicals, etc." ("The Significance of Recent Common Market Developments in Latin Amer-

ica," Publication by UN Economic and Social Council, Dec., 1960, p. 83)

4. It would tend to stabilize prices, because
   a. "The United States should help to stabilize the prices of Latin American raw materials sold on the world market. If this were done, it would do more to help Latin America than any amount of financial assistance through loans and grants. Costa Rica, for example, sells coffee at whatever price the world market allows and buys wheat from the U.S. at controlled prices. Many Costa Ricans think they are being cheated by the United States whenever they buy bread at a high price and sell their coffee at a low price." (Harry Kantor, "U.S. and Latin American Relations," *Vital Speeches,* Dec. 15, 1961, p. 145)

C. It would be beneficial to the United States, because
   1. The balance-of-payments problem would be improved, because
      a. "Our international balance-of-payments position can and should be strengthened through increasing our export surplus." (Leonard Weiss, *Department of State Bulletin,* August 7, 1961, p. 250)
   2. Our markets in the Western Hemisphere would expand, because
      a. "Increased production abroad will cause an increase, not a reduction, of American exports abroad. Manufacturing countries provide a far greater market for exports of manufactures than non-industrial countries. In 1955, although trade restrictions existed, exports of manufactures from industrial to other industrial areas amounted to about $55 per capita, and exports of manufactures from industrial areas to non-industrial areas amounted to $11 per capita. Industrialization of underdeveloped countries will boom the U.S. export market." ("The Administration Proposed Foreign Trade Expansion Act of 1962," *Congressional Digest,* Aug.–Sept., 1962, p. 222)

D. Canada's economic-development problem could be reduced, because
   a. "An economic merger with the U.S. would be expected to bring about a heavy flow of American capital northward to speed Canada's development." (*United States News and World Report,* Feb. 19, 1962, p. 65)

CONCLUSION

(Usually a short paragraph of summary or recapitulation plus an appeal for acceptance)

NEGATIVE CASE OUTLINE

INTRODUCTION

(This is the place for the negative's reactions to the affirmative's definitions, interpretations, analysis, etc., and for any negative admissions or waivers.)

DISCUSSION

I. The need for a common market in the Western Hemisphere is greatly exaggerated, because

   A. The internal conditions in Latin America are improving significantly, because
      1. The middle class is growing, because
         a. "We are seeing in Latin America the emergence of the most powerful new economic force in the western world —the new Latin American urban middle class. It has long been a commonplace observation of traveling in Latin America that it seemed to consist of the very rich and the very poor. This is no longer true and this is a wonderful thing." (J. Peter Grace, *VITAL SPEECHES*, October 15, 1957, p. 22)
      2. Per capita income is rising, because
         a. "Postwar economic growth in Latin America has been considerably more rapid than in most other underdeveloped areas. High rates of growth in per capita output have also been achieved despite a high rate of growth in population." (*United States–Latin American Relations*, Study of the Committee on Foreign Relations United States Senate, No. 6, 1960, p. 23)
      3. The Alliance for Progress is promoting land reform, because

a. "It was agreed at Punta del Este that in order to be eligible to participate in the benefits of the Alliance for Progress program, the individual countries of Latin America will be expected to have under way certain fundamental changes in their economic and social institutions. First will be agrarian reform (if a given country has not already carried out such a program) for the redistribution of the nation's land property. Second will be the reorganization of the tax system, to end the traditional situation whereby the poor have paid virtually all the cost of government." (Robert J. Alexander, "New Directions: the US and LA," *CURRENT HISTORY*, 42:68, February, 1962)

4. The Alliance is urging tax reform, because

    a. "To reform tax laws, demanding more from those who have most, to punish tax evasion severely, and to redistribute the national income in order to benefit those who are most in need, while, at the same time, promoting savings and investment and reinvestment of capital." (Charter of Punta del Este—Declaration to the People of America, *Department of State Bulletin,* Sept. 11, 1961, p. 459)

5. The Alliance is encouraging industrial development, because

    a. "To accelerate the process of rational industrialization so as to increase the productivity of the economy as a whole, taking full advantage of the talents and energies of both the private and public sectors, utilizing the natural resources of the country and providing productive and remunerative employment for unemployed or part-time workers. Within this process of industrialization, special attention should be given to the establishment and development of capital-goods industries." (*Ibid.*)

B. There is enough common-market activity in Latin America already because

  1. The Alliance for Progress is working on it, because

    a. "To strengthen existing agreements on economic integration, with a view to the ultimate fulfillment of aspirations for Latin American common market that will expand and diversify trade among the Latin American countries and thus contributing to the economic growth of the regions." (*Ibid.*)

  2. Regional arrangements are active, because

    a. Latin American Free Trade Association is lowering trade barriers, because

        1) "Agreement on a Free-Trade Area Plan Article I. The Contracting Parties hereby establish a free-trade area which shall be fully operational within a period not longer than ten years from the date on which the agreement enters into force." (*The Latin American Common Market,* United Nations, Economic and Social Council, p. 103)

    b. The Association is diversifying the economies, because

        1) "At present, Latin America's trade is essentially an exchange of farm commodities and minerals for manufactured goods from the U.S.A. and Europe. LAFTA hopes to speed 'import substitution' by setting up its own plants to make heavy machinery and equipment. The big market envisaged by LAFTA will provide a framework within which such plants can operate efficiently." (*Business Week,* June 9, 1962, p. 78)

    c. Central American Common Market is removing trade barriers among its members, because

        1) "Common Market in Central America is already a going concern. Guatemala, Honduras, El Salvador and Nicaragua . . . have abolished most trade barriers and will eliminate the rest of them within five years. As a result, trade between members is expanding at the rate of about 15% annually . . ." (*Ibid.*)

C. Trade barriers to the U.S. from Latin America are low, because

    1. Basic commodities from Latin America enter the U.S. duty-free, because

        a. "Many of Latin America's most important raw material exports to the United States—notably coffee, cocoa, bananas, and iron ore—are on the free list." (*United States–Latin American Relations, op.cit.,* p. 11)

    2. Other Latin American produce has low tariff.

        a. "Over half of U.S. imports from Latin America enter the country duty-free. The United States is virtually the only country in the world that does not impose a duty on coffee, Latin America's number one export." (*Journal of Inter-American Studies,* October, 1961, p. 462)

D. The basic economic situation of Latin America is improving, because

1. Foreign investment there is expanding, because
   a. "United States investment in Latin America in 1955 was $6.4 billion. By 1960 it has reached $9.3 billion. US investment in Europe was only $4.2 billion in 1955. Today it remains 50% less than that in Latin America, only six and a half billion dollars. (*Economic Policies Toward Less Developed Countries, op.cit.*, p. 62)
2. Industrialization in Latin America is growing, because
   a. An official study found this to be true. (*United States–Latin American Relations, op.cit.*, p. 29)
3. The balance of payments is not a serious problem, because
   a. "Over the 1948–58 period, Latin America has had a trade deficit with the United States in most years, and a substantial aggregate deficit for the period as a whole. Latin America has tended to have a merchandise surplus with the rest of the world during this period however." (*United States–Latin American Relations, op.cit.*, p. 79)

II. A common market would be undesirable for the Western Hemisphere, because

A. The U.S. would not find it beneficial, because
   1. It would conflict with other essential trade agreements, because
      a. There are such, with individual nations and groups of nations.
   2. Some of our small businesses would be driven to failure, because
      a. "High-Rated Commodities US Tariff, 1961 (% of value)

Clocks, watches & parts	51–67
Safety razors	85–255
Surgical instruments	45
Nail clippers	45
Cigarette lighters	50
Household Chinaware	30–60
Citrus fruit juices	99
Tungsten ore	50
Plywood	40
Ethyl alcohol	56
Lenses	40

Talc products	30–45
Colors, dyes, stains	40 up
Woven woolen fabrics	49
Barium dioxide	93
Lace curtains	63–75
Pruning shears	65
Surveying instruments	35"

("Trade and Tariffs," *Current History*, August, 1962, p. 107)

    3. The Latin American market is not great, because
        a. "The fact that the bulk of Latin American population is made up of subsistence farmers with scant purchasing power limits the market for manufactured goods." ("Latin America," *Business Week*, September 22, 1962, p. 172)

B. The Latin American countries would not find it beneficial, because
    1. Their infant industries would be hurt, because
        a. "The Latin American countries are determined to bring about as rapid economic development and the great growth of as many manufacturing industries as possible within their borders. They are convinced that in order to industrialize they must protect their new manufacturing enterprises—and principally, they must protect them against real or potential competition from the United States." ("Trade Policies in Latin America," *Current History*, August, 1962, p. 80)
    2. They need tariff restrictions, because
        a. They need the revenue, because
            1) "Most Latin America countries impose severe restrictions on the import of goods from abroad and many also impose export taxes, but these are usually only for revenue purposes." (*United States–Latin American Relations, op.cit.*, p. 27)
        b. Their industries need protection, because
            1) "Virtually all Latin American countries employ import duties, or quota, or licensing controls (usually both) as a means of providing protection to domestic industries." (*United States–Latin American Relations, op.cit.*, p. 98)

3. Incompatible governments would be involved, because
   a. Nationalism would be troublesome in some countries, because
      1) "Such a philosophy (the complete abolition of all trade barriers and the planned utilization and completely free interchange of labor and raw materials) would be incompatible with the nationalistic attitude that exists throughout these nations at the present time." (General W. E. Potter, *Vital Speeches,* March 15, 1960, p. 340)

   b. Unstable governments would pose a serious problem, because
      1) "Argentina . . . has been ruled by a puppet president and a military dictatorship for three and a half months. The treasury is about bankrupt, the peso has fallen from 83 to a dollar to as low as 137 to a dollar, the cost of living has risen 42.7% since April, and one of the most powerful of the Peronist unions last weekend threatened to take over the factories themselves unless they were paid long-overdue wages." (*Time,* July 20, 1962, p. 32) and
      2) "Peru . . . was split by a bitterly fought presidential election in which none of the candidates got more than $\frac{1}{3}$ of the votes. Amid cries of electoral fraud and threats of a military takeover, the 3 proud candidates have been jockeying for 5 weeks and no one has given way." (*Time,* July 20, 1962, p. 32) and
      3) "Brazil has been spinning adrift for eleven months ever since President Janio Quadros quit. Now, in place of a strong presidency it has a two-headed parliamentary system that isn't working." (*Time,* July 20, 1962, p. 32)

C. The common external tariff of a common market would harmfully exclude non-member nations, because
   1. ". . . there is the possibility, however, unfortunately, that the regional bloc might lead to an economic and political schism within the Free World, a course which could mutually weaken the common defense against aggressive Communism." (*Foreign Trade Policy for the 60's,* New York Chamber of Commerce, June, 1961, p. 10)

CONCLUSION

(Usually a short paragraph of summary or recapitulation plus an appeal for acceptance.)

THE SPEAKER'S OUTLINE

Distinguished from the case outline. Every speech should be delivered from an outline, although the notes need not be taken to the platform. Whether written or memorized, however, the speaker's outline should consist of such notes as will most readily recall the *ideas* which have been carefully worked out in the longer outlines and selected for presentation. It differs from the case outline, from which it is derived, in these respects: it is more condensed; it is for the speaker's use only; it serves to recall ideas during presentation rather than to organize the composition of the case; it may be based upon a direct or an indirect order of argument. The direct or so-called "deductive" order of argument may be seen in the brief and the case outline. The indirect order of argument may involve the same materials, but the sequence of main points and subpoints is inverted. This process of beginning with evidence, illustrations, and lesser points and leading up to main points is thought to be more effective in the presence of an unfavorable audience.

The following speaker's outline is based upon the specimen brief.

A specimen speaker's outline:

FIRST AFFIRMATIVE SPEAKER'S NOTES

I. Two Barometers Indicate Third World War
   A. Propaganda
      Gallup poll—Roper poll

B. Armaments
   N.Y. Times quote—Bonn quote
II. Two Causes
   A. Russia
      1. Weak peace organization
         Byrnes quote—give statistics
      2. Strong army
         Tribune—AP dispatch
      3. Propaganda
         Osborne
      4. Neighboring states
         Time—Newsweek
   B. United Nations
      1. Veto
         Quote charter
      2. Money
         Budget quote
   Conclude

ORGANIZATION OF
INFORMAL ARGUMENT

It is erroneous to believe that organization is not important in arguments for which there has been little specific preparation. The need for organization is just as great in those forms of argument for which carefully written outlines cannot be prepared as in those types which may be so outlined. There is little persuasive force in disorganized, rambling speaking or writing. The person who wishes to become effective in arguments on short notice must learn to organize his thinking and speaking as the argument proceeds. He must have an outline, but it must suggest itself at the time of speaking and unfold during the argument. The best way to learn the basic techniques of organization is to prepare and deliver arguments which do permit the deliberate preparation of written outlines. Exercises for the development of facility may be used later.

EXERCISES

1. Prepare a short sample of topical outlining on some familiar subject which lends itself to this kind of treatment. The subtopics are to be descriptive parts, narrative parts, and expository parts of the main topics.

2. Prepare a short sample of logical outlining. It may be wise to use one proposition in all the assigned chapter exercises. Restate the argument thus outlined in as many enthymemes as are necessary to state this argument correctly. Revise the outline until it can be stated in a series of enthymemes.

3. Prepare a long specimen brief. Avoid the mistakes made in the short outlines.

4. Draw from the brief a case outline.

5. Prepare speaker's notes based upon a portion of the case outline.

6. Hand in a case outline of a speech or an essay you have read, or a speech or a debate you have heard. One side or both sides in Appendix A or B would serve this purpose.

Chapter 14

THE COMPOSITION
OF ARGUMENT

We discuss here the composition of the language of argument. This is dictated in part by the structure of the argument, especially when a logical case outline is followed to the letter, but considerable opportunity remains for the speaker in the way he develops this structure—in the selection and arrangement of words, phrases, sentences, and paragraphs. Clearness, directness, suggestiveness, and strength in argument are achieved in no small degree by putting into practice the principles of style which are presented in this chapter.

MODIFYING THE CASE
OUTLINE

When one goes beyond the reporting of his analysis and his logical case formulation, he gets into persuasion. This, in turn, usually imposes some nonlogical considerations, such as the psychological effectiveness of his pattern of arrangement. We know that the strictly logical outline which enables the writer or speaker to test the cogency of his proof may not be the most effective pattern for his presentation. He may decide to use an indirect or even an implicative order. The following specimens will suggest two of the many ways to modify case outlines into more interesting patterns of arrangement.

This indirect-order outline enabled a classroom speaker to reach a conclusion by means of an inverted enthymematic structure:

"WHO SHOULD JUDGE?"

1. D.U. Fraternity
   a. Hazed pledges
   b. Administration put fraternity on probation
2. Triangle Fraternity
   a. Pledge "walkout"
   b. Administration put fraternity on probation
3. Sigma Chi Fraternity
   a. Pledge "hell week"
   b. Administration put fraternity on complete probation
4. Kappa Kappa Gamma Sorority
   a. Senior class "walkout"
   b. Two school functions cancelled by administration

A. All disciplinary actions concerning Greek organizations have taken by the administration alone.
   1. SAE lion-painting case
      a. Two boys caught painting the SAE lions
      b. Administration suspended them for ten days
   2. *Daily*-stealing case
      a. Three boys caught stealing a day's issue of the *Daily*
      b. Administration suspended them for ten days

B. All disciplinary actions concerning individuals have been taken by the administration alone.
   1. Minnesota has a student judiciary.
   2. Michigan has a student judiciary.
   3. Purdue has a student judiciary.

C. At least three comparable institutions have student judiciaries that assist the faculty in solving disciplinary problems.

I. We ought to try the student-judiciary plan.

The following implicative outline was used by a student speaker who acted upon the theory that doubtful or disbelieving listeners are more likely to be persuaded if they are led to a conclusion by easy stages.

"THE ANSWER TO KOREA"

I. There are only four possible solutions
   A. Truman's policy
   B. Use of A-Bomb
   C. Withdrawal from Korea
   D. MacArthur's policy

II. Truman's policy of localizing war in Korea is unwise
   A. Now is making no headway
   B. Communists can pour in troups almost indefinitely
   C. Involves more than just Korea; it is based on Communism throughout Europe and Asia

III. Use of A-bomb is too risky
   A. Costly in lives and cities
   B. Where to bomb?
   C. Might get a few dropped on us

IV. Withdrawal means defeat
   A. Means appeasement
   B. Lives lost already would be wasted
   C. Money in war material used would be lost

V. MacArthur's policy is, therefore, the most realistic

Exactly how much more effective than the traditional, didactic patterns these newer arrangements are has not been shown, but there is a growing body of experimental literature on this question.[1] At least it has seemed easier to develop a more interesting style after modifying the case outline.

[1] Carl I. Hovland, ed., *The Order of Presentation in Persuasion* (New Haven: Yale University Press, 1957); Raymond K. Tucker, "An Experimental Study of the Effects of the Implicative Sequence in Persuasive Speaking," Unpublished Doctoral Dissertation, Northwestern University, 1956.

234 · THE COMPOSITION OF ARGUMENT

ACHIEVING CLEARNESS

Our words for the desirable qualities of style are inexact; they represent subjective impressions of language usage. In the case of clearness there are several words that we use to get at the idea: perspicuity, accuracy, precision of connotation and denotation, specificity, nuance of meaning, and lucidity.

Although we cannot actually convey our ideas to others, we can and do use audible and visible symbols which our listeners and readers interpret in their own terms. The association of symbol and meaning in the receiver's mind must be essentially like that in the sender's mind if understanding is to be achieved. Thus we say that clearness of style refers to the ability of discourse to arouse definite, specific meanings, and preferably on the instant.

There are several ways to improve the clearness of one's speaking and writing. The first essential step is, of course, the clarification of one's own thinking. After doing this, he should strive to use more specific and concrete language than some are wont to do. There is a proper use for general and abstract statements in the main topics of a discourse, but specific, concrete, and familiar terms are needed to call up the desired associations in the minds of listeners and readers. Thus, "a tall, slender, sharp-featured man" is more specific than "a man." Concreteness, on the other hand, is an absolute; a term is either concrete or abstract. It is concrete if it refers to a material substance. "Honesty" is abstract, while "Honest John Doe" is concrete.

Other aids to clearness include the minimal use of involved sentences, adaptation to the language of the audience, and the development of a smooth progression of ideas which makes the "drift" of the discourse clear. The discriminate use of several methods of definition is often helpful, too. These include classification, etymology, synonyms, context, example, negation, etc.

Observe in the following speech quotations, the first from Brougham and the second from Burke, the difference in clearness which the addition of specificity makes:

(1) In all the despotisms of the East, it has been observed that, the further any part of the empire is removed from the capital, the more do its inhabitants enjoy some sort of rights and privileges; the more inefficacious is the power of the monarch; and the more feeble and easily decayed is the organization of the government.

(2) In large bodies, the circulation of power must be less vigorous at the extremities. Nature has said it. The Turk cannot govern Egypt, and Arabia, and Kurdistan, as he governs Thrace; nor has he the same dominion in Crimea and Algiers which he has at Brusa and Smyrna. Despotism itself is obliged to truck and huckster. The Sultan gets such obedience as he can. He governs with a loose rein, that he may govern at all; and the whole of the force and vigor of his authority in his center is derived from a prudent relaxation in all his borders.

Grammatical correctness, precision of denotation and connotation, fidelity of sentence to idea, specificity and concreteness of words, and the ability to express shades of meaning are the familiar constituents of accuracy as a characteristic of style. One's style is said to be accurate, for instance, if it achieves clarity by referring to a thing instead of its attributes. Among the devices used to improve the accuracy of style are illustration, vivid description, the use of specifics, and the habit of searching for the best expression.

Verbal hypocrisy is probably the worst violation of the principle of clarity. One case in point involves a business leader who extols the glories of competition while practicing restraint of trade, price fixing, and the like. Familiar pharisaical phrases include: "If I don't get the money, someone else will." "Some of my best friends are Jews, but . . ." "She's a good wife and mother, but . . ." "Of course you're my best friend, but business is business."

In the following paragraphs from a magazine article we can observe the achievement of clarity through the employment of several means which have been explained. Notice how tersely President Kirk states the primary functions of a college and points out where higher education is failing:

The primary functions of a college are to develop intellectual discipline, orderly processes of reasoning, ability to use the English language accurately and gracefully and to cultivate the good taste that is the most basic quality of an educated person. A college that defaults on these responsibilities is perpetrating a fraud on its students.

My principal criticism of higher education today is that we do not stretch the minds of superior students to their full capabilities. By the same token, marginal students who go to college to mark time before taking jobs—to play on teams, get husbands or wives or simply because it's the thing to do in their parents' social set—are permitted to slide by on what was called in my day "a gentleman's C." The curriculum is studded with snap courses that contain minimal mental nourishment and teach skills that can be learned faster and more cheaply in vocational schools.[2]

ACHIEVING DIRECTNESS

Directness is a complex quality of discourse which characterizes the best face-to-face conversation. It stems from a speaker's or a writer's eagerness to communicate. A direct style is easy to read or listen to; it is unobtrusive and genuine. An individual listener or reader is made to feel that he is being personally addressed.

Mental directness can be improved by adapting one's language to the audience, to the type and the purpose of the discourse, to the author's personality, and to the occasion. "Appropriateness" is a general term for all this. Specific rhetorical devices include stories, conversations, questions, personal pronouns, and perhaps an occasional light touch or bit of humor. In extemporaneous speaking, wherein the composing is done at the moment of speaking, we advise students to make changes as they proceed, that is, to insert reinforcement where needed, to repeat if necessary, to omit whatever seems superfluous, to refer to incidents of the moment, to tone down impulsive remarks, and in various ways to sharpen their ideas. In the more formal situations, however, the

[2] Grayson Kirk, "College Shouldn't Take Four Years," *Saturday Evening Post*, March 26, 1960, p. 109.

expectation is that a formal level of usage will be employed. Informal or colloquial English would be in poor taste.

Style is said to have the quality of ease or unobtrusiveness if it does not call attention to itself, either because of its polish or because of its roughness. If there be figurative language, it should be used without display. A written speech should not "smell of the lamp" or seem to strain for effect. Some notable speakers and writers have achieved ease of style with figurative language and rhythmic prose, while others have done equally well with severely plain styles. There is no standard formula for success, but simplicity of style is generally more in demand today than it apparently was early in the nineteenth century.

Much of what we have said about directness is observable in the following extract from Professor Morgan's address to the fraternity pledges at Northwestern in 1959. It "gets under the skin."

Correspondingly, it is up to you students to show us that you can behave as adults; as soon as you do so, important segments of the academic faculty will move to restore the university to its proper research and teaching functions. Stop thinking of our university as a Big Brother, cop and judge; stop griping at regulations (like the new, fantastic seven-hour party rule) as unwelcome impositions from above. Start acting like grown-ups, and thinking and feeling as responsible individuals. Earn our respect. We shall then be delighted to let you run your own private lives, for our proper educational concern is with the student mind, not with the student body.

When an upperclassman urges you to study in order to keep the house average up, or in order to be eligible for activities, or to keep off probation, remind him that, however worthwhile all of these other goals may be, knowledge is the purpose of study. Never, never feel that you have to apologize to anybody for being intellectually curious and working hard. Rather apologize to yourself for those occasions on which you cheapen your own individuality by becoming merely organizational. Learn to study as a man, to decide as a man, to live as a man, and to love as a man, not as an Alpha or a Beta or a Gamma. A fraternity man must be a *man* first and fraternal only afterwards.

You will, probably unconsciously, find yourself choosing among images—men to admire and emulate. Your choice will be your own and will reflect you; no one should try to dictate it. But I do ask at least your sympathetic respect for the lonely, serious graduate student, and for that rare mature upperclassman to whom ideas and ideals are more important and even more exciting than mere prowess in beer drinking and amorous automotive athletics. Ask yourself this: At your own very best, what kind of a man can you become? Answer honestly, and live that way.

ACHIEVING
SUGGESTIVENESS

Expressions which not only communicate meaning accurately but also call up associated meanings are called suggestive. Other words for this general quality are freshness, variety, and vividness; they refer to the power of language to stimulate the imagination of the listener or reader. Figures of speech are the most suggestive, but the level of usage which one employs is another source of this quality; it suggests the kind of person the communicator is. Crude expressions, for instance, suggest an uncouth person. "Loaded" words and many other striking statements are effective because they call to mind indirectly some ideas that are not explicitly stated. Finally, the rhythm of one's style reveals something about his emotional state, sometimes more truly than his words.

Variety, which implies originality and imagination as opposed to monotony and banality, influences attention through changes in words, phrases, and types of sentences. The meaning of variety or freshness in words and phrases is probably self-evident, but variety in sentences may not be. Variations in sentence length, order, and purpose are meant here. Sentence order refers to loose, balanced, parallel, and periodic structure; while the purposes of sentences are indicated by the designations of them as exclamatory, interrogative, declarative, and imperative.

Expressing himself in suggestive prose, a letter writer stated his opposition to the proposal that local citizens should be informally "deputized" to report traffic violators:

When nervous housewives, binoculars in their shaking hands, lurk behind the lace curtains in the living room, waiting to report me to your chief of police. . . . When grandfathers, whose glasses were broken three weeks ago and haven't been fixed yet, can sit on the front porch and decide that I was one-half inch out of my lane at the stop light and called the chief of detectives. . . .[3]

Notice the forceful, positive suggestion which F. D. Roosevelt achieved through the use of rhythm, repetition, anaphora, and parallel structure in his Democratic Victory Dinner speech of March 4, 1937.

Here is one-third of a nation ill-nourished, ill-clad, ill-housed—NOW!

Here are thousands upon thousands of farmers wondering whether next year's prices will meet their mortgage interest—NOW!

Here are thousands upon thousands of men and women laboring for long hours in factories for inadequate pay—NOW!

Here are thousands upon thousands of children who should be at school, working in mines and mills—NOW!

Here are strikes more far-reaching than we have ever known, costing millions of dollars—NOW!

Here are spring floods threatening to roll again down our river valleys—NOW!

Here is the dust bowl beginning to blow again—NOW!

If we would keep faith with those who had faith in us, if we would make democracy succeed, I say we must act—NOW!

Freshness or variety of style is often wanting in the speeches of school debaters. There is a tendency to conduct most debates in a stylized pattern and to repeat the traditional debate jargon to a degree that does violence to the principles of style which are treated in this chapter. One teacher of school debating, while conceding that judges may tire of hearing these hackneyed phrases, nevertheless contends that such locutions are indispensable to effective debating. But he makes a six-page concession to the importance of variety when he lists many different ways to introduce a speech, to conclude a speech, to open refutation, to interpret a quotation, etc. This is helpful advice, and more will be said of it in the last chapter.

[3] Evanston (Illinois) *Review,* July 14, 1960.

ACHIEVING STRENGTH

As a quality of style, strength is an abstraction which is compounded of many specifics. It can be defined in terms of its synonyms: force, emphasis, energy, intensity, and impressiveness. A strong style is pithy, telling, and forceful—not weak, tame, or colorless. Since not all ideas in an argumentative speech or essay are equally important, the author needs some devices to make the big ideas *sound* big.

Among the means of achieving strength are numerous techniques of word choice, selection of supporting details, and sentence arrangements. In order to achieve forceful language, writers and speakers use short and specific words, active voice, emotional words, and brevity of expression. They achieve strength through supporting details by using figures of speech, recalling vivid experiences, quoting reliable authorities, citing striking facts, using vivid description, and dramatizing their material generally. They develop forceful arrangements of sentences by using the climax order of ideas, by interspersing some antithesis and balance, by varying their types of sentences, and by striving for emphasis by place and by space. Emphasis by place means the use of strong words to open and close the key sentences. Emphasis by space is accomplished by iteration (packing more into a paragraph), restatement (repeating in different words), and repetition, if not done to excess. Forceful style is characterized by movement; it seems to go somewhere. The following newspaper editorial is a case in point: [4]

AN OUTRAGEOUS INTRUSION

In an astounding intrusion of politics into the fields of science and education, a group of state legislators is attempting to promote the controversial cancer treatment, Krebiozen, and its sponsor, Dr. Andrew C. Ivy.

Dr. Ivy acquired a political claque when the dispute over Krebiozen

[4] Chicago *Daily News,* June 8, 1961, p. 16.

first arose back in 1951. The sensational nature of its announcement engaged Dr. Ivy in a row with Dr. George D. Stoddard, then president of the University of Illinois.

Dr. Stoddard was already highly unpopular with a group of legislators, and these found Dr. Ivy's cause a handy stick with which to beat the U. of I. president. They got him, too. He resigned in 1953 under the pressure of the university board of trustees. Dr. Ivy also lost his position as vice-president in charge of professional schools.

Dr. Ivy is scheduled to retire Sept. 1. He now heads a department of clinical science in the U. of I. College of Medicine. The faculty senate of the college voted to discontinue the department, distributing its functions among other divisions.

At this point, the Legislature got into the act. First came a resolution in the House lauding the eminence of Dr. Ivy as a physiologist and extolling the "substantial promise" of Krebiozen. Then came two bills, one to raise the retirement age from 68 to 70, to cover Dr. Ivy, the other to re-establish the department of clinical science and raise its budget from $75,000 to $100,000.

The purpose of the department is defined in the bill as "research, testing, evaluation and teaching in the medical field." This appears designed to permit Dr. Ivy to do research on Krebiozen—now banned under a never-rescinded order of Dr. Stoddard's.

The merits, if any, of Krebiozen as a cancer treatment are wholly outside the question that is raised here. Plans are under way for tests of that drug by the federal National Cancer Institute, pursuant to arrangements made by U.S. Judge Julius H. Miner in a libel suit.

The issues now raised is whether the College of Medicine of the University of Illinois is going to be directed by its administrators and its faculty, or by a group of legislators with political axes to grind and who couldn't distinguish between carcinoma and chow mein.

Responsible members of the Legislature should rise in anger at this crass interference in matters outside the proper scope of that body. The University of Illinois has suffered enough from the unfortunate controversy over Krebiozen. It is time now to leave that decision in the hands of the experts in the field, to whom it has been consigned.

EXERCISES

1. Convert a logical case outline into an indirect-order outline as explained at the beginning of this chapter. Presumably a case outline was made in connection with the study of briefing and outlining.

2. Convert a logical case outline into an implicative sequence as explained at the beginning of the chapter.

3. Critically analyze a specimen in the Appendices in terms of the principles of style. For instance, what do you think about the language in Appendix B?

4. Write an editorial or a letter for or against a proposition. Strive to epitomize the principles of style which have been studied.

5. Present a short argumentative speech, drawing upon the advice given here and adapting the message to the class audience.

6. Convert an argumentative essay into a suitable speech for the purpose of demonstrating the differences between oral and written styles.

THE ADVOCATE AS SPEAKER

THE ROLE OF THE
SPEAKER

Range of activities. The advocate appears as a speaker wherever oral argument takes place. His activities range from formal public debate to the most informal conversations. In considering the role of speaking in advocacy, it is important to recognize that much of this speaking is conducted in conversation with others on controversial issues of every kind and variety. Competence in "public speaking" is an asset to any advocate and indispensable to success in many situations, but not all arguments by any means are presented from a public platform. In this chapter we are mainly concerned with the qualities of good speaking, public or private, which affect *all* oral argument wherever it is conducted.

Personal identification. The advocate is usually identified with his subject in a more personal way than are other speakers. This factor, more than anything else, distinguishes the speaking of the advocate. He always recommends a position, point of view, or course of action to others, and in this capacity he stands as a sponsor of a cause. Indifference or detachment on his part is usually interpreted to mean a lack of conviction. He is asking his listeners to accept the proposition which *he* represents. Unless his presentation is such as to convey personal enthusiasm, interest, and conviction, his proposition may suffer an undeserved fate. By the same token, we must confess, a weak position may often be given an acceptance which it does not merit, because of the force of the personality supporting it. Psychologically, the advocate and his cause are one, at least while he is speaking. They are likely to stand or fall together.

This phenomenon is peculiarly associated with advocacy. It applies in all speaking, but speakers who seek primarily to entertain or inform are much less intimately associated with their ideas. The speaking advocate, more than any other speaker, must concern himself with those personal qualities which recommend him *and* his cause to his listeners.

THE ETHOS OF THE
ADVOCATE

For more than twenty centuries the kind of persuasion which is produced by the listeners' impression of the speaker has been known as "ethos." The term, as a rhetorical concept, apparently originates in Aristotle's *Rhetoric*. He says of it:

The character [ethos] of the speaker is a cause of persuasion when the speech is so uttered as to make him worthy of belief; for as a rule we trust men of probity more, and more quickly, about things in general, while on points outside the realm of exact knowledge, where opinion is divided, we trust them absolutely. . . . We might almost affirm that the speaker's character [ethos] is the most potent of all the means to persuasion.[1]

In another place, Aristotle gives us his analysis of ethos:

As for the speakers themselves, the sources of our trust in them are three, for apart from the arguments (in a speech) there are three things

[1] Aristotle *Rhetoric*, I.2 (Lane Cooper's translation).

that gain our belief, namely, intelligence, character, and good will. Speakers are untrustworthy in what they say or advise from one or more of the following causes. Either through want of intelligence they form wrong opinions; or, while they form correct opinions, their rascality leads them to say what they do not think; or, while intelligent and honest enough, they are not well-disposed (to the hearer, audience), and so perchance will fail to advise the best course, though they see it. That is a complete list of the possibilities. It necessarily follows that the speaker who is thought to have all these qualities (intelligence, character, and good will) has the confidence of his hearers.[2]

There can be no question that the impressions which listeners get of the speaking advocate, consciously or otherwise, constitute a persuasive element of great importance. We say "consciously or otherwise" because many of our reactions to persons are based upon stimuli of which we are not aware. Many persons have been heard to say, "I don't know why, but I don't think I'm going to like him." Listeners inevitably form impressions of a speaker's intrinsic merits or flaws on the basis of his voice, appearance, language, topics, reasoning, and many other clues. These impressions affect audience reactions, which are rooted in basic attitudes and habits. An experimental study has found positive correlations between successful persuasion and the factors of likeableness, attractiveness, sincerity, and general competence.[3]

From the speaker's point of view, the use or non-use of some kind of ethos is scarcely a matter of choice; he will be judged on the basis of whatever he says or does. Therefore, he should strive to make this factor of ethos work in his favor instead of against him.

The records of the characters and the utterances of many eminent American speakers reveal pertinent instances of ethical persuasion. When Theodore Roosevelt, who was known as an "Eastern goldbug," spoke in "free-silver" Colorado in 1900, the audience expected him to make an embarrassed retreat from his position. Instead, he shouted, "We stand on a *gold* platform. . . . We

[2] *Ibid.*, II.1.
[3] Franklyn S. Haiman, "An Experimental Study of the Effects of Ethos in Public Speaking," *Speech Monographs,* XVI, 1949, 190–202.

stand for the same thing in Colorado that we stand for in New York!" His audience "stopped the show" with their cheers for his courage, honesty, and seeming defiance of political expediency. Woodrow Wilson's ethical appeal stemmed from his academic status, his analytical ability, his language skill, and the high, moral quality of his principles. Ralph Waldo Emerson's earnestness and simplicity on the lecture platform bespoke sympathy and respect, particularly on the part of the more intellectual audiences. As a spokesman for organized labor, Samuel Gompers inspired trust because of his honesty and courage. To his followers he proved his devotion to the labor cause by refusing bribes, resisting intimidation, and declining salaries from businessmen. He not only sensed and expressed the prevailing spirit of labor, but also adapted his tactics to the conservatism of business audiences. Among the spokesmen for the farmers, perhaps no one was more sensational than Benjamin "Pitchfork" Tillman of South Carolina. He achieved his position of authority and leadership by virtue of his honesty, courage, sincerity, intelligence, and devotion to the welfare of his constituents. These are but a few of the many illustrations of ethical persuasion which could be cited.

FACTORS AIDING
THE ETHOS OF THE ADVOCATE

The ethos of the speaker is ultimately determined by the *choices* he makes—by the kind of propositions he elects to defend, by the materials he uses, by his attitudes toward persons and things, by the emotions he displays, by the language he uses—indeed by all the factors which enter into the speech situation, all the cues or signs available to the listener for interpretation. The speaker is likely to succeed as an advocate in the degree that his listeners interpret these choices, cues, and signs to mean that he is a man of intelligence, character, and good will.

The best way to make a listener think you are a man of intelligence, character, and good will is to *be* such a person! No artifice is a satisfactory substitute for long with very many people! The best we can do here is to suggest factors which will enable the advocate to put his best self forward. No speaker will do his cause full justice with less.

Assurance. When an advocate speaks with reasonable assurance, his apparent confidence and poise exert a positive suggestion in his favor. His voice and general manner bespeak sincerity and conscientious preparation. We advocate *reasonable* assurance because excessive self-confidence or "cockiness" exerts negative suggestion. The fact is that an audience is more receptive when the speaker seems to be in a good emotional state with respect to the proposition, the audience, and himself.

Although there are some advocates who seem to have too much confidence in themselves, it is generally true that students of this activity need some bolstering in this respect. Their psychological weakness may stem from a fear of failure, a dread of the unfamiliar, the memory of an embarrassing experience, or a complex of other causes. The symptoms of anxiety, such as oral dryness, trembling, moist palms, mental blockage, and the like, affect both the speaker and his audience. No one needs to be reminded of the effects upon the speaker. However, when the listeners notice the signs of nervous tension, the process of communication is hampered still more.

An advocate should, therefore, strive to bring his confidence level up to a point of efficient behavior. This requires perserverance, an understanding of the situation, proper attitudes toward the job, thorough preparation, practice, and intelligent criticism. One ought to realize that some tension is normal and necessary for efficient operation. Since it must be present, the wise procedure is to keep it under control and make it work *for* rather than against the speaker. In fact, a reasonable amount of tension tends to stimulate one to greater efforts in thought and delivery. Some speakers are helped by the thought that others are in the same state and that most listeners are considerate. Another attitude is one of eagerness to share an enthusiasm with the audience. Still another is that of losing oneself in a cause to the extent that he forgets to be afraid; of this situation we might say that the proposition chose the speaker. In a teacher-pupil situation, the lessons should be arranged in the order of gradually increasing difficulty, one fault should be corrected at a time, the directions should be explicit, and the criticism should be constructive and not embarrassing.

Preparation. Intellectual competence is apparent in the speaker's grasp of the proposition. Listeners are more likely to be convinced or persuaded by a speaker who knows what he is talking about. The thoroughness of preparation is observable in the speaker's statement of his proposition, his analysis, his evidence, his reasoning, his organization of ideas, his oral composition, and other processes of which argumentation consists.

Intensity. Any advocate whose proposition really means a great deal to him will speak with intensity, unless it is inhibited by fear. His intensity expresses itself in his voice, bodily action, and language. He leaves no doubt that he "means business." Some speakers who are skillful in a technical sense can simulate intensity more or less successfully, but their impact would undoubtedly be greater if they spoke from real conviction. In short, the intensity of the advocate's speaking gives the audience his appraisal of the significance of the proposition and his position with respect to it.

Flexibility. Another contributing factor to the ethical persuasion of an advocate is his flexibility or adaptability. This ability can be seen in his freedom from "canned" speeches, his adaptation of evidence and reasoning to the specific audience, his skill in refutation when the occasion calls for it, his method of dealing with questions from the floor, etc. A speaker who does not seem to be able or willing to adapt his demeanor and his remarks to the nature of the situation at hand generally loses some of his potential effectiveness. In extreme cases such inflexible speakers have been known to lose more by speaking than they would have by remaining silent.

Sincerity. This contributing factor includes the personal qualities which are known as genuineness, honesty, fairness, and sympathy. An advocate should reveal his true worth in the way he behaves. If his true worth will not bear revelation, he had better work on self-improvement. Sincerity, rather than artifice, should characterize a speaker's attitude. Artifice and simulation are poor substitutes for sound mastery of the subject, for honest conviction from which sincerity springs, and for the personal warmth which prompts one to respond to the needs of others. There is wisdom in the saying, "What you are speaks so loudly that I cannot hear what you say."

Honesty and fairness should be apparent in one's handling of arguments—both his own and those of an opponent. This can be accomplished by avoiding the sophistry which makes the worse appear the better reason. It can be accomplished also by distinguishing between probable truth and absolute truth. Finally, it can be achieved through sincerity and reasonable modesty. In this connection, an advocate should not allow his enthusiasm or competitive spirit to lead him into overstatements or extravagant claims.

Sympathy and good will can be revealed in the manner of a speaker's adaptation to his audience. He should show his awareness of their problems, express genuinely friendly sentiments, refer to current affairs, advise the best course as he sees it, and use language which is suited to the audience without indulging in stereotyped phrases and shallow platitudes.

Directness. This factor of ethical persuasion is usually considered to be a matter of delivery, but it is more than that. Directness stems from a compelling eagerness to communicate with others. It is revealed in the advocate's physical behavior, voice, ideas, composition, and whatever makes for conversational presentation.

Physical, mental, and vocal indirectness can be discovered quite simply. If, when a speaker is interrupted by a questioner, he changes his manner of delivery or perhaps his style of composition, it is likely that he was indirect. This fault may be manifested in elocutionary delivery, lack of eye contact because of note-reading or staring blankly at something, an uninterested attitude, and many other mannerisms.

Indirectness reduces a speaker's effectiveness, possibly in a serious degree. Persons prefer to be looked at by a speaker, and they will not become enthusiastic about a proposition if the advocate seems indifferent. A speaker should watch his audience for signs of approval, doubt, disagreement, or boredom. In addition, he should adjust to these conditions as he would in a conversation. The most effective modern speaking, according to our values, is that which has been characterized as enlarged conversation.

References to oneself. When a speaker makes references to himself for the purpose of enhancing his ethos, he is said to be using direct ethical persuasion. To be sure, many such attempts are obvious, negatively suggestive, and therefore ineffective, but some personal references have been used successfully. For instance, an advocate might refer to his associations with persons, places, institutions, and the like which have prestige value to the audience, provided that he does so with a sense of appropriateness. Similarly, he might mention his experiences and his sincerity for the purpose of establishing his authority to speak. John M. Thurston's "A Plea for Cuba" (1898) is a case in point:

Mr. President—I am here by command of silent lips to speak once and for all upon the Cuban situation. I trust that no one has expected anything sensational from me. God forbid that the bitterness of a personal loss should induce me to color in the slightest degree the statement that I feel it my duty to make. I shall endeavor to be honest, conservative, and just. I have no purpose to stir the public passion to any action not necessary and imperative to meet the duties and necessities of American responsibility, Christian humanity, and national honor. I would shirk this task if I could, but I dare not. I cannot satisfy my conscience except by speaking, and speaking now.

I went to Cuba firmly believing that the condition of affairs there had been greatly exaggerated. . . . I never saw, and please God I may never again see, so deplorable a sight. . . . I can never forget to my dying day the hopeless anguish in their despairing eyes. Huddled about their little bark huts, they raised no voice of appeal to us for alms as we went among them. Men, women, and children stand silent, famishing with hunger. They have no homes to return to; their fields have grown up to weeds; they have no oxen, no implements of husbandry. . . .

THE EXTEMPORE
METHOD

The method explained. Extemporaneous speaking, which is often confused with impromptu speaking, involves the more preparation. The advocate who speaks extempore knows in advance what his proposition and side are to be. He has time to think, read, discuss with others, prepare an outline, and in other ways prepare himself, short of writing a manuscript. In the best extempore speaking, only the final pattern of language is composed while the person speaks. This pattern of language can be improved through continued practice in writing and speaking. Extempore speaking which is prepared as indicated here is usually the best suited to the presentation of argument; in fact, it is a practical necessity in a give-and-take situation. It permits careful preparation and, in addition, it is flexible, direct, and spontaneous. When it is poorly done, extempore speaking has some weaknesses in common with the other methods.

Its superiority to other methods

Impromptu speaking. Done without any *specific* preparation, this is not limited to public occasions; it occurs in informal, argumentative conversations. One speaks impromptu when he has not taken time to prepare his remarks, but this does not rule out his drawing upon his background or *general* preparation. Facility in this kind of presentation is an asset because of the frequency of its use. However, beginners will do well to practice with prepared arguments first. Impromptu efforts are expected to measure up to the standards of analysis, reasoning, evidence, presentation, and so forth, which are met by the best speakers who are present. An advocate who is inexperienced, poorly informed, and conceited may display glibness, but his logical weaknesses can easily be pointed out. The superiority of the extempore method to the impromptu is obvious.

Reading from manuscript. This is a familiar type of delivery. There is some justification for it in situations which demand verbatim accuracy or exact timing. Persons whose every word may be scrutinized, or those who speak via radio, may deem it wise to read from carefully prepared manuscripts. Most speakers, however, can rarely use this excuse legitimately. They should realize that many factors of effectiveness may be sacrificed by reading. Directness, animation, and adaptability always suffer unless the oral reader is uncommonly expert.

Speaking from memory. As the name indicates, this activity means that the speaker commits to memory the kind of manuscript which we referred to in the preceding paragraph. This type of delivery is required in school oratorical contests, for example. The disadvantages are those of reading, except that directness may not be so easily impaired. There remain the difficulties of adjustment to the situation and the hazard of forgetting. In fact, the uncertainty of recall and the concentration upon the exact language frequently inhibit genuine responses to meaning and mood, and the delivery becomes artificial, monotonous, or otherwise indirect. Both reading and memorization are inadvisable in arguments in which both sides are represented. The demands of adaptation, attack, and defense can rarely, if ever, be met properly with a manuscript or a memorized speech.

SOME SUGGESTIONS ON DELIVERY

A point of view on delivery. Any advocate who presents his case orally must communicate his ideas and feelings through audible and visible symbols. In other words, the elements of basic importance in delivery are voice, bodily action, and platform decorum. Without laboring the obvious premise that skill in delivery is important, we shall offer some practical suggestions concerning the elements of effective delivery in public speaking. In so doing, we do not pretend to offer a condensed substitute for chapters on delivery in the elementary public-speaking textbooks. Neither do we mean our separate treatments of voice, action, and the like to be construed as a denial of the many and complex interrelationships which exist among the several elements of delivery, and between delivery and other constituents of the speaker's task.

Desirable characteristics of voice. One's voice is of considerable importance; it reveals much about him, and it has effects upon others. Attitudes, personality traits, moods, and physical conditions are often revealed in the voice. That is why actors adapt their voices to their roles. If the voice is to communicate, which means to have an effect upon others, it must be heard, it should be pleasant to hear, and it should not be so unusual as to divert attention from the message.

Pitch. One of the desirable characteristics of voice is an acceptable range and flexibility of pitch. A speaking voice which is deficient in this respect is called a monopitch, and it is incongruous with the sincere, animated, intense expression of a conviction. In other words, much of a speaker's meaning can be conveyed by his variety in pitch or melody. This is the principal reason for varying one's pitch, but it is not the only one. A speaker who does not use his optimum pitch with some variety is likely, if he must talk a great deal, to experience throat tension and hoarseness, huskiness, breathiness, or a general weakness in the voice.

Time or rate. A second desirable quality is appropriate time or rate. We customarily think of variety, pause, and rhythm in this connection. Vocal sounds have duration in time; some may be drawled, while others are clipped. Some voices have pauses, but others seem not to be interrupted by inhalation. There are singsong rhythms, staccato rhythms, and patterns that lack any meaningful rhythm. Variety in these elements of time prevents a monorate, which is a form of indirectness. The direct communication of nuances of meaning demands vocal variety.

Force, or adequate and varied loudness. This has to do with the carrying power and emphasis of a voice. An advocate should speak loudly enough to be heard, and he should vary his loudness or intensity to indicate the stress he wishes to place upon each word. While doing this he should keep a reserve of force which can be brought to bear on the few high points in his speech. In order to project vocal sounds with ample intensity but without harshness, a speaker must maintain adequate breath support up to each pause for breathing, produce tones of good quality, and avoid excessive tension in the vocal musculature.

Voice quality. Observable in the resonance, clarity, purity, and general timbre of the speech sounds, this is intimately associated with the sincerity and intensity of a speaker's emotional reactions. An advocate's voice should be a responsive instrument which registers emotional color that springs from genuine, appropriate feelings.

Articulation. If this is not clear and distinct, understanding, to say nothing of conviction, is difficult to secure. Articulation which will not distract attention from the speaker's message can be achieved through the proper use of the tongue, lips, palate, soft palate, and related structures in the shaping of consonants.

Action. Bodily action is the visible code of communication—posture, movement, and gesture. This part of delivery is important both to the speaker and the audience. It frees the speaker for more effective communication, conveys additional meaning to the listeners, and is, therefore, an important aspect of directness. Precise, mechanical instructions on how to stand and move must not be given, but a few basic principles are useful. First, effective movement is coordinated; all of the body must work as a unit. In other words, the entire person should convey the desired, single impression. Secondly, the entire body should be animated and should be responding actively to what the voice and language are saying. Third, all action is better when it is integrated with the ideas, inwardly motivated, and mostly uninhibited. Fourth, a speaker's action should indicate some reserve. That is, gestures should be spontaneous, but they should not give the impression of going the limit. Some control is preferable to complete abandon.

General appearance. Some of a speaker's effectiveness, or lack of it, can be attributed to his platform manner and personal appearance. Platform behavior includes taking the platform, sitting in the view of the audience, and indicating an attitude toward the situation. Before he rises to speak, the advocate ought to appear interested in the proceedings and courteous toward the persons present. When a speaker takes the platform, he should do so confidently and deliberately, acknowledge the introduction gracefully, face the audience pleasantly and quietly for a few seconds, and then begin speaking in a conversational manner. Such behavior indicates poise and good breeding.

Personal grooming likewise reveals the real person, or at least most listeners think it does. Neatness of clothing and the person, good taste in the manner of dress, discriminate use of cosmetics, and a fitting choice of coiffure are obvious principles of personal grooming. This aspect of general appearance affects attention and suggestion just as platform decorum does.

EXERCISES

1. Let each member of the class write a rank-order list of the five most persuasive speakers he has heard. One person or a committee might then prepare a list of the speakers who were ranked on several ballots. When the second list is issued to the class, each student will rank each speaker he has observed, using these criteria of ethical persuasion: assurance, evidence of preparation, intensity, flexibility, sincerity, and directness. Observe the relationships between the rankings on general persuasiveness and ethical persuasion.

2. Write a critique of a public speech of advocacy which you have heard recently. This speech may be a lecture outside the classroom situation, or it may be one speech in a school debate. Evaluate the delivery and the ethical persuasion.

3. Deliver a short extemporaneous speech based upon one point in partition from your case outline. Exemplify the principles of ethical persuasion and delivery.

4. In terms of the printed record which appears in Appendix A or B, set out what seem to be the instances of ethical persuasion in the remarks of one of the debaters.

Chapter **16**

FALLACIES AND STRATAGEMS

The overlapping terms "fallacies" and "stratagems" are used to cover the many varieties of what we know as "crooked thinking." Fallacies are often defined as defects in proof or as instances of erroneous thinking which render arguments logically unsound. Stratagems are likewise unsound, but they are distinguished by the deceptive intentions of the user. These tricks are used to divert, distort, or confuse arguments.

Speakers, listeners, writers, and readers urgently need to understand the more common obstacles to sound thinking and reasoning. Experiments have shown that resistance to propaganda is a function of sound thinking, and that the teaching of sound thinking is the most successful educational procedure in developing resistance to propaganda. Speakers and writers who understand how thinking can go astray should be able to strengthen their own arguments against refutation and to detect their own opportunities for refutation in case they reply to another speaker or writer. Practically the entire content of this book is relevant to these purposes.

Our discussion of fallacies and stratagems is closely related to our treatment of the kinds of arguments, the structure of argument, the rules of evidence, analysis, refutation, and, to a greater or lesser degree, all the principles of argumentation. We shall refer back to these principles as we show how any violations of them result in obstacles to straight thinking. By drawing together in one place the many obstacles to straight thinking, we hope to provide a convenient review and to facilitate the teaching of a separate unit on the topic.

In addition to knowing these principles, one should realize that illogical thinking is more likely to occur in relation to subject matter about which one is poorly informed, and that fallacies are more difficult to detect in real-life context than they are in their simplified, shortened, textbook form.

FAULTY USE OF EVIDENCE

Any treatment of evidence (including the absence of it when some was needed) which fails to meet some of the tests discussed in Chapter 7 may be regarded as an obstacle to critical thinking. Since each test of evidence under the five categories of tests has been illustrated with a fallacy, we shall at this time merely list and occasionally comment upon the ways in which evidence may be unsatisfactory.

Questionable substance

1. Outdated material. New data may have been found, or the quoted expert (or one at least as well qualified) has given different testimony more recently.
2. Irrelevant material. The so-called evidence does not relate to the point in question.
3. Internally inconsistent material. The material does not "hang together"; the parts are not in agreement.
4. Externally inconsistent material. It is contradicted by experience, by other evidence, etc.
5. Insufficient material. This may mean none or some, and

the standard of sufficiency is variable. The requirements of logical adequacy may be quite different from the demands of an audience. In either case, circumstantial evidence should be cumulative.

6. Not the best kind of material. This means that ordinary opinion was quoted when expert testimony could have been cited, or that opinions were used when facts were available, or that hearsay was used when original evidence was obtainable.

7. Misused statistics.

  a. Items are compared while the definitions of terms or the values of units are not held constant.
  b. Percentage of change is not computed on a constant base.
  c. Figures are used for phenomena which cannot be quantified.
  d. A generalization is based upon a sampling error.
  e. A trend line is erroneously projected because of inadequate data.
  f. Some important variable has not been taken into account.
  g. The kind of average is not given.
  h. The kind of correlation is not stated.
  i. The level of significance is not specified. In this situation we do not know how much better than mere chance the result is.

Questionable source

1. Flaws in ordinary witnesses.

  a. Personal stake in the issue and poor reputation for veracity may be moral disqualifications, but they are not uniformly so.
  b. Lacking opportunity to get the information.
  c. Lacking the necessary mental ability.
  d. Lacking the necessary physical ability to observe.

2. Flaws in expert testimony.

  a. Used when not required by situation.
  b. Source not adequately qualified as expert.

Questionable reporting

1. The medium ("scandal sheet," for instance) may not be credible.
2. Vagueness or ambiguity may mar the report.
3. Slanting may make the report unfair.
4. There may be insufficient context to provide adequate basis for understanding.
5. Fact and opinion may be confused.

Insufficient documentation

1. See "Documentation" in Chapter 7. A speech should not be expected to have as much documentation as a doctoral dissertation, but this does not mean that it should be expected to have none.

Unacceptability to an audience

(This is pertinent only when we are dealing with persuasion; it has very little to do with a prima-facie case, for example.)

1. The listeners or readers refuse to believe the content.
2. They do not adequately understand it.
3. They do not accept the source.

FAULTY ANALYSIS

When one prepares to speak or write in reply to a case, the following flaws (and others) become opportunities for refutation; but when one is only a reader or a listener, these kinds of crooked thinking should still be detected and guarded against.

Confusion of presumption and burden of proof. Either through ignorance or design, one might behave as if he had the presumption in his favor when, in fact, he had the burden of proof. An accuser who demands that the accused defend himself before any proof of guilt has been given has confused presumption and burden of proof.

Misconception of proof required. As we explained earlier, the degree of proof required in the kind of discourse we are concerned with is called probability, not certainty. Thus one should not claim to have "proved beyond a shadow of doubt," nor should he demand that degree of proof from others.

Misunderstanding of burden of rebuttal. Occasionally a disputant is uncertain of whose move it is or when he is obliged to reply. It will be recalled that the actual affirmative on a properly worded proposition has the burden of proof and speaks first. If he makes a logically adequate case (or his part of it in a team effort), the negative has the burden of rebuttal or the obligation to reply. If this reply is logically adequate, the burden of rebuttal is shifted to the affirmative, and so it goes back and forth.

Faulty interpretation of proposition. Failure to define key terms or in other ways to explain the meaning of the proposition is a nearly certain source of misunderstanding. The respondent should promptly point out either the lack of definition or the inadequacy of the given one, and he may properly offer his definition as a basis for discussion.

Inadequate statement of issues. The mere fact that the issues are not explicitly verbalized in an advocate's discourse does not always constitute an inadequate statement of issues. More often than not, the issues are implied, which means that readers or listeners may infer the issues after perceiving the points in partition.

Inadequacy of statement in an affirmative case usually means that at least one potential issue was not admitted, waived, or answered. In other words, some inherent and vital matter was omitted. In a negative case, inadequate statement may mean that no potential issue was taken up and thus made actual, or it may mean that a nonissue was brought up. This last error can be made by an affirmative as well. Instead of indulging in needless repetition at this point, we refer the reader to the instructions on finding and stating issues in Chapter 4 on analysis.

FAULTY ARGUMENT
FROM SIGN

Any argument from sign which fails to meet the requirements as set out in Chapter 8 is likely to be an obstacle to critical thinking. A familiar abuse of the correlative relationship may be seen in the argument that the American Civil Liberties Union must be guided from the Kremlin because both are critical of the House Un-American Activities Committee. Sign reasoning may lead to error in any of the following five ways:

1. When a sign is mistaken for a cause or a functional inter-dependency.
2. When a nonreciprocal sign is used reciprocally.
3. When one ignores the context which alters a sign relationship.
4. When too much weight is given to too few signs.
5. When the sign relationship is only coincidental.

FAULTY CAUSAL
ARGUMENT

Causal scapegoating and the predicting of future events lead to many fallacies. The following are some of the circumstances which lead to difficulty:

1. The connection between cause and effect is not close and unbroken.
   a. The fallacy of "after this, therefore because of this" (*post hoc ergo propter hoc*) should be avoided.
   b. The fallacy of "noncause for the cause" (*non causa pro causa*) may otherwise occur, as in the statement, "Since thrifty people have money, the way to make people thrifty is to give them money."
   c. The fallacy of "it does not follow" (*non sequitur*) applies here and in other situations in which the conclusions do not follow from the premises.
2. The possible operation of other causes to prevent or alter the alleged effect is not considered.
3. The alleged cause is not adequate to produce the known effect. Thus a fallacy of part cause is committed.
4. The known cause is not understood in terms of the alleged effect and other possible effects.

5. Conditions or reciprocal relations are mistaken for causes, and fallacies of false cause result.
   a. Poor housing may be a condition favorable to crime, but it is not in itself a cause.
   b. Political conditions foster some type of political philosophy, and the prevailing philosophy fosters certain conditions, but one is not the cause of the other.

FAULTY ARGUMENT BY EXAMPLE

1. Selected examples are not fair in terms of the point involved.
2. The size of the sample is insufficient to represent the range of variability among the members of a group.
3. Unfavorable instances are not accounted for.
4. Selected cases do not clearly show the relation which is being generalized.
5. The "gambler's fallacy" occurs when one assumes that a generalization enables him infallibly to predict the nature of the next specific instance.

FAULTY ARGUMENT BY ANALOGY

1. Figurative analogy is used as proof.
2. Compared cases are dissimilar in some essential respect.
3. Differences between the compared cases are not accounted for.
4. Too much weight is given to one analogy.

INCONSISTENT STATEMENTS

Any of the modes of reasoning may become involved in an inconsistency, which is the name given to a pair of contradictory assertions. For instance, one would invite the charge of inconsistency if he deplored the influence of the national government in state and local affairs and then urged larger Congressional appropriations for "pork barrel" projects in his district.

DIVERSIONS AND
SUBSTITUTIONS

Diversions to other arguments. These familiar fallacies and stratagems occur when disputants change the subject, get off the point, or use "red herring" tactics. Since these have not been discussed previously, we shall explain briefly the most common ones.

The fallacy of irrelevant conclusion occurs when (1) some point which is not contradictory is proved in an attempt to disprove the point in question, or (2) some conclusion other than the one demanded is proved. In order to disprove the argument that labor unions coerce their members, one must prove that at least some unions don't do it. If, instead of proving this, one were to prove that coercion is reprehensible, he would commit a fallacy of the first kind. To illustrate the second kind, suppose that instead of proving that the accused is guilty of forgery, one proves that forgery must not be condoned.

Appeals to interests, motives, or prejudices (*argumentum ad hominem*) are diversions from an intellectual appeal.

Attacking the person instead of his ideas (*argumentum ad personam*) is a fallacious procedure. We are reminded of the lawyer who said to his assistant, "No case—abuse the other attorney." This and other irrelevancies belong in the general class of fallacies of *ignoratio elenchi* (ignorance of the point at issue).

Diversions to stop argument on a point. These occur when persons find themselves near defeat on the point at issue and introduce statements which lead the opponent to concede the real point or to defer to the influence of the diversionary statement.

1. The use of specialized language, technical jargon, or abstruse statements is a familiar example.
2. The reliance upon appeals to authority (*argumentum*

ad verecundiam) rather than to reason involves an invalid use of evidence from authority or expert opinion.

3. Appeals to tradition or custom are fallacious if one argues that something should not be done because it has not been done before.

4. Mob appeal or "playing the gallery" is known as the fallacy of *argumentum ad populum*. This is the stock-in-trade of demagogues.

5. Closely related to mob appeals are those of pity and sympathy (*argumentum ad misericordiam*). An attorney might use this appeal to "soften" a jury.

6. Arguments based upon ignorance (*argumentum ad ignorantiam*) attempt to shift the burden of proof or the burden of rebuttal, as the case may be. For instance, one might argue, "Communication with deceased persons must be possible, for no one can prove otherwise."

Substitutions of nonrational matter and manner. These occur when one attempts to substitute irrelevant material or a contentious manner for the materials and attitudes of critical thought. Appeals to force (*argumentum ad baculum*) involve "using the big stick." Among nations this means war, or at least a threat of war. This appeal says, in effect, "Will you agree, or must I twist your arm?" The more obvious substitutions include the use of humor, ridicule, irony, bombast, and anger.

MANIPULATION TO
DISTORT AND CONFUSE

An arguer who uses this type of crooked thinking does not abandon the point at issue; he manipulates it so as to distort the idea and to confuse other persons.

Unreasonable extension of the argument. This may occur when one alters the adjective "some" to "all," or when one unfairly uses *reductio ad absurdum* in refutation. Such extensions may take the form of urging an opponent to an unreasonable position or deliberately misrepresenting and broadening his statement.

Special pleading. This device is sometimes defined as the use in one situation of an argument which would not be accepted in another. A citizen of the United States might urge the United Nations to take some action with respect to the internal affairs of Russia, but he might not agree that, under similar circumstances, the United Nations should treat the United States in the same way. Another definition of special pleading refers to the omission of evidence which is relevant to the point but at variance with the intended conclusion. It is one-sided reasoning in support of a preconceived conclusion. Partisans often omit facts and reasons which are at variance with their own conclusions. For instance, a politician might boast of his party's economical administration of the state by citing the absence of bonded indebtedness, state sales taxes, corporation taxes, etc., but fail to mention the inequitable tax base, the low state of the public schools, and the neglect of social services.

Genetic fallacy. When the truth or falsity of an idea is made exclusively dependent upon its source, this fallacious manipulation is present. Thus an idea is said to be "good" if a "good" person or group originated it, but "bad" if the source is in poor repute—"The Fair Employment Practices Act is impractical because it was sponsored by 'do-gooders.'"

Forcing ideas into arbitrary categories. Such torturing of ideas may take the form of making sharp distinctions between items on a continuum, or of calling an idea valid because it is the "mean between extremes." Thus a person need not be a "radical" or a "reactionary," but this does not mean that his ideas are "right" if they are at the halfway point between the extremes.

Pigheadedness. A participant in a controversy exemplifies this personality trait if he refuses to admit something from which the point under discussion immediately follows, or if he admits the premises but denies the conclusion. Thus he might admit a theory but deny its practical application, thereby erecting an obstacle to straight thinking.

Stressing weak arguments. This occurs when an advocate refutes the weakest proof and claims complete refutation, or when he meets a superficial argument with another one of his own for the purpose of ridiculing his opponent.

"Trick" questions. In a give-and-take situation in which opposing advocates exchange questions and answers, we often observe this kind of dialectical stratagem.

1. Instead of asking questions in a logical order, such as cause and effect, for instance, a person asks one on a cause, two on an effect, one on a cause, etc., so as to confuse the respondent who does not see the relationships in perspective.

2. The questioner might also use the respondent's answers for a purpose or a conclusion which their content does not warrant.

3. In a similar vein, the trickster might ask questions with several meanings and quickly advance the argument on the basis of a partial answer to one of the elements of the compound question.

4. A fourth variation involves asking the converse of an intended question in order to mislead the respondent. Thus, if the respondent consistently gives negative answers to questions which the interrogator wishes affirmed, the questioner may ask the converse as if it were that which he wished to have affirmed.

5. A fifth variant involves the use of a series of questions which will establish a sort of habitual "yes" response before the crucial question is put.

6. The device known as the "complex question" rests upon the fallacious assumption that when one says he has not stopped doing something, he must still be doing it; whereas, he may never have done it at all. For example, "Have you stopped cheating during examinations?"

MISUSE OF LANGUAGE

Ambiguity. This much-abused pattern of language usage often impairs communication seriously, but it does serve a basic purpose in humor and poetry. We shall identify three common forms of ambiguity.

Equivocation. Otherwise known as "ambiguity of a single term" or as "equivocation in quality," this is often a fallacy of four terms. The single term appearing in two or more premises is treated as if its meaning were constant when it is not. Note these examples: "Some dogs have pointed ears; my dog has pointed ears; therefore, my dog is *some dog.*" "A dandelion is better than heaven, because a dandelion is better than nothing, and nothing is better than heaven." The Bill of Rights did not require revision after the freeing of the slaves because of the ambiguity of the word "person" in the Constitution.

Composition and division. These two variants stem from the ambiguous use of "all." They are equivocations in quantity. When used collectively, "all" means the total group, as in "all the building" (the whole building). When used distributively, "all" means each and every one, as in "all the members." The fallacy of composition occurs when one takes collectively that which should be taken separately: "High prices of grain are beneficial to farmers; high prices of clothing help the textile industry; high prices of machines help the manufacturers. Thus a general price rise would be economically beneficial to the country." The fallacy of division occurs when one takes separately that which should be taken collectively. "The Student Governing Board is a very active group. Joe Zilch, who is a member, must therefore be very active."

Amphiboly. The fallacy or stratagem of amphiboly arises from an ambiguous construction of the sentence as a whole. The misconception is usually traceable to confused antecedents, word order, relative and demonstrative pronouns, dangling participles, etc. The consequences may be amusing or serious. These are examples of amphiboly: "Wanted: An apartment by a young couple with a southern exposure." "Homemakers: save soap and waste paper." "Respectable entertainment every night except Sunday."

When King Croesus of Lydia planned a war against Persia, he asked the Delphic oracle how the venture would turn out. The oracle replied that a great kingdom would fall. Croesus assumed that he would win, but he lost. The oracle had not specified *which* great kingdom would fall.

Vagueness. This results from the use of a term which has no well-defined meaning. Thus, it can be more confusing than an ambiguous term, which has two possible meanings. Some common kinds and sources of vagueness include technical jargon, argot, cant, abstractions, and a general lack of correspondence between words and their referents. However, we do not condemn all abstractions used by competent theorists in the process of conceptualizing a maze of specifics into a systematic theory. Some instances of vagueness follow: The defeat of France in 1940 was attributed by some commentators to the "*weakening* of the *moral fiber*" of the French people. Some ordinances forbid the wearing of "a bathing suit which *indecently exposes* any part of the wearer's person." Our troubles beset us, according to some persons, because we "don't read the Bible *enough*."

Accent. The stratagem or fallacy of accent occurs as a result of improper word stress. The unfair separation of a word from its context or the use of vocal inflection may create a false impression. The meanings of most sentences can be altered by either of these devices. These are some examples: "He spake to his sons, saying 'Saddle me an ass,' and they saddled him." In W. L. White's *Report on the Russians* we can find many isolated sentences which, if removed from context, would suggest a pro-Russian author. However, most reviewers classified the book as anti-Russian in general tone. As another example, note how the censorious words are deleted from a critic's review before it is quoted in advertisements for movies, plays, books, etc.

"Loaded" words. Language is used not only to inform, but also to express subjective feeling or to arouse emotional behavior in others. The matters of probability about which we argue seem to be most seriously plagued by the mixing of the informative and the affective functions of language. At any rate, all speakers, writers, listeners, and readers should be constantly aware of the use to which the language is being put. A few samples will indicate the type of suggestive pressure technique which abounds in propaganda: "un-American handout to incompetents," "court-packing scheme," "Constitution defender (or wrecker)," "yes-man," "the American way."

Figure of speech and hypostatization. The first device is used in two ways: one may argue from a grammatical or linguistic form to the nature of a real thing, or he may use figurative language as if it were literally intended. We cite, as an instance of the first type, the argument that a representative should be a mere "rubber stamp" for his constituents because etymologically the word "representative" means passivity. The misuse of figurative language might occur in an expression such as Ingersoll's "Life is a narrow vale between the cold and barren peaks of two eternities."

The second device, hypostatization, is employed when one uses abstract terms as if they represented specific and concrete entities which are capable of independent existence and of producing real effects. The process of reification in mental stereotyping is a distressing case in point. These are examples of hypostatization: "Nature designed us to act, not to be acted upon." "His conscience told him what was right." "History has a way of calling the period an age of defeat." "We live in a world, as the poet Jeffers has it, that turns back upon itself terribly in incestuous relationship." In a lighter vein, we recall the grinning cat (in *Alice in Wonderland*) which walked away and left its grin behind.

TAUTOLOGY AND
BEGGING THE QUESTION

Definition. Some textbooks in logic distinguish between tautology and begging the question. They state that the former is formally valid and the latter is not. In the literature of argumentation, however, the two phenomena are treated as one under the heading of begging the question (*petitio principii*), which consists in having assumed in the premises that which is "proved" in the conclusion. Instead of analyzing this vexed question in detail, we shall simply point out that both patterns, as illustrated below, should be considered as obstacles to straight thinking.

Four forms of tautology

Argument in a circle. "Because the testator had sufficient ability to do business, therefore it is to be inferred that he read and understood the letters; and because he read and understood the letters, therefore he is to be inferred to have been of sufficient ability to do business." (Wright *v.* Doe EX. DEM. TATHAM.)

Question-begging words. "Abolish the bungling bureaucracy." "Newfangled school subjects should be dropped." "Vote to clean the rascals out."

Question-begging definitions. "The Office of War Information is a New Deal propaganda mill." "College-bred means a four-year loaf." "The A.A.U.P. is a professors' union."

Nonevident premise. "Everyone knows that military training teaches discipline; it would therefore make the country more law-abiding." "I did not want aerial warfare," said Hitler on January 1, 1941. "Since tariff protection has made American what it is, we should retain it."

The fallacy of begging the question. "The belief in luck is universal, for everyone believes in it." "When war is no more, the nations will progress as never before, for in all their endeavors they will move forward more rapidly than before."

EXERCISES

1. Select from advertisements, editorials, letters, or printed speeches one example of each of the eleven classes of fallacies and stratagems. Record the results of your "fallacy hunt."

2. Identify the obstacle to critical thinking in each of these items:
   a. All Socialists are interested in social reform.
      John Doe is a Democrat.
      John Doe is interested in social reform.
   b. All conservatives are opposed to Medicare.
      All physicians are opposed to Medicare.
      All physicians are conservatives.
   c. All Republicans are conservatives.
      No Southerners are Republicans.
      No Southerners are conservatives.
   d. Some men are conceited.
      John Doe is a man.
      John Doe is conceited.
   e. According to a Soviet diplomat, the United States was the aggressor in Korea because there were 100,000 American troops in Korea but no Koreans in the territory of the United States.
   f. Autos should be barred from the downtown streets, because

Julius Caesar barred all chariots from downtown Rome, and thereafter Rome grew great.

g. A woman's intelligence does not scare suitors away. I know of a woman whose mental tests classed her as a genius, yet she married a fellow scientist and bore eight children in eleven years.

h. If we integrate our city park, we shall soon have a Negro mayor.

i. Small Wonder floor polish gives three times better results.

j. In trying to prove that high taxes are a cause of national decline, Professor Parkinson compares the tax burdens of the United Kingdom, the United States, Italy, and Japan without taking into account the differences in income.

k. We made a pool on the main street in town on the question of a 5-per-cent tax raise to improve the school system. The replies of the first hundred people we asked are pretty conclusive: yes—56, no—14, don't know—30. It is obvious that of the interested citizens a vast majority want better schools and are willing to pay for them.

l. The constant demands of labor for higher wages are the cause of inflation.

m. Anybody ought to know how to vote in this election. Only the present administration could have brought peace and general prosperity. These achievements can't be gainsaid.

n. The play *Trees Are Green* is a lively farce which has won a good reception in Boston. Producer and cast alike are confident of a long run when they hit Broadway next month. And with good reason, too.

o. Sound financial policies for a nation are comparable to the prudent management of a household. If, year after year, the householder goes into debt, he must eventually face bankruptcy. So, too, the state that neglects to balance its budget is pursuing a course that can end only in bankruptcy.

p. Eastern University is the nation's most outstanding school, and that means that the paleontology department there must have an outstanding faculty and facilities.

q. If the children are provided with a TV set, they will become spectators at the expense of healthful play out-of-doors, and if they do not have a set they will miss part of the culture of contemporary times.

r. Automation is an electronic monster, subjugating our industry to a veritable robot tyranny.

s. A company personnel board is discussing the age limit to be specified for applicants for a certain job. One member of the board argues, "This company has always followed the policy of taking only young men into its labor force. So the younger we set the age limit, the better."

t. Teachers are people who never got out of school. They don't have to worry about competition, prices, payrolls, strikes, government red tape, and so on. It's a good life in the ivory tower. Schools have their place. But when it's a question of deciding the practical problems of a city-planning commission, then we need a man with business experience. You are businessmen, and you know what experience is.

u. A businessman says to a friend, "I won't pay any attention to what Jones says about the strike. He's a labor leader, so he couldn't be impartial even if he wanted to."

v. A dismissed teacher charges that the teaching load in the Pleasantville School District is actually heavier than reported. At a teachers' meeting the Superintendent of Schools remarks, "Every school district has to expect incidents like this from teachers who have proved themselves misfits, and who are dissatisfied and uncooperative."

w. At the very kickoff of this campaign, let me say that if anyone is arrogant enough to use smear tactics against our President, I will meet those tactics with merciless exposure.

x. I don't know what the affair that George got into was all about. At any rate, "Where there's smoke there's fire," and I'll not have my daughter going out with him.

y. You suggest to a friend that the violence of crime comics is a factor conducive to juvenile delinquency. "Well," remarks the friend, "many fairy tales abound in violence and lurid scenes of horror. So if you're going to condemn crime comics, you'll have to take a stand against fairy tales, too."

z. If it's true, as you say, that GI's don't like their officers, then they don't like discipline, because that's what officers represent —discipline.

REFUTATION AND REBUTTAL

THE NATURE OF
REFUTATION

General definition. Refutation is a part of the broader group of processes which in modern argumentation is known as attack and defense. Attack refers to the destruction of opposing proofs, while defense refers to the rebuilding of an argument which has been attacked. Actually the two are nearly inseparable, because the process of rebuilding may involve an attack upon the objections to one's case. Refutation, which is the older term for attack, consists in the destruction of opposing proofs. Although it is destructive in form, it is no less serviceable than constructive proof in terms of its purposes and results.

With respect to any given proposition, if we can induce a hearer to reject the position of our opponent, we are thereby preparing him to accept our own view. There are two basic methods by which we may weaken or destroy the hearers' belief in our opponent's case: by attacking directly what our opponent has said in support of his case, and by building up a counterproposition or argument until its acceptance makes the acceptance of the opponent's position impossible. Under the first, we attack the evidence or the argument, showing its weakness. Under the second, we argue that the accused was insane, or too young, or not present, and that therefore the case against him cannot possible be true, regardless of the evidence.

Aristotle's names for these basic forms of refutation were "objection" and "countersyllogism." Objection consists in attacking the premises, evidence, or reasoning of an argument in such ways as to weaken it or render it improbable. A countersyllogism consists in offering argument and evidence to support a proposition which is logically incompatible with the proposition it is presented to refute. If the counterargument is more convincing (more probable) than the argument it is offered to refute, it is presumed that the audience will accept the more probable of the two. Actually, these two methods are often used in combination to good effect. Thus, a debater will object to his opponent's argument on one or more grounds and will go on to offer a line of argument of his own which is more convincing than the opposing argument in its now weakened condition. Refutation pure and simple is rarely, if ever, sufficient, so that to destroy without building up will usually not serve our purpose. Refutation, therefore, is properly auxiliary and supplementary to positive proof.

Its importance. When two or more rival advocates take turns in presenting their cases, there is likely to be a burden of rebuttal on all except the first speaker or writer. This points up the theoretical importance of refutation. But there is also a practical importance: one must use contrast to undermine belief in a rival idea while building belief in one's own. In our attempts to persuade others, we must realize that they will almost surely have in their own minds many preconceived ideas about the matter under discussion, and that many of those ideas are likely to be antagonistic to what we are trying to get them to believe. In such circumstances, our success must often depend upon our ability to destroy these hostile conceptions, thus preparing the way for the acceptance of our own contentions. The necessity for such destructive effort is, of course, peculiarly pressing in any form of argument in which the advocate is confronted by some definite opponents, as in debate, be it an oral dispute or a newspaper controversy. Here the audience or readers are balancing the two sides of the question, and the competent debater tries to make them see that his side overbalances the other. Direct answers to *what the opponent has said,* if well done, counts heavily in the final balancing. This is refutation.

Skill in this activity distinguishes a superior advocate from a merely clever speaker or writer. It is one thing to set out one's own case, but it is quite a different matter to single out, restate, analyze, and repel attacks which are made against it. To allow rival arguments to stand is to invite defeat. Thus a salesman copes with objections and rival claims, a legislator answers rejoinders and amendments, and a political candidate replies to charges.

WHAT TO REFUTE

Opportunities for refutation. At this time the opportunities for refutation will be set out only briefly, because a detailed treatment will be given under "Specific Methods" later in this chapter. For the present we may say that there are three major opportunities for refutation: faulty analysis, faulty evidence, and faulty reasoning. Faulty analysis may be seen in the lack of a prima-facie case, the use of questionable assumptions, the stressing of a minor point, and the use of ambiguous key terms. Faulty evidence simply means that which fails to satisfy the appropriate tests. It may be insufficient, misrepresented, unqualified, irrelevant, inconsistent, contradictory, etc. Similarly, faulty reasoning fails to meet the appropriate tests, as we shall see in greater detail under "Fallacies." The more common faults include the use of the wrong mode of reasoning for a given context, formal fallacies, diversions, misquotations, and miscellaneous stratagems.

How much to refute. Knowing the opportunities for refutation is not enough; one needs to use judgment in selecting the best ones and a suitable number of them. In school debates or other situations in which logical rigor is expected, a debater would be well advised to reply to the points which could affect the decision on an *issue.* Selection of clash points in terms of their importance to the cases, rather than in terms of ease of refutation, number of items, or location in a case, is the principle we endorse. Novices tend to believe that they must reply to everythng an opponent says, but this is seldom true, either in school debate or in real-life controversy. In the latter situation one should reply to any material which seems to be influential against him. Time can be saved by grouping several related objections together for purposes of refutation.

Avoid attacking "straw men." Whenever an advocate suppresses, obscures, or misquotes an opponent's message and then attacks the substitute instead of the original, he is guilty of answering himself. It is easy to set up "straw men" and knock them down, but it is dangerous and contemptible. To suggest possible arguments, unless you are sure either that they have already been advanced or that they must be advanced by the other side, is foolish. If the arguments are worthwhile, do not help your adversary by suggesting them; if they are not worthwhile, it is a waste of time to notice them. Furthermore, it gives an opponent the opportunity to ridicule the effort, by admitting or ignoring the points thus suggested.

STRUCTURE OF
REFUTATION

Position of refutation.   Sometimes the location of refutation in a speech or an essay depends upon the general format of the exchange. The precedents or rules of some situations stipulate that replies belong in certain places, constructive arguments in others, and questions and answers in still others.

It often happens that an opponent makes a point which must be overthrown before the following speaker or writer can safely proceed with his own proof. In such circumstances, clearly, the answer must be made at the beginning of the rejoinder. "Clearing away the barriers" and "taking one hot off the bat" are figurative expressions for this process. The following short excerpt from the end of one of Lord Boothby's remarks and the beginning of Mr. Lodge's reply illustrates this position of refutation:

The United Nations, of course, belies its name as Mr. Lodge well knows with his experience. There is nothing united about the United Nations. But it is a point of contact and the only point of contact between the Communist and the democratic world and I think as such it has immense potential value. But if it is to go on being a point of contact we got to have them in. Otherwise we might as well pack up the United Nations altogether and have done with it and try something else.

Mr. Lodge: With great respect to Lord Boothby, it's not the only point of contact. As I said, we have contacts with the Chinese Communist representatives now in Warsaw on the subject of prisoners. You don't need to be in the United Nations in order to conduct business with another government. . . .[1]

With respect to the method of handling refutation, a common word of advice is to follow up refutation with positive proof. This suggestion, however, is of a general nature and is open to exceptions. But it must not be forgotten that refutation is destructive; it demolishes but does not build up. To make men act or thoroughly believe, it is not enough to make them see that there is no reason why they should not be convinced; they must be made to see that there is a positive reason why they should be convinced. Consequently, pure refutation is weak and lacks the strongest elements of conviction; it is a necessary help, but it is not sufficient in itself. It is, therefore, generally an anticlimax to place refutation at the end of the discussion or at the end of any important division of the argument. Positive proof rather than refutation should be given the most emphatic place.

This procedure was followed by Professor Linus Pauling in his letter to the *New York Times* in reply to an earlier letter by Professor Edward Teller on the subject of testing nuclear explosives. In the first 20 per cent of the twelve column inches, Pauling outlined Teller's case in favor of resumed testing. Then he disagreed "on every point" for 66 per cent of the column. In the final paragraph, or 14 per cent of the column, he presented his con-

[1] Transcript of Henry Cabot Lodge and Lord Robert Boothby on "Face the Nation" Debate: Should Red China Be Admitted to the United Nations Now? Broadcast over the CBS Television Network, March 23, 1961.

structive alternative to continued testing (moratorium, complete disarmament, control, and inspection.) [2]

With respect to the strength and the weakness of the points of refutation, the same principles apply as in constructive proof; the more emphatic places are the beginning and the end, other factors being constant. If, then, the answer to be made is strong, it may well be put first or near the last. Weaker or less fully developed answers are best placed between stronger points. In one rejoinder of approximately one hundred lines, a writer placed a five-line point between two well-developed points which ran from twelve to seventeen lines each. The longer paragraphs attacked the alleged facts on job opportunities and the criticism of lower tuition charges at the state institutions, while the short paragraph between them merely asserted that the opponent had equated a college education with a job.[3]

Finally, there is the question as to whether it is best to make the answer a distinct point in the discussion, or to introduce it merely as an incident to some other point. This depends upon the importance of the argument to be answered, and is therefore a question of personal judgment in each particular case. In general, however, such answers are best given in connection with those parts of one's own proof with which they are naturally associated. In fact, they should always be considered wherever they happen to arise in the course of one's own argument, except where there is a particular definite reason (such as extreme importance of the point made or effective challenge of the previous speaker) for setting this rule aside. Then usually such refutation should be given before constructive argument. It is therefore true in general that, with the exception of the most vital of the proofs of the opposition, *refutation is best made as the occasion for the answer arises in the course of one's own demonstration.* These individual points that may be taken up as they arise are sometimes called "special refutation." But if the answer to an opponent's argument is, under the circumstances, of such importance as to make any large part of the question depend upon it, there should be no

[2] *New York Times*, November 19, 1961, p. 8E.

[3] President Millett's reply to Professor Freeman in "Letters to the Editor," *Wall Street Journal*, November 10, 1961.

hesitation in making it one of the *main points of the proof* and emphasizing it as such. Such a main point may be taken up wherever it most logically fits into the case. These large fundamental points that make an important part of the case are sometimes called "general refutation." Whether one interweaves refutation with his own case or deals with refutation separately, he should conclude with his own case.

In the Acheson essay on national defense we have an affirmative rebuttal which illustrates this point. The writer restates the affirmative charge that the Eisenhower defense effort is inadequate; next he represents the negative as saying that our nuclear deterrent is effective; then he refutes this point by saying that the so-called deterrent force would be destroyed by an enemy's first strike; finally, he concludes with a review of the case for the affirmative.[4]

Steps in refutation. Since the whole point of refutation is to show that there are two opposing views which clash and that one defeats the other, there is much to be said for following a clear-cut procedure. An examination of some particularly good specimens of refutation reveals these steps: (1) something *worth* refuting was chosen for attack; (2) the item to be refuted was clearly stated; (3) *how* it was to be refuted was specified; (4) *results* in terms of the opposing cases were pointed out; (5) some use was made of either the affirmative or the negative case outline in organizing the refutation. An affirmative advocate is well advised to use his own case outline as a basis for attack and defense. The negative, however, not wishing to strengthen the affirmative case by repetition, is likely to use a revised affirmative outline in order to reveal its flaws, or he may use the negative outline in an attempt to draw the affirmative off its case. In the latter situation the negative would use predetermined positions against the anticipated points.

The following is an example of Webster's method in forensic refutation, a model of clearness in introducing refutation. The quotation is from his speech in the case of Ogden *vs.* Saunders:

[4] Dean Acheson, "The 'Debate' on Defense," *The Reporter,* March 3, 1960, p. 27.

Here we meet the opposite arguments, stated on different occasions in different terms, but usually summed up in this, that the law itself is a part of the contract, and therefore cannot impair it. What does it mean? Let us seek for clear ideas. It does not mean that the law gives any particular construction to the terms of the contract, or that it makes the promise, or the consideration, or the time of performance, other than is expressed in the instrument itself. It can only mean that it is to be taken as a part of the contract or understanding of the parties, that the contract itself shall be enforced by such laws and regulations respecting remedy and for the enforcement of contracts as are in being in the State where it is made at the time of entering into it. This is meant, or nothing very clearly intelligible is meant, by saying the law is part of the contract. . . .

Against this we contend:
1st. That, if the proposition were true, the consequence would not follow.
2nd. That the proposition itself cannot be maintained.

Let us take an illustration from a deliberative oration. Webster, in replying to Calhoun in the Senate, on the question of protective tariff, divided his speech into five parts, corresponding to the five main points of his opponent. The following are the sentences introductory to these parts respectively:

I. In treating of protection, or protective duties, the first proposition of the honorable member is, that all duties laid on imports really fall on exports; that they are a toll paid for going to market.

II. Another opinion of the honorable member is, that increased production brings about expansion of the currency, and that such increase makes a further increase necessary. His idea is, that, if some goods are imported, the amount of exports still keeping up, the whole export being thus paid for by the import, specie must be brought to settle the balance; that this increase of specie gives new powers to the banks to discount; that the banks thereupon make large issues, till the mass of currency becomes redundant and swollen; that this swollen currency augments the price of articles of our own manufacture, and makes it necessary to raise prices still higher, and this creates a demand for the imposition of new duties. This, as I understand it, is the honorable member's train of thought.

III. There is a third general idea of the honorable gentleman, upon which I would make a few observations. It is, that the South and West are the great consumers of the products of the North and East; that the capacity of the South to consume depends on her great staples; and that the sale of these depends mainly on a foreign market.

IV. A fourth sentiment of the honorable member is, that the removal of all duties increases the exportation of articles manufactured at home.

V. Finally, the honorable member is of the opinion that the whole system of protection was prostrated, and is prostrated, cut up, root and branch, and exterminated forever, by the State interposition of South Carolina.

SPECIFIC METHODS OF REFUTATION

In any thorough treatment of the methods of refutation there must be many cross-references to other topics such as analysis, evidence, reasoning, and fallacies. One who refutes inevitably attacks on one or more of these fronts. For this reason we classify the specific methods of refutation under attacking the analysis, attacking the evidence, attacking the reasoning, and using special devices.

Attacking the analysis. This is frequently done by questioning an expressed or an implied assumption which serves as a premise, by criticizing the selection of isues, by pointing out the evasion of an issue, or by objecting to the definition of a key term. In reply to the argument that the United States postal authorities should do all they can to prevent the circulation of *Pravda* and *Izvestia* in this country, George F. Kennan, former Ambassador to Russia, questioned the implicit assumption in these words:

FEAR OF COMMUNIST THOUGHT

In conclusion I can only raise again the question I have raised on previous occasions: Are there really people in our Government who believe that our own political philosophy is so unconvincing, our attachment to it so weak, our youth so bewildered and gullible—and the outlook of our adversaries, on the other hand, so forceful, so logical, and so persuasive—that we must shield our people physically from every confrontation with Communist thought?

How ironic that such suggestions should so often come from those whose stock in trade is the claim to be the most ardent devotees and guardians of the national virtues. And how pertinent Milton's contempt for "a fugitive and cloistered virtue, unexercised and unbreathed, that never sallies out and sees her adversary, but slinks out of the race where that immortal garland is to be run for, not without dust and heat." [5]

Since an attack upon the selection of issues is similar to an attack upon the evasion of an issue, one specimen will serve. After *Forbes* editorially urged an extension of the Reciprocal Trade Program, a considerable volume of correspondence in opposition to the editorial poured in. In reply, the editor charged the objectors with ignoring the rights of the millions of Americans whose jobs depend on exports, the need of our allies for trade instead of aid, and the stake of the consumers who pay for tariffs. [6]

Instances of attacking an opponent's analysis by objecting to the defintion of a key term can be seen in school debates on federal aid to public schools. Typical affirmatives defined equalization of educational opportunity in terms of a minimum acceptable standard, while the negatives insisted that the standards in the poorest states be raised to those of the wealthiest. Many teams also differed in their definitions of needy states: per-pupil expenditures were used by some, while others preferred teachers' salaries, etc.

Attacking the evidence. Typical attacks of this sort allege unsupported assertion (no evidence), insufficient evidence, biased evidence, misquotation, the existence of contrary evidence, and irelevancy. In replying to these attacks, one must rebuild his evidence or add corroborative evidence. In his review of a controversial television documentary, a critic said, in part, "The entire script neither answered the question, nor addressed itself directly to the matter at any time." [7] He charged that the factual evidence

[5] "Letters to *The Times*" (New York), dated March 3, 1955.
[6] *Forbes*, April 15, 1958, pp. 11–12.
[7] R. L. Shayon, "Sorry, Wrong Number," *Saturday Review*, February 7, 1959, p. 28.

and the expert-opinion evidence were either lacking or irrelevant.

Attempted refutation by the method of citing contrary evidence may be seen in the next specimen. A Chicago alderman, using thirty-eight affidavits from diary workers as evidence, charged that local dairies predated their milk containers and that unsold milk from stores was being sold to institutions in bulk as fresh. In reply, the president of the Board of Health said that there was a constant check on the milk supply: "Just last week my inspectors dumped 816 gallons of milk because it was predated." [8]

One method of attacking a point based upon expert-opinion evidence consists in casting doubt upon that whole class of evidence, as in this dispute over the executive span of control in the theory of management:

A good question is, "How is this number arrived at?" There seem to be essentially three lines of evidence:

First, there is the reference to the accumulated wisdom of experience. This includes both the appeal to authority (i.e., generals and other public figures) and to common practice (in which a survey of company executives showed the median number of subordinates reporting to superiors was six). . . .

First, what of the appeal to authority? This we can dismiss rather summarily. History is full of instances in which famous men were just plain wrong about things.[9]

Attacking the reasoning. As we show in the chapters on reasoning and fallacies, there are many potential weaknesses, such as inconsistencies between statements, which may provide opportunities for refutation. Space permits the illustration of only a few of the more important types of attacks upon reasoning. One whose argument is attacked in this way has to either discredit the objection or rebuild his argument.

An attack upon sign reasoning occurred in a debate on alleged illegal detentions of prisoners by the Chicago police. First, the American Civil Liberties Union charged in a report that thousands of prisoners each year are held for illegally long periods of time. In reply, the corporation counsel's office cited the small number

---

[8] Chicago *Daily News*, January 27, 1953.
[9] *Business Scope*, "Blue Report," No. 7, 1957.

of successful damage suits against the city for false arrest. Attacking this sign inference editorially, a city daily countered with the argument that the scarcity of successful claims against the city may mean that the victims were ignorant of their rights, that the police probably did not aid the plaintiffs, and that some juries may not take someone else's detention seriously.[10]

In the controversy about the danger of dumping radioactive wastes, one writer challenged an analogy based upon evidence which both sides accepted. He began by stating that the Atomic Energy Commission of the United States often refers to the British experience with offshore dumping of radioactive wastes as a reason for our not needing to be concerned. Then he quotes the British report, which stipulates that in estimating the permissible radioactivity of the beach sand, it was assumed that no one regularly spends more than one hundred hours per year on the beach. Finally, the writer attacked the analogy by pointing to the fact that in the Cape Cod area many persons spend two or three hundred hours on beaches, and in Florida the exposure may be as high as a thousand hours.[11]

Attacking the causal argument that increased competition among television channels would improve the quality of the programs, a critic retorted that this argument has no basis in experience. He pointed to movie theaters, magazines, and newspapers which competition has forced to close. Quality will be improved only by the emergence of a new kind of public demand, he concluded.[12]

A *non sequitur* (does not follow) was charged against the writers of the education message to Congress by an editorialist who opposed federal aid to education as specified in a particular bill. Granted that our children should have excellent schooling, it does not automatically follow that a comprehensive plan of federal support should be established.[13] As in the other cases men-

[10] Chicago *Daily News,* March 4, 1959.

[11] *The Reporter,* March 17, 1960.

[12] Gilbert Seldes, "Is Luce for Light?" *Saturday Review,* December 20, 1958, p. 33.

[13] "The Ubiquitous Non-Sequitur," *Wall Street Journal,* February 21, 1961, p. 12.

tioned above, the debate does not end here; we are viewing segments out of context.

Sometimes, recasting an opponent's line of argument into a syllogism will make strikingly clear the logical confusion in it. Lincoln used this attack upon the reasoning of Douglas in their Galesburg debate:

Now, remembering the provision of the Constitution which I have read, affirming that that instrument is the supreme law of the land; that the judges of every state shall be bound by it, any law or constitution of any state to the contrary notwithstanding; that the right of propery in a slave is affirmed in that Constitution, is made, formed into, and cannot be separated from it without breaking it; durable as the instrument, part of the instrument,—what follows as a short and even syllogistic argument from it? I think it follows, and I submit to the consideration of men capable of argument, whether as I state it, in syllogistic form the argument has any fault in it?

Nothing in the constitution or laws of any state can destroy a right distinctly and expressly affirmed in the Constitution of the United States.

The right of property in a slave is distinctly and expressly affirmed in the Constitution of the United States.

Therefore, nothing in the constitution or laws of any state can destroy the right of property in a slave.

I believe that no fault can be pointed out in that argument; assuming the truth of the premises, the conclusion, so far as I have capacity at all to understand it, follows inevitably. There is a fault in it, as I think, but the fault is not in the reasoning; the falsehood, in fact, is a fault in the premises. I believe that the right of property in a slave is not distinctly and expressly affirmed in the Constitution, and Judge Douglas thinks it is.

Special devices. These are frequently classified as "rhetorical" methods, but that designation implies the mistaken notion that the methods defined above are not. The following methods might be termed "special" or "miscellaneous," because they have less in common than do those in the preceding groups.

Reductio ad absurdum. One of the most commonly used methods of refutation is that of reducing an argument to an absurdity, or, as it is named, the *reductio ad absurdum.* The refuter adopts for the moment the line of argument of his opponent, then, by carrying it out to its logical conclusion, shows that it results in an absurdity. For example, when a lawyer asserted in court that a corporation can make no oral contract because it has no tongue, the judge exposed the fallacy by saying simply, "Then, according to your own argument, a corporation could not make a written contract because it has no hand."

Macaulay makes striking use of this device:

> Many politicians of our time are in the habit of laying it down as a self-evident proposition, that no people ought to be free till they are fit to use their freedom. The maxim is worthy of the fool in the old story, who resolved not to go into the water until he had learned to swim. If men are to wait for liberty until they become wise and good in slavery, they may indeed wait forever.

This method is effective because of its simplicity and directness; it also has in it an element of ridicule that is persuasive against an opponent.

Posing a dilemma. As a method of refutation, this procedure consists in reducing an issue to an alternative, and then showing that both members of the alternative are untenable. These two members are called the "horns of the dilemma." The refuter says, in substance, "Now, with respect to this point at issue, there are two and only two possibilities—A and B. But A is not true, and B is not true; consequently your contention fails." In order to make the dilemma conclusive, obviously two things are necessary: (1) the horns of the dilemma must include all the possibilities in the case—that is, *the alternative must be exact;* and (2) both members of the alternative must be destroyed.

James Wilson, speaking in the convention for the province of Pennsylvania, in vindication of the colonies, in January, 1775, used the dilemma as follows:

> In the first place, then, I say that the persons who allege that those employed to alter the charter and constitution of Massachusetts Bay act by virtue of a commission from his majesty for that purpose, speak improperly, and contrary to the truth of the case. I say they do not act by virtue of such a commission. What is called a commission either

contains particular directions for the purpose mentioned, or it contains no such particular directions. In either case can those, who act for that purpose, act by virtue of a commission? In one case, what is called a commission is void; it has no legal existence; it can communicate no authority. In the other case, it extends not to the purpose mentioned. The latter point is too plain to be insisted on; I (will) prove the former.

Sometimes the possibilities with respect to the point in issue cannot be reduced to two. There may be a choice offered of any one of three or more possible conditions or courses of action. In such a case, to state the issue in the form of a dilemma, presenting a single alternative, would not be an exact disjunction, and so would be fallacious; to be truthful it is always necessary to state *all* the possibilities of choice, whatever their number. When more than two possibilities are to be considered, the method is, properly speaking, not a dilemma; but the *modus operandi* is similar. Webster, in his argument in the case of the Providence Railroad Co. *vs.* the City of Boston, made a division into three possibilities. Mr. Webster is here contending against the proposition that a certain street or piece of land is a public highway:

If this street, or land, or whatever it may be, has become and now is a public highway, it must have become so in one of three ways, and to these points I particularly call your honor's attention.

1st. It must either have become a highway by having been regularly laid out according to usage and law; or

2nd. By *dedication* as such by those having the power to dedicate it, and acceptance and adoption so far as they are required; or

3rd. As a highway by long use without the existence of proof of any original laying out, or dedication.

It is not pretended by any one that the land in question is a highway, upon the last of these grounds. I shall therefore confine myself to the consideration of the other two questions; namely, "Was there ever a formal and regular laying out of a street here? or was there ever a regular and sufficient dedication and acceptance?"

Sometimes there is *faulty disjunction* of the dilemma. In this situation an opening is left for an opponent which may result in great discomfiture to the author of the defective dilemma.

Thus, Lincoln, in his speech on the Dred Scott Decision, refused to accept either of the horns of the dilemma presented by Douglas. Lincoln said of Douglas:

> He finds the Republicans insisting that the Declaration of Independence includes all men, black as well as white, and forthwith he boldly denies that it includes negroes at all, and proceeds to argue gravely that all who contend it does, do so only because they want to vote, to eat, and sleep, and marry with negroes. He will have it that they cannot be consistent else. Now I protest against the counterfeit logic which concludes that because I do not want a black woman for a slave, I must necessarily want her for a wife. I need not have her for either. I can just leave her alone.

Applying the method of residues. Like that of the dilemma, this method is founded upon a division of the point in question into parts. The difference is that in the dilemma all the parts are destroyed, whereas in the method of residues one of the parts is left standing. By the method of residues, the matter in dispute is divided into two or more sections, which include all the possibilities in the case; then all but one of these are demolished, the one left standing being the aspect of the issue which the refuter wishes to establish. "There are," says the refuter, "three possibilities: A, B, and C. But A and B are false, consequently the presumption is that C is true." This method is not, strictly speaking, a method of refuting; it is rather a method of using refutation. The ultimate purpose of the speaker or writer is not destructive, but constructive; he destroys some of the parts into which he divides the question, in order that he may establish the remaining part. He uses refutation to accomplish his end, but the end itself is constructive proof.

The first requisite in using the method of residues is that *the division of the whole into parts shall be exhaustive.* The strength of the method depends entirely upon the assumption that all the possibilities in the case are destroyed save one. If, then, the disputant, in his division, omits one of the possibilities, he has proved nothing, for it still remains uncertain which possibility is true— the one he seeks to establish, or the one he failed to mention. Again, in order to make the work complete, it is usually necessary that the residual part be enforced by positive demonstration. The refutation of all but one of the possibilities leaves a presumption that the remaining possibility is true; but there may well be a suspicion that even this last part, too, is false, or that there is some fallacy in the division. Consequently, to be at all convincing, the residual part must be enforced by positive proof.

Burke, in his speech on conciliation with America, used the method of residues. He began:

> Sir, if I were capable of engaging you to an equal attention, I would state, that as far as I am capable of discerning, there are but three ways of proceeding relative to this stubborn spirit which prevails in your Colonies, and disturbs your government. These are:—to change that spirit, as inconvenient, by removing the causes; to prosecute it as criminal; or, to comply with it as necessary. I would not be guilty of an imperfect enumeration; I can think of but these three. Another has indeed been started, that of giving up the Colonies; but it met so slight a reception that I do not think myself obliged to dwell a great while upon it. It is nothing but a little sally of anger, like the forwardness of peevish children, who, when they cannot get all they would have, are resolved to take nothing.

He then considered the first two ways at length, proved them impracticable, and concluded:

> If then the removal of the causes of this spirit of American liberty be, for the greater part, or rather entirely impracticable; if the ideas of criminal process be inapplicable, or if applicable are in the highest degree inexpedient, what way yet remains? No way is open, but the third and last, to comply with the American spirit as necessary; or, if you please, to submit to it as a necessary evil.

Turning the tables. By this is meant showing that something presented by your opponent really supports your case and not his. It is "stealing his thunder." To turn the argument of an opponent against him is not often possible, but circumstances sometimes give the opportunity. A piece of testimony may be used by a writer who has not fully considered all the interpretations that may be put upon it. It not infrequently happens that evidence or argument is introduced to give support to some particular point, and, in its bearing on that phase of the question, the evidence may be favorable to the speaker or writer who introduces it; but as the discussion proceeds, it may turn out that, with respect to some other phase of the question, the evidence or the argument may be interpreted in another way, adversely to the one who introduced it. The effect of such an unexpected turn of affairs is obvious; the opponent is "hoist with his own petard."

Lincoln turned the tables admirably in his speech at Cooper Union in February, 1860:

Some of you delight to flaunt in our faces the warning against sectional parties given by Washington in his *Farewell Address*. Less than eight years before Washington gave that warning he had, as President of the United States, approved and signed an act of Congress enforcing the prohibition of slavery in the Northwestern Territory, which act embodied the policy of the government, upon that subject, up to and at the very moment he penned that warning; and about one year after he penned it, he wrote Lafayette that he considered that prohibition a wise measure, expressing in the same connection his hope that we should at some time have a confederacy of free states.

Bearing this in mind and seeing that sectionalism has since arisen upon this same subject, is that warning a weapon in your hand against us or in our hands against you? Could Washington himself speak, would he cast the blame of that sectionalism upon us who sustain his policy, or upon you who repudiate it? We respect that warning of Washington and we commend it to you, together with his example pointing to the right application of it.

Using questions or exploratory refutation. In cases of direct confrontation which permit questioning, particularly in cross-examination formats, a debater may ask questions the answers to which will prepare the way for subsequent refutation. This is colloquially called "setting up" a point for refutation. It is accomplished by revealing a weakness such as an inconsistency or a lack of evidence. A classic example of this maneuver may be seen in the transcript of the Stassen-Dewey radio debate in 1948 on the proposal to outlaw the Communist party in the United States. Governor Dewey asked Governor Stassen what instrument he would use to outlaw the party, and the answer stipulated the Mundt-Nixon bill. Dewey then refuted the "plan" case by showing that the recommended bill could not, and was never intended to, outlaw the Communist party.[14]

Exploratory refutation is the more hazardous procedure; it attacks something which has not yet been expressed by an opponent. The chief risk in using this form of anticipatory refutation is that the opponent may embarrass the refuter by pointing out that he had no intention to use the material which had been attacked. A counterattack would probably include terms such as "tilting at windmills" and "hitting straw men." At times, though, a stand which an opponent seems reluctant to divulge can be "smoked out" by exploratory refutation which is phrased conditionally.

Attacking the truth of a conclusion. Several of the previously mentioned methods of refutation, particularly those involving attacks upon reasoning, might be classified here. However, the point in identifying the sixth and seventh categories here is to distinguish between attacks upon the truth of a conclusion and attacks upon a conclusion even if true. In the former class are three variants: those which cast doubt upon a conclusion, those which deny a conclusion, and those which prove a contrary.

Attacking a conclusion even if true. Even though a point may have been made with satisfactory evidence and impeccable logic, it can perhaps be refuted on the ground that the conclusion is inconsequential or irrelevant. After a minor office-seeker finished accusing the opposite party of communistic tendencies, citing new tariff legislation and laws to protect natural resources as suspicious signs, a metropolitan daily which often endorsed candidates of his party took pains to point out that several of his points were irrelevant to the issue of communism. The same paper took a criminal-court judge to task for a similar breach of relevancy. After a jury acquitted the defendant of a morals charge, the presiding judge argued two matters which had not come up in the trial, namely, the competence of the arresting officer and the quality of law enforcement in that district.[15] Additional speci-

---

[14] *Vital Speeches of the Day,* XIV, 16, 1948.
[15] Chicago *Daily News,* February 23, 1959.

mens of irrelevancy may be seen in the chapter on fallacies and stratagems. Attacks on personality, appeals to tradition, and similar tricks are familiar types.

When an affirmative speaker on a national, tax-supported medical-care program argued that the scarcity of complete hospitals in rural areas proved the need for his plan, a negative speaker replied that the lack of an expensive facility in a sparsely populated township or county does not prove the wisdom of providing it regardless of cost. Because of modern communication and transportation, he countered, it is economically wiser to develop health centers in or near the centers of population. The first part of the negative reply attacked the affirmative point as inconsequential.

REBUTTAL

Definition. Refutation and rebuttal are not synonyms in our view; the former denotes the presentation of evidence and reasoning designed to weaken the case of an opponent, while the latter may denote both the attack upon an opponent's case and the defense of one's own against the refutation attempted by an opponent. In other words, refutation means attack, while rebuttal means both attack and defense (rebuilding).

Rebuttal has another meaning in certain specialized contexts, such as school and courtroom debating. It is the almost universal practice in courts, in contest debating, and in actual debates in assemblies of various sorts to provide for special periods after the main cases have been completed in which evidence and argument can be advanced in attack and defense of the main cases. Such periods are called rebuttal periods. Speeches made at such times are called rebuttal speeches. In law, rebuttal is "the giving of evidence on the part of a plaintiff (affirmative) to destroy the effect of evidence introduced by the defendant (negative) in the same suit" (Webster's Dictionary). In some debates, both contest and real, this legal precedent is more closely followed, and only the affirmative has rebuttal speeches. Of course, all speakers on both sides may have more or less refutation in the main speeches. Since the order of speaking and the nature of negative cases give the negative speakers superior opportunities for refutation in the main speeches, it is well to give the affirmative some compensating advantages in rebuttal. So even where both sides have equal rebuttal speeches, the negative leads in rebuttal, giving the affirmative the last rebuttal speech.

Rebuttal as defense. When defending or rebuilding his own point, a methodical debater would take these steps: (1) restate his point and the attack made upon it, (2) indicate the importance of the point and the relation of that attack to the cases, (3) set out his stand on the point, (4) rebuild his point or refute the attack upon it, (5) restate his position.

Several methods are available for the defense or the rebuilding of a point that has been attacked. One is hardly a defense; it is a tactical concession. When a fallacy has ben obviously refuted, the best procedure is to admit it. Or one might concede a point, if need be, but then go on to show that its effect is diminished or offset by one's own point.

Defenses against attacks upon analysis (definitions, issues, premises) will now be considered. When an important definition has been questioned, it is wise to cite standard, authoritative sources in the appropriate field. The reason for this is that a general dictionary is not the "last word" in specialized fields such as international law, economics, medicine, etc. Sometimes a negative will try to press an affirmative into equating "should" with "will" or "would" in a proposition of policy. The affirmative may and should refuse on the ground that these verbs are not synonyms. If an attack is made upon the selection of issues (alleged omission, or the inclusion of a nonissue), the defense must be made in terms of the theory of analysis as given in Chapter 4. In case a premise or an assumption is called into question, the best course is to explain and defend it. Both sides of the debate on tax-supported medical care for the aged under Social Security often neglect to reveal their philosophical assumptions.

Defenses against attacks upon evidence should be chosen to suit the nature of the refutation. If the charge is "too little evidence," one might be justified in explaining that little is needed on a matter of common knowledge (as in judicial notice in court), or he might produce more evidence. In case a source of evidence is attacked, one might point out that this does not prove the content to be false or unreliable, or he might defend his source, or he might add corroborative data. Occasionally one's evidence is over-matched by more or better material. In this situation he might add more and better evidence, but the better course is to reason more cogently from the evidence. A card-quoting contest is a poor sub-stitute for an intellectually satisfying debate. Finally, when the truth of the evidence is doubted, one might determine whether a confusion of fact and inference had taken place, or he might add corroborating evidence.

The obvious defenses against the charge of fallacious reasoning are two: admit it if true, or explain why the inference is sound when understood as intended. Much of what is given in our chapters on reasoning and fallacies applies here.

Defenses against five of the special devices of refutation will now be explained briefly. An attempted reduction to the absurd should be scrutinized as a possible stratagem of unfair extension of an opponent's argument. A so-called dilemma may not be one; perhaps one of the "horns" can be broken, or there may be a third way out. Similar advice applies to the handling of a "residues" attack: break down the disqualification of one or more of the choices, or suggest another choice. Successful replies to table-turning tactics have been made by questioning the opponent's frame of reference, by showing that he admits the argument, or by pointing out that he has shifted ground. Finally, five ways to deal with questions and exploratory refutation will be men-tioned. Legitimate questions of information should, of course, be answered. However, any time-wasting tactics and irrelevant ques-tions should be pointed out for all to note. The best defense is adequate preparation; anticipate the basic questions, and have answers ready. One way to discourage the "heckling" type of question is to insist that the questioner explain the relevance of his question before the respondent wastes any time on it. With respect to exploratory refutation, we suggest that it be viewed as a possible candidate for the "straw man" category.

General principles of rebuttal speeches

Use no new, main constructive points. Only such material as can be used *against the opponents' case as presented* should be permitted. It has already been suggested that in a debate where a man may speak more than once, it is well to hold material in reserve for rebuttal. It is, of course, possible to repeat or refer to arguments and evidence already given, but such repetition or reference must be subordinate to rebuttal and must be used destructively or for purposes of rebuilding. The constructive cases may not be added to in this period. Thus it would be improper for a negative speaker in a school debate to introduce the "impracticability" argument in a rebuttal speech. It would be equally improper for the affirmative to introduce its "plan" case in the rebuttal period.

But repeating or referring back to materials previously given is never so strong as the presentation of new, supplementary support. For this reason it is sometimes good strategy, even at the cost of taking something away from the strength of a first speech, to hold back some good evidence as a reserve. The judges of contest debates, moreover, should always penalize debaters who simply repeat or continue their main speeches during the time allowed for rebuttal. All that has been said above concerning refutation applies to rebuttal speeches in debate. Refutation is the very essence of debate, and the power to refute well is one to be sought by a debater as earnestly as he would seek any single power that a public speaker may hope to possess.

Answer the crucial parts of the whole case. Too much emphasis cannot be given to the remarks made earlier concerning what to answer in refutation. It is probably worthwhile here to discuss this question with particular reference to the rebuttal speeches in formal debate. The great fundamental principle which should guide the preparation of all rebuttal speeches is, *Answer the crucial parts of the whole case of the other side.* One of the fatal weaknesses in the equipment of any debater, and a weakness that is almost invariably displayed by a beginner, is the weakness of attacking only a part of an opponent's proof. It is easiest in refutation to pick out the weak points of the opposition and attack them, leaving the more formidable points standing. It demands less careful preparation and a less accurate analysis of the case of the other side, and it often seems to make the greatest impression on the audience. Consequently there is a temptation to pick up the more obvious errors of an opponent and dramatically expose them, or to seize upon some foolish word or phrase and ridicule it; this brings a laugh or a burst of applause, whereas, in an attempt to refute any of the stronger proofs, success is not so easy, for the audience, feeling that there are two sides to the issue, is not so readily convinced. But in the end, the audience will probably adhere to the man who has made it believe that his case, as a whole, is the stronger. Consequently, to achieve final success, the debater must endeavor to make the audience see not that he has destroyed an argument here and there, but that he has overwhelmed the essence of the proof against him.

In order to make an attack upon the whole case of the other side, *two things* are necessary. First, *the speaker must analyze the entire proof of his opponents and pick out the few basic points in it.* It is necessary to determine upon the few fundamental points of an opponent's proof, for the same reason that it is necessary to determine upon one's own. It is necessary for the sake of *clearness;* to give the same attention to the large and the small points of the other side perplexes a hearer in his understanding of the question as a whole. It is necessary for the sake of *emphasis;* it is only by neglecting or slighting trivial facts and dwelling upon the important ones that the vital points of the question can be brought out into a clear light. It is necessary for the sake of *saving time;* rebuttal speeches are usually short, and they are definitely limited. To give attention to the facts of secondary importance is to waste part of these precious minutes. If the vital points of an opponent's contentions are destroyed, his subordinate points fall with them and so do not need special rebuttal. These main contentions must be answered if an opponent is to be defeated at all, and, if they are answered, *to do more is superfluous.*

But, second, it is not enough for a debater merely to select the important points of the other side and proceed to refute them; *he must make it clear to the audience that in answering these points he is meeting the whole case against him*—that these *are* the foundations of the opposing case. To give the rebuttal its full effect requires that the audience be made to see that the speaker is attacking the entire proof in opposition and that if he succeeds, he has won his case. To do this requires that the arguments to be answered shall be stated clearly beforehand and shall be explained in such a way as to make it evident that in them is contained the whole case of the other side. It is very often desirable, as a means of making it evident that the whole case of the other side is being attacked, to *analyze openly* before the audience the proof of an opponent, and explain just what his argument as a whole amounts to. For instance, a speaker in rebuttal might well begin in some such manner as this: "Everything of any importance that my opponent has had to say on this question may be reduced to these three propositions: first, etc., second, etc., third, etc.," or "My opponent's case, as far as it has been presented to us, can be stated in his own words, as follows: etc." In some such way the audience may be made to have faith in the speaker's sincerity and in the importance of his efforts in rebuttal, and so be made ready to acknowledge the full force of his refutation.

For example, Webster, in his "Reply to Hayne" in the debate on the Foote Resolution, devoted a great deal of his speech to the refutation of Senator Hayne's theory of states' rights under the Constitution. Before entering on this task, he set forth in full the case presented by Senator Hayne, stating all the essential propositions of his doctrine and making it evident that, taken together, they embraced everything that demanded refutation:

There yet remains to be performed by far the most grave and important duty, which I feel to be devolved on me by this occasion. It is to state, and to defend, what I conceive to be the true principles of the Constitution under which we are here assembled. I might well have desired that so weighty a task should have fallen into other and abler hands. I could have wished that it should have been executed by those whose character and experience give weight and influence to their opinions, such as cannot possibly belong to mine. But, sir, I have met the occasion, not sought it; and I shall proceed to state my own sentiments, without challenging for them any particular regard, with studied plainness, and as much precision as possible.

I understand the honorable gentleman from South Carolina to maintain, that it is a right of State Legislatures to interfere, whenever, in their judgment, this Government transcends its constitutional limits, and to arrest the operation of its laws.

I understand him to maintain this right, as a right existing under the Constitution; not as a right to overthrow it, on the ground of extreme necessity, such as would justify violent revolution.

I understand him to maintain an authority, on the part of the states, thus to interfere, for the purpose of correcting the exercise of power by the General Government, of checking it, and of compelling it to conform to their opinion of the extent of its powers.

I understand him to maintain that the ultimate power of judging of the constitutional extent of its own authority is not lodged exclusively in the General Government, or any branch of it; but that, on the contrary, the States may lawfully decide for themselves, and each state for itself, whether in a given case, the act of the General Government transcends its power.

I understand him to insist that, if the exigency of the case, in the opinion of any State Government, require it, such State Government may, by its own sovereign authority, annul an act of the General Government, which it deems plainly and palpably unconstitutional.

Try to keep the opponent on the defensive. Negative spokesmen typically challenge the evidence, demand more evidence, ask detailed questions, raise numerous objections, and in other ways try to make the affirmative's burden of proof more onerous and to shift the burden of rebuttal to that side as well. This strategy is intended to keep the affirmative so busy answering questions and objections that its case cannot be given sufficient attention. The listeners or readers find their attention dominated by the negative's ideas.

Affirmative advocates generally have fewer opportunities to use this strategy; they have more constructive responsibilities to occupy their time. However, one way to place the negative on the defensive is to insist that they prove that their dire predictions are likely to come true and will be serious. Thus, when the negative cries "socialism" whenever any social legislation is proposed, the affirmative shifts the burden of rebuttal by challenging the negative to prove that the change will lead to socialism and that such a trend will inevitably be bad. Another affirmative tactic consists in demanding that the significance of each negative question or objection be shown before an answer is attempted. Negatives who are merely heckling the affirmative or trying to make them waste time are readily thwarted by this affirmative defense.

Be honest, fair, and courteous. The final principle relating to rebuttal speaking is, *Be fair, courteous, good-humored, and honest in dealing with the opposing case.* State the opposing arguments fairly. Do not color them to suit yourself by rephrasing, or substituting, or inserting words not used by your antagonist. In the use of charts and maps, in asking to examine evidence, in giving opponents an opportunity to examine your evidence, be courteous. You will hurt your own case and make your audience uncomfortable by being churlish and ill-tempered. It is probably not necessary here to advocate and advise common honesty. An honest man will be an honest debater. Manufacturing evidence, garbling quotations, falsifying references, misstating facts—these things are not "strategy" or "part of the game." They are simply cheap dishonesty—plain lies. No self-respecting debater will indulge in such practices. In contest debating, when the stupid or dishonest are detected in such practices, permanent disbarment from platform activities should be the minimum penalty.

Preparation of rebuttal speeches.   While this should be carefully done, it does not mean that rebuttal speeches should be memorized or read from manuscript. Rebuttals in a printed debate, as in the cases of editorials and letters to the editor, will, of course, be written.

Use extemporaneous procedure in speaking.   The material out of which to fashion rebuttal speeches should be carefully gathered and arranged for rapid use. Many contest debaters fail in this phase of their work. In debate, rebuttal is *no less important than positive proof;* in intercollegiate debates it is most often the rebuttal that is decisive. In any discussion it is the last speech that is coveted; Webster's famous "Reply to Hayne" was almost pure refutation. And it is very seldom that successful refutation is impromptu. *Good rebuttal speeches are practically always extempore,* not impromptu or memorized. Preparation of material to meet extemporaneously *any* stand taken by the opposition is good preparation; anything else is weak and dangerous. Daniel Webster declared that all the material of his "Reply to Hayne" had been gathered and waiting in his desk for months before the debate. Speaking of Senator Hayne, he said to a friend, "If he had tried to make a speech to fit my notes, he could not have hit it better. No man is ever inspired with the occasion; I never was."

Memorized preparation, however, is always to be avoided (if

possible) in debate, and should rarely be attempted by beginners, especially in contest debating. There is, in the first place, too great danger that the opposition will not say just what you are prepared to answer; and there is in debate no greater exhibition of incompetence, no greater indication of weakness, than a memorized rebuttal that does not *fit*.

Mere words and gestures do not make refutation any more than they make positive proof. There must be just as much evidence in the one as in the other. Rebuttal demands as careful a choice of weapons and as accurate a method of handling them as any other kind of proof. Invention, selection, and arrangement demand as much preliminary planning here as elsewhere.

These foregoing suggestions are especially applicable in preparation for school or college debates. There the limitations of time are very stringent. Not the smallest fraction of a minute can be lost in confusion or unnecessary deliberation; the answer must be in the debater's head as soon as the argument has left his opponent's lips. This necessity for such preparation—important everywhere, but here intensified by the circumstances—constitutes one of the most valuable phases of contest debating.

Know both sides; avoid surprises. Clearly, the primary necessity in preparing rebuttal is to know just what points we may be called upon to answer; we must have a clear and accurate understanding of the points our opponents need to establish and of the methods they may adopt in the attempt. Would any capable general ever lay the plans for a battle without first considering the position of his enemy, his location, his points of strength and weakness? As we discovered earlier, the selection of the main heads of the brief in debate depends very largely upon what the opposition may be able to "do about it." Those points must be chosen for emphasis—points that hit hardest and straightest at *the necessary* proofs of the other side (when we are able to tell in advance what such necessary proof will be). And at the same time we must remember that these main heads will surely be attacked, and we must take up a position that is defensible against assault. All this means a study and comparison of the two sides of the question so as to find out what arguments need to be attacked and, on the other hand, how one's own arguments may be best defended against the particular attack the other side will have to make.

But it is rarely possible to foresee every argument that an opponent may advance. No two persons reason just alike; an opponent may well look at the question from some peculiar standpoint, or, as more often happens, he may plan a surprise. Then, too, there are many minor questions that are raised in such a discussion which it is hardly worthwhile trying to anticipate or which escape notice in preparation. Commonly, these minor points are best left unanswered; but sometimes circumstances make them worth notice. Whatever the reason, it is certain that all the incidents of a debate cannot be foreseen; we must always expect the unexpected. A successful debater must always be ready to meet strange situations and to manufacture more or less of refutation and of proof on the scene of action. A debater who has read only on those phases of the question that are of interest to him, or who undertakes only those parts of the discussion that he treats in his own proof, is helpless in such circumstances. He has no resources to draw upon. If the discussion were in writing, he might think it over, consult new authorities, and plan his answer; but in oral debate there is no such opportunity. He must act at once. He is in the predicament of a military expedition that sets out on a long campaign with a day's rations and no base of supplies. When a debater is thus surprised, his only hope must lie in having a thorough knowledge of the question *as a whole, and in all its details*—a knowledge so thorough as to be ready at the call of any exigency. Furthermore, a broad understanding of the foundations and general conditions of the question is necessary, in order to be able to estimate rightly the force and bearing of arguments that are made by opponents. A debater who does not understand the basic assumptions or premises on which his own and his opponent's cases rest is almost hopeless in rebuttal. A superficial preparation always distorts the mental vision of a speaker and confuses in his mind the real issues in the discussion. But debate demands an especially clear perception and quick judgment of what is vital; the debater must think as quickly and act as decisively as the broker on the exchange; superficial information or a confused understanding mean as sure disaster in the one case as in the other. A debater in action must be able, when any argument or any evidence is brought against him, to estimate in a few seconds just what the matter amounts to, how it is related to his own case, how much to say about it, and where (in what part of his speech) to answer it. Here a stock of ready-made arguments becomes useless. *Only a deep understanding of the subject to the very bottom* can give the clear, ready insight and the steady judgment that alone avails.

Have a clear, careful method. The natural tendency of inexperienced debaters in rebuttal is toward carelessness of method. It is true even of more experienced debaters that speakers who are careful in arranging and presenting their original proofs, when they come to the work of refutation, forget themselves and degenerate into a weak informality, wandering from the point and mixing up their materials without regard for clearness of statement, the proper arrangement of evidence, or the natural sequence of the proofs. Rebuttal is not necessarily more informal than any other part of a debate or discussion, and it requires just as much care in presentation. The materials for it must be selected as judiciously, arranged as logically, and stated as clearly.

When attacking an opponent's point, a debater usually does well to take these steps: (1) state the clash point, (2) give the opponent's view of it, (3) make his attack on that view, (4) summarize his own position, (5) point out what remains for the opponent to do.

Division of duties in school debate. Only a brief sketch of the rebuttal work of each team member will be given here. We are assuming the traditional two-member team and a rebuttal period consisting of four five-minute speeches. Any suggested division of labor is secondary to the importance of teamwork.

First in the order of appearance is the first negative rebuttal, which, when added to the second negative constructive speech, makes a total of fifteen consecutive minutes of negative speaking. This being the case, these two persons must plan their work so that they will supplement, not duplicate, each other. Sometimes an arrangement similar to the "zone" assignment in basketball is used. If the second negative constructive speaker works on the "need" and "practicability" points (under a proposition of policy), the first negative rebuttal speaker concentrates upon "disadvantages." In general, the first rebuttalist continues from the point at which his colleague stopped. He answers additional points, presses the attack upon vulnerable and important topics, and stresses the effect of this upon the affirmative case. However, he should keep the negative stand in the foreground.

Second in the order of speaking is the first affirmative rebuttal. Since it follows fifteen minutes of negative presentation, it often must "come from behind" to win. Efficiency in the use of time is critically important; not everything can be answered, and the replies must be terse. After dealing briskly with the closing remark of the preceding speaker, the first affirmative rebuttalist rebuilds the main points of his team's case, answering negative attacks in terms of the affirmative position. It is important to keep one's own case in the foreground; otherwise the speaker seems to be on the defensive. This speech usually closes with a brief recapitulation of the affirmative stand.

The last rebuttal for the negative comes next. After countering the effect of the preceding speaker's closing remark, this speaker presses the negative objections or counterproposition, points up what has not been answered, summarizes the effect upon the affirmative case, and places the negative viewpoint in the foreground.

In last position comes the final affirmative rebuttal. This speaker adapts to the preceding speaker's most telling sentence, uses a rebuilding summary of the affirmative case, avoids defensiveness and the temptation to reply to minor diversions raised by the negative, keeps the focus on his own case, and perhaps closes with a hortatory remark.

EXERCISES

1. Identify the opportunities for refutation which you see in a specimen of argumentative discourse, such as an editorial, a printed speech, or a letter to an editor.

2. Analyze a printed debate in terms of assigned topics from this list: (a) how much was refuted, (b) the position of refutation, (c) steps in refutation, and (d) specific methods of refutation.

3. Select opposing rebuttal speeches in a printed debate (as in Appendix B), and evaluate them in terms of the advice given in the section on rebuttal in this chapter.

4. Oral assignment—a direct-clash exercise. Divide the class into groups of four or five persons. Each group should be assigned a carefully phrased clash point which has been drawn from a familiar proposition. Let the first speaker lead off with a five-minute defense of the point as phrased. Thereafter, all other members of the group should alternate by sides in attacking and defending that point in four-minute speeches. The criticism and evaluation should incorporate the doctrine of this chapter.

Chapter 18

KINDS OF DEBATE

In Chapter 1 we defined argumentation and debate and indicated some of the more important areas in which these forms of discourse operate. Here we are concerned specifically with debate and its applications in a free society. The five kinds, or applications, of debate are not discrete classes, and they are not based upon a single standard of classification. A school debate, for example, may be legislative in form, political in subject matter, and educational in purpose. Although some specimens of debate defy classification, a method of grouping based upon central tendencies seems to have pedagogical usefulness.

WHAT DEBATE IS

Debate consists of opposing arguments on a given proposition between a supporting affirmative and an opposing negative. As such, it provides some of the more important applications of the principles of argumentation with which this book is concerned. Debates may take place wherever opposing arguments (but not necessarily arguers) meet, whether it be a street corner, a microphone, a court of law, a political campaign, a legislative assembly, or the printed page. Thus, we may speak of the debate on states' rights which has been going on since the formation of our federal government. Formal rules or no rules at all may govern these arguments, and the purposes of the participants may vary tremendously.

The discourse among persons in which debate plays an important role is conducted primarily for purposes of learning and action. And of these two, debate is more concerned with action. It is first and foremost a policy-determining technique. It is in this capacity that debate serves a social purpose of great practical importance. Indeed, it is difficult to conceive of a democratic society of any kind in which its members did not resort to debate as a means of resolving issues and determining policy. Problems, differences, conflicts are inevitable in any society. Where these problems are of a sort that they must be settled in one way or another, and where differences persist after every reasonable effort to secure a consensus, the logical and sensible recourse for civilized human beings is debate. The most usual form of this debate is parliamentary debate, or legislative debate under the regulations of parliamentary procedure. Motions are made, debated, and acted upon, and the motions so adopted (usually by majority vote) become the law of the land or the policy of whatever group has taken the action. This kind will be treated last.

JUDICIAL DEBATE

Judicial or forensic debate is conducted for the purpose of adjudicating questions, mostly of fact and usually in a court of law or some other tribunal organized for this purpose. The affirmative is the plaintiff and the negative the defendant in such actions. Decisions are usually rendered by judges or juries.

As in legislative debate, a speaker in judicial debate makes use of most of what has been said in this book about propositions, issues, evidence, kinds of argument, briefing, and other matters.

The debate, however, is conducted under the special rules and conventions which obtain in the jurisdiction under which the court operates.

Although most judicial propositions are called factual, there are some which are otherwise. Injunction proceedings seek a policy decision, and the long-range purpose of some criminal trials is to change value judgments and possibly to influence future legislation. The Scopes trial was an instance of the latter; Bryan and Darrow probably were not primarily concerned with the fate of the person on trial.

This kind of debate is conducted for a decision, as has been stated, and it is pursued with varying degrees of rigor. The greater rigor is generally expected of pleaders before the higher tribunals, while somewhat lower standards have been known to prevail in jury trials in lower courts.

POLITICAL DEBATE

Political or campaign debate is conducted in democratic societies for the purpose of selecting candidates and electing persons to public office, and for the purpose of reaching decisions on public issues which have been referred to the people for vote. No body of procedural regulations, such as parliamentary law or the rules of legal pleading, exists to govern political debate. The only limitations imposed are the regulations governing elections and the general laws governing libel and slander. The end sought is a decision, but it is based upon the "results" criterion. Thus we see in action popular persuasion more often than intellectual rigor.

Propositions of policy predominate in political debating, but some individual clashes occur on allegations of fact or on value judgments. There have been debates on the evaluation of a party or an administration, for instance, even though the longer-range unstated proposition was one of policy. Again in terms of the immediate context, there are debates on propositions of fact such as, "The Democratic party is the war party," and "The G.O.P. is the depression party."

SCHOOL DEBATE

Academic or school debate is conducted for the purpose of developing skill in the art of debate. Such school debates are frequently organized to simulate legislative, judicial, political, and philosophical debate. It is hardly necessary to observe that only the most naive student of the subject would seek to limit the applications of argumentation and debate to school debates, valuable and useful as they are for educational purposes.

Most school debates take place on propositions of policy. Whether or not this is wise would make an interesting proposition of value. However, reporting the status quo accurately, we must say that in school debating, propositions of value are uncommon and propositions of fact are rare.

In this kind of debate, too, there is a variable quality of rigor. When a critic's decision is sought, the quality of the proof tends to resemble that of a judged trial; in an audience-decision or nondecision debate, the proof tends to be less rigorous but more persuasive in a popular sense. More will be said of this in the last chapter, "Debate as Training."

PHILOSOPHICAL DEBATE

Again speaking of central tendency, propositions of value predominate in this kind of debating. Decisions, if any are made, are incidental, not usually voted, and perhaps not even made known. "Understanding" is a more accurate name for the desired outcome than "decision."

Strictly speaking, philosophical argumentation refers to the nature of argument as it is used in philosophical discourse.[1] This meaning will be expounded later, but at present the term "philosophical debate" will be used to include the countless informal,

[1] See H. W. Johnstone, Jr., *Philosophy and Argument*, State College of Pennsylvania, 1959; and M. Natanson, "Rhetoric and Philosophical Argumentation," *Quarterly Journal of Speech*, XLVIII, 1962, pp. 24–30.

decisionless disputes which defy classification under judicial, political, school, or legislative debate. Two or more persons, even in a "bull session" atmosphere, might exchange arguments on "Should high-school students 'go steady'?", "Is the Presidency too much for one man?", "Is thrift old-fashioned?", and countless other questions of these sorts.

Somewhat different questions are associated with philosophical argumentation when it is used in a strict sense: "Is human will free?", "Is a belief unreasonable if no reason can be given for it?", "Is the law of contradiction only a thought?" But the difference between the two sets of questions is mainly one of depth or sophistication rather than kind.

Strictly speaking, philosophical arguments have several distinguishing features. One is that they are neither factual, as in science, nor formal, as in logic. Another is that they are more expository than persuasive. Thus it follows that they aim at free choice rather than exploitation; their technique is open, not concealed. A third feature is that the arguer seeks to understand himself in relation to the truth. The important thing for us to understand is the fundamental intent of the philosophical arguer, not the specific arguments used. Socratic dialectic, which is treated in another chapter, represents a fusion of rhetoric and philosophy which epitomizes this feature.

LEGISLATIVE DEBATE

Legislative debate is conducted for the purpose of reaching a group decision on matters of policy in organized meetings in which motions are made. All that has been said in this book about propositions, issues, evidence, kinds of arguments, cases, and other matters applies to such debate. We present here the rules of procedure under which such debate is usually conducted. Further advice may be obtained by consulting handbooks on parliamentary law.[2] Most of the propositions (motions) are of

[2] See P. A. Carmack, "Evolution in Parliamentary Procedure," *Speech Teacher*, XI, 1962, pp. 26–39; A. F. Sturgis, *Standard Code of Parliamentary Procedure* (New York: McGraw-Hill, 1950); H. M. Roberts, *Rules of Order,*

policy, the debate is for a decision, and the degrees of rigor are extremely varied.

Rationale of parliamentary procedure. The general object of parliamentary procedure is to provide a set of rules and principles for the orderly conduct of meetings which typically involve oral debating of controversial matters. It is the means by which the intent of the majority can be determined in an honest, orderly manner.

Parliamentary procedure is complex, but not as complex as some persons think. Nor is it intended as a means by which a devious manipulator can serve his own ends. Although occasionally abused, it is intended as a defense against chicanery. It provides a fair hearing for all persons, it is flexible enough to serve the needs of every type of meeting, and it can be used with varying degrees of formality.

Rules of procedure make more sense when their underlying principles are understood. Five of them can be stated briefly: one item of business at a time, majority rule with safeguards for the minority, free and full debate, equality of opportunity, and diplomacy and common sense.

Related to these general principles are several specific duties and rights of members of a parliamentary body. An individual member has these rights: (1) to appeal from a decision of the chair to the assembly, (2) to call for a point of order, (3) to explain or debate, except in violation of the rules, (4) to make a motion, if in the proper manner, and (5) to take the floor, upon being recognized, until he concludes his remarks or until a time limit expires. With these rights go the following duties: (1) to abide by the spirit and the rules of proper procedure, (2) to obtain recognition before speaking, (3) to speak only on matters that are in order, (4) to interrupt a member only when it is worth doing and when the motion permits it, and (5) to keep debate on an impersonal basis.

Revised (Chicago: Scott Foresman, 1951); J. F. O'Brien, *Parliamentary Law for the Layman; Procedure and Strategy for Meetings* (New York: Harper & Bros., 1952).

Conventional sequences

1. *Typical Order of Business*
   a. Call to order
   b. Roll call, if customary
   c. Reading, correction, and approval of minutes
   d. Presentation and acceptance of officers' reports
   e. Reports of *ad hoc* committees
   f. Reports of standing committees
   g. Old business
   h. New business
   i. Announcements
   j. Adjournments
2. *Steps in a motion*
   a. Member obtains floor
   b. Motion is made
   c. Motion is seconded
   d. Motion is restated
   e. Motion is debated
   f. Amendment, referral, etc., may occur here
   g. Debate is stopped
   h. Motion is put
   i. Vote is taken (aye—no, hands, rising, roll call, and ballot)
   j. Vote is announced

Motions and their purposes

1. Introduce business
   a. Main motion or resolution
2. Alter a motion
   a. Amend (add, insert, delete, substitute), **or**
   b. Refer to committee, or
   c. Divide question
3. Defer action
   a. Postpone indefinitely, or
   b. Postpone definitely, or
   c. Refer to committee, or
   d. Table, or
   e. Make a special order
4. Suppress a motion
   a. Object to consideration, **or**

   b. Postpone indefinitely, or
   c. Table, or
   d. Move previous question, or
   e. Withdraw motion
5. End or limit debate
   a. Move to limit, or
   b. Move previous question
6. Reconsider a matter
   a. Take from table, or
   b. Reconsider, or
   c. Rescind, or
   d. Consider at time to which postponed, or
   e. Consider at time of committee report, or
   f. Consider as new business after indefinite postponement, or
   g. Discharge committee if it fails to report
7. Reverse a decision
   a. Reconsider and defeat, or
   b. Rescind, or
   c. Contrary motion
8. Set aside rule
   a. Suspend rule, or
   b. Create committee of whole sometimes
9. Protect members or enforce rules
   a. Inquiry, or
   b. Appeal, or
   c. Point of Order, or
   d. Privilege
10. Close a meeting
   a. Recess, or
   b. Adjourn

Table of Selected Motions and Rules

MOTIONS IN ORDER OF PRECEDENCE	NEEDS A SECOND?	AMEND-ABLE?	DEBAT-ABLE?	SIZE OF VOTE?	MAY INTERRUPT A SPEAKER?
1. Privileged (in this order)					
a) Fix time of meeting	Yes	Yes	No	Maj.	No
b) Adjourn (2)	Yes	No	No	Maj.	No
c) Take recess (2)	Yes	Yes	No [8]	Maj.	No
d) Question of privilege	No	No	No	(1)	Yes
e) Make Special Order	Yes	Yes	Yes	⅔	No
2. Incidental (in any order)					
a) Suspend a rule	Yes	No	No	⅔	No
b) Withdraw motion	No	No	No	Maj.	No
c) Object to consideration	No	No	No	(3)	Yes
d) Point of order	No	No	No	Chair	Yes
e) Appeal from chair	Yes	No	(4)	Maj.	Yes
f) Division of motion	Yes	Yes	No	Maj.	No
g) Division of house	No	No	No	No	Yes
h) Parliamentary Inquiry	No	No	No	No	Yes
3. Subsidiary (in this order)					
a) To table	Yes	No	No	Maj.	No
b) Previous question	Yes	No	No	⅔	No
c) Limit or extend debate	Yes	Yes	No	⅔	No
d) Postpone definitely	Yes	Yes	Yes	Maj.	No
e) Refer to committee	Yes	Yes	Yes	Maj.	No
f) Amend	Yes	Yes	Yes [5]	Maj.	No
g) Postpone indefinitely	Yes	No	Yes	Maj.	No
4. Main (in any order)					
a) Original, main	Yes	Yes	Yes	Maj.	No
b) Reconsider	Yes	No	Yes [5]	Maj.	Yes [6]
c) Rescind	Yes	Yes	Yes [5]	Maj. [7]	No
d) Take from table	Yes	No	No	Maj.	No
e) Make general or special order	Yes	Yes	Yes	Maj.	No

Notes on table of motions:

[1] If chair decides that question is one of privilege, it is made and handled as main motion.

[2] Not always privileged.

[3] A two-thirds negative vote needed to defeat motion.

[4] Not debatable in some circumstances.

[5] Except when motion to be amended, reconsidered, or rescinded is not debatable.

[6] Interruption permitted only to make motion. Consideration has rank of motion to be reconsidered.

[7] Some exceptions.

[8] Not debatable if made when another question is before the body.

EXERCISES

1. Select a problem for class debate. Each member of the class is asked to investigate the problem and phrase a proposition as a motion expressing the action he wishes to propose. Be prepared to present this motion and defend it in a three-minute speech. Use the table of parliamentary motions given in this chapter as a basis for guiding parliamentary debate on the motions. Appoint a chairman and make it a rule that each member of the class be prepared to support each main motion, amend it, or oppose it in a manner best suited to accomplish his purpose. Use this exercise as a drill in parliamentary procedure. Experiment with different types of motions until you understand them and know how to use them.

2. Was the Eisenhower-Stevenson campaign of 1956 a political debate? Explain your position.

3. Were the four televised meetings of Kennedy and Nixon in 1960 properly classified as political debates?

4. How should we classify a printed dispute in a mass-circulation magazine on the question, "Which is better in a compact car—front engine or rear engine?"

5. Practice parliamentary procedure in a realistic setting as described by J. W. Cleary, "A Parliamentary Procedure Teaching Method: The Formation Of A Realistic Organization," *Speech Teacher,* XI, 2, March, 1962, pp. 124–129.

DEBATE AS TRAINING

DEBATE AS AN
EDUCATIONAL METHOD

Its origin and development. Debate and its predecessor, disputation, were among the earliest known teaching devices. Protagoras, who taught in Athens approximately 2,400 years ago, is referred to as the "father of debate." He is said to have been the first to encourage regular discussions on set subjects and to organize argumentative contests among pupils. Aristotle, who taught a century later in Greece, commented on debate as a school exercise in his *Rhetoric*. Historically, the teaching and the practice of debate have flourished and declined concomitantly with democracy. Tyrants have had no use for debaters and their teachers.

Contest debating began in this country as an intramural activity of college literary societies. Some writers have erroneously stated that the first intercollegiate debate took place between Harvard and Yale in 1892. The first intercollegiate debate in which Northwestern University took part was held twenty years earlier, in 1872.[1] Decision debates between Northwestern and Michigan took place in 1894 and 1895. A "Forensics" course was inaugurated at Northwestern in 1892. The movement spread to hundreds of colleges and thousands of high schools across the land. There are countless leagues and tournaments, and teams travel in all states and even to foreign countries. This tremendous growth has raised questions concerning the place of debate in the educational scheme. These will be considered in the following comments on objectives and criticisms.

Important objectives. A confrontation of advocates, such as one finds in a debate, affords excellent training in argument. The presence of opposition stimulates the participants to greater endeavor and compels them to consider both sides of the question. The real issues are more likely to develop if both sides are represented by carefully prepared advocates. The presence of such opposition motivates greater consideration of the logical adequacy of evidence and reasoning. The rules of debate, furthermore, promote the observance of certain standards of decorum which keep the controversy within bounds and insure to both sides a fair hearing.

A second objective is improvement in extemporaneous speaking. Competent debating demands, and provides practice in, this kind of speaking. The debater learns to think on his feet, to adapt his arguments to those of his opponent, and to adjust himself in various ways to the situation at hand. Debating can develop a self-reliant, ready speaker who is able to meet situations as they arise.

Ability in the analysis and investigation of public questions is a third objective. Rarely in other situations do school and college students study these questions with the enthusiasm and thoroughness which debaters exhibit in preparation for debates. They know that they cannot do a good job unless they are well prepared. The importance of these skills and habits of mind should be obvious.

Skill in critical thinking is a fourth general objective which in part comprehends the others. It is useful in speaking, listening,

---

[1] Otto F. Bauer, "A Century of Debating at Northwestern University: 1855–1955," Unpublished M.A. Thesis, Northwestern University, 1955.

writing, and reading. A critical thinker habitually applies the precepts of argumentation: he discerns propositions, he discovers issues, he knows how to study a subject, he is aware of the proof requirements of a proposition, he applies the tests of evidence, he distinguishes between valid and fallacious reasoning, he identifies implicit assumptions, and he recognizes the nonlogical means of persuasion. This skill in critical thinking is no mere by-product if the debating is based upon the sound principles of argumentation.

We look upon school debate as a preparation for policy-determining debate such as we observe in the courtroom, the legislative assembly, and in countless less-formal situations of life. As such a preparation it is one of the most valuable educational experiences in which competent students can take part. Some of the many types of debate have been used successfully as teaching devices in classes in public speaking, argumentation, and social studies. An exposition of each of these types of school debate appears later in this chapter.

Criticisms of the activity. For the purpose of this discussion we shall ignore the superficial objections which have to do with the number of students who receive the benefits of debate, the classes missed because of trips, and other allegations of overemphasis. These are superficial because they do not allege inherent faults in debate as training. Abuses can and should be corrected without abolishing the worthwhile activity. We shall direct our attention to the more significant attacks. In this connection we refer our readers to the defense of real-life debate in Chapter 1.

Several criticisms can be grouped under the general charge of intellectual perversion. This charge is stated in the following ways: debate fosters insincerity for the sake of victory; a debater's mental activity is characterized by wish-thinking and opportunism; young people are harmed by being forced to argue against their convictions; debaters do not search for truth, because their thoughts and feelings are predetermined.

It is easier to make the charge of dishonesty and sharp practice than to prove it. Persons with little knowledge and strong prejudice, which they dignify as "conviction," find it hard to believe that those who espouse the opposite side are anything but knaves or fools. From the point of view of the audience, the issue is not how strongly the debater believes his argument, but whether it is significant and valid. If it is not, the opposition should point out this fact. The presence of a competent opponent is a deterrent to dishonesty. The assumption of democracy is that when both sides have been advocated, the listeners can be trusted to make a wise decision.

The charge that school debaters are harmed because of their being forced to argue against their convictions has not been proved. Neither the extent of the practice nor its harmfulness has been substantiated. We state that the only responsibility of a debater is to set up the best possible case for his side in terms of the available proof. His convictions are in no way at stake. The rhetorical competence which is sought in school debates must not be confused with the ethical question of how one may use that competence in the policy-determining debates of later life. Our observations of thousands of debaters lead us to conclude that one is a better advocate for having prepared not only his side but the other as well. Then, too, a vast number of school debaters have no preference for one side until they have debated both. Frequently, those who have an initial preference change their minds after they work on the other side. Practicing on both sides forces one to entertain the possibility that a rival idea has merit. Why take so seriously a "conviction" which often is merely a snap judgment based upon little or no study?

Let us consider another aspect of the first general charge of intellectual perversion—that debaters cannot seek the truth because their thoughts and feelings are predetermined. Debate does not require one to investigate a problem by first deciding what he will think about it. There is a place for open-minded investigation, and that place is in the investigation and analysis which precede debate. Even so, there are times when we must work from axioms and beliefs. From the audience's point of view, this is better than listening to speakers explore their minds in public while the listeners wait for an intelligible statement. Debate need not be characterized by sketchy and opportunistic investigation. Nor does the so-called "deductive" method of presentation inevitably mean that no "inductive" inquiry preceded it.

We see no reason to discard the eagerness to declare a conviction, the practice of stating proof concisely, and the willingness to change one's belief as investigation and argument may direct.

A second criticism of debate is that competition encourages contentiousness or fosters attitudes of conflict. A debater, according to this view, represents militarism in intellectual life. We recall that Aristotle cautioned against drawing a point of issue when it could be avoided, but he also provided most systematically for vigorous attack and defense if conciliation failed. As we stated before, there is no wisdom in glossing over real clashes of interest as if they did not exist. If feelings run high in debate, the form of the activity is not the cause; the fact that personal interests are at stake brings out conflict. If labor and management spokesmen debate, is it because these men were school debaters, or is it because their drives for wages and profits clash? As we have said, if exploitation and force are to be avoided in such cases, we must have available an orderly method of handling these differences. Debate is such a method. Since this is the case, training in the method merits a place in the educational scheme.

A third criticism is that school debate seeks only a temporary decision rather than a solution to the problem about which the controversy centers. "Solution" has a noble sound, but discussions of current problems do not reach ultimate or final answers. The "solutions" reached in discussions, either in real-life situations or in school exercises, are a series of temporary decisions en route to the ultimate, just as are those of debate. What, for instance, is the "solution" to a labor-management disagreement over wages, and would it be permanent? We see that in many practical matters there is not time for endless quest of certainty. There are important differences between the laboratory ideal and the expedient handling of pressing current problems. Realities of life demand decisions. If we delay, we may lose all power to act.

Fourth, school debate is accused of harmful emphasis upon "two-sidedness" or "two-valued orientation." The same has been said of real-life debates, and that charge has been answered in Chapter 9. The same reply fits this situation, because we view school debate as preparation for the debates of life.

Finally, let us consider the fifth general objection: debate is futile because an advocate can seldom, if ever, convince his opponent.

> A man convinced against his will
> Is of the same opinion still.
> A woman convinced against her will
> Is of the same opinion, but is never still.

It is said that one may vanquish an opponent but still not persuade him. This is obviously sometimes true and sometimes not. Even if it were always true, it would not be a very discerning criticism. Under normal circumstances a debater is attempting to convince some third party rather than his opponent. This third party may be an audience, or it may be a judge; but it is some man or group of men whose judgment on the matter is significant to him. The very fact that the debaters have found themselves unable to agree is usually the precise reason why the debate takes place. Ideally, at least, people will first make every effort to come to some kind of agreement on a problem through reflective deliberation or discussion. Failing in this, they will then resort to debate, wherein the decision is submitted to a popular vote or to some supposedly neutral third party. In a debate, both parties frankly and openly *desire* to maintain their proposition, and the debate is over as soon as one party concedes the position of his opponent. Convincing one's opponent may be one purpose of a debater, but in the great majority of cases this is only incidental to winning the support of others.

APPROACHES AND
ATTITUDES IN DEBATE

The strategic approach.   Some ingenious persons have written chapters and even books on the ways to gain unexpected advantage over an opponent in an argument. A few of them have gone so far as to express these tricks in sophistic terms, such as "not showing one's hand," "bottling-up the enemy," and "splitting hairs." We do not subscribe to this doctrine, which attempts to exploit the audience at the expense of one's opponent and at the expense of a reasonable decision on the proposition. A less philosophical objection is that trickery can usually be exposed by a seasoned debater. Furthermore, the tricksters do much harm to the repute in which debate is held by thoughtful persons. About the only strategy that cannot be exposed to the discomfiture of the person who is trying to use it is that of sound, vigorous argument; and, of course, this is not strategy in the sense in which we have used the term.

The straightforward approach. The best approach in almost any argument, from both the logical and the psychological points of view, is that of a sound analysis supported by as few carefully chosen lines of argument as will constitute prima-facie or logically adequate support for this analysis, with each of these lines of argument thoroughly bolstered with the best available evidence. A case built along these lines has the merit of being simple, clear, and at the same time completely fortified from every point of view. Scattered and complex cases are seldom so effective as those which are organized around a few simply stated and well-supported arguments. If this be strategy, then it is the kind which will not thwart intelligent deliberation.

Desirable personal attitudes. "Magnanimity" or "fair play" is the best term to characterize the desired personal behavior of a debater. He should not be a little pettifogger "skilled in delays, sophisms, and misapprehensions." Rather, he is a person whose interest in the issue is unmistakable and who is capable of rising above personal embroilments, petty trickery, meanness, and vindictiveness. The attitude that we are describing here is not stuffy self-righteousness, but the kind of earnestness, tempered with generosity and frankness, which makes pettiness suffer by comparison. Edmund Burke once said that magnanimity in politics is "not seldom the truest wisdom." Assuming this to be true, we say that the attitude which we recommend not only makes for more intelligent deliberation, but is good persuasion as well.

BUILDING THE CASES

Most of the principles of case construction have been discussed in Chapter 12. At this time we shall indicate some specific applications to school debating.

Suggestions for affirmative debaters. If the issues as set out by the first affirmative speaker are accepted as the basis of the argument, the affirmative case becomes the ground on which the contest will presumably be conducted. Affirmative speakers will do well to make their case stand out clearly throughout the debate and to press the negative to meet it. We stress this because negatives often seek to draw the argument toward their stand. Negative objections should be answered in terms of the affirmative case, either by meeting them with a reinforced case point or by showing the objection to be irrelevant or inconsequential in terms of the affirmative case point as stated.

The burden of proof should be accepted and met specifically. However, the negative must be prevented from avoiding its logical responsibilities and foisting undue burdens upon the affirmative. To meet a reasonable burden of proof on a proposition of policy, the affirmative must establish the extent and seriousness of the problem, the inherency of causal factors in the present situation, the workability of the proposal in terms of meeting the cause for action, and the probability that the solution will not entail new and greater problems. It seems that most of the weak affirmative cases are so because of a failure to clinch the second point—the inherency of causal factors in the status quo.

Affirmative cases on propositions of value and fact must also meet the burden of proof, but the issues and the points in partition are unlike those of propositions of policy. These matters are treated basically in Chapter 4. Since propositions of value are used infrequently in school debates, we shall refer here to only one example in order to make our point about the building of a debate case. In debates on the proposition of value which declared chain stores to be detrimental to the public welfare, the most successful affirmative teams first set out and defended their criteria for judging a system of retail distribution in terms of public welfare. Then they went on to show that chain stores as defined did not measure up to those criteria.

We have urged affirmatives to prevent their opponents from foisting undue burdens upon them. There are situations in which the affirmatives take undue burdens upon themselves without any urging from the negative side. This happens when the affirmative case goes beyond the requirements of the proposition. For instance, if the proposition demands the nationalization of basic, nonagricultural industries, any affirmative case which stands for total nationalization is really affirming a new proposition or motion, or at least a motion as amended. In terms of basic industries, this stand is more nearly a negative case, but not necessarily a safe one.

Suggestions for negative debaters. The negative case must constitute a vital objection to the proposition. As in the case of the affirmative, it is generally advisable to take a conservative position and to concentrate on a few decisive points. Some negative cases on propositions of policy have stood on one point: "It won't work."

The suggestions concerning affirmative cases indicate some potential weaknesses which the negative should be prepared to attack. To this end, the negative debaters should prepare not only a case of one of the four types discussed in Chapter 12, but also several optional blocks of material which can be adapted to the peculiar weaknesses of various affirmative cases. This flexibility of attack distinguishes the best negative teams.

A reminder of the special risks involved in a counterproposition attack is in order at this point. The negative counterproposition must be clearly stated and must be truly counter. If the affirmative can adopt it as a means to their end, the negative case fails. However, as we also said previously, the negative plan need not be adopted if it defeats the affirmative. That adoption may grow out of another debate. Thus the proposal of a new rural school building might be defeated by a counterproposal of a fleet of school buses, but the latter should be debated as a new proposition before it is adopted.

REBUTTAL PRACTICE

How to prepare for it. Effective rebuttal requires careful preparation. In fact, it is more difficult, and may be more important to the outcome, than the constructive effort is. Debaters who view rebuttal as an impromptu exercise are deluding themselves.

Both the constructive and the rebuttal speaking should be extemporaneous. Both should be prepared equally well. A sound case is harder to attack, and prepared rebuttal enables a debater to defend his case and attack that of the opposition more efficiently.

Rebuttal preparation differs somewhat from constructive preparation. A team or a squad ought to consider all the individual arguments and all the case plans which they may face. Each argument should be written on a separate card or added to a large rebuttal chart. Below this statement on the card, or in columns to the right in the instance of a chart, the argument should be followed through three or four possible exchanges between the two teams. This should prevent mere repetition of old evidence and reasoning which do not suffice to meet a new attack. It might be called defense in depth. The debaters who will use this material should do the major portion of the work on it. The faculty director should only direct, guide, or advise.

Such preparation is not "canning" rebuttal. The objectionable "canned rebuttal" is written and memorized in advance and used regardless of the trend of the debate. Rebuttals which are read from cards or papers are likewise objectionable; neither type of presentation develops the debater.

One convenient type of oral practice effectively discourages the "canning" of rebuttal material. It is a practice rebuttal session conducted according to a modified direct-clash sequence. The director designates an affirmative speaker to present one small point in three minutes, calls on a negative speaker to reply for two minutes, calls on an affirmative to reply for two minutes, and calls on a negative to close for his side. The second clash may be started with a negative point, and so on. Other devices, such as cross examination, also discourage improper preparation.

How to conduct it.   As we have said in a previous connection, every speech in a debate after the first affirmative should include some rebuttal. We refer the student to Chapter 17 for the methods of refutation. The use of some rebuttal in most constructive speeches follows logically from the fact that proof in a debate is cumulative; that is, the second speaker of a team builds upon a foundation laid down by the first speaker. Thus, a second affirmative should re-establish his colleague's cause for action before going on to set out the plan and its advantages. Each speaker after the first one in a debate should open his speech by "taking one hot off the bat." This is done by isolating and refuting tersely and effectively the last telling point made by the preceding opponent.

Although adaptation and refutation are needed in constructive speeches, these processes must not cause one to neglect his constructive responsibilities. Affirmatives are more likely to spend so much time refuting that they fail to present a prima-facie case. A similar danger confronts a negative whose attack includes a preconceived case.

Furthermore, the use of refutation in constructive speeches should not result in a loss of organization and coherent development. Both sides have this risk. Otherwise well-organized cases become muddled if refutation is poorly handled. If the attack or defense is germane to a constructive point to be taken up in the speech, all can be woven into one argument. If the refutation material does not apply to the constructive point under discussion, it is better to take up the refutation first and then turn to construction. Even in negative speeches based entirely on refutation there should be evidence of planned progression. Both sides are expected to present sequences of arguments which can be followed.

There should always be some guiding plan in rebuttal. This includes the general strategy, the division of labor between teammates, and the organization of each rebuttal speech. Such planning is important because it may prevent fuzziness of statement, overlapping of coverage, omission of essential matter, and wasting of time. The gain in focus or emphasis alone makes advance planning worth the effort.

We shall consider first the distribution of duties between teammates. Whatever plan is devised must not be thought inflexible; provisions need to be made for freedom to meet important arguments as they arise and to handle unforeseen situations promptly. One scheme of rebuttal is called "man to man" defense. The first speaker on one team handles what is said by the first speaker on the other side, the second speaker meets the arguments of his opposite speaker, and so on. A more effective plan is called the "zone" defense, in which each debater is assigned specific ideas or portions of a case to attack or defend. A rough division may be made according to the cause for action, the plan, counterpropositions, etc. In general, we prefer that division of labor which assigns to each speaker the handling of whatever points seem to need prompt attention when he gets up to speak. No one can reliably predict what those will be. This scheme stresses the timeliness of rebuttal and demands versatility in a debater.

Another aspect of this division of labor concerns the proper function of the last rebuttal speaker for each side. In general, it is the presentation of a contrasting summary rather than a sketchy treatment of many scattered points. Roughly two-thirds of the allotted time is sufficient for this purpose. One method is to summarize only what has been said against each main opposing argument, and then climax the statement with a terse review of one's own case. Another method is the contrasting summary of the main points of conflict under the headings of ultimate issues. Herein one not only "boils down" the arguments, but also attempts to point out his team's advantage. For the latter purpose, it is often better to organize the rebuttal around one's own case.

The second aspect of the guiding plan is the organization of each rebuttal speech. Definite points should stand out in a clear relationship to the case as a whole. Hit-or-miss rebuttal consisting of a disconnected series of remarks is not effective. It is better to use topic sentences, carefully selected forms of support, transitions between points, and a conclusion which clinches the main ideas.

The following miscellaneous items of advice on the use of rebuttal in debate have been given by many coaches and judges:

1. Don't try to hit everything. Use few points, and group related questions and arguments under each.
2. If necessary, use anticipatory refutation to dispel common misconceptions before they are stated, but do not set up "straw men."
3. Show the relationship to the whole case when defending or attacking a point.
4. When refuting a point, state it tersely but fairly, in-

dicate its importance to an issue or the case, attack it, and assess the damage.

5. Keep running notes, possibly in parallel columns, for convenience in checking what remains to be done.

6. When on the affirmative, press the negative to show how the repairs or the counterproposition will meet the need better than your plan will. If the counterproposition is not truly counter, adopt it as a part of your plan.

7. It is not enough merely to repel an attack; the strong points of one's own side and the admissions and the omissions of the other side should be stressed.

8. In making a second reply, do not repeat the proof; use new evidence and reasoning. New constructive argument, however, is not admissible.

9. In the interest of appropriate style, avoid the specialized vocabulary of argumentation and the use of stereotyped expressions such as: "we have proved," "my constructive speech," "Mr. Chairman, honorable judges, worthy opponents, ladies and gentlemen," etc.

10. Observe the standards of delivery that characterize the best public speaking.

11. Finally, avoid overstatement, mere assertion, misquotation, personal attack, and, in general, the "hammer and tongs" approach.

CONDUCTING THE
DEBATE

Presiding officer. Anyone who participates in a debate, either educational or policy-determining, should know and observe the customs of the activity. A debate is usually presided over by a chairman who opens the meeting, introduces the speakers, and perhaps sets the tone of the program. He announces the decision of a panel of judges or introduces a single critic judge who gives a critique. The chairman announces the proposition, but does not discuss it. This is good advice for all introducers of public speak-

330 DEBATE AS TRAINING

ers. The chairman should announce a speaker and remain standing until the speaker approaches the lectern and recognizes him.

Salutation. When the speaker reaches the front of the platform, he should pause momentarily and then address the audience. "Ladies and Gentlemen," "Ladies," "Gentlemen," or "Members of the Tuesday Study Club" suggest the approproate kind of salutation. It is both superfluous and in poor taste to call the roll as in "Mr. Chairman, Honorable Judges, Worthy Opponents, Ladies and Gentlemen." The timekeepers may feel slighted. Instead of addressing the opponents or the judges during the debate, it is better to speak to the audience. It is assumed that the judges and the opponents will hear what is said.

In case a visiting team is being entertained, the first speaker for the home team may give a brief and genuine expression of welcome. The following speaker for the visiting team may respond appropriately.

Judges or critic. The panel of judges or the critic judge should be seated in the audience and be provided with satisfactory facilities for writing notes. If the decision and critique are to be given orally by the critic judge in the presence of the audience, he should be apprised of the arrangement when he is engaged. At the close of the debate the chairman should introduce the judge. If, as in the case of a three-judge panel, no oral critique is presented, the ballots should be collected by ushers or timekeepers and brought to the chairman for announcement.

Audience. When the debaters have achieved sufficient competence to be worthy of an audience, a public situation adds much to a debate. Although one campus affords only a few opportunities per season, the program can be expanded by taking debates to civic clubs, school assemblies, and other such groups. This is not to say that tournament debating needs to be dropped from the schedule. Audience interest can be built up by using propositions that concern them and by modifying the traditional pattern through the use of direct-clash contests, a cross-examination period, an open forum, and shift-of-opinion ballots. The audience situation can be educationally more useful if the debaters are taught to address the listeners as persons who are to settle the question at the close of the debate.

Attitude toward opponents. The behavior of debaters toward each other should be fair, courteous, considerate, and honest. Any evidence of poor sportsmanship turns an audience against a speaker. This includes the conduct of debaters at their tables while another person is speaking. Loud whispering, talking aloud, grimacing, noisy handling of papers, yawning, and other evidences of bad manners should be avoided.

Timekeepers. Most formal debates in this country are conducted according to customs or rules, one of which concerns the time limit of each speaker. Ten-minute constructive speeches and five-minute rebuttals are the most common. Rarely there is a three-minute intermission between the constructive series and the rebuttal series.

Two timekeepers, usually one from each of the competing schools, sit near the front and signal each speaker. During a ten-minute speech, the timekeepers display ten cards, changing them at one-minute intervals to show the remaining time. As the speaker begins, the card marked "10" is shown, and after one minute has elapsed, card "9" is shown, and so on. The expiration of the allotted time is indicated by the time-keepers' rising or by the use of an audible signal. The speakers and the timekeepers should "check signals" before the debate begins.

Properties. The stage setting for a debate customarily includes a table and the required number of chairs for each team, a chair for the presiding officer, and a speaker's stand. Occasionally, water pitchers and glasses are provided. It is customary to place the affirmative team on the right side of the platform. It is the left side as seen by the audience. Charts are sometimes added to the list of properties. The little they add to the effectiveness of a team can readily be offset by their susceptibility to damaging refutation. If a chart is used, it should be large enough for all to see and should be left in view until the debate is concluded.

EVALUATING A DEBATE

Criticism and judging. The criticism of a debate and the decision in a debate should not be confused. It is possible to have a criticism without a decision, and vice versa. In interscholastic debating, criticisms are rarely given without a decision. The decision is seldom accompanied by a critique when three judges are used, but a single critic judge customarily offers suggestions. This critique may be given in the presence of the audience or presented to the interested persons after the presiding officer has read the decision to the audience.

A competent, thorough criticism contributes greatly to the educational opportunities presented by a debate. After a debate in the classroom or on the public platform, such criticism should be given by someone whose understanding of argumentation and debate qualifies him to evaluate the work of the debaters. His function is that of a teacher.

Types of votes. There are three different kinds of decisions which can be given in debates. Each has its unique purpose, method, and meaning. The first of these is the legislative vote. The judge bases his decision upon the merits of the proposition; that is, he votes for the side in which he believes. This type of decision should not be given by a judge or a board of judges in school debates. The legislative vote belongs in legislative assemblies where policy-determining debate takes place.

However, in audience-decision debates, a legislative vote is used. This situation is different in that the average listener does not assume competence to give a critic's vote. The outcome should not be construed as a critical decision. If there is to be an expression of opinion from the audience, a legislative vote in the form of a shift-of-opinion ballot should be used. The Woodward ballot shown below is issued to each listener before the contest, and he records his general opinion before and after the debate.

BEFORE THE SPEECH   AFTER THE SPEECH

Mark only one Place

—YES (This expresses my belief on this question)

—I am UNDECIDED

—NO (This expresses my

I have heard the entire discussion, and now:

—The only change in my original opinion is that I am LESS SURE my opinion is right.

belief on the
question)

—The only change in my original opinion is that I am MORE SURE my opinion is right.
—My original opinion has been changed to YES.
—My original opinion has been changed to NO.
—My original opinion has been changed to UNDECIDED.
—NO CHANGE. I vote the same as before the speech.

A brief explanation of the scoring procedures is pertinent here. The point values of the several degrees of shift following a *single speech* in favor of a given policy are these:

from no to yes = 4
from no to undecided = 3
from undecided to yes = 1.5
from yes to more sure = 1
from no to less sure = 1
no change = 0
from yes to less sure = −1
from no to more sure = −1
from undecided to no = −1.5
from yes to undecided = −3
from yes to no = −4

For a *debate,* use the following formula instead of the foregoing. Whichever team has the larger numerical shift is the winner of the legislative decision.

Affirmative shift = $\dfrac{\text{number original no}}{\text{number original yes}}$ × (number shifted from yes to more sure) + (number shifted from no to less sure) + $\frac{3}{2}$ (number shifted from undecided to yes) + 3 (number shifted from no to undecided) + 4 (number shifted from no to yes).

Negative shift = (number shifted from no to more sure) + $\frac{3}{2}$ (number shifted from undecided to no) +

$$\frac{\text{number original no}}{\text{number original yes}} \times [(\text{number shifted from yes to less sure}) + 3 \text{ (number shifted from yes to undecided)} + 4 \text{ (number shifted from yes to no)}].$$

The juryman's vote, which is the second type, is one in which the decision is based solely upon the evidence submitted. In the opinion of the judge, the weight of evidence lies with the side to whom he awards his decision. Since the matters of evidence constitute only one of several criteria in school debates, a decision based solely upon the weight of evidence is obviously inadequate. Furthermore, the juryman's vote is suited to propositions of fact, not policy. Finally, in the juryman's vote the jury is under oath to vote for the negative unless the affirmative proves its case beyond a reasonable doubt. In a school debate the time limit might prevent the affirmative's proving its case so conclusively, and thus the negative would have an advantage.

The critic's vote, which is the third type, is based upon the quality of the debating. The judge indicates which team, in his opinion, did the more effective debating. This does not mean that he agrees with the arguments or the side of the winning team, or that one side had merely the greater weight of evidence. It is his educational job to point out the strong and the weak points of the debaters in terms of acceptable criteria such as those which appear in the ballot below. The debaters should be able to learn something about their activity as a result of this kind of decision. For this reason it is the best one to use in school debates.

Criticism blanks and rating scales. The critic's vote may be registered by the writing of one word ("Affirmative" or "Negative"), by giving credits for items on a score card, or by assigning quality ratings. The list of criteria may vary in length from four to ten items, but it should cover analysis and case, evidence, attack and defense, and delivery. Below are types of ballots used in tournaments.[2]

Instructions to critics. If an unqualified person is asked on short notice to judge a school debate, it is unlikely that a set of instructions will improve his performance to an acceptable level.

[2] Used by permission of the American Forensic Association.

American Forensic Association Debate Ballot

FORM **C**

vision _____ Round _____ Room _____ Date _____ Judge _____

irmative _____ Negative _____

heck the column on each item which, according to the following scale, best describes your eval-
tion of the speaker's effectiveness, and indicate the RANK for each speaker in the space following
name.

| 1—poor | 2—fair | 3—adequate | 4—good | 5—superior |

	1st Affirmative	2nd Affirmative	1st Negative	2nd Negative
	1 2 3 4 5	1 2 3 4 5	1 2 3 4 5	1 2 3 4 5
alysis				
asoning & vidence				
ganization				
utation *				
livery				
	Total _____	Total _____	Total _____	Total _____

a cross-examination debate, this should incorporate evaluation of the cross-examination.

am Ratings: AFFIRMATIVE: poor fair adequate good superior
NEGATIVE: poor fair adequate good superior

MMENTS:
Aff. (name) _____ RANK ( )

COMMENTS:
1st Neg. (name) _____ RANK ( )

Aff. (name) _____ RANK ( )

2nd Neg. (name) _____ RANK ( )

ny opinion, the better debating was done by the _____
(AFFIRMATIVE OR NEGATIVE)

JUDGE'S SIGNATURE   SCHOOL

American Forensic Association Debate Ballot

FORM **D**

Division............... Round................ Room.............. Date............. Judge...............................

Affirmative... Negative...............................

INSTRUCTIONS

Rank the debaters in their order of excellence in this debate: 1 for best, 2 for second best, 3 for third best and **4** for least best.

Rate the effectiveness of each debater in a manner similar to the way you grade in school; i.e., A, B, C., etc. However, on the ballot use rating points as indicated by the following table:

A+ = 15;	B+ = 12;	C+ = 9;	D+ = 6;	E+ = 3;
A = 14;	B = 11;	C = 8;	D = 5;	E = 2;
A— = 13;	B— = 10;	C— = 7;	D— = 4;	E— = 1.

Name	Rank	Rating points
1st Affirmative	....	....
2nd Affirmative	....	....
1st Negative	....	....
2nd Negative	....	....

(NOTE: Rank and Rating points should correlate with the decision; i.e., the winning team should receive the higher total in rating points and get the lower total in ranking. In close debates the rank might be tied but the rating points should favor the winning team.)

COMMENTS:

1st Aff.:

COMMENTS:

1st Neg.:

2nd Aff.:

2nd Neg.:

In my opinion, the better debating was done by the ....

(AFFIRMATIVE OR NEGATIVE)

JUDGE'S SIGNATURE   SCHOOL

However, some educators issue instructions to presumably qualified judges with the view to standardizing the procedures and
making certain that the students are evaluated on specific criteria
which are deemed important. Each critic judge who serves in the
televised high-school tournament described in the next section of
this chapter is given in advance some printed instructions similar
to the following:

1. Particular attention should be paid to evaluating the effectiveness with which the debaters adapt their arguments and evidence to
the television audience. They are instructed to adapt to the television
audience, not to the judges or other people in the studio.

2. An argument is to be considered established if it is supported by
evidence and reasoning sufficient to convince an intelligent but previously uninformed person that it is more reasonable to believe the
argument than to disbelieve it.

    a. You should base your decision entirely on the materials pre-
sented, *without regard for other materials with which you may be
acquainted.*

    b. Since you are to decide which of the two teams did the bet-
ter job of debating, and not the "truth" inherent in one position or another, you should *accept as true all arguments supported by reasonable
proof until such arguments are refuted by the opposing team.*

    c. You should not accept statements unsupported by reasonable
proof.

    d. You should not expect the debaters to use as much evidence
as they would present in a standard debate. Evaluate the adequacy of
evidence in terms of the limited time available to the debaters.

3. When arguments may be introduced

    a. Each team's arguments must be introduced in the constructive
speech.

    b. New arguments must not be introduced in the rebuttal
speeches; however, additional evidence in support of arguments introduced in the constructive speeches may be presented in the rebuttal
speeches.

4. The following procedure is to be followed by the participants in
the cross-examination period:

    a. The questioner may ask any fair, clear question that has a di-
rect bearing on the debate. The questioner may use the period (1) to
build up any part of his own case, (2) to tear down any part of the
opposition's case, or (3) to ascertain information, such as the opposi-

338 · DEBATE AS TRAINING

tion's position on a certain issue, that can be used later in the debate.

b. The questioner controls the time. He may interrupt the respondent to request shorter or more direct answers, or to indicate that the answer is sufficient.

c. The questioner must confine himself to questions and not make statements or comments.

d. The respondent must answer every question unless he can show that it would be unfair or unreasonable to expect him to answer.

e. The respondent may request that the question be repeated or rephrased if it is not clear.

f. The respondent must give answers as short and clear as the questions warrant, but he is not confined to yes-or-no answers.

g. *The respondent must confine himself to answers,* and not question the questioner or make comments on other subjects.

h. A debater should be penalized for rudeness.

5. Guard against the following errors in judging:

a. Voting for the team upholding the position in which you believe.

b. Holding preconceived opinions about how a particular position should be developed and penalizing a team for not developing it according to these opinions.

c. Being unduly influenced by arguments dealing with subjects of special interest to you.

d. Stressing one aspect of debating out of proportion to its importance and then rewarding or penalizing the debater more than he deserves for excellence or weakness in this regard. Avoid placing too much emphasis on delivery or personality and not enough on content.

e. Being unduly influenced by the last rebuttal or underestimating its importance.

f. Being swayed by such irrelevant factors as the sex of the speaker, the reputation of the school which the speaker represents, and the personal mannerisms, quality of voice, dress, or appearance of the speaker.[3]

Possibly one more item of instruction or interpretation would serve to reduce the confusion and bickering surrounding the judging of a school debate in which the affirmative fails to complete a prima-facie case. In a *judicial* debate, especially before a

[3] Prepared by Frank Nelson for "Rebuttal" on CBS-WBBM-TV, Chicago, 1962.

judge, the affirmative loses if it does not present a prima-facie case. However, a school debate is frequently judged in terms of *several* criteria, such as we have seen in Form C of the A.F.A. ballot. To vote against an affirmative which lost on only the "analysis" criterion means that a weight of more than 50 per cent has been assigned to that single criterion. Clearly, the affirmative which ignored a vital element should lose on the "analysis" criterion, even if the negative failed to comment on the omission; but this does not mean that the affirmative must inevitably lose on all or most of the five criteria. On the other hand, a negative which ignores or comments weakly upon a serious omission should be penalized, albeit somewhat less, under "Refutation."

Even if some critic judges still insist upon assigning a weight of more than 50 per cent to "analysis," we think there is one circumstance in which this view is mistaken, and that is when the negative is caught lying, as in the case of fabricating evidence. Our assumption is that an ethical breach is worse than a logical one. According to this view, the guilty team, whether affirmative or negative, must lose even when clearly ahead on all other counts.

TYPES OF SCHOOL
DEBATE

Definition of school debate. We use the term "school debate" to designate the various types of this activity which may be undertaken for the purposes of informing an audience on public questions and training students in certain speech skills. It should be understood that debate and some types of discussion are more often used as policy-determining techniques in legislative, forensic, and political deliberation. The chief purpose of educational speech activities is to develop attitudes and skills which will enable individuals to participate more competently in the important discussions and debates of life.

Discussion-debate modification

Three-team debate. A slight modification of debate in the direction of discussion is seen in a debate among three sides or teams, each of which supports a solution or plan. The three positions may be a defense of the plan embodied in the proposition, a defense of the status quo, and a defense of a counterproposition or alternative plan. The element of intentional reasoning, which is inherent in advocacy, is present in this modified form of debate. Assuming that team A represents the status quo, team B defends the proposed plan, and team C advocates an alternative plan, the following sequence of speeches might be used:

First speaker of B team attacks the status quo for 8 minutes.
First speaker of A team defends the status quo for 8 minutes.
First speaker of C team attacks the status quo for 8 minutes.
Second speaker of B team advocates the proposed plan for 12 minutes.
Second speaker of A team defends status quo against the B plan for 12 minutes.
Second speaker of C team advocates the alternative plan for 12 minutes.
First speaker of C team attacks the B plan for 8 minutes.
First speaker of A team attacks the C plan for 8 minutes.
First speaker of B team attacks the C plan for 8 minutes.

Debate-forum. The open-forum debate commonly consists of any of the other types followed by a discussion in which the audience participates. Questions are directed to specific speakers through the presiding officer of the debate. The chairman has discretionary authority to rule out questions, to restate questions, to assign questions to speakers, and to call for certain types of questions. The open-forum debate is usually a no-decision contest. It is a modification toward discussion in the degree that audience participation takes place in the final stage.

Parliamentary session debate.[4] Several educational debate procedures have been patterned after the parliamentary methods of policy-determining groups. This one, as developed at Pennsylvania State College, requires a chairman, a secretary, four discussion leaders, and an audience. After the chairman opens the meeting and states the question, the first visiting speaker gives an

[4] See J. F. O'Brien, "The Place of Extra-Curricular Speech in the College or University of Today, *Quarterly Journal of Speech,* November, 1935, pp. 583–584.

eight-minute committee report on the matter of "evils" and their sources. If no "evils" are reported, the discussion is on the validity of the report. If "evils" are reported, the speaker moves the adoption of a solution. A second visiting speaker then talks for eight minutes on the plausibility of the solution. Next, each of the two-home-team speakers has eight minutes in which to support, amend, or offer a substitute motion. Since no debate can take place if four speakers support the one motion, the home team might plan to offer an amendment and a substitute motion, or a substitute motion and its defense. After thirty-two minutes of platform speaking, the discussion is opened to the assembly.

English debate.[5] Visiting debaters from Oxford and Cambridge have attracted considerable attention in American forensic circles because of their unusual practices. The most noticeable of these are their use of entertaining wit and philosophic-literary style, their easy platform manner, their lack of teamwork, and, more fundamentally, their attitude toward the contest situation. This attitude, which is foreign to American debaters, is observable in the Oxonians' behavior. They are unusually open-minded in their concessions of points, their readiness to praise an opponent's ideas, and their general indifference to pugnacity. Their preparation is brief and casual; they do not use "set" case outlines and card-index boxes, and they are not directed by a faculty sponsor.

These differences, which are dramatized whenever English and American debaters meet, stem from the practices of the Oxford Union Society. Hundreds of students from twenty-odd colleges of Oxford meet to discuss major public questions in this old literary-social club. It duplicates the House of Commons in that it has a chairman's dais, benches for the government and the opposition, party leaders and "aye" and "no" exits. Each of the four main speakers for the evening is assigned to the side in which he believes. Evening dress is customary. Without much reference to his colleague, he speaks fifteen or more minutes without a prepared brief or manuscript. A note from the secretary is the only notification of the elapsed time. The occurrence of heckling and the fact

[5] See *Quarterly Journal of Speech Education,* June, 1923, pp. 215–222; *ibid.,* February, 1925, pp. 45–48; *Quarterly Journal of Speech,* February, 1948, pp. 46–53.

that the audience will vote serve to make the speaker use wit, informality, and general persuasion instead of debate evidence in the American sense. After an open-forum period, the audience divides and votes by exits—not on debating excellence, but on the merits of the question. The motivation for this activity is the possibility of a career in public life.

Some persons have become enamored of the Oxford Union style and have advocated its adoption in place of our present programs. But there is a possibility that the foreign procedure is overrated. An American Rhodes Scholar and a don of Balliol College have agreed that most of the speaking in the Oxford Union Debating Society is very dull.[6]

British and American debaters who have recently exchanged visits have pointed out additional differences between the practices in the two countries. In the Cambridge and Oxford Unions, as well as in Parliament, all remarks are addressed to the President or the Speaker. The members of student societies occasionally invite outside speakers of distinction to participate in debates. There is always an audience of at least fifty or sixty persons for the weekly debates, each one of which lasts longer than an American intercollegiate contest. In this connection, it is interesting to note that the Unions do not engage in inter-university forensics or have more than one debate on a proposition, except when two of their members tour this country for fees.

An American version of the English-style debate involves changes which impose time limits, maintain orderly procedure, and equalize participation. From four to eight persons are required to assume responsibility for the delivery of speeches. The following are eleven rules of procedure:

(1) The President calls the House to order and announces the motion for debate.

(2) Ten-minute speech by a previously designated speaker moving the adoption of the motion.

(3) Ten-minute speech by a previously designated speaker opposing the motion.

[6] "Oxford: Two Views in Vivid Contrast," *New York Times Magazine,* April 30, 1950.

(4) Seven-minute speech by a previously designated speaker seconding the adoption of the motion.

(5) Seven-minute speech by a previously designated speaker opposing the motion.

(6) At this point the floor is open to any member of the House who desires to speak. The time limit on these speeches is five minutes. No member may speak more than once, points of order or information excepted. Members favoring the motion and those opposing it speak alternately. The President indicates the side entitled to the floor by announcing, "I will now recognize a speaker for the motion," or "I will now recognize a speaker opposed to the motion." (In so far as practicable, each school represented splits its delegation so that it has an equal number of speakers favoring and opposing the motion.)

(7) Any speaker except the one who opens the debate may be interrupted by any member of the House at any time. Such interruptions take one of two forms. (1) If the rules have been infringed, a member is entitled to rise and point this out to the President, at the same time describing the infringement which he believes to have taken place. (2) The second type of interruption permitted is a direct request for information addressed to the speaker who has the floor. To make this sort of interruption a member must first rise to his feet in such a manner as to attract discreetly the attention of the President. The speaker, if he wishes to be interrupted, will sit down. If he does not sit down, and ignores the member who desired to interrupt, the latter must resume his seat. An interruption on a point of information must be made in the form of a question, and is addressed to the speaker through the President. The interrupter may not himself impart information to the House; he may only seek to elicit information from the speaker. The President will rule the speaker out of order if his interruption does not constitute a genuine request for information.

(8) The debate on the motion proceeds in the fashion outlined for one hour and thirty minutes, at which time the speaker who originally moved the adoption of the resolution presents a five-minute speech answering the arguments which have been presented against it and summarizing the discussion. Immediately following this speech there is a division of the House. Abstentions are intimated by informing the tellers. The numbers having then added up, the President announces the results from the Chair.

(9) Members favoring the motion sit facing those who oppose it, the former ranging themselves on the President's right, the latter on his left . . .

344 · Debate as Training

(10) The speeches are clocked by a timekeeper. Members must bring their remarks to a close upon receiving his signal.

(11) A member may speak on any phase of the subject he desires. The President will, however, rule out of order any member who attempts to introduce material which is obviously not germane to the discussion.[7]

Problem-solving debate.[8] The schemes of problem-solving debate provide for three sets of speeches (analysis, solution, and evaluation) by two teams of two or three speakers each. The problem is phrased as a question rather than a proposition. All of the speakers attempt to solve the problem, and in doing so they may agree or disagree with any other speaker, including their own colleagues. Those who favor this mixed type of procedure say that it provides greater freedom to argue one's convictions, it encourages reflective and cooperative thinking, it prevents the choosing of sides too soon, it informs audiences more effectively, and it provides excellent early-season practice for school debaters. However, unless some precaution is taken to organize teams whose convictions on the problem are identified with different proposals, there may be no semblance of a debate.

The sequence and functions of speakers require special attention. "Analysis" speakers attempt to interpret the question, to set out what they conceive to be the disturbing factors and their causes, and to develop criteria by which solutions may be judged. Each "solution" speaker explains and defends a solution which his team believes to be the most satisfactory in terms of the analysis of the problem. The function of an "evaluation" speaker is to compare and evaluate the proposals. His responsibility is not to attack or defend any proposal, but rather to interpret, compare, and evaluate in terms of available evidence and argument. According to one version of the problem-solving debate, two "analysis" speakers have ten minutes each, two "solution" speakers have twelve minutes each, and two "evaluation" speakers have eight

---

[7] D. Ehninger, "Outline of Procedure for the English-Style of Debate," *The Gavel*, copyright March, 1948. Used by permission of Delta Sigma Rho.

[8] See F. W. Orr and A. L. Franzke, "The University of Washington Plan of Problem-Solving Debate," *Bulletin of the University of Washington* (Extension Series), No. 8, January, 1938.

minutes each. This scheme is often modified to include only one "analysis" speech, from two to four "solution" speeches, and only one "evaluation" speech. The latter sequence eliminates any possibility of repetitious speeches in the first and third stages, and it provides for the introduction of more than two solutions. If periods of questioning are desired, the following order would be followed by two-man teams: (1) an eight-minute analysis by the first speaker of team A, (2) an eight-minute solution by the first speaker of team B, (3) a five-minute questioning of the first speaker of team B by the second speaker of team A, (4) an eight-minute solution by the second speaker of team A, (5) a five-minute questioning of the second speaker of team A by the first speaker of team B, (6) an eight-minute evaluation by the second speaker of team B.

Student congress or legislature.[9] Like the problem-solving debate, the student congress or legislative assembly works on one or more problems rather than a proposition. The students' investigation consists in a study of the subjects, which are announced two months prior to the opening of the session. The purpose of this investigation is to analyze the problems and to consider solutions, to the end of drawing a bill or resolution which will be introduced in the meetings. On an intercollegiate basis, individual school delegations come prepared to introduce and defend their respective bills. The delegates need to understand committee work, parliamentary procedure, and other details of routine in addition to the subject-matter aspects of the assembly.

The National Student Congress of Delta Sigma Rho usually involves a three-day series of meetings, including the opening assembly, preliminary committee meetings, main committee meetings, joint conference committee meetings, and general assemblies. The opening assembly provides for the election of a speaker of the house, the appointment of a parliamentarian, and the announcement of committee assignments. In subsequent committee meetings the bills which have been brought in by the several delegations are analyzed, discussed, and reported out as one bill

---

[9] See L. S. Judson, ed., *The Student Congress Movement* (New York: the H. W. Wilson Company, 1940); also *The Gavel* of Delta Sigma Rho.

per committee. Minority reports may be made also. The ensuing general assemblies take action on the committee proposals under the usual rules of parliamentary procedure. This pattern may be varied in terms of the number of problems discussed, the length of the session, the number of houses (unicameral or bicameral), and the rules of procedure.

This type of educational speech activity provides a variety of experiences in conversation, discussion, debate, and in giving nominating speeches. The benefits of research and democratic participation are equally obvious. However, serious limitations become apparent if committee chairmen are unskilled, if a few dominant students hold the floor, or if parliamentary wrangling supplants sincere deliberation.

Forensic experience progressions. Several combinations of discussion, extemporaneous speaking, and debate have been used in lieu of intercollegiate tournaments. An intercollegiate conference held at Northwestern University in 1945 included a lecture-forum, a series of round tables corresponding to the steps in reflective thinking, a parliamentary meeting to frame resolutions, an extemporaneous speaking contest, and three rounds of debating. The number of round tables may vary from three to six or more.

The forensic experience progression, as developed by Elwood Murray, includes three forum-panel discussions, one extemporaneous talk, and six one-man-team debates, organized around five subtopics as indicated in the following stages. Each student's work in each stage is rated by a critic. The first is the problem phase, in which a forum-panel discussion takes place on the question, "What is the problem, and to what extent is it significant?" Each participant presents a five-to-seven-minute speech of definition, analysis, and interpretation. This includes (1) the nature and extent of the problem, (2) analysis of divergent points of view, (3) possible future effects, and (4) the speaker's personal "stake" in the matter. Following the talks, each participant is allowed five minutes in which to comment on other talks and to defend or modify his own position. The chairman conducts a forum at the end of each phase.

As a continuation of the problem phase, the second stage is

conducted as a formal panel discussion on the question, "What are the major causes of the problem?" The speaking procedure of the first stage is continued, but the analysis is deeper. Each talk is concerned with these points: (1) origin and causes of the problem, (2) the accepted criteria for the evaluation of any solution, and (3) the differences in criteria which must be resolved.

The third stage, called the solution phase, consists in a series of extemporaneous talks on the question, "What are the solutions to the problem?" Each person has five to seven minutes in which to outline solutions but not to argue them. All speakers after the first may need to adapt their remarks to prevent repetition.

Continuing the solution phase, the fourth stage involves debates on the question, "What is the best solution?" A proposition is formulated by the speakers and the critic at the end of the third stage. Each speaker chooses a solution which he will advocate in the fourth stage. He will engage in six debates, in three of which he defends his plan and in three of which he opposes other plans. An affirmative speaker is allowed periods of six, six, and three minutes. A negative speaker is allowed periods of eight and seven minutes.

Stage five, the action phase, is conducted as a forum-panel discussion on "What, as citizens, will be our program to put into effect the necessary remedies?" The speaking procedure is the same as that in stages one and two. Each talk includes (1) a statement of the effects of participation upon the speaker's thinking, (2) a summary of his favorite solution, (3) an indication of the obstacles to be confronted by this solution, (4) proposed procedure to deal with obstacles, and (5) an outline of the speaker's program for preparing himself for action on the problem.

Debate symposium.[10] The debate symposium provides for four two-man teams. The first speaker for each team states his team's position, and the subsequent speakers may amplify their colleagues' remarks, cross examine any of the speakers of the other teams, refute any of the preceding arguments, or restate and summarize their own positions. A forum for audience participation usually follows the series of debate speeches.

[10] See H. F. Harding, "A Debate Symposium," *The Speaker,* Vol. XX, May, 1938, p. 6.

Cooperative investigation.[11]   In the cooperative investigation, a problem is analyzed in a manner similar to that of Dewey's steps in problem-solving. Each of the six speakers is given a topic. The first three topics relate to "understanding the problem," and the last three pertain to "suggested solutions." The first three speeches are explanatory and investigative, whereas the last three are advocatory.

Intercollegiate forum.[12]   The intercollegiate forum provides for a group of four speakers, the first of whom explains the background and present status of the problem. Each successive speaker then presents a proposed solution and restates or refutes other plans. One need not maintain his original point of view, as in a traditional debate; in fact, he may withdraw his proposal and defend that of another speaker. This is a mixture of debate and discussion for these reasons: (1) it includes advocacy, (2) it provides for definition and analysis of a problem, (3) it presupposes the introduction of several proposals, and (4) it permits the modification of one's original position.

Variations in traditional debate

Two-man debate.   A convenient short form of the traditional debate for classroom use is that in which only two persons speak. This permits debating when team work is difficult to arrange. The affirmative opens the debate with a ten-minute constructive speech, the negative replies with a fourteen-minute rejoinder, and the affirmative closes the debate with a four-minute rebuttal. These time limits may be changed to suit the occasion, but each side must have the same amount of time. The chief variation in method lies in the negative rejoinder, which includes attack and defense in one speech.

Two-man teams.   Traditional debates ordinarily take place between affirmative and negative teams of two or three speakers each. The trend in school and college debating is toward the exclusive use of two-man teams in contest situations. A typical arrangement of speeches is as follows:

[11] See H. L. Ewbank, "The Wisconsin Public Discussion Contest," *The Gavel*, Vol. XX, May, 1938, p. 54.
[12] See A. B. Williamson, "A Proposed Change in Intercollegiate Debating," *The Quarterly Journal of Speech*, Vol. XIX, February, 1933, pp. 192, 200–202.

Constructive Speeches

First affirmative .... 10 minutes
First negative .... 10 minutes
Second affirmative .... 10 minutes
Second negative .... 10 minutes

Rebuttal Speeches

First negative .... 5 minutes
First affirmative .... 5 minutes
Second negative .... 5 minutes
Second affirmative .... 5 minutes

The affirmative opens the constructive speeches, and the negative opens the rebuttal speeches. In other words, the affirmative opens and closes the debate, and the negative has two consecutive speeches in the midst of the debate. The first affirmative states the proposition, gives the affirmative interpretation of it, and develops the affirmative answer to at least one issue. The following negative speaker must react to the preceding speaker's interpretation and reply to the opponent's argument. The affirmative's interpretation must be scrutinized to make sure that it places a legitimate construction upon the language of the proposition. The second speakers on both sides will offer necessary refutation, complete their constructive arguments, and summarize briefly. Rebuttal speakers will attempt to attack opposing arguments, to defend their constructive arguments, and to focus the debate upon the contested issues.

Short forms for radio and television. When a half-hour period on the air is available, the speaking time is likely to be somewhat less—perhaps twenty-five minutes. The following distribution of time has been used for several seasons of thirty-one weeks each in the WBBM-TV and Northwestern University high-school debate tournament:

First affirmative constructive speech .... 5 minutes
Second negative questions the first affirmative 3 minutes
First negative constructive speech .... 5 minutes
Second affirmative questions the first negative 3 minutes

Consultation break in which student journalists report and debaters plan rebuttals	2½ minutes
Second-negative rebuttal	3 minutes
Second-affirmative rebuttal	3 minutes

Instructions to participating teams stress the importance of adapting their language, delivery, evidence, and reasoning to the television audience. There is, in addition, an explicit rule that the affirmative on a proposition of policy shall present only a "need" case. Thus, there is no contest on "plan" or "advantages."

One-rebuttal debate. This simple variation of the traditional debate reduces the length to forty minutes and still utilizes four debaters. It encourages adaptation and rebuttal throughout the debate, since three of the speakers have no other opportunity to present refutation. The schedule of speeches may be arranged as follows:

Constructive Speeches

First affirmative	5 minutes
First negative	10 minutes
Second affirmative	10 minutes
Second negative	10 minutes

Rebuttal Speech

First affirmative	5 minutes

Split-team debate. In an effort to remove the element of institutional rivalry between debate teams, this deviation from the traditional debate was developed. One serious defect, however, is the difficulty or impossibility of teamwork and serious effort. If one considers team activity an important aspect of debating, he will not care to have competing schools or societies exchange one speaker unless there has been ample time for thorough collaboration before the contest.

Cross question debate.[13] This is a more radical departure from the traditional type of educational debate in that it includes

[13] See J. S. Gray, "The Oregon Plan of Debating," *Quarterly Journal of Speech Education,* April, 1926, pp. 175–179.

constructive speeches, periods of cross-questioning by opponents, and rebuttal summaries. The following schedule of speeches involves four debaters and requires eighty minutes:

First affirmative presents an entire case	20	minutes
First negative questions the first affirmative	10	minutes
Second negative presents an entire case	20	minutes
Second affirmative questions the second negative	10	minutes
First negative presents rebuttal	10	minutes
Second affirmative presents rebuttal	10	minutes

The schedule above may be modified for classroom use by reducing the case speeches to twelve minutes each, the questioning periods to four minutes each, and the rebuttals to five minutes each. Three-man teams may be used if the third speaker on each team gives the rebuttal summary. Still another schedule enables each speaker to join in the cross examination:

First affirmative speech	10	minutes
Cross examination by second negative	3–5	minutes
First negative speech	10	minutes
Cross examination by first affirmative	3–5	minutes
Second affirmative speech	10	minutes
Cross examination by first negative	3–5	minutes
Second negative speech	10	minutes
Cross examination by second affirmative	3–5	minutes
Negative rebuttal summary	5	minutes
Affirmative rebuttal summary	5	minutes

Since the most unusual aspect of this type of debate is the question-and-answer period, we shall offer some suggestions for conducting it. The time belongs to the questioner for use in drawing out the respondent, but not for the delivery of a speech. Questions and answers must be brief and clear. The respondent may request a restatement of an unclear question, and the questioner may insist upon brief answers. The questioner should lead up to the admission of a premise or an analogy, but he should not press for a final admission; it can be deduced in rebuttal. This type of debate, perhaps more than any other, demands for its success an attitude of fair play and an honest attempt to get at the real issues. The participants must be courteous and abide by rulings from the chair, rather than indulging in quibbling about procedure. It is better to reserve direct rebuttal for the final period, in which one deals with the final bearing of the cases, the answers, and ignored questions. Since the purpose of questions is to get at analysis, evidence, and inference, it is advisable to group one's questions under the case headings. Obviously, a questioner must be ready to adapt to any of the possible answers which may be given. Finally, both speakers should stand near the lectern and speak loudly enough for all to hear.

It is apparent that this type has certain advantages and limitations. One advantage is the considerable audience interest which is stimulated by the similarity to hearings and trials, the spontaneous adaptations which are made, and the sharp focus upon contested points. Another advantage, in terms of the training of speakers, is the necessity of careful preparation. As we pointed out earlier, the question-and-answer period will degenerate into mere bickering unless there is fair play and an honest effort to deal with issues. Then, too, the debaters should adjust their questions to the opposing case and make some use of the answers. In short, the technique of questioning is vital.

Direct-clash debate.[14] This departure from the traditional debate form was first tried in the season of 1931–1932. In addition to providing variety in the forensic program, it disciplines debaters in extemporaneous speaking and in clashing directly on the point at issue.

Although the same propositions that are used in other debates may be used in the direct clash, there are differences in the size of teams and in the method of judging. A team may consist of no more than five and no fewer than two debaters, and opposing teams need not be of equal size. The speaking order need not be fixed, but no one may speak twice in succession during a clash, and no one may begin successive clashes. If the unique scoring procedure which is described later is not used, the debate may be a nondecision or an audience-vote affair.

[14] See Edwin H. Paget, "Rules for the Direct Clash Debate Plan," *Quarterly Journal of Speech,* October, 1937, p. 431.

The opening phase of the debate consists in definition and analysis by both sides. An affirmative speaker has eight minutes in which to define terms, explain the proposed plan, and set forth what his team believes to be the issues. Proofs are not advanced in this phase. A negative speaker then has eight minutes in which to indicate the issues which his side accepts for clash and to outline a counterproposition if one is to be used. Thus the debate is limited to those issues upon which disagreement exists. If the clash is on only one issue, it must be subdivided for use in subsequent phases.

Following the two eight-minute speeches, each side may speak for another three minutes to clarify some points or, in the case of the affirmative, to indicate its attitude toward the counterproposition. In some tournaments these two stages are replaced by a general meeting in which clash points are selected.

The first clash is opened by an affirmative speaker in a three- or four-minute speech which presents a point in partition or one of its main subpoints within an issue upon which the teams have agreed to clash. The judge is instructed to penalize a team for presenting irrelevant or inconsequential points. The first negative speaker has two minutes for a pointed reply to the specific argument of the preceding speaker. The second affirmative must then, in two minutes, answer directly the first negative. This exchange continues until each side has given three two-minute speeches. The closing speech is a two-minute, affirmative summary. Hence, the total elapsed time is fifteen or sixteen minutes per clash.

At the end of each speech after the first five minutes, the chairman shall await a signal from the critic judge before allowing the debate to proceed. This permits the judge to terminate the clash and award a point to the team whose opponent replied weakly, dodged the point, or shifted ground. An even clash is allowed to continue for seven speeches before a decision is given on the merits of the debating.

The second clash is opened by the negative, and the routine continues as in the first clash. No point may be initiated twice in a series of clashes, except that the side losing a clash may initiate the same one again.

The affirmative and the negative alternate in initiating clashes until one side has won three. The judge may waive the score-by-points rule if he believes that one team has conceded or has won the all-important point in the debate. If no critic judge is used, each side shall present two or three points, and each clash shall continue for seven speeches. A shift-of-opinion ballot may be used to obtain an audience decision.

Mock trial.[15] This plan grew out of a search for new and interesting varieties of public-speaking events for off-campus audiences. In essence it is a modified jury trial based upon a debate proposition. Its appeal may be traced to the dramatization of conflicting ideas. In one of the experimental debates an injunction was sought restraining the United States from protecting, by armed force, the lives and properties of her nationals abroad in the event of foreign war. Three students who carried major roles represented the judge of the court, the Attorney General of the United States, and the attorney seeking the injunction for the plaintiff. Seven minor roles were those of three witnesses for the plaintiff, three for the defense, and a bailiff. Each witness represented a prominent authority and confined his testimony to statements of historical fact or to the printed statements of the person he represented. Some witnesses impersonated the originals. The bailiff opened court and swore in the witnesses. Twelve members of the audience served as jurors.

The following is a sketch of the procedure:

1. The bailiff calls the court to order.
2. The judge gives a three-minute speech on the background of the question (as in a first affirmative speech).
3. The attorney for the plaintiff has three minutes in which to outline the case he hopes to establish through the examination of his witnesses.
4. The attorney for the defense has three minutes for a similar presentation.
5. The attorney for the plaintiff calls his three witnesses singly. He may have four minutes for the direct examination of each. The

[15] See Warren Guthrie, "The Reserve Plan for Intercollegiate Discussion," *Quarterly Journal of Speech*, October, 1939, pp. 392–396; also *University Debaters' Annual*, 1937–1938 (New York: H. W. Wilson Company), pp. 327–388.

attorney for the defense may ask three questions of each witness in cross examination.

6. The same plan is followed for the defense.
7. The attorney for the defense has three minutes in which to summarize his case and make a final plea to the jury for the rejection of the injunction.
8. The attorney for the plaintiff makes a similar summary and plea for the granting of the injunction.
9. The judge instructs the jury to decide the case solely on the evidence and to return a verdict.

If the proposition calls for the adoption of a new policy instead of the abandonment of an old one, a decree of specific performance or a writ of mandamus may be sought by the plaintiff.

Heckling debate.[16] The practice of heckling opponents is not new, but the procedure described here was introduced into intercollegiate debating in 1926. The originator sought to stimulate interest among debaters and audiences by introducing a life-situation element which intensifies conflict. Perhaps there is "never a dull moment" in such contests, but there is some danger that the exchanges will degenerate into a chaotic wrangle in which the speakers as well as the audience will become lost. At least this is not the type for novices.

The following principles or rules have been offered for the conduct of heckling debates:

1. The speaking order is first affirmative, first negative, second negative, and second affirmative. Each one has ten minutes (or fifteen to eighteen if agreed upon in advance) to present a speech and answer a heckler. There are no rebuttals.
2. Only the heckled speaker may reply. Each debater is assigned to heckle one opponent. Team members may confer quietly.
3. Before asking his first question, a heckler rises, asks the chair for permission to speak, and turns to face the speaker. He reseats himself during the reply. Thereafter the heckler does not address the chair.
4. The speaker should resume the speech as soon as he has answered a question briefly, pertinently, and politely.

[16] See Charles H. McReynolds, "A New System of Debate," *Quarterly Journal of Speech*, February, 1940, pp. 6–11.

5. The chairman should insist upon brief and pointed questions, he should curtail heckling if audience interest is jeopardized, and he should enforce the rules of courtesy.
6. Heckling should be aimed at developed points, not isolated sentences. Its purpose is to get at vital matters, not merely to harass a speaker. Interruptions are sometimes restricted to a five-minute period in the middle of each speech. In this case the last affirmative must not use a new argument in the nonheckling period.

Direct-question or dialectic debate.[17]   The essence of this procedure is that the constructive speeches are replaced by dialogues between colleagues. It may be used with the cross-question or other types of debate. Although it has possibilities in variety and audience interest, there is a problem of maintaining unity and continuity.

In an experimental debate in 1935, the affirmative used fifteen minutes to present their case through a dialogue between the two colleagues. This team was then cross-examined by the negative for ten minutes. Following this, the negative developed their case in a fifteen-minute dialogue and were cross-examined by the affirmative for ten minutes. One negative speaker and one affirmative speaker concluded the debate with five-minute summaries.

Congressional-style debate.[18]   A combination of the usual procedure, cross-questioning, and heckling was developed at Purdue University about 1931. The number of speakers is variable, but two-speaker teams are recommended. The time limit of constructive speeches is twelve minutes, one-third of which may be used for heckling by the opposition. At any time after the third minute of the speech of either team's first speaker, heckling may commence. The limit is three interruptions per speech, but more than one question may be asked during one interruption. If interrupted in his last minute, a speaker shall have an extra minute for a conclusion. Each rebuttal speaker is allotted six minutes, one minute

[17] See C. P. Lahman, *Debate Coaching* (New York: The H. W. Wilson Company, 1936), pp. 34–35.
[18] *Ibid.*, pp. 35–36.

of which may be used for an interruption by an opponent, and the remaining five minutes are available for rebuttal or cross-examination of the opposition. The last rebuttal speaker on each side shall not be interrupted during his last two minutes. Two timers are needed—one for speakers and one for interrupters. The order of speakers is the same as that in a traditional debate.

Tournaments. Tournament debate is not essentially another type. Rather, it is a scheme which enables several schools to secure numerous debates for their teams in a short time and at less cost per debate. In every season there are countless one-day and two-day tournaments, usually during Fridays and Saturdays. The host school invites each visiting school to furnish one or more units, each one consisting of a judge and two or four debaters. In some cases each team remains on one side, while in others the teams alternate sides.

The schedule is usually divided into three or more rounds. Under the heading of each round are posted the affirmative teams, the negative teams, the judges, the rooms, the chairman-time-keepers, etc. The most difficult part of this scheduling is the pairing of teams and the assigning of judges so that no teams meet each other more than once, and so that a judge does not hear one team twice or judge a team before his own team meets it. The following scheme of pairing teams allows the preparation of brackets in advance, even if the number of schools exceeds or falls short of the expected number. The important point is that each four-man delegation be given a number upon arrival.

ROUND I			ROUND II	
Aff – Neg	*J*		*Aff – Neg*	*J*
1 – 3	2		1 – 5	3
2 – 4	3		2 – 6	4
3 – 5	4		3 – 7	5
4 – 6	5		4 – 8	6
5 – 7	6		5 – 9	7
6 – 8	7		6 – 1	8
7 – 9	8		7 – 2	9
8 – 1	9		8 – 3	1
9 – 2	1		9 – 4	2

ROUND III		ROUND IV	
Aff – Neg	*J*	*Aff – Neg*	*J*
1 – 7	4	1 – 9	5
2 – 8	5	2 – 1	6
3 – 9	6	3 – 2	7
4 – 1	7	4 – 3	8
5 – 2	8	5 – 4	9
6 – 3	9	6 – 5	1
7 – 4	1	7 – 6	2
8 – 5	2	8 – 7	3
9 – 6	3	9 – 8	4

This basic pattern can be adapted to more rounds and more school units. It has been used in five rounds for forty schools and in four rounds for seventy schools competing at Northwestern University. In case a school enters more than one unit, then numbers at least ten points apart should be assigned to those units before other schools draw numbers.

The foregoing arrangement does not apply to an elimination tournament. The determination of a championship is based upon the percentage of victories or upon high-point totals of quality ratings. If an elimination tournament is desired, and if one defeat is sufficient to eliminate a school, a bracket such as the following can be used:

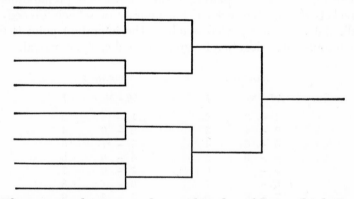

These two schemes can be combined to form a third. Some tournaments have several nonelimination rounds, after which some of the highest-ranking teams are placed into elimination brackets, as in the illustration above.

Tournament directors often introduce some controls, in addition to a numbering scheme, for the purposes of spreading the geographical distribution of each team's opponents and "seeding" the entries in terms of ability.

There are several additional matters of tournament administration which often make the difference between a successful event and a hopeless confusion. These details require advance planning and several good workers to carry out the plans. Emotional stability is useful, too. The first decision which needs to be made concerns the kind of tournament, its size in relation to available classroom, hotel, and restaurant space, and the date. The dates of other campus events and those of nearby tournaments should be checked to avoid embarrassing conflicts. Concerning the kind of tournament, the director and his assistants should determine whether to have only debate or to add events in discussion, oratory, extempore speaking, etc. Although one may wish to have something more unique than "just another debate tournament," he need not adopt the extreme to which some tournaments have gone. Even a large circus has only three rings. The maximum size of the tournament should be established by a survey of the local facilities. After all, size is less important than the quality of the competition and the availability of competent criticism.

Following these steps, the announcements or invitations should be sent to the schools which have been listed. These notices should announce the date, place, events, rules, housing accommodations and rates, fees if any, time schedule, etc. Some sort of reply form or advance registration card is usually enclosed. When these replies are received, the director should send acknowledgements of entries and give any necessary additional information. If each school delegation is limited in size, a reminder to this effect is appropriate. Generally speaking, a delegation consists of two or four debaters and a judge.

Before the delegations arrive, everything must be in readiness. Chairman-timekeepers must be on hand, signs should be posted to direct the traffic, registration facilities must be ready, a general meeting room should be open, and all mimeographed materials which are to be issued must be on hand. Time cards, ballots, schedules, campus maps, instructions to chairman-timers, registration forms, receipt blanks, and the like should be ready at the headquarters.

Each unit and the accompanying judge should be assigned a serial number in the registration process, if the flexible numbering system as described in this chapter is used. If the expected number of participants does not appear, the mimeographed schedule for round one must be revised and perhaps written on a large board in the general meeting room. During the first round the schedule of all rounds can be duplicated and be ready for distribution between the first and second rounds.

If the proper planning has been done, the management should be able to issue results and the evaluation sheets or rating scales within approximately thirty minutes after the final round ends. In the meantime, some diversionary entertainment might well be provided. If a more detailed tabulation of results is to be issued, it can be made, duplicated, and mailed within a few days after the tournament.

THE ROLE OF THE
DIRECTOR

Attitude toward the job. One who directs debating should consider it his job to teach argumentation and debating. Obviously he should have been selected because of his ability to do so. There ought, of course, to be an academic offering as well as co-curricular work in this field in a college or a university. These remarks lead us to our distinction between teaching and coaching. One is teaching debating when his efforts enable students to become competent debaters of any proposition in the future, but he is coaching when he strives merely to enable his students to win a given contest.

This distinction means that the director or teacher should direct or lead, but not drive or "spoon feed," his students. He will direct the reading, lead some discussions, criticize practice debates, and help in other ways short of compiling reference cards, drawing case outlines, and writing speeches.

In many an institution the debating program is the "lengthened shadow of a man"—the director. It is usually he who shapes the goals, sets the tone, and builds the tradition. Fortunate is the school that has had an unbroken succession of competent directors and helpful administrators.

Promotional activities. Often the most difficult of the promotional activities consists in the inauguration of a program where none has existed. Some who have met this problem have started with a nucleus of former high-school debaters or a small group of interested students in speech classes. Others have announced propositions of interest to some students in political science, history, or economics. In some cases an intramural event has been developed among classes, fraternities, or societies, using a proposition of campus interest. Still others have presented entertaining demonstration debates featuring visiting teams of recognized ability.

These and other devices have more prospect of success if the administrative officers provide moral and financial support. This important support may be obtained if the case for forensics is convincingly presented. We have suggested some arguments in our treatment of the educational objectives and the criticisms of the activity.

After the activity has been started with official sanction and support, there remains the problem of motivating the participants. They are typical human beings in their desire for recognition and interesting experiences. These may be provided by means of interesting propositions, attractive schedules, academic credit, school awards, membership in honorary societies, and publicity.

News stories of forensic activities are of interest not only to the town and campus papers, but also to the papers of the participants' home towns. Appropriate news stories and editorials tend to interest other students in participating, stimulate attendance at debates, and show the community that the activity is making progress. The publicity should continue from the announcement of tryouts to the publication of the awards which are made at the close of the season. Newspaper publicity may be supplemented by pictures, posters, oral announcements, yearbook features, and off-campus appearances before community audiences. The peculiarities of the local situation will govern the relative emphasis which is given to each of these media of publicity.

Selecting the squad. If the prospective debaters exceed the number that can be taught properly, the personnel of the squad may be determined by means of tryouts. These are held in the fall, usually a month or six weeks before the first intercollegiate engagements. The time intervals between the first meeting and the tryouts, and between the tryouts and the first contests, vary because of local conditions—the experience of the students, the difficulty of the propositions, the available meeting time, and the standard of achievement which the director holds.

There is much difference of opinion among directors concerning the number of debaters who should be retained on the squad through the season. Some believe that the squad should be reduced from time to time until a first team remains to enter the principal contests. Others use the squad system, which means that different teams from the squad are chosen to represent the school in each contest. These alternatives are said to constitute the dilemma between winning and training, because only a few schools are able to use many debaters and still maintain superior records. The use of several teams during a season is educationally sound, but novices ought not to be foisted upon public audiences. Their first experiences are obtainable in intrasquad practices, intramural programs, and novice tournaments.

Practice experiences. These practice experiences are essential, but not of such importance that regular class work may be disrupted for a considerable period. It is advisable to establish a regular meeting time so that the debaters may budget their time. If regular squad meetings are not desired, one can schedule practice debates and small group meetings. Sometimes there are separate meetings for affirmatives and negatives, and at other times there are separate squad meetings for men and women, or for varsity men, varsity women, and freshmen.

In order to make the most of the intrasquad practices, several procedures may be used.[19] One is the unvarying practice of criti-

[19] Week-by-week training schedules may be found in C. P. Lahman's *Debate Coaching* (New York: H. W. Wilson Company, 1936), pp. 140–142.

cizing each oral presentation. Another is the insistance upon the use of extemporaneous delivery. A third is the use of various types of debate. Fourth, an occasional shifting of sides and team personnel has much to recommend it. Occasional changes in cases or methods of handling specific arguments constitute a fifth suggestion. Finally, a short version of the direct-clash debate form may be used with profit as a rebuttal practice device. We have discussed the basic skills and the principal methods of preparation in previous chapters.

Intercollegiate competition is the next stage in the series of practice experiences. It is available in many invitational practice tournaments which provide a maximum of experience at a minimum cost. Some of these tournaments are divided into novice and experienced sections. They are scheduled between late November and April. Typically, the visiting teachers serve as judges without fee. Each entrant usually receives a quality rating and perhaps an oral critique. If only a decision is rendered, the educational value of the experience is less than it might be. Individual debates between schools are quite common also. They may be held before assemblies, classes, campus organizations, or off-campus audiences.

In planning the practice situations for a season, the director will find it to his long-range advantage to arrive at philosophically defensible answers to questions such as these: Am I providing sufficiently varied kinds of forensic experiences? Do I allow winning to become an end in itself? Should I arrange debates on more than one proposition per season? Do I teach research techniques, or just use handbooks? Do I enforce ethical standards?

OUTLINE OF PRINCIPLES
FOR DIRECTORS AND TOPICAL REVIEW FOR
STUDENTS

    I. Variables which influence a program
       A. Director's philosophy, time, energy, etc.

See also Kenneth Hance, "Adapting 'the Teaching Cycle' to Debate," *Quarterly Journal of Speech,* December, 1944, pp. 444–450.

B. Attitudes of administrators and faculty members
C. The tradition of this activity in the school
D. Budget, travel restrictions, etc.
E. Assistance, teaching-load credit, etc.
F. Number and experience level of interested students
G. Relevant curricular offerings
H. Ratio of resident and commuter student population
I. Kind of institution (liberal arts, tech., etc.)

II. Assumptions underlying the kind of program described herein
A. That advocacy in the best rhetorical tradition is important in our society
B. That critical perception of advocacy is needed by our citizens
C. That advocacy and the critical perception thereof *can* be taught by means of school debating
D. That school debating *should* be so conducted that it produces these outcomes
E. That the co-curricular program should stem from curricular offerings in public speaking, discussion, argumentation, and the like

III. Essential matters of knowledge and of skill, the former of which may be too often slighted
A. Relationships of inquiry and proof
B. Logical and ethical responsibilities of an advocate
   1. Probability, presumption, burden of proof, burden of rebuttal, etc.
   2. Ethical limits of strategy
C. Nature and functions of propositions
D. Finding issues in three kinds of propositions
E. Investigation, inquiry, or research
F. Evidence: kinds, tests, uses of
G. Implication and linear inference: kinds, tests, fallacies, etc.
H. Building cases
   1. Prima-facie case
   2. Steps in development
   3. Types of cases

          4. Principles of logical outlining

    I. Refutation and rebuttal

          1. Nature of

          2. Opportunities for

          3. Methods of

          4. Preparation for

    J. Kinds of debate and their special problems

          1. In terms of the contexts in which they are conducted

             a. Legislative

             b. Judicial

             c. Political

             d. Academic

             e. Philosophical

          2. In terms of the procedures employed

             a. Parliamentary session

             b. English parliamentary

             c. Problem-solving

             d. Progression

             e. Direct clash

             f. Cross examination, etc.

    K. Criticism, evaluation, and judging of student performance.

    L. Miscellaneous, related matters

          1. Composition

          2. Delivery

          3. Ethos

          4. Motivation, etc.

IV. Attitudes and overt behavior to be insisted upon

    A. Courtesy toward opponents, judges, and others

    B. Magnanimity and fair play

    C. Honesty in use of evidence and in the representation of an opponent's argument

    D. Employment of only that kind of strategy which does not thwart intelligent deliberation

    E. Conceiving of debate speaking as direct, sincere, competitive, problem-solving communication with real people

EXERCISES

1. If circumstances permit, have some demonstration debates in class. It is usually more interesting to use a variety of types, such as a modified English debate, a problem-solving debate, a cross-question debate, a direct-clash debate, a mock trial, etc.

2. Use the shift-of-opinion ballot in an audience situation, and apply the formula in measuring the shifts.

3. Advanced students who are preparing to direct forensics may be asked to prepare study outlines, briefs, cases, discussion outlines, bibliographies, evidence files, or rebuttal charts on a question or a proposition, as the case may be, which will be used in the following season.

4. Advanced students in a coaching course should have supervised practice in giving critic decisions. The demonstration debates or intercollegiate debates on campus may be used for this purpose.

5. Prepare lesson plans, a training schedule, or a syllabus for use in a debate class, a debate squad, or a social-studies class in which debate is used as a teaching device.

6. Using the A.F.A. ballot, Form *C*, but omitting "delivery," evaluate the school debate in Appendix *B*.

WRITTEN DEBATE

"FAIR PLAY" IN CRIMINAL
INVESTIGATIONS AND PROSECUTIONS *

Fred E. Inbau, Professor of Law, Northwestern University

To what extent can criminal investigators and prosecuting attorneys function effectively, if at all, within the "fair play" concept that is so characteristic of the American way of life? How much individual civil liberties can we grant to all persons and still maintain the degree of public safety and security necessary for our collective existence and enjoyment? In seeking to answer these questions, let us first direct our attention to the social requirements of *criminal investigation* and then consider the ethical standards that should or can be imposed. Thereafter we shall make a similar analysis of the problem as regards *criminal prosecution*.

The social and ethical requirements of criminal investigation:

The social requirements of criminal investigation may be stated as follows, at least for purposes of beginning our discussion: 1)

* *Tri-Quarterly,* Northwestern University, Evanston, Illinois, Winter, 1961. Reprinted by permission.

the apprehension of the criminal, and 2) the procurement of the proof of guilt.

Police efforts to satisfy these two requirements give rise, first of all, to the issue of the ethics of their activities with respect to the particular individuals who may be affected by the investigation. For instance, what ethics should prevail as to the criminal himself? As to a suspect? As to the victim, perhaps? As to witnesses, and other prospective informants? Or as to others who by reason of certain circumstances must be questioned or investigated?

In instances where the criminal is caught in the act, or where his identity as the perpetrator of the offense is known and there is adequate proof of his guilt, the problem of ethics is not a serious one, and the occasional breaches that do occur are relatively minor and easily correctible. The same holds true for the victim and the witnesses to such crimes, and others who may become involved in one way or another. The real difficulties are presented, however, in cases where the offender is not presently known, or where the proof of guilt is not presently on hand. It is this type of case which may necessitate the questioning of law-abiding citizens; the arrest of actual suspects or the detention of other persons who may or may not be guilty; the interrogation of suspects; the search of arrestees, or of their automobiles, homes, or places of business; and the use of various other investigative tactics and techniques, such as wiretapping or other electronic eavesdropping devices. It is here that we encounter, not only the problem of the ethical requirements respecting the particular individual involved, but also a larger and far more important issue—the ever present conflict between the concepts and ideals of individual civil liberties and the collective welfare and best interests of the general public.

There is such a close affinity between the issue of ethics respecting the particular individual suspect, witness, informant, or other person, and the civil liberties issue in general, that we may treat both issues as though they were but one. We may then proceed to a discussion of the area of basic conflict between the social or public need requirements of protective security from criminal conduct and the concepts and ideals of individual civil liberties.

In the course of my discussion I shall not only analyze the basic differences but shall also seek to arrive at some resolution of the differences into a workable plan that will permit both interests—civil liberties and public protection—to survive side by side.

One anomalous aspect of this whole problem of the social and ethical requirements of criminal investigation is that we demand of the police that they satisfy the social requirement of public protection, but then we compel them to function within a strait-jacket of antiquated, impractical laws, rules, and regulations imposed by either the legislatures or the courts. The police officers then find themselves on the horns of a dilemma. Either they abide by the prescribed rules and render ineffective service, or else they break or circumvent the rules and perform the service required of them. In my opinion this is not only unfair to all parties concerned but also completely unnecessary. And I believe this difficulty could be resolved by a concerted intelligent effort on the part of the legislatures and the courts to understand and appreciate the practicalities of law enforcement; and, in turn, for the police to understand and appreciate the true objectives of well-intentioned legislative acts and rules of court.

Arrest and detention:

A major segment of the strait-jacket to which I have referred involves the laws and court rules governing arrest and police detention. In the United States the requirement generally prevails that a police officer may only arrest when a crime has been committed and he has reasonable grounds for believing that the person he is about to arrest has committed it. (This, incidentally, refers to major offences; as regards misdemeanors the officer may not, as a general rule, arrest unless the offense is committed in his presence.) Moreover, except in a very few states, an officer does not have the right, unless he makes an actual arrest, to detain anyone for investigation or questioning as to his identity or purpose in being at the place where the officer finds him. Nor is there the right to search such persons for weapons or anything else unless incidental to an actual, lawful arrest. And once an arrest has been effected it is generally required that the arrestee must be taken, without unnecessary delay, before the nearest magistrate for a preliminary hearing (or arraignment, as it is called in our federal courts).

The practical difficulties that confront a police officer by reason of these various requirements and restraints can be readily seen in the following case situation:

At 3 o'clock in the morning an officer in a police car observes the figure of a man in an alley or in a dark and otherwise deserted street. The man darts behind a telephone post. What police action is warranted and permissible under these circumstances?

In many jurisdictions of the United States, unless a crime has been committed and the officer has reasonable grounds for believing the man behind the post has committed it, there is no legally authorized action the officer can take other than drive by and merely observe the man behind the post. As a practical matter, however, the officer will take further action. He will approach the man, with gun drawn; he will ask some questions and he may also effect a search to be sure his quarry is disarmed, if necessary. But in doing so the officer is acting without legal authorization. Moreover, if a concealed weapon is found as a result of the search, in about half of our states the evidence would not be usable because it was illegally obtained.

Suppose the officer in this case took no action because of his lack of legal authorization, and it later developed that the unidentified man behind the post had just committed a murder or a rape, or was a participant in a kidnapping. What do you suppose the public reaction would be? Dismiss such a numbskull from the force! And in all probability his commanding officer would transfer him to another assignment for the purpose of placating the complaining public. But of this you can be sure: there would be no public committees formed to have the law changed. In a short time the incident and the police problem it presented would be lost in the public memory.

Another dependable prediction can be made about subsequent developments. The police officers and police organizations of the community or state would not band together in an effort to obtain remedial legislation. They too would move on to other things and to the handling of future case situations in the most practical, unobtrusive way known to them.

I will venture another prediction. If anyone submitted a piece of remedial legislation, there would be a tremendous hue and cry from civil liberties groups to alert the public to the dangers of this insidious attempt toward the development of a totalitarian police state. And the inarticulate police interests would not likely offset this attack; their appeals would have to be pitched on a non-emotional, rational plane that would be very difficult to get across, largely because of the general lack of public understanding regarding the practicalities of law enforcement, and a failure on the part of the general public to recognize the fact that much more is required for totalitarianism than an effective police force.

Problems of the type represented by the case of the man behind the post could be made far less troublesome if law abiding citizens were willing to accept the risk of this kind of inconvenience and embarrassment which they might very innocently acquire by taking a short cut through an alley at 3 o'clock in the morning. It seems to me that the remote risk of an innocent encounter with the police under reasonable circumstances such as this should be accepted as a risk of citizenship itself. The innocent citizen is sometimes asked to subject himself to far greater risks in the public interest—risks of real, grave danger as well as inconvenience. Witness, for instance, his call to the colors in defense of his country.

All this is not to say, of course, that the police should be granted unlimited freedom of action. But it does suggest that we accord to them the reasonable and necessary ways and means to accomplish the difficult tasks assigned to them. A few of our states, but only a very few, have faced up to the issue and have adopted a so-called Uniform Arrest Act which permits the officer in my hypothetical case to act lawfully and effectively. In those jurisdictions he is authorized to detain, for a reasonable time, anyone discovered in suspicious situations such as the one just described, for the purpose of establishing his identity, or until a check can be made as regards any crimes that may have been recently committed in the vicinity, or as to whether the detained person is wanted elsewhere as a fugitive. These jurisdictions also permit arrests to be made upon less technical requirements than usually prevail; and, in addition, they authorize a reasonable police delay between the time of arrest and the time of presentation before a magistrate.

As already suggested, what concerns the legislatures, the courts, and the general public—and what accounts for the stagnant situation I have just described—is the fear of police abuses and the loss of civil liberties. But we can protect ourselves from these risks and at the same time permit the police to function effectively. That happy situation cannot be attained, however, by some simple expediency in the form of controls imposed on the police by legislative proscriptions or court-formulated rules. An unfit police force cannot be transformed into a good one by legislative fiat or judicial decree. A respect for civil liberties, coupled with effective law enforcement, can only result from the adoption of a system whereby our police are selected and promoted on a merit basis, properly trained, adequately compensated, and accorded a freedom to protect the public and enforce the law with a minimum of politically inspired interference. Public opinion and an alert and vigorous press would furnish the required controls with respect to the issue of civil liberties and abuses.

If this analysis appears naive, I offer the example of the Federal Bureau of Investigation. It is an effective law enforcement body that is also thoroughly mindful of the requirements of individual civil liberties.

Another illustration of the point that criminal investigators are strait-jacketed by many unwise and unnecessary legal rules and restrictions is to be found in the rules and restrictions governing the police interrogation of criminal suspects and of other persons in the course of a criminal investigation. In this field there is perhaps more back-turning by the legislatures and the courts on the practicalities of law enforcement than in any other area.

Criminal interrogation:

One completely false assumption accounts in large measure for the technical and practical restrictions on police interrogations. It is this, and the fallacy is certainly perpetuated to a very considerably extent by mystery writers, the movies, and TV: Whenever a crime is committed, if the police will only look carefully at the crime scene they will almost always find some clue that will lead them to the offender and at the same time establish his guilt; and once the offender is located, he will readily confess or disclose his guilt by trying to shoot his way out of the trap. But this is pure fiction; in actuality the situation is quite different. As a matter of fact, the art of criminal investigation has not developed to a point where the search for and the examination of physical evidence will always reveal a clue to the identity of the perpetrator or provide the necessary proof of his guilt. In criminal investigations, even of the most efficient type, there are many, many instances where physical clues are entirely absent, and the only approach to a possible solution of the crime is the interrogation of the criminal suspect himself, and of others who may possess significant information. Moreover, in most instances these interrogations, particularly of the suspect himself, must be conducted under conditions of privacy and for a reasonable period of time; and they frequently require the use of psychological tactics and techniques that could well be classified as "unethical," if we are to evaluate them in terms of ordinary, everyday social behavior.

To protect myself from being misunderstood, I want to make it unmistakably clear that I am not an advocate of the so-called "third degree," for I am unalterably opposed to the use of any interrogation tactic or technique that is apt to make an innocent person confess. I am opposed, therefore, to the use of force, threats, or promises of leniency—all of which might well induce an innocent person to confess; but I do approve of such psychological tactics and techniques as trickery and deceit that are not only helpful but frequently necessary in order to secure incriminating information from the guilty, or investigative leads from otherwise unco-operative witnesses or informants.

My position, then, is this, and it may be presented in the form of three separate points, each accompanied by case illustrations:

> 1. Many criminal cases, even when investigated by the best qualified police departments, are capable of solution only by means of an admission or confession from the guilty individual or upon the basis of information obtained from the questioning of other criminal suspects.

As to the validity of this statement, I suggest that consideration be given to the situation presented by cases such as these. A man is hit on the head while walking home late at night. He did not see his assailant, nor did anyone else. A careful and thorough search of the crime scene reveals no physical clues. Then take the case of a woman who is grabbed on the street at night and dragged into an alley and raped. Here, too, the assailant was unaccommodating enough to avoid leaving his hat or other means of identification at the crime scene; and there are no other physical clues. All the police have to work on is the description of the assailant given by the victim herself. She described him as about six feet tall, white, and wearing a dark suit. Or consider this case —and we have one in Illinois just like it. Three women are vacationing in a wooded resort area. Their bodies are found dead alongside a foot trail, the result of physical violence, and no physical clues are present.

In cases of this kind—and they all typify the difficult investigation problem that the police frequently encounter—how else can they be solved, if at all, except by means of the interrogation of suspects or of others who may possess significant information?

There are times, too, when a police interrogation may result not only in the apprehension and conviction of the guilty, but also in the release of the innocent from well-warranted suspicion. Here is one such actual case within my own professional experience.

The dead body of a woman was found in her home. Her skull had been crushed, apparently with some blunt instrument. A careful police investigation of the premises did not reveal any clues to the identity of the killer. No fingerprints or other significant evidence were located; not even the lethal instrument itself. None of the neighbors could give any helpful information. Although there was some evidence of a slight struggle in the room where the body lay, there were no indications of a forcible entry into the home. The deceased's young daughter was the only other resident of the home and she had been away in school at the time of the crime. The daughter could not give the police any idea of what, if any, money or property had disappeared from the home.

For several reasons the police considered the victim's husband a likely suspect. He was being sued for divorce; he knew his wife had planned on leaving the state and taking their daughter with her; and the neighbors reported that the couple had been having heated arguments, and that the husband was of a violent temper. He also lived conveniently near—in a garage adjoining the home. The police interrogated him and although his alibi was not conclusive his general behavior and the manner in which he answered the interrogator's questions satisfied the police of his innocence. Further investigation then revealed that the deceased's brother-in-law had been financially indebted to the deceased; that he was a frequent gambler; that at a number of social gatherings which he had attended money disappeared from some of the women's purses; that at his place of employment there had been a series of purse thefts; and that on the day of the killing he was absent from work. The police apprehended and questioned him. As the result of a few hours of competent interrogation—unattended by any abusive methods, but yet conducted during a period of delay in presenting the suspect before a committing magistrate as required by state statute—the suspect confessed to the murder. He told of going to the victim's home for the purpose of selling her a radio, which she accused him of stealing. An argument ensued and he hit her over the head with a mechanic's wrench he was carrying in his coat pocket. He thereupon located and took some money he found in the home and also a diamond ring. After fleeing from the scene he threw the wrench into a river, changed his clothes and disposed of the ones he had worn at the time of the killing by throwing them away in various parts of the city. He had hidden the ring in the attic of his mother's home, where it was found by the police after his confession had disclosed its presence there. Much of the stolen money was also recovered or else accounted for by the payment of an overdue loan.

Without an opportunity for interrogation the police could not have solved this case. The perpetrator of the offense would have remained at liberty, perhaps to repeat his criminal conduct.

> 2. Criminal offenders, except, of course, those caught in the commission of their crimes, ordinarily will not admit their guilt unless questioned under conditions of privacy, and for a period of perhaps several hours.

This point is one which should be readily apparent not only to any person with the least amount of criminal investigative experience, but also to anyone who will reflect momentarily upon the behavior of ordinary law-abiding persons when suspected or accused of nothing more than simple social indiscretions. Self-condemnation and self-destruction not being normal behavioral characteristics, human beings ordinarily do not utter unsolicited, spontaneous confessions. They must first be questioned regarding the offense. In some instances, a little bit of information inadvertently given to a competent interrogator by the suspect may suffice to start a line of investigation which might ultimately establish guilt. Upon other occasions, a full confession, with a revelation of details regarding a body, the loot, or the instruments used in the crime, may be required to prove the case. But whatever the possible consequences may be, it is impractical to expect any but a very few confessions to result from a guilty conscience unprovoked by an interrogation. It is also impractical to expect admissions or confessions to be obtained under circumstances other than privacy. Here again recourse to our everyday experience will support the basic validity of this requirement. For instance, in asking a personal friend to divulge a secret we carefully avoid making the request in the presence of other persons, and seek a time and place when the matter can be discussed in private. The very same psychological factors are involved in a criminal interrogation, and even to a greater extent. For related psychological considerations, if an interrogation is to be had at all, it must be one based upon an unhurried interview, the necessary length of which will in many instances extend to several hours, depending upon various factors such as the nature of the case situation and the personality of the suspect.

> 3. In dealing with criminal offenders, and consequently also with criminal suspects who may actually be innocent, the interrogator must of necessity employ less refined methods than are considered appropriate for the transaction of ordinary, everyday affairs by and between law-abiding citizens.

To illustrate this point, permit me to revert to the previously discussed case of the woman who was murdered by her brother-in-law. His confession was obtained largely as a result of the interrogator adopting a friendly attitude in questioning the suspect, when concededly no such genuine feeling existed; by pretending to sympathize with the suspect because of his difficult financial situation; by suggesting that perhaps the victim had done or said something which aroused his anger and which would have aroused the anger of anyone else similarly situated to such an extent as to provoke a violent reaction; and by resorting to other similar expressions, or even overtures of friendliness and sympathy such as a pat on the suspect's shoulder or knee. In all of this, of course, the interrogation was "unethical" according to the standards usually set for professional, business and social conduct. But the pertinent issue in this case was no ordinary, lawful, professional, business or social matter. It involved the taking of a human life by one who abided by no code of fair play toward his fellow human beings. The killer would not have been moved one bit toward a confession by subjecting him to a reading or lecture regarding the morality of his conduct. It would have been futile merely to give him a pencil and paper and trust that his conscience would impel him to confess. Something more was required —something which was in its essence an "unethical" practice on the part of the interrogator. But, under the circumstances involved in this case, how else would the murderer's guilt have been established? Moreover, let us bear this thought in mind. From the criminal's point of view, *any* interrogation of him is objectionable. To *him* it may be a "dirty trick" to be talked into a confession, for surely it was not done for his benefit. Consequently, any interrogation of him might be labeled as deceitful or unethical.

Of necessity, criminal interrogators must deal with criminal offenders on a somewhat lower moral plane than that upon which ethical, law-abiding citizens are expected to conduct their everyday affairs. That plane, in the interest of innocent suspects, need only be subject to the following restriction: Although both "fair" and "unfair" interrogation practices are permissible, nothing shall be done or said to the subject that will be apt to make an innocent person confess.

If all this be so, why then the withholding of this essential interrogation opportunity from the police? And we do, insofar as the stated law is concerned. It comes in the form of statutes or rules that require the prompt delivery of an arrested person before a magistrate for a preliminary hearing or arraignment. Moreover, the United States Supreme Court has decreed that in federal cases no confession is to be received in evidence, regardless of its voluntariness or trustworthiness, if it was obtained during a period of unnecessary delay in delivering the arrestee to a federal commissioner or judge for arraignment. In the federal jurisdiction of Washington, D.C., which must cope with a variety of criminal offences and problems similar to any other city of comparable size, this federal court rule has had a very crippling effect on police investigations.

One incongruity of the prompt arraignment rule is this. It is lawful for the police to arrest upon *reasonable belief* that the arrestee has committed the offense, following which they must take him before a magistrate, without unnecessary delay, and charge him with the crime; but for legal proof of the charge, his guilt at the time of trial must be established *beyond reasonable doubt*. Moreover, when the accused gets into the hands of a magistrate for the preliminary hearing, the opportunity for an effective interrogation is ended, many times because of the advice he receives from his attorney to keep his mouth shut.

If we view this whole problem realistically, we must come to the conclusion that an interrogation opportunity is necessary and that legislative provision ought to be made for a privately conducted police interrogation, covering a reasonable period of time, of suspects who are not unwilling to be interviewed, and that the only tactics or techniques that are to be forbidden are those which are apt to make an innocent person confess.

At one time it was fashionable in the United States for jurists and law professors to refer to the "Judges' Rules" which the English and Canadian courts have laid down for the "guidance" of police interrogators, and say: "If the British and Canadian police can be effective under such rules, then our officers have no cause to complain." Such naïveté seems to have dissolved since the appearance in print of the frank admissions of at least two prominent English police officials to the effect that the Judges' Rules could not be honored because of practical limitations. These writers actually revealed how the Rules were circumvented—by the simple devices of (a) postponing the time when the officers were satisfied of the guilt of the person they were interrogating, and (b) by pretending to search only for ambiguities when questioning a person already in custody.

The eminent English criminal law authority, Glanville Williams, recently stated that in England the Judges' Rules have, in effect, been abandoned by tacit consent, and he gave as the reason that they had been found to be "unreasonable restrictions upon the activities of the police in bringing criminals to book."

There are other ways to guard against abuses in police interrogation short of taking the privilege away from them. Moreover, we could no more afford to do that than we could stand the effects of a law requiring automobile manufacturers to place governors on all cars so that, in order to make the highways safe, no one could go faster than twenty miles an hour.

The only real, practically attainable protection we can set up for ourselves against police interrogation abuses (just as with respect to arrest and detention abuses) is to see to it that our police are selected and promoted on a merit basis, that they are properly trained, adequately compensated, and that they are permitted to remain substantially free from politically inspired interference. In the hands of men of this competence there will be a minimum degree of abusive practices. And once again I suggest that the real interest that should be exhibited by the legislatures and the courts is with reference to the protection of the innocent from the hazards of tactics and techniques that are apt to produce from them confessions of guilt or other false information. Individual civil liberties can survive in such an atmosphere, alongside the protective security of the public.

Wiretapping and electronic eavesdropping:

The police employment of wiretapping and other electronic eavesdropping devices poses another sharp issue respecting social requirements and the ethics of criminal investigation.

To cope with jet-age criminals, particularly those engaged in organized, syndicated crime, it is imperative that the police be given the authority—under controlled conditions of one sort or another—to resort to wiretapping and also to the use of other kinds of electronic eavesdropping for the purpose of crime detection and the apprehension of criminals.

Civil liberties pressure and sentiment have generally succeeded, in the United States anyway, in not only preventing the police from securing this privilege, but in actually taking it away from those who at one time had it or had exercised it under the assumption of permissibility. But sooner or later the force of serious circumstances and events will compel the grant of that privilege to the police. We certainly need it for national defense purposes; and we also need it in order to cope effectively with organized crime and other serious offences.

The big bugaboo about eavesdropping is the understandable fear of its being used to probe into our private lives, to ascertain business secrets for competitive purposes, and to tap us or our parties for political purposes. Any such practices are unethical and ought to be outlawed. But here again effective controls are available to insure the proper exercise of police wiretapping privileges. New York, for instance, has a workable compromise. It is a felony in New York for anyone other than the police to tap a telephone wire; and the police can do so only upon court authorization for each particular case situation. (However, the continued existence of the New York procedure is presently in a state of grave uncertainty, by reason of a recent United States Supreme Court decision.)

In my opinion the New York compromise between individual civil liberties and social requirements is a far better solution than a blanket prohibition of the practice.

In terms of a stated principle, here is what I have been trying to say with respect to the basic issues of social requirements and the ethics of criminal investigation. The legislatures, the courts, and the public must recognize the fact that individual liberties cannot exist in a vacuum. They are meaningful only if they are to be exercised within the medium of a safe, stable society.

As with so many other problems of life and living within a free and democratic society, we should be able to find, and we can find, with respect to the social and ethical difficulties involved in the area of criminal investigation, a workable compromise. Once we reach an understanding on both sides as to the basic and fundamental issues and differences, intelligent consideration should carry us the rest of the way.

The social and ethical requirements of criminal prosecution:

Although it seems clear to all of us that it is socially desirable to prevent all crimes and to apprehend all criminals, there is actually a different philosophy that prevails, in effect, anyway, with respect to criminal prosecutions.

Have you ever stopped to consider thoroughly the *real* reason why we tolerate so many restrictions on the prosecution's efforts to convict and at the same time give so much leeway to defense counsel and to the defendant in their efforts to avoid a conviction? Perhaps you may be inclined to say: "Certainly; it's for the protection of the innocent." This, of course, is one reason—and it is generally accepted as the only one. But there is another and a more basic one. Before suggesting it, however, I would like to raise a few points to indicate, at least to my way of thinking, that the only or major reason is not the usually stated one of protection of the innocent.

First of all, why is it that in a criminal prosecution the defendant—the one person who should be able to enlighten the fact-finders more than anyone else—need not take the stand and testify?

Why, in most jurisdictions, is it necessary that the jury be unanimous in its verdict, when democratic determinations of utmost importance—questions of group survival—are made upon the basis of a two-thirds vote, or even a majority vote of Congress, Parliament, or of some other body charged with similar responsibilities?

Why exclude unerring proof of guilt, as about half of our state courts do, solely because the police did not follow the prescribed procedures in obtaining it?

Why do we who are members of the legal profession, and why does the public at large, tolerate a standard of legal ethics that permits defense counsel to cross-examine, and by cross-examination "destroy" a prosecution witness when counsel knows, from what his own client has told him, and from what his own evidence clearly establishes, that the prosecution's witness is telling the absolute truth? And upon this point, give consideration to these words of an eminent and respected defense counsel; they appeared in an article of his which was published in a Bar Association journal: "If he [defense counsel] is defending a guilty person, and he usually is, his job is to prevent that fact from coming to light." The article further stated: "When I succeeded in enabling a malefactor to escape his just desserts I had a glowing gratification of having accomplished a professional *tour de force.* This gratification was intensified by the knowledge that I had lived up to my obligations as an officer of the court, and had acted in accordance with the codes of legal ethics."

Why the toleration of a rule that requires the prosecutor to disclose to the court evidence or witnesses favorable to the defense, when a similar obligation does not rest upon counsel for the accused? And why should the prosecution be required to make available, for the inspection of defense counsel, written statements obtained from the defendant and from the prosecution's witnesses, without placing a comparable obligation upon defense counsel?

Why not, as a prerequisite to the *defense of alibi*, require the defendant to serve notice and set forth the essential details of the alibi?

Why is it that the defendant may appeal from a conviction, but (in the United States, anyway) not the prosecution, and especially in cases where the judge has grossly erred in his instructions to the jury or in his rulings upon the evidence? And why is it that the defendant may appeal on the ground of improper conduct by the prosecutor, without according a similar right to the prosecution when defense counsel has engaged in unethical or even outrageous conduct that may have affected the jury verdict?

Why, at the conclusion of a criminal trial, do we not prosecute for perjury defense witnesses who have unquestionably lied under oath, and that fact is readily susceptible of proof? Why let the defendant himself get by with it? In fact, we are rather thoroughly committed to the view, tacitly anyway, that it is all right for him to do just that. Interestingly enough, one appellate court recently held that once an accused is acquitted he could not be tried for perjury regarding his testimony at the trial because the verdict of not guilty was *res judicata* of the issue as to whether he lied or not. In other words, the verdict of not guilty was a court decision that he had told the truth. And yet the case is one where the evidence of perjury is now obvious beyond a reasonable doubt.

While on the subject of perjury, why, may I ask, do we not try to convict for perjury, witnesses who have unquestionably lied during the course of a divorce trial? Occasionally we do prosecute if the case is an outrageous frame-up and has been exposed on the front pages of the newspapers, but otherwise no prosecution is ever undertaken. If it should be attempted, the chances of a conviction would be slim. And this last observation prompts me to raise another question of a little different nature from the ones previously mentioned.

Why do we tolerate a system or a practice that makes it so very difficult to convict such accused persons as paramour killers, mercy killers, and motorists who kill by reckless driving? And why do we permit defense counsel in such cases to employ the tactics they are generally known to employ for purposes of getting their client off? Recall, if you will, the tactics of defense counsel as regards the insanity defense of the husband in "Anatomy of a Murder."

The true answer to most, if not all, of the questions I have raised is certainly not—"For the protection of the innocent."

To get the real answer, what may be needed is to stretch the mind of the general public out on a psychoanalyst's couch. If we did that here is what I believe would be discovered:

> *We, the public at large, really do not want to convict all criminals, but only enough to discourage criminal conduct!*

If you will ponder over this statement you will have to agree, I believe, that the psychoanalyst came up with a very plausible explanation for the behavior referred to in my various questions.

Assuming the validity of the couch revelation, what then may account for the patient's deep-rooted feelings?

Perhaps we, the public, and particularly the jury in a specific case, harbor some sort of psychological self-identification with the offender. In cases involving paramour killings, mercy killings, negligent homicides, and the like, this factor may be more apparent than in various other kinds of case situations. But in theft cases, also, and particularly as regards the offense of embezzlement, we may find the same self-identification factor. After all—and I submit this to you fully confident of its validity as to the approximation of percentages—about 85 out of every 100 persons will "steal" if the opportunity to do so is presented to them. I feel confident that this figure is about right and I base it upon the professional experiences some of us have had in the investigation of thefts and embezzlements committed by employees of banks, merchandising companies and other commercial houses. To be sure, I am not talking about large thefts and embezzlements, but thievery nevertheless. And I include such things as one's own enrichment by the padding of an expense account, the carrying home, by an employee, of merchandise belonging to the store where he works, and the pocketing of small overages in a bank teller's account at the end of the day. All this, of course, is a form of theft. And I wonder if our propensity for such conduct does not in some measure explain our laxity with respect to the legal prosecution of persons accused of thievery.

Before concluding our analysis, perhaps a few more points are in order.

If I recall correctly, as kids, in playing the game of "cops and robbers," most of us wanted to be cops. In college or law school, some students are attracted by positions in the field of criminal investigation; a number of them in the United States pursue a career in the FBI and other such law enforcement agencies. But how many law students express a desire to make a career of prosecuting attorney? I am not talking, of course, about using the office of assistant prosecutor as a tide-over or as preparation for becoming a criminal lawyer practitioner on the side of the table; I am talking about a burning desire to be a prosecutor, rather than counsel for the defense. I know, of course, that there are economic and other factors that feature in such decision making, but the real reason must be a more deep-rooted one. It may be this, by way of differentiation between a desire to be a criminal investigator and the lesser interest in becoming a prosecutor.

When the criminal case reaches the prosecution stage, the matter becomes quite personalized. Here stands X, the defendant, a particular individual, with his sympathy provoking background or situation. Our self-identification may come much easier and quicker at this point than when the police were searching for the unknown someone who committed the crime. Maybe that is one reason why we tolerate the practices and the kind of ethical standards that prevail in a criminal prosecution. That, perhaps, is why the position of counsel for the defense is more glamorous in the public eye than that of prosecutor.

It also seems to me that the feeling sometimes prevails that once an offender has been caught and has been in police detention and has been subjected to exposure for what he is, that may be punishment enough.

Undoubtedly, too, there is the economic factor of the public not being able to afford to keep in the penitentiary all the people who may technically belong there.

From what I have said up until now my readers may well be assuming that I deplore the philosophy that we do not want to convict all criminals; that we want to convict only enough to discourage that kind of conduct. But I do not. It does not disturb me at all, and I am prepared to accept that philosophy as a desirable way of life. However, I do object to *the excesses* that have developed, like barnacles on an otherwise good ship. I feel that the legislatures and the courts, and particularly the courts, have gone much too far. And not only is that fact itself disturbing, but also the reasons for their doing so.

Here are two case examples of what I mean by excesses. One is a United States Supreme Court decision; the other a decision of the British Columbia Supreme Court.

In the 1957 case of *Mallory v. United States* (354 U.S. 449)—and this is the case I had in mind in one of my previous instances —the trial court conviction of an accused rapist was reversed solely because of the fact that the police had interrogated him and obtained a confession from him at a time when they were delaying (for a few hours) the taking of the accused before a committing magistrate, as prescribed by a federal rule which requires that the police must do so "without unnecessary delay."

Soon after the release of the accused, he committed another offense; and he was sentenced to sixty days for assaulting the female
complainant. A few months ago he was prosecuted in Philadelphia
on a charge of rape and burglary, and was found guilty of burglary and aggravated assault upon a housewife. In my opinion,
the release of persons of this type for the purpose of disciplining
the police is going much too far.

About the same time of the Mallory case, the Supreme Court of
British Columbia, in the case of *R. v. McLean and McKinley*
(1957) 31 W.W.R. 89, held a confession to a criminal assault
upon a girl to be void because the police interrogator had made
an untrue statement to the defendant when he was told that the
police had talked to the defendant's accomplice, whereas in fact
no such conversation had occurred. Since the officer's untruthful
representation was not the sort of thing that might make an innocent person confess, this decision, in my opinion, is another example of a court going much too far.

If space permitted, many other similar examples could be re-
cited, particularly from our federal courts. But these two are
quite illustrative of an undesirable judicial philosophy that has
developed in recent years.

What accounts for the present "turn 'em loose" philosophy
which the courts have adopted? The answer, as I see it, is more
serious and disturbing than the individual case decision themselves.

It has become far too fashionable in judicial circles to line up
"on the liberal side." In their zeal to become "great judges," the
formula of some judges seems to be: adopt a "turn 'em loose"
policy or count yourself out as a great judge. This amounts to the
writing of one's own epitaph, and we have had too much of that
from some of our judges in recent years.

Another factor accounting for this "turn 'em loose" trend of the
past fifteen or twenty years is the failure of the police and prosecution adequately to present to the courts, legislatures and general public the police-prosecution side of the issue, whereas the
civil liberties viewpoint has been enthusiastically voiced and effectively presented. Moreover, the civil liberty lawyers and other
civil liberty exponents are constantly on the alert for any develop-

ments of the police-prosecution viewpoint; they are always on hand to rush in and stamp it out if they can.

We urgently need a moderation of the trend and developments of recent years, and a workable compromise of the two major competing interests; and I submit that it ought to be something along this line:

1. Make reasonably possible—though by no means certain —that the guilty will be convicted.
2. Make certain—insofar as reasonably possible—that the innocent are not convicted.

This should be the real concern of the courts—making it *reasonably* possible to convict the guilty, and setting up *reasonable* judicial safeguards for the protection of the innocent.

The courts have no right to police the police. That is an executive and not a judicial function. Furthermore, the courts have enough troubles of their own. Witness what goes on in some of the municipal or magistrate courts of our large cities. In my opinion there are, in such courts, more hurts to the innocent and more trampling over of basic individual civil liberties and ethical considerations than you will find in most police departments. Much of the concern, energy, and efforts that the courts expend with respect to police conduct could be better spent on getting their own house in order.

THE PARADOX OF THE PROFESSOR AND THE POLICEMEN: A REPLY TO MR. INBAU *

Joel Sprayregen, practicing lawyer and former staff counsel to the Illinois Division of the American Civil Liberties Union.

A practising lawyer who sets forth to joust in print with a legal scholar is at once confronted by the peril of venturing into his adversary's camp to do battle with his adversary's chosen weap-

* *Ibid.*, Spring, 1961. Reprinted by permission.

ons. The realization is all the more sobering when that adversary is Professor Fred E. Inbau. Any of us who attempt to think seriously about problems of criminal law and administration are to an invaluable extent students of Professor Inbau through the auspices of his many books and articles, as well as the courses and lectures he has given for law students, lawyers, law enforcement officers, newsmen, and others. I myself have been privileged to attend, under grants procured by Professor Inbau, two of these professional institutes, and I sincerely hope that nothing in this essay will be interpreted as ingratitude for these opportunities.

When to Professor Inbau's impressive scholarly accomplishments are added his experience as the nation's foremost authority on scientific crime detection, the burden of rebuttal becomes even more formidable. Last year, the Chicago Police Department utilized his experience and skill as a lie detector operator in helping separate the criminals from the policemen in the "Summerdale scandal." His practical and scholarly skills are displayed at their best in his article, *Fair Play in Criminal Investigations and Prosecutions,* in the Winter, 1961, edition of this journal.

Nevertheless, as I read this article I was haunted by a paradox about which I have speculated, without solution, in the past: why are the people who should be most immune so often myopically victimized by their own naïveté? Why do I believe Professor Inbau is naïve? Because of the nature of man in general and policemen in particular. I rest my case, though reserving the right to clarify some ambiguous terms, on the following sentence which I believe is the heart of Professor Inbau's article:

The only real, practically attainable protection we can set up for ourselves against police interrogation abuses (just as with respect to arrest and detention abuses) is to see to it that our police are selected and promoted on a merit basis, that they are properly trained, adequately compensated, and that they are permitted to remain substantially free from politically inspired interference.

In short, Professor Inbau wants the police substantially left alone. And by "politically inspired interference" his text makes clear that he means, in large part, decisions by the courts. Can we let the police alone?

At base my differences with Professor Inbau are philosophic. The depth of these differences is illustrated to me by the rhetorical question he poses at the outset of his article: "How much individual civil liberties can we grant to all persons and still maintain the degree of public safety and security necessary for our collective existence and enjoyment?" The phrasing indicates that Professor Inbau conceives of civil liberties as something the government grants, or doles out—like hot lunches, crop subsidies, or social security benefits. I believe that in a democratic society the values we call civil liberties are inherent and that it is beyond the competence of the men who populate the government payroll at any particular moment to take them away or dole them out. This was true in 1787 when Jefferson wrote to Madison: "A bill of rights is what the people are entitled to against every government on earth." [1] It has been reaffirmed in 1961 by the successor to these great men when President Kennedy spoke in his inaugural address of our "belief that the rights of man come not from the generosity of the state but from the hand of God."

The architects of our constitutional system knew man. They knew that he enjoys the taint of original sin and has an immense capacity for venality, corruption, brutality, and injustice. They knew that this capacity is likely to be strained when man is given the power to take away the liberty of his fellows (as in the exercise of the power which we give all policemen) and they sought to guard against abuse by distributing power among the various branches of the government and making its exercise subject to review or, if you will, interference. When they rose to fight King George, they recognized an ancient foe. Indeed, the *Politics* of Aristotle had taught them that "the most typical form of tyranny . . . is just that arbitrary power of an individual which is responsible to no one . . ." [2]

If this be considered an unduly cynical view, I submit that our republic was founded on precisely this cynical knowledge that men are not angels. The *Federalist*, a remarkable pre-Freudian document, tells us:

[1] Koch and Peden (eds.), *Life and Selected Writings of Thomas Jefferson,* 438 (Mod. Libr. Ed., 1944).

[2] Aristotle, *On Man in the Universe,* 336 (Classics Club ed., 1943).

It may be a reflection on human nature, that such devices [e.g., separation of powers] should be necessary to control the abuses of government. But what is government itself, but the greatest of all reflections on human nature? If men were angels, no government would be necessary. If angels were to govern men, neither external nor internal controls on government would be necessary.[3]

But, it will be rejoined, I am the one who is being naïve and impractical. The policeman observing the figure dart behind the telephone pole at 3 a.m., to use one of Professor Inbau's vivid examples, can not be expected to understand Jefferson or the Constitution. Nor will the policeman's problem be answered by reciting the tired quotations I have set out above. Since I fear that much of this objection is true, I turn immediately to the principal of "reforms" advocated by Professor Inbau: he asks that the powers of the police to arrest, detain, and interrogate people be substantially broadened. In blunter language, he wants to make it easier for policemen to lock people up, secretly confine them in police stations, and work on them to confess their guilt. The present rules, we are told, put the police in a "strait-jacket."

The stone tablets with which Professor Inbau would lead us out of the strait-jacket and into the Promised Land have already been inscribed: they are the Uniform Arrest Act, which he laments that only three states (Delaware, New Hampshire, Rhode Island) have adopted since its formulation 20 years ago. Moses, not endowed with the patience of the proponents of the Act, smashed to pieces the original tablets bearing the Decalogue in much less time. The contents, wisdom and constitutionality of the Act as such will not be discussed fully here; these have already been the subject of extensive and illuminating comment.[4] For present purposes, only these major "reforms" contemplated by the Uniform Arrest Act need be set out:

[3] *The Federalist,* No. 51, 337 (Mod. Libr. ed., 1937).
[4] See, e.g., Bibliography, 50 Jour. Crim. L. & Crim. 175 (1959); Warner, *The Uniform Arrest Act,* 28 Va. L. Rev. 315 (1942); Foote, *Safeguards in the Law of Arrest,* 52 Northwestern L. Rev. 16 (1957); Bellow, *The Uniform Arrest Act—Its Impact on Illinois Law* (memorandum on file at American Civil Liberties Union, Ill. Div.).

1. The Act would give every policeman in the land the absolute right to lock up in secret for two hours, without ever bringing any charge, any person against whom he harbors "suspicion."

2. The Act tells the police that they can hold and interrogate in secret every person whom they arrest for 24 hours (48 hours where Sundays or holidays intervene); further, if the police persuade a judge that there is "good cause," they can keep this up for *two days* more.[5]

At the outset it may be conceded that these "reforms" would make the task of the police easier. But this argument proves too much: all of our constitutional guarantees were fashioned precisely to make the lot of the government more difficult whenever it seeks to deprive a citizen of his liberty in order to preserve a free society. Professor Inbau says that we seem to want to convict only enough criminals to discourage criminal conduct. I would rather put it that we fear to attempt to convict all criminals because in so doing we would necessarily convict many of the

---

[5] Section 2 of the Uniform Arrest Act provides:
   (1) A peace officer may stop any person abroad who he has reasonable ground to suspect is committing, has committed or is about to commit a crime, and demand of him his name, address, business abroad and whither he is going.
   (2) Any person so questioned who fails to identify himself or explain his actions to the satisfaction of the officer may be detained and further questioned and investigated.
   (3) The total period of detention provided for by this section shall not exceed two hours. The detention is not an arrest and shall not be recorded as an arrest in any official record. At the end of the detention the person so detained shall be released or be arrested and charged with a crime.
Section 11 of the Uniform Arrest Act provides:
   If not otherwise released, every person arrested shall be brought before a magistrate without unreasonable delay, and in any event he shall, if possible, be so brought within twenty-four hours of arrest. Sundays and holidays excluded, unless a judge of the (district) court of the (district) where he is detained or of the (district) court of the (district) where the crime was committed for good cause shown orders that he be held for a further period of not exceeding forty-eight hours.

innocent and lose our character as a society in which individual liberty is fundamental. It may be supposed that the Germans, if it is not uncharitable to recall that they once were not our loving allies, exterminated all the plotters in *Lidice;* some of us still feel that the price was too high.

The rights of the 'Suspect' and Other Citizens

Intelligent appraisal of these "reforms" requires that they be considered in context together with the other obstacles which our Constitution, laws, and procedural rules erect in the path of the police. Would not the destruction of some of these guarantees likewise make the life of the police easier? For example, the right of the defendant to remain free on bail makes it certain that some criminals will flee to escape; yet most defendants are admitted to bail because this right is the vital corollary of the presumption of innocence. For another example, the right of the defendant to cross-examine the prosecution's witnesses may mean that a skillful defense lawyer will save his client by destroying a truthful but unpersuasive state witness; no one objects to this because we believe that every man should be able to confront his accusers. And most obviously our eschewal of torture is intended to deprive our police of one of the historically most effective weapons of law enforcement. Dean Griswold reminds us that "torture was once used by honest and conscientious public servants as a means of obtaining information about crimes which could not otherwise be disclosed." [6]

Why, then, do Professor Inbau and the Uniform Act single out the area of arrest, detention, and interrogation for drastic "reform?" What might the police accomplish with these added powers? The answer is simple and frightening: they could use them, as the record shows they have too often been inclined to do, to abolish or curtail a number of other important rights of the "suspect" and other citizens. These rights include:

1. *The right to be free from arbitrary arrest:* The requirement that the police arrest only upon reasonable cause is *not* an obsolete technicality. In an age before relativistic social "science" had

[6] Griswold, *The Fifth Amendment Today,* 7 (1955).

made it possible to reduce human liberty to the status of one variable in a complex social equation, Sir William Blackstone, the great 18th century English legal commentator, explained why:

> For if once it were left in the power, of any, the highest, magistrate to imprison arbitrarily whomever he or his officers thought proper (as in France it is daily practiced by the Crown) there would soon be an end of all other rights and immunities.[7]

More recently, a pair of uniquely qualified legal scholars have explored the continuing viability of the Anglo-American law's prohibition of arbitrary arrests on suspicion:

> The round-up or dragnet arrest, the arrest on suspicion, for questioning, for investigation or on an open charge all are prohibited by the law. It is undeniable that if those arrests were sanctioned by law, the police would be in a position to investigate a crime and to detect the real culprit much more easily, much more efficiently, much more economically, and with much more dispatch. It is equally true, however, that society cannot confer such power on the police without ripping away much of the fabric of a way of life which seeks to give the maximum of liberty to the individual citizen. The finger of suspicion is a long one. In an individual case it may point to all of a certain race, age group or locale. Commonly it extends to any who have committed similar crimes in the past. Arrest on mere suspicion collides violently with the basic human right of liberty. It can be tolerated only in a society which is willing to concede to its government powers which history and experience teach are the inevitable accoutrements of tyranny.[8]

The requirement that arrests be made only upon reasonable cause is so deeply rooted in our law that last year the Supreme Court of Deleware, one of the states which has enacted the Uniform Arrest Act, assumed that the Act does not change the historical requirements.[9] In so reading the Act, the court removed one of its most objectionable and dangerous features.

---

[7] 1 Blackstone, *Commentaries,* 98 (Field ed., 1827).

[8] Hogan and Snee, *The McNabb-Mallory Rule,* 47 Georgetown L. Jour. 1, 22 (1958).

[9] *De Salvatore* v. *State,* 163 A. 2d 244 (Del. Sup. Ct., 1960).

2. *The right to counsel in the police station:* The Chicago Bar Association, many of whose members probably need the reminder as much as anyone else, recently performed a valuable public service by publishing and circulating an interesting little pamphlet by Erle Stanley Gardner which makes this point:

> There is one thing, and only one thing, which stands between the citizen and the possible wrongful conviction of crime, and that is a body of lawyers so courageous, so fearless, and so willing to fight for the safeguards which the law has given us that they will impair their own popularity if necessary to see that we are given the protection of the law.[10]

The right to counsel—which enables a citizen charged with a crime to understand his rights and intelligently defend himself— is generally thought of only in connection with trials. But there is little doubt that the right to counsel extends into the police station. In Illinois, for example, a state law makes it a crime for policemen to deny the request of a prisoner in their custody to contact a lawyer (or family or friends).[11] The police ordinarily disregard this law until the prisoner is "booked"—although the statute explicitly makes this excuse irrelevant—and the inarticulate victims of this kind of flagrant violation of a criminal law are unable to demand its strict enforcement. One authority has said this of the early need for counsel:

> Although competent counsel is of great value at [trial], the time when the accused person really needs the help of a lawyer is when he is first arrested and from then on until trial. The intervening period is so full of hazards for the accused person that he may have lost any legitimate defense long before he is arraigned and put on trial.[12]

What kind of hazards? For one, as this essay will later make clear, the "Third Degree," which can and has made innocent

---

[10] Gardner, *The Case of the "Guilty" Client* (Chicago Bar Assn. Ed., 1961).

[11] Ill. Rev. Stats. 1959, Ch. 38, Sec. 449.1.

[12] Miller, *Lawyers and the Administration of Criminal Justice*, 20 A.B.A. Jour. 78 (1934): see Allison, *He Needs a Lawyer Now*, 42 Jour. Am. Jud. Soc. 113 (1948).

persons confess. More subtle hazards are revealed in one of Professor Inbau's most widely read books, *Lie Detection and Criminal Investigation* (2d ed., 1948), a manual for police interrogators, which prescribes various deceitful techniques for the police to employ on "suspects." It is readily apparent that these techniques will be largely unavailing in the cases of seasoned criminals, who know of their right not to talk and will be reinforced soon after arrest by their lawyer and bondsman. But it is just as apparent that these techniques can ensnare the frightened and bewildered into making incriminating statements. Such "suspects" are just those who most need a lawyer's help in combating deceitful police techniques and who most often will be unable to have such help—the poor, the ignorant, the foreign speaking, the young, the person who has never before been arrested. Statistics set out later in this essay show that many thousands, and perhaps the majority, of arrested persons who may face these police tactics are guilty of no crime.

Like most kinds of discrimination, then, attempts to curtail the right to counsel under the guise of giving the police more latitude for private interrogation, will harm just those persons who are most vulnerable.

It is true that the U.S. Supreme Court has held that a confession was not made unlawful by the failure of the police to comply with the defendant's request to consult with his lawyer during his interrogation.[13] But the pivotal fact in this case was that the prisoner had attended law school and thus was presumed to know his rights. In a very recent case, a high federal court has upset a state murder conviction because the defendant was not provided with counsel during a pre-trial police interrogation culminating in a confession and conducted while he was hospitalized for surgery and drugged—even though he had not requested the aid of counsel.[14]

Professor Inbau acknowledges that the "reforms" are designed to curtail the right to counsel in the police station because "the opportunity for an effective interrogation is ended, many times because of the advice [the 'suspect'] receives from his attorney to

[13] *Crooker v. California*, 357 U.S. 433 (1958).
[14] *Griffith v. Rhay*, 282 F. 2d 711 (C.A. 9, 1960).

keep his mouth shut." As a lawyer in criminal cases, I have sometimes exercised my judgment—and, I believe, fulfilled my obligation both to my client and my professional oath—to advise a
client not to talk. I have also, when I thought the circumstances
proper, advised clients to give statements, *in my presence,* to the
FBI and state prosecutors. The crucial point is this: the judgment
as to whether or not a lawyer is needed, and what advice is to be
given at any stage of a criminal prosecution can not safely be left
in the hands of the police.

So I do not agree that the interests of justice will be served by
curtailing the right to counsel in the police station. Rather, I believe that the right to counsel should be extended to the hundreds
of thousands of cases annually in which Americans are sent to
jail without seeing any lawyer but the prosecutor.[15]

3. *The right to Habeas Corpus:* The writ of *habeas corpus*
would apparently be unavailable during the preliminary two-
hour incarceration and the 24-to-48-hour secret detention urged
by Professor Inbau and the Uniform Arrest Act. The "Great Writ"
is one of Anglo-American law's great contributions to the armory
of liberty. The Constitution forbids its suspension except in cases
of "Rebellion or Invasion." [16] The writ commands a jailer to produce forthwith the person whom he is detaining so the court may
inquire into the legality of the detention. In Chicago and in other
places, in many cases the writ has been the only way to end an
illegal detention or, worse yet, police torture, as in the famous
case of Hector Verburgh, discussed below. The suggested "reforms" would broaden the powers of the police, instead of the
courts, to determine when the detention should end. Justice
William C. Douglas has made clear why the power should remain with the Courts:

"What happens behind doors that are opened and closed at the sole
discretion of the police is a black chapter in the history of every country—the free as well as the despotic, the modern as well as the
ancient . . ." [17]

---

[15] See *Equal Justice for the Accused* (report of Assn. of the Bar of City
of N.Y. and Natl. Legal Aid Assn., 1960).

[16] U.S. Const., Art. I, Sec. 9.

[17] *U.S.* v. *Carnigan,* 342 U.S. 36, 46 (1951) (concurring opinion).

The truth of this observation was certified before a congressional committee by a former Washington, D.C. policeman who—in one of the most remarkable conversions since that of St. Paul—had become a criminal defense lawyer:

"I have had the opportunity to be behind those doors . . . My experience leads me to the conclusion that the statement [that Justice Douglas made] is correct." [18]

4. *The right to be admitted to bail:* The "suspect" would not be eligible for bail during the expanded secret interrogation period which Professor Inbau and the Uniform Arrest Act advocate. The discussion above has indicated why our Constitutions guarantee the right to bail in almost all criminal cases. In one case where the Chicago police held a suspect for 36 hours in an attempt to exhort a confession, they were reminded by the state Supreme Court that:

Our statutes are intended to insure that persons who are arrested shall not be detained without reasonable cause, and to afford them an opportunity to be released upon bail. The fact that there is as yet insufficient evidence to justify preferring charges against a criminal suspect is not an excuse for detention, but is precisely the evil which the statute is aimed at correcting.[19]

5. *The privilege against self-incrimination:* Professor Inbau concedes that the "privately conducted police interrogation, covering a reasonable period of time" which he advocates, should apply only to "suspects who are not unwilling to be interviewed . . ." And in a fine book he has revealingly stated that the privilege against self-incrimination today "exists mainly in order to stimulate the police and prosecutor into a search for the most dependable evidence procurable by their own exertions; otherwise there probably would be an incentive to rely solely upon the less dependable that might be obtained as a result of compulsory interrogation." [20]

[18] Testimony of James R. Scullen, Hearings of Special Judiciary Committee Subcommittee to study decisions of the U.S. Supreme Court 153 (Aug. 2, 1957).
[19] *Fulford* v. *O'Connor*, 3 Ill. 2d 490, 500 (1954).
[20] Inbau, Self-Incrimination 6–7 (1950).

Yet, as the discussion above of the right to counsel indicates, Professor Inbau is not fully pleased by the defendant's freedom "to keep his mouth shut." We have this freedom today largely because Freeborn John Lilburne preferred to keep his mouth shut—and be whipped and pilloried for it—when the Star-Chamber sought to question him about his "seditious and heretical" books in 1637.[21] So today the Fifth Amendment is available to petty criminals as well as to United States senators, and the rule against self-incrimination still serves its principal historic function: it discourages police torture because the state must prove its case by independent evidence, not by compelling the defendant to incriminate himself. As one authority observes, "It is significant that the shadow of the rack and the thumbscrew was part of the background from which the [self-incrimination] rule emerged." [22] The suggested enlarged opportunities for detention and interrogation in the secrecy of the police station would give the police vastly increased opportunities to subvert the prisoner's right not to incriminate himself; they would place less of a premium on efficient police work and more of a premium on coercive interrogation and brutality.

6. *The right to a prompt court hearing and a judicial determination of guilt:* Almost all American jurisdictions require that arrested persons be brought before a magistrate "without unnecessary delay." [23] This requirement is the focal point of the attacks of Professor Inbau, the Uniform Arrest Act, and many police spokesmen. Until the prisoner is brought before a judicial officer, the detention is likely to be secret and the police can manage to keep the previously enumerated rights of the prisoner unavailable, if not unknown, to him. For example, he may be unable to call a lawyer and will be unable to be released on bail. Thus, a prompt court hearing is indispensable to the preservation of other important legal safeguards. Conversely, as Professor Inbau points out, "when the accused gets into the hands of a magistrate for the preliminary hearing, the opportunity for an effective interroga-

---

[21] Taylor, Grand Inquest 188 (1955); Griswold, op. cit. *supra*, n. 6 at 3.
[22] McCormick, *Handbook of the Law of Evidence,* 155–57, 252–57 (1954).
[23] E.g., Fed. Rules of Crim. Procedure, Rule 5; Ill. Rev. Stats. 1959, Ch. 38, Sec. 660.

tion is ended . . ." Blackstone supplied a rationale for the prisoner's right to a prompt hearing that still holds true after 200
years:

> To bereave a man of life, or by violence to confiscate his estate,
> without accusation or trial, would be so gross and notorious an act of
> despotism, as must at once convey the alarm of tyranny throughout the
> whole nation; but confinement of the person, by secretly hurrying him
> to jail, where his sufferings are unknown or forgotten, is a less public,
> a less striking, and therefore a more dangerous engine of arbitrary
> government.[24]

The magistrate at the preliminary hearing, or arraignment,
must determine whether a crime has been committed *and* whether
there is probable cause to believe the prisoner guilty. If not, the
prisoner must be set free. If so, the magistrate may decide a case
involving a minor crime; in felony cases, he will hold the prisoner
to the grand jury which determines whether or not to indict. In
the case of all felonies and most minor offenses, the defendant
may choose to be tried by a jury instead of a judge, and may be
convicted only upon proof beyond a reasonable doubt.

I have provided this elementary exposition of a rather elaborate
legal structure to make clear one basic error which appears to
permeate Professor Inbau's article and many policemen's thinking: it is *not* the job of the police to decide the question of guilt.
Their job is to present the evidence to the court. In a symposium
a few years ago, Judge Samuel S. Leibowitz, whose record as a
criminal court judge has definitely *not* been marked by the
leniecy toward the accused which some would expect of a former
great criminal defense lawyer, wrote:

Professor Inbau seemingly suggests different rules for the guilty and
the innocent. There can be only one set of rules and that is for the
protection of all persons accused of crime. Whether a particular suspect
is guilty or innocent can be determined only after and not before the
trial, and a predetermination of his guilt cannot be permitted to indicate or prescribe proper investigation procedures.[25]

---

[24] 1 Blackstone, op. cit. *supra*, n. 7 at 98 (Field ed., 1827).
[25] Leibowitz, *Safeguards in the Law of Interrogation and Confessions*, 52
Northwestern U. L. Rev. 86–87 (1957).

Yet Professor Inbau still tells us that police interrogation "need only be subject to the following restriction: Although both 'fair' and 'unfair' interrogation practices are permissible, nothing shall be done or said to the subject that will be apt to make an innocent person confess."

Given this advice, the "suspect" whom the policeman judges "guilty" becomes fair game. Detention itself may be employed as punishment when the police decide who is guilty and arrogate the judicial function unto themselves. The Chicago police for many years had a rule to this effect in cases of "well-known criminal(s)" (i.e., those so judged by the police). The rule survived even after a high federal court held it invalid.[26] So we are back to the *Federalist* and its reminder that the "accumulation of all powers . . . in the same hands . . . may justly be pronounced the very definition of tyranny."[27] As Jack Mabley, a Chicago newspaperman who is willing to speak out frequently against police illegality, put it: "Complications enter, however, when the police arrest a man, classify him as a wise guy or probably guilty, and beat him up. The complication is that he is not guilty."[28] That such mistakes are frequently made—even after a trial where the defendant has had the benefit of many safeguards—is too well known to require elaboration. The last book written by the late Jerome Frank, the most intellectually gifted judge this country ever had, supplied frightening documentation of a quantity of such miscarriages of justice, many of them induced by police brutality based on usurpation of the judicial process:

> When a police official declares that he tortures no one but criminals, he unwittingly exposes the real menace of the third degree: He is asserting the police have a right, without a trial, to determine the guilt of an arrested person. Once we concede any such right to the police, we potentially endanger all men. For then we authorize the police to torture anyone they, in their uncontrolled discretion, decide is a criminal.[29]

[26] *Wakat* v. *Harlib*, 253 F. 2d 59 (C.A. 7, 1958); see *Secret Detention by the Chicago Police* (a report by the American Civil Liberties Union, Ill. Div.), 19–21 (1959).

[27] Op. cit. *supra* n. 2, at 313.

[28] Chicago *Daily News*, May 20, 1958, P. 3.

[29] Frank and Frank, *Not Guilty*, 183 (1957).

The Third Degree and Police Lawlessness

It is time to inter a rather disingenuous assumption on which this essay has, in part, been proceeding. This assumption is that the enumerated rights of the defendant weigh heavily upon the consciences of our policemen and that, like good Knights of the Round Table struggling with the codes of chivalry, they would sooner suffer bitter heartbreak than break the rules. The new police administration in Chicago inspires admiration and hope in many of us, but a brief look at the past record, with an emphasis upon the police department Professor Inbau knows best, does not give us much confidence in police respect for individual liberty. In 1929, a group of distinguished lawyers appointed by President Hoover to survey American law enforcement reported:

The methods . . . in Chicago include the application of rubber hose to the back or the pit of the stomach, kicks in the shins, beating the shins with a club, blows struck with a telephone book on the side of the victim's head. The Chicago telephone book is a heavy one and a swinging blow with it may stun a man without leaving a mark.[30]

Another study found "lawless law-enforcement [against the uninfluential offender in Chicago] so extreme as to have the look of a sadistic release from the repressions damming police work in other directions." The methods are described as including rubber hoses across the abdomen, tear gas injected into a box placed over the suspect's head, the application of acid to the sex organs, and hanging suspects by the ankles.[31] In the case of Hector Verburgh, the janitor who was the famous "wrong man" in the Suzanne Degnan murder case, the use of a sadistic technique which has often been alleged was apparently proved against the Chicago police. The technique involves shackling a prisoner's hands behind him, looping a rope through the handcuffs and over a door top, and hoisting the prisoner until his feet dangle, with his toes barely touching the floor. The allegations have persisted. *The*

[30] 6 *Lawlessness in Law Enforcement*, report of National Commission on Law Observance and Enforcement (Wickersham Commission), n. 8, p. 126.
[31] Hopkins, *Our Lawless Police*, 167, 218–19 (1931).

Kohn Report quoted an anonymous Chicago policeman as follows in 1953:

Third degree methods of brutality are still being practiced in most stations. It is usually confined to hard slapping and a few well directed punches but occasionally an 'uncooperative' prisoner may be 'strung up' or seated in a position extremely painful to the spine.[32]

In at least 12 separate cases decided between 1948 and 1956, the Illinois Supreme Court either found that police had extorted an involuntary confession or ordered the trial court to reconsider the case because the State had failed to meet the burden of proving that its policemen had acted lawfully.[33] And of course only the minutest fraction of charges of police brutality can be preserved for review by high courts.

The reports of the U.S. Supreme Court tell the same bloody tale. In 1936, Chief Justice Charles Evans Hughes wrote a landmark opinion [34] reversing the murder convictions of Mississippi Negroes whose confessions were secured, with the aid of deputy sheriffs, by methods including the following: being strung up and down from a tree by a rope tied around the neck, and whipping with a buckled leather strap which cut their backs to pieces. A steady stream of coerced confession cases, from north and south, with white and black defendants, has followed. Just last year the Court decided a case in which a mentally incompetent robber suspect had been subjected to 8 or 9 hours of intensive questioning in a room no larger than six by eight feet (and perhaps smaller) which at times was filled with three police officers.[35] In reversing the conviction, Chief Justice Earl Warren wrote:

[32] Kohn, *Crime and Politics in Chicago,* 27 (I.V.I. ed., 1953).

[33] *People* v. *Dugan,* 401 Ill. 442, 82 N.E. 2d 482 (1948). *People* v. *Sloss,* 412 Ill. 61, 104 N.E. 2d 907 (1952). *People* v. *Rogers,* 413 Ill. 554, 110 N.E. 2d 201 (1953). *People* v. *Kirkpatrick,* 413 Ill. 595, 110 N.E. 2d 519 (1953). *People* v. *Wakat,* 415 Ill. 610, 114 N.E. 2d 706 (1953). *People* v. *Heirens,* 4 Ill. 2d 131, 122 N.E. 2d 231 (1954). *People* v. *Evans,* 4 Ill. 2d 213, 122 N.E. 2d 730 (1954). *People* v. *LaFrana,* 4 Ill. 2d 261, 122 N.E. 2d 583 (1954). *People* v. *Wagoner,* 8 Ill. 2d 188, 133 N.E. 2d 224 (1956). *People* v. *Adams,* 1 Ill. 2d 446, 115 N.E. 2d 630 (1953). *People* v. *Hiller,* 2 Ill. 2d 323, 118 N.E. 2d 11 (1954). *People* v. *Thomlison,* 400 Ill. 555, 81 N.E. 2d 434 (1948).

[34] *Brown* v. *Mississippi,* 297 U.S. 278 (1936).

[35] *Blackburn* v. *Alabama,* 361 U.S. 199, 206 (1960).

A prolonged interrogation of an accused, who is ignorant of his rights and who has been cut off from the moral support of friends and relatives, is not infrequently an effective technique of terror.

Justice Douglas summed up the observations gained from sitting at a unique vantage point during most of this period:

> One who sits, as I have, on an appellate bench for twenty years knows beyond peradventure that the third degree still flourishes underground in this country. No section is immune from it. In my lifetime it has reached in America the extremes other nations have known— from burning a suspect's feet with live coals to drilling holes through his live teeth. These are not standard police practices in America; but they recur too frequently for complacency. And they commonly strike at the lowly, inarticulate members of our communities, not at the elite.[36]

The kinds of excuses to which police officers are driven in the rare cases where they are actually prosecuted for brutality, as disclosed in two recent cases under the Federal Civil Rights Act, are revealing. In a civil suit for damages, brought by a man wrongly convicted and imprisoned for burglary because of a coerced confession, Chicago policemen testified that the prisoner had sustained multiple fractures and bruises by falling down the stairs after grappling with an officer for his gun.[37] And Nevada policemen, indicted for brutality including raining blows with a heavy flashlight on a prisoner, produced a police report attributing the severe bruises to an attempt by the prisoner to jump from a police car traveling at 50 m.p.h. In both cases, the federal juries disbelieved the policemen, and their verdicts were ultimately affirmed.[38]

This sordid background notwithstanding, Professor Inbau wants the police to be largely freed from court-imposed restraints in determining the limits of fair interrogation techniques.

The right to be free from police brutality could have been discussed, for the sake of symmetry, along with the rights of the de-

[36] Douglas, *The Means and the End*, 1959 Wash. U.L.Q. 103, 107.
[37] *Wakat v. Harlib*, 253 F. 2d 59 (C.A. 7, 1958); *Secret Detention*, op. cit. *supra* n. 26 at 15–17.
[38] *U.S. v. Pool*, 260 F. 2d 57 (C.A. 9, 1958).

fendant enumerated above. It has been given special treatment here for two obvious reasons: (1) many of the other rights exist largely as means to prevent police brutality, and (2) this is the most gruesome kind of police lawlessness when it occurs.

Of course no one article can completely catalogue all the kinds of illegal police conduct which may violate civil liberties. But brief mention of a few of these practices which are directly related to the "Third Degree," will help make clear the dimensions of the problem:

1. *Lengthy secret detentions:* A study of the Chicago police department's own records, conducted by the American Civil Liberties Union, showed that in 1956 more than 20,000 prisoners were secretly held in police stations for 17 hours or more without being booked—despite the legal requirement that prisoners be brought to court "without unnecessary delay." The same study showed that almost 2,000 of these prisoners were held without charge for two days or more, and 350, for three days or more.[39] The accuracy of this study has never been challenged, perhaps because of police fear of revealing the unknown: in almost one-third of the studied cases the police arrest slips on file with the Municipal Court failed to show the length of detention. There is good reason to believe that these cases involved the worst abuses.

The same study verified an observation made by many of us who have handled criminal cases in Chicago: prisoners are left in a lock-up for *at least 16 hours* while the arresting officers go home and sleep; the prisoner is booked and charged only after these officers return for their next shift on duty. I have investigated cases where it was apparent that prisoners were left in the lock-up overnight without being charged solely because of the personal antagonism of the arresting officers.

2. *Dragnet arrests:* One veteran Chicago police reporter, breaking free from the rules of the craft which often seem to prescribe that nothing is to be reported which may disturb police news sources, wrote:

In my two score years as a police reporter I have covered many murder investigations. I have seen police officials drag in dozens of

[39] *Secret Detention,* op. cit. *supra* n. 26 at 25–26, 45–46.

persons a day for intensive questioning—just for the record and without any real belief it would aid solution of the case.[40]

In Washington, D.C., at the height of local furor over whether or not the Supreme Court had unduly restricted proper police investigations, the police sought three 17-year-old Negroes who had committed a robbery. In one neighborhood 90 "suspects" were arrested, of whom 65 were over 50 years of age; 67 of these "suspects" were held in jail overnight; all were released by the next day without being charged with the crime. The local police chief, who of course is a vigorous critic of court decisions involving his men, admitted that this roundup had been carried "a bit too far," but said that he had issued no written orders to prevent similar illegal dragnets "because every crime must be investigated on its own merits." [41] Two astute local observers appropriately queried: "One wonders if those who sent up such a clamor when Andrew Mallory (see discussion below) was set free had much to say about this gross act of illegality on the part of the police." [42]

Professor Inbau would have us assume that broadening police arrest powers would have little effect on the average citizen. The published statistics of police departments, sketchy and unreliable as such self-serving documents are, indicate otherwise. In Chicago in two recent years 84,634 arrests were made on apparent mere suspicion, the charges of "loitering" and disorderly conduct later being dismissed by the police courts. In 1955, 22,477 "suspects," or 83% of those "detained for investigation," were released by the Detroit police without being charged. In Cleveland during two recent years 67% of the 25,400 persons "held for investigation" by the Detective Bureau alone were released without charge.[43] With loose arrest practices thus institutionalized in our police departments, one may rightly question—and fear—the conse-

[40] Chicago *American*, Aug. 29, 1957.
[41] *Trilling* v. *U.S.*, 260 F. 2d 677, 690 (1958) (dissenting opinion); Testimony of Myron Ehrlich, *Admission of Evidence*, Hearings before Senate Judiciary Committee Subcommittee 78 (July 17, 1958).
[42] Hogan and Snee, op. cit. *supra* n. 8, at 23.
[43] Foote, *Safeguards in the Law of Arrest*, 52 Northwestern U.L. Rev 16, 25–29 (1957).

quences of giving the police further power to indulge their often groundless "suspicions" by locking citizens up.

3. *Convicting the innocent and the "frame-up"*: The realization that innocent men can be sent to prison, or executed, because of extorted false confessions and/or police-inspired "frame-ups" is even more shocking than the "Third Degree"—both because the wrong is more enduring and because this represents the basest perversion of the judicial process, which is designed to serve truth and justice. How often does this happen? Of course no one knows. The guiltiest culprit can often sing a persuasive song of "frame-up." But does it happen?

Ask Leslie Wakat, who spent seven years in prison for "burglary" because five Chicago detectives took six days, during which time he suffered a broken hand and serious injuries to many other parts of his body, to beat false confessions out of him.[44] Ask Joe Majczek and Ted Marcinkiewicz, who spent twelve and seventeen years respectively in prison for the "murder" of a chicago policeman, whose surviving colleague threatened a witness into giving false testimony.[45] They were ultimately freed largely because of the unwavering faith of Majczek's mother and some fine work by Chicago *Times* newspapermen. Or ask Rudolph Sheeler, who spent six years in prison for the murder of a Philadelphia policeman, because police had brutally tortured a false confession out of him.[46] And then read the book written by Judge Frank and his daughter *Not Guilty*, which provocatively discusses a number of similar cases.

I have shared in the heavy responsibility of presenting to a court the claim that private detectives, working with a policeman, successfully contrived to "frame" a real estate appraiser for the theft of a 10c shopping bag because he refused to sign a false confession; ultimately, the larceny conviction was reversed.[47]

Within the past two years in Chicago, two separate cases have shown an ominous common pattern. Two men of apparent good

[44] See *People* v. *Wakat*, 415 Ill. 610 (1958), *Wakat* v. *Harlib*, 253 F. 2d 59 (C.A. 7, 1957), *Secret Detention*, op. cit. *supra* n. 26 at 15–17.
[45] Frank and Frank, op. cit. *supra* n. 29, at 1–30.
[46] Id. at 167–80.
[47] *People* v. *Caine*, 26 Ill. App. 2d 364 (1960).

standing complained of police illegality—one of wide-open vice in his neighborhood, the other of a police assault on him. Both quickly found themselves indicted on improbable sex charges, and the police produced a claimed "confession" from one. Both men were eventually acquitted on the sex charges—thereby supporting, though concededly not proving, their charges of police "frame-ups." The effect of these cases—even with the acquittals —on persons thinking of challenging police illegality needs no explanation. Congressional records report the surprise of Washington, D.C., officials when they realized that a rape to which they had just secured a confession had been cleared by the conviction of a different man only two days before.[48]

These and other like cases make three things clear: (1) Despite Professor Inbau's desire to place far greater reliance on confessions in order to convict criminals, we have learned that confessions can be most unreliable where police coercion is sufficiently ingenious, painful, and persistent, (2) we are being asked to broaden substantially the same dangerous powers which our policemen have often seriously misused; and (3) at the same time we are being asked to curtail severely judicial review of police lawlessness.

I have perhaps been remiss in failing to show until now what Professor Inbau says in his article:

I want to make it unmistakably clear I am not an advocate of the so-called 'third degree,' for I am unalterably opposed to the use of any interrogation or technique that is apt to make an innocent person confess.

Undoubtedly this is sincere. But unfortunately Professor Inbau's quixotic view of the police persuades him to oppose the most, or perhaps the only, effective remedies which we have *at present* to prevent the police from relying on the "Third Degree." In his manual for police interrogators, one of the tactics Professor Inbau recommends "to cause the subject to lose the equilibrium" is the

[48] *Admission of Evidence in Certain Cases*, Hearings of Subcommittee No. 2 of the House Judiciary Committee 111 (Dec. 10, 1943).

so-called "friend and enemy act." [49] This means that the combination of one policeman acting tough to a suspect and the other appearing sympathetic may help induce a confession. Of course Professor Inbau goes on in the same book to warn against physical abuse and threats or promises.[50]

But why should we expect policemen who are unable to comply with unambiguous laws which tell them to bring their prisoners before a judge promptly and that the "Third Degree" is illegal to accept of their own volition the limitations which Professor Inbau suggests? Isn't it much more likely that policemen, who are not ordinarily verbal sophisticates, will apply the "friend and enemy" act by doing what comes naturally: the "bad" policeman will prove his enmity with his fist or blackjack and the "good" policeman will prove his goodness with soothing promises of leniency. This same naive view of policemen leads Professor Inbau to attack with special vigor the rules by which many courts exclude evidence obtained from prisoners as a result of unconstitutional police tactics, or during periods of illegal detention, and the related decisions of the U.S. Supreme Court in the celebrated *McNabb* [51] and *Mallory* [52] cases.

Illegally obtained evidence and the McNabb and Mallory Cases

The McNabbs were illiterate Tennessee mountaineers. During a raid on their backwoods still in 1940, a federal revenue agent was shot and killed. Arrested and thrust into a barren cell in the middle of the night, the McNabbs were subjected for several days to "unremitting questioning by numerous officers" *in camera* and without the benefit of seeing attorneys or friends. The ensuing confessions helped convict the McNabbs of murder.

Justice Felix Frankfurter, whose formidable legal skills have

[49] Inbau and Reid, *Lie Detection and Criminal Investigation,* 119–20 (2d ed., 1948).
[50] Id. at 149.
[51] *McNabb* v. *U.S.,* 318 U.S. 332 (1943).
[52] *Mallory* v. *U.S.,* 354 U.S. 449 (1957); see Hogan and Snee, op. cit. *supra* n. 8.

frequently been used in recent years to explain why the Court should *not* honor claimed deprivations of civil liberties, delivered an opinion which eloquently summed up many of the arguments advanced in this essay. He first explained the importance of the "impressively persuasive requirement" that arrested persons be brought to court promptly:

> For this procedural requirement checks resort to those reprehensible practices known as the 'third degree' which, though universally rejected as indefensible, still find their way into use. It aims to avoid all the evil implications of secret interrogation of persons accused of crime. It reflects not a sentimental but a sturdy view of law enforcement. It outlaws easy but self-defeating ways in which brutality is substituted for brains as an instrument of crime detection.[53]

After examining the record, which failed to show that the Mc-Nabbs had been taken before a judicial officer as the law plainly required, Justice Frankfurter explained why the courts could not accept the confessions:

> Plainly, a conviction resting on evidence secured through such a flagrant disregard of the procedure which Congress has commanded cannot be allowed to stand without making the courts themselves accomplices in willful disobedience of law ... We are not concerned with law enforcement practices except in so far as courts themselves become instruments of law enforcement. We hold only that a decent regard for the duty of courts as agencies of justice and custodians of liberty forbids that men should be convicted upon evidence secured under the circumstances revealed here.[54]

Before the *McNabb* decision, "federal law enforcement agents had long been accustomed to look upon the various provisions demanding prompt arraignment . . . as empty of force or consequence." [55] But federal officers would, or perhaps could, not be sure that the Supreme Court meant to apply seriously the prompt

[53] 318 U.S. at 344.
[54] Id. at 345–47.
[55] Hogan and Snee, op. cit. *supra* n. 8 at 3.

arraignment requirement until the Mallory decision was handed down in 1957. In that case Justice Frankfurter, for a unanimous Court, held that failure of the Washington, D.C., police to bring a rape suspect before a judicial officer between the time of his arrest at 2:30 p.m. and his confession the same evening invalidated the confession. The Court concluded that only by insisting on prompt arraignment can the stigma of the "Third Degree" be removed from the police and judicial processes.

The dilemma posed in such cases for courts which earnestly wish to eliminate the "Third Degree" has been probed by two outstanding high court judges. Justice Walter Schaefer of the Illinois Supreme Court, a jurist of singular erudition and perception, said in a memorable lecture a few years ago (which he concluded with the telling observation that "The quality of a nation's civilization can be largely measured by the methods it uses in the enforcement of its criminal law"):

> The confession cases generally follow a rather set pattern. Following the commission of a crime the police take the accused into custody. During the course of his detention he is not permitted access to counsel and he is interrogated about the crime. The period of detention varies, but it is almost always longer than the local law allows. The interrogation terminates with his confession. He is then brought before a magistrate and formally charged with the offense. When the confession is offered at the trial the defendant does not usually deny having made it, but he repudiates it. Violence and threats on the part of the interrogating officers are alleged. These allegations are almost always denied. On rare occasions there will be objective evidence that the prisoner suffered injuries while in custody; in such cases there will be conflicting testimony as to how they were incurred . . . The record is often barren of the evidence which would help resolve this conflict. It frequently fails to show the actual mental and physical condition of the defendant, or more important, the course of the interrogation itself . . .[56]

Justice Douglas has made the same point more forcefully:

[56] Schaefer, *Federalism and State Criminal Procedure*, 70 Harv. L. Rev. 1, 11, 26 (1956).

When the police hold a man incommunicado the opportunities for coercion are great. Proof of it is always difficult. There is the word of the accused against the word of the police. The judge—or the jury—that has to decide where the truth lies often has a difficult, if not impossible, task.[57]

The *Mallory* case, then, attempted to answer the vexing problem caused by the fact that the "Third Degree" and other illegal pressures employed to extort confessions, are usually not objectively verifiable in court. The Court's answer was that the police should be denied the *opportunity* to practice the "Third Degree": Confessions secured during a detention where the police confined the suspect long enough to apply illegal coercion would not be accepted by the federal courts. The federal courts, it was declared, would no longer be a party to the practice of lengthy secret detentions by the police—the practice which makes possible the "Third Degree."

A great outcry followed. Such champions of human liberty as the Hon. Jim Eastland of Mississippi came forward with bills to overrule the *Mallory* decision. None passed, but the margin was close. It was charged that it would be impossible to enforce the laws prohibiting the kinds of conduct which are considered illegal in the nation's capital. Professor Inbau says that the *Mallory* rule "has had a very crippling effect on police investigations" in Washington. But there are published figures which belie these charges. The chart set out below, which appears in the testimony of a District Commissioner at a Congressional hearing,[58] makes it appear doubtful that the *Mallory* decision, handed down in June, 1957 has had a serious effect on the ability of Washington police to solve crimes. Note that the total solution rate was higher in 1958 —the year following *Mallory*—then it had been in five out of the last six preceding years:

[57] Douglas, *The Right of the People*, 155 (1958); see also Hogan and Snee, op. cit. *supra* n. 8 at 27.
[58] Testimony of Commissioner Robert McLaughlin, Hearings of House Appropriations Committee, Subcommittee on District of Columbia, 86th Cong., 1st Sess., p. 441.

Classification				Percent solved			
	1952	1953	1954	1955	1956	1957	1958
Criminal homicide	96.4	88.2	97.2	100.	96.5	97.7	93.8
Rape	95.6	92.9	93.6	93.4	91.8	92.0	91.9
Robbery	70.5	58.6	57.5	63.3	59.2	54.8	61.3
Aggravated assault	82.8	81.3	85.1	88.5	86.8	88.8	84.3
Housebreaking	46.3	37.5	44.0	52.6	51.1	47.2	50.5
Larceny—theft	34.9	36.1	35.2	40.5	36.9	37.4	40.8
Auto theft	31.9	23.2	26.9	28.4	38.7	34.7	31.9
Total	49.3	46.0	49.4	55.6	50.2	49.5	51.0

Comparable evidence is found in a recent speech by Oliver Gasch, another able critic of the *Mallory* decision, who as federal prosecutor for the District of Columbia is most directly confronted with the decision. While continuing to deplore the rule and its results, Mr. Gasch admitted that *"Mallory* questions, that is to say confessions or admissions, are of controlling importance in probably less than 5% of our criminal prosecutions," and further that because of the courts' insistence on legal arrests for probable cause and prompt arraignment "police work is generally more thorough and exact" and "reliance on confessions generally has been minimized." [59]

Professor Inbau and I agree that the F.B.I. is living proof that effective law enforcement and respect for civil liberties are not incompatible. The F.B.I. operates subject to the *Mallory* rule and without a Uniform Arrest Act; its conviction rate is better than 90%. Do we dare give our local police departments, on their proven records, far broader powers than the F.B.I. has to arrest, detain, and interrogate "suspects"?

Certainly we all favor the kinds of measures Professor Inbau suggests to improve the quality of our police—better training, more adequate compensation, a merit system, freedom from unwholesome political influences, and adequate internal supervision and discipline. This is the challenging core of Orlando Wilson's great experiment in Chicago, which appears to be making distinct progress. But even in that distant day when our local

[59] Gasch, *Law Enforcement in the District of Columbia and Civil Rights,* 3–4 (1960).

police departments may be raised to the calibre of the F.B.I., I suggest it would be naive tampering with liberty to enlarge their powers along the lines suggested by Professor Inbau. The F.B.I. proves that the job can be done without such powers.

The record shows that we do not yet have sufficient remedies against police lawlessness. It is a fair bet that *none* of the police officers responsible for the flagrant illegalities described in this essay were ever appropriately disciplined by their superiors. Most are still on the force, or have been honorably retired, and many have been promoted. One of the officers involved in the Hector Verburgh incident later became Chicago's police commissioner. Damage suits against wrongdoing police officers are generally a waste of a lawyer's, and the injured person's, time,[60] though there are some indications that this may be changing. Criminal prosecutions based on police violations of civil liberties are sporadic; prosecutors are not likely to indict those whom they need to build their cases.

With such remedies against police lawlessness largely ineffectual, Professor Inbau nevertheless tells us: "The courts have no right to police the police." But the courts do have an unshakable responsibility to interpret and apply the Constitution and the laws, as well as their own procedural rules, in the trial of criminal cases and in deciding what evidence shall be considered lawful. This is precisely what the Supreme Court did in the *McNabb* and *Mallory* cases. When the California Supreme Court, plagued by years of persistent and willful police violations of civil liberties, finally adopted a rule excluding evidence obtained through illegal police actions, it stated:

> Other remedies have completely failed to secure compliance with the constitutional provisions on the part of police officers with the attendant result that the courts under the old rule have been constantly required to participate in, and in effect condone, the lawless activities of law enforcement officers.

[60] Foote, *Tort Remedies for Police Violations of Individual Rights,* 39 Minn. L. Rev., 473 (1954); Wilson, *Police Arrest Privileges in a Free Society: A Plea for Modernization,* 51 Jour. Crim. L. & Crim. 395, 400 (1960).

When, as in the present case, the very purpose of an illegal search and seizure is to get evidence to introduce at a trial, the success of the lawless venture depends entirely on the court's lending its aid by allowing the evidence to be introduced.[61]

Of course, many police spokesmen in California howled at this decision—including the police chief of Los Angeles, whose subordinates, according to the published court reports, have been involved in numerous violations of defendants' constitutional rights. But listen to the California Attorney General, the state's chief law enforcement officer:

I believe further that because of this decision the police are doing better work. Their investigations are more thorough and within American constitutional concepts. More guilty pleas have resulted because of intensive pre-arrest work.[62]

In sum, then, there are three principal reasons for my conclusion that it would be dangerously naïve to give the police the added powers sought by Professor Inbau:

1. The ideal of individual liberty in a free society.
2. The record of our police forces, which proves that we need more—not less—safeguards to prevent abuse of the very powers which Professor Inbau would expand.
3. The probability that such powers would encourage attempts to solve cases by dragnet arrests and coercive interrogation, rather than by civilized and efficient police methods.

Now to face two of the "hard cases" offered by Professor Inbau to show the injustice of present restrictions on the police. It should be noted that this kind of argumentation cannot prove wholly satisfactory because, as long as defendants possess *any* legal safeguards, some cases will be difficult—or insoluble—for the police. But even the most sensational examples offered do not detract from my conclusions:

[61] *People* v. *Cahan*, 44 Cal. 2d 434, 445 (1955).
[62] *Kamisar, Wolf and Lustig Ten Years Later: Illegal State Evidence in State and Federal Courts*, 43 Minn. L. Rev. 1083, 1158 (1959).

1. *The Starved Rock murders:* Despite Professor Inbau's fears that restrictions on police interrogation might prevent solution of the horrifying murder of the three matrons in an Illinois state park, a young man is on trial for the crimes as this essay is written. Of course he gave a confession. Of course he says it was coerced. Of course the police say it wasn't. Ultimately, the defendant's fate will largely rest on whether or not the jury or reviewing courts believe that the confession was coerced.

The well-known attachment of many of our police departments to "Third Degree" tactics may conceivably lead a jury to disbelieve a true confession in some cases and thus let a guilty person go free; many Criminal Courthouse observers in Chicago felt this was why the State lost a recent highly publicized murder trial there, despite the fact that a confession was received in evidence.

2. *The no-eye-witness case of the woman murdered by her brother-in-law:* In this case, Professor Inbau says, a confession was secured during a period of unlawful detention before bringing the prisoner before a magistrate. Apparently the courts were satisfied that the confession was voluntary. If the prisoner was willing to talk, why couldn't the police interrogate him after they had complied with the law? (In a murder case, bail would ordinarily not be available.) By unlawfully detaining the prisoner in the secrecy of the station house, the police could have raised a substantial doubt in the minds of a court or jury as to the voluntariness of the confession, and thus bungled away a good case.

It may be retorted that all of the above shows that police now substantially exercise the powers which the Uniform Arrest Act would "grant" (and then some)—so why not codify existing practice into law? My answer would be that at the same session of the Legislature a bill should be introduced to repeal the Ten Commandments. Our civilization has had a hard time living with *that* too for the past few thousand years. But both the Decalogue and the Bill of Rights represent moral ideals; the farther we retreat from these ideals, the more they become worth pursuing.

I have left only a few minor quibbles with Professor Inbau—and one major quarrel.

Professor Inbau assumes that public opinion, that elusive democratic deity, has been seduced by the civil libertarians. The conquest, if there was one, was most evanescent. Occasionally when the police have made an incredible mistake—such as the physical mistreatment a few years back in an abandoned Chicago police station of a "suspect" who turned out to be a distinguished judge [63]—the public and press clamor for curbs on police misconduct. But despite the staggering volume of dragnet arrests, the well-fed and articulate members of society, such as those who read this journal, rarely are touched by police lawlessness and thus do not really care about it. A recent Illinois governor, apparently operating on the theory that what they don't know won't hurt them, vetoed a bill which would have simply required the posting of prisoners' constitutional rights in detention places! And remember that it was not the insitutionalization of callous disregard for individual liberties which led to the "new order" in the Chicago police department; only after the policemen-as-burglars scandal exploded did a surprised Chicago awake one morning to find that it had a Police Superintendent who was a Californian and a college professor.

Professor Inbau says that we should realize that "much more is required for totalitarianism than an effective police force." Maybe—but an effective police force lacking concern for individual liberties and subject to little outside control will give you an awfully good head start. The Nazis were only a minority party in the German government when Herman Goering became boss of the Prussian police; the Communists repeated the same tale in Eastern Europe. The demand that the courts leave the police alone should also be considered in the light of the 1933 decision of the Prussian administrative court that Goering's secret police were not subject to judicial control.[64]

Professor Inbau seems to be heartened by claims that the English police are breaking the famous "Judge's Rules." By some retrogressive transcultural process, the English have recently picked up some vulgar American habits, such as racial discrimination, commercial television, and rock and roll music, apparently together with a little of police brutality. A recent book by a Lord

---

[63] *Secret Detention,* op. cit. *supra* n. 26 at 5.
[64] Fraenkel, *The Dual State,* 26 (1941).

Justice of the English High Court reveals a basic difference between the two countries: "There is a convention that the English
police will act fairly, and the judges are the guardians of it too."[65]
Unfortunately, despite the fact that our society—unlike the English who maintain liberty without a written Constitution—has had
a Bill of Rights for 170 years, too often we have lacked that "convention" of police fairness. In England, one isolated act of police
brutality may result in the convocation of an inquiring commission. The authority on whom Professor Inbau relies for his view
of the English police describes this typically English response to
police transgressions:

> In 1959, two Birmingham detectives struck and kicked a Jamaican
> in the police station when they were questioning him about his be-
> havior towards a white woman in the street. They were convicted and
> resigned from the police force.[66]

This did not happen in Birmingham, Ala. In the same article,
the English authority, who has lived in this country, notes the
force of Professor Inbau's plea for the police to use "unethical"
and "deceitful" tactics on "suspects," and then states:

> It is important to consider whether the adoption of tactics that
> would contravene ordinary standards of honest dealing may not harm
> the police in the eyes of the public and cause a loss of confidence. In
> the United States, one of the chief problems confronting the police is
> that the public (with some reason) has no trust in them and will not
> co-operate by giving them information of crime.[67]

Now, it may be asked, is not the picture of the police painted
in this essay rather one-sided? If by that, it is meant that I have
marshaled the evidence in order to support a point of view, I
certainly plead guilty. What about the many decent policemen
who work competently and fairly and are underpaid? Their story

---

[65] Devlin, *The Criminal Prosecution in England*, 16 (1958).
[66] Williams, *Questioning by the Police: Some Practical Considerations*,
1960 Crim. L. Rev. (Eng.) 325, 343–44.
[67] *Id.* at 337.

deserves to be told—but not in response to a plea for "reforms" of the kind Professor Inbau suggests.

I am congenitally unable to deliver the unctuous disclaimer which assures the audience that I must be a decent fellow because "some of my best friends are . . ." (the blank can be filled in appropriately for any social occasion). As an American citizen, my best friend is my liberty.

I hesitate to utter my final thought because it is peripheral to the main topic of this essay; but I do so because I regard it as central to a more important subject. Professor Inbau concludes with a blast at Supreme Court judges who "line up 'on the liberal side'" and "adopt a 'turn 'em loose'" policy in order to write their own epitaphs as "great judges." To me, it seems more "conservative" than "liberal" to protect individual liberty against state encroachment.

But I am profoundly disturbed by these remarks because they seem to carry an implication that the Supreme Court is not doing its conscientious best to decide each case before it. Like most young lawyers I would yield to no one in asserting that the Court —like police departments, churches, universities, and other mortal institutions—has made many wretched mistakes in its long history, before and after *Dred Scott,* in and out of the police field, and right down to the movie censorship decision at the present term. But I also appreciate the tremendous burden of responsibility which the Court bears in adjusting competing claims involving fundamental national interests and enabling us to settle bitterly divisive controversies in an orderly manner. As Professor Harry Kalven has recently written of the Justices, "The rest of us are fortunate indeed that our job is so much easier and less responsible." [68]

For this reason, and one other, I feel that a scholar or a lawyer is obligated to state his criticisms of the Court with particularity and not to suggest that the Justices' motives are improper. The other reason is obvious: We are presently engaged in a great national struggle testing whether the racist theories which we had hoped were buried with Hitler shall rule our schools or whether

---

[68] Kalven, *Metaphysics of the Law of Obscenity,* in Kurland (ed.), *The Supreme Court Review,* 1, 45 (1960).

the American promise of individual dignity can be fulfilled for *all* our citizens. And since the *School Desegregation* cases, the Supreme Court has filled a unique and rather exposed position in that struggle as the firm articulator of the national conscience.

Now of course I do not suggest for a moment that Professor Inbau sides with the racists. But neither do many of the other good people who join the ominous attack on the Court as an institution and thus on the ideal of equal justice under law. At any conclave where members of dissident minority blocs gather, you will hear the complaints that precedents are being overthrown (i.e., that past mistakes are being recognized and corrected), some mumbling about Supreme Court "usurpation," and a call for curbs on the Court's appellate jurisdiction in civil rights cases. The principle complainants, of course, are those few faded flowers of the fallen Confederacy who prate of "interposition" and "massive resistance"—which mean official racist lawlessness— and who find the sublimest manifestation of their Christian morality in throwing the first stone at little Negro schoolgirls. We can help the Supreme Court with tough, pointed criticism of its work; we can help only the racists with scattergun attacks on the Justices' motives.

At the recent Northwestern University Law School Symposium on the Administration of Criminal Justice, my colleague, Bernard Weisberg, general counsel of the Illinois Division of the ACLU, closed his talk [69] with this provocative thought: We hear much about experiments, such as the Uniform Arrest Act, to *decrease* personal liberty; it would be refreshing to hear instead about experiments to *increase* personal liberty. Some obvious experiments suggest themselves in the police and criminal law field—*e.g.*, use of summons rather than arrest in minor cases, making appeals less expensive, providing for impartial and objective records of what actually occurs during police interrogations, and making available expert-witness and investigatory help, as well as attorneys, to indigent defendants. We can hopefully look to our law schools and foundations to help think of and devise others.

Do we have too much crime, and do we need effective ways to

[69] To be published in a forthcoming issue of the Jour. Crim. L. & Crim.

fight it? Of course. But do we have too much personal liberty? In the past 44 years we have seen societies willingly give up their liberty "temporarily" and in the supposed interest of some overriding societal good—only to find it irretrievably lost. Who can really say that we would not be similarly deluded if we follow Professor Inbau's suggestions and forfeit a significant portion of our personal liberty to the tender and substantially uncontrolled discretion of the police?

AN INTERCOLLEGIATE DEBATE

(*West Point Final, 1962*)

RESOLVED: THAT LABOR
ORGANIZATIONS SHOULD BE UNDER THE
JURISDICTION OF ANTITRUST LEGISLATION

AFFIRMATIVE: Baylor University

NEGATIVE: Ohio State University

1st affirmative: Cal Kent

Thank you very much. Mike and I, in reviewing *the 1955 report of the Attorney General's Commission to study the antitrust laws,* discovered that labor unions can be prosecuted under the antitrust laws only in three instances: (1) when their acts involve fraud or violence, (2) when they act in collusion with business groups, and when their acts lie outside of the legitimate functions of a labor union, and (3) when they are not involved in a labor dispute as defined by the Norris-LaGuardia Act. It is because Mike and I feel that this limited application of antitrust to labor does not provide sufficient protection to the American economy from the anticompetitive acts of labor that we stand resolved: that labor organizations should be under the jurisdiction of antitrust legislation.

In order to define terms, "labor organizations" means any employee groups which meet with management for the purpose of negotiating wages and conditions of employment. "Antitrust legislation" simply means a legal prescription against an unreasonable restraint of trade.

Since 1932, United States policy in applying antitrust to labor has been predicated upon the supposition that the legitimate functions of labor unions must be safeguarded at all costs. As a consequence of this supposition, unions—acting alone and in their own self-interest—are today free to restrain trade in manners which businesses or even unions themselves, if they acted in combination with business groups, are not allowed to do—a curious and, we believe, unjustified legal inconsistency. The consequences of this inconsistency and the misplaced emphasis of our labor policy have proven extremely detrimental, both in the areas of production and distribution of goods for the American economy.

Let's take a look at some examples. First of all, turning to the area of production, excessive union power resulting from an antitrust immunity allows unions to perpetrate makework and featherbedding practices which raise prices and pinch productivity. These are restraints of trade and have these effects, as was determined by the Supreme Court in the precedent-setting case, *U.S. v. Brims*, in 1926. Makework and featherbedding are restraints of trade because they tend to raise prices or to otherwise take from the buyers or consumers the advantages which would occur to them from free competition within the market.

We could look at some examples. We could turn to the railroad industry, which has been forced to suffer since 1919 under the same set of work rules—work rules which demand, for instance, that an unnecessary fireman ride in the cab of a locomotive even though this locomotive is diesel—which require that train crews be paid a full day's wages for each 100 miles they travel just because back in 1919 that's all the further a train could go. And today's trains can go 300, 500, sometimes 600 miles. In commenting on this situation, Lawrence Fertig, in his new book on *Prosperity Through Freedom*, tells us this: that the estimated figure of the cost to the consumers and the industry is over 500 million dollars a year.

We could proceed to the construction industry, where the list of makework is almost endless. For example, there is a limit on ˈthe number of outlets which any electrician may install on a given day, while carpenters may not hang more than a limited number of doors. Plenty of money could be saved if threaded pipe could be delivered for installation, but this would violate union rules. Bricklayers who used to lay a thousand bricks a day are not allowed to lay more than 500. As a result, the on-site labor costs involved in building a home are up 20% due to this form of waste.

And then we could turn to the entertainment industry. Last Tuesday, Mike and I went and saw "Carnival," and we enjoyed the show; but our ticket cost us $6.90. The reason: superfluous electricians, stage hands, and musicians had to be hired and paid for. In commenting on the problem which exists within this industry, Frank Chandrow, formerly of the Yale Economics Department, tells us this: "The union decrees that no show may open without the presence of a full crew, consisting of at least one carpenter, an electrician, a curtain raiser, and helpers who help do nothing. A one-set show requires only the pushing of buttons to raise and lower the curtain, something which could be done by the stage manager; but the union, nevertheless, requires the presence of five men."

This, then, becomes the affirmative need area in this field of production. Well, you may be asking yourself, "Why aren't the unions prosecuted for these anticompetitive acts?" For the simple reason the Supreme Court has ruled in the precedent-establishing case of *U.S.* v. *American Federation of Musicians* that these are legitimate labor activities. The union's conduct, featherbedding and makework, was held to involve a labor dispute concerning terms and conditions of employment and, thus, not subject to the antitrust laws.

The problem in the area of production, then, is one of makework and featherbedding practices. But we could turn to another area today, and that is the area of distribution. And here the unjustified union exemption leads us to other problems. First of all, unions are free to discriminate against one employer in favor of another employer. The case in point here is *Adams Dairy* v. *St.*

Louis Dairy, heard October 14, 1958. What transpired was simply this. The Adams Dairy Company was forced by the union to pay a higher rate to its drivers than the union forced St. Louis Dairy to pay to its drivers. As a result, Adams Dairy was forced to raise its price and thus was forced out of the competitive market. It lost its competitive advantage. In commenting on this particular situation, Professors of Law, Meriweather and Smith, in their 1960 text, *Labor Relations Law*, tell us this: "The union's purpose was to force the one dairy which was adversely affected to adopt uneconomical practices which lessened its capacity to compete with home deliveries." Why wasn't there prosecution in this particular case? Proof of the essential element of a union conspiring or conniving with a combination of businessmen to suppress competition was found to be lacking. This, then, is the reason why unions can discriminate against one employer in favor of another.

But, then, there is another area, and that is: the union today is free to control the internal operations of an industry. Turning to the 1958 report of the Washington State Economics Department, "In some industry the right to do business is openly and legally controlled by the unions. The unions decide who will be allowed to operate, who will be permitted to hire men, and who will receive delivery of materials." The case in point here is *Davis Pleating and Button Company* v. *California Sportswear and Dress Association,* heard in the courts January 27, 1956. What transpired was this: Davis was involved in selling pleatings and buttons to each of the individual members of the California Sportswear and Dress Association. What then happened was he successfully resisted an attempt at unionization. The union then forced each individual member of the association into a contract whereby they agreed not to buy from any nonunion firm. And the court found this all legal because only one union, one employer, was involved.

And then I think the third area which we can delineate is that unions today are free to force businesses out of business. The case in point here which established the precedent was *Weier* v. *Chicago Plasterers Institute,* heard December 23, 1959. Now, what transpired in this precedent-setting case was that Arthur Weier had received the exclusive franchise for the Quickbric plastering process within the Chicago area. He continued to proceed with operations for almost two years, thinking he had the approval of the union. It was a prerequisite for doing business that you had the approval of the union, and the union's president had given him the go-ahead signal. Two years later it turned out that the union's president was not in a position to approve him, but the union's board had to. The union withdrew their support, he was not able to get union plasterers, and his subcontractors who were using union plasterers were not able, because of union pressure, to buy from him. As a result, he lost his contract, his subcontractors, his job, and his business. What was the result of this particular precedent which was established in this case? The 1961 report of the Small Businessmen's Association tells us this: "Over 10,000 small businesses have been forced out of business by this type of union activity in the past two years since the Weier decision took place."

Then what is it that Mike and I are trying to tell you? We have an unjustified legal inconsistency today, which means that unions are free, acting alone, to do what they cannot do acting in collusion, or what business cannot do acting in business' own self-interest. As a result, we have restraints of trade—the restraints of trade of makework and featherbedding—and we delineated three examples. And then we could turn to problems in the area of distribution. And the net result of all of these has been the same effect. That is, prices have been raised, productivity has been pinched, and even men have been forced out of business. It is because Mike and I feel that it is time to put the public interest in the place of primacy in our national labor relations today that we think that the antitrust laws should be extended over more union activities.

1st negative: Dale Williams

Having had the opportunity in the past to listen to some of the tapes of these final rounds, I know that usually the speakers start off by saying how happy they are to be here. I will simply say that at this point I cannot convey my feeling at being here in this particular position. I simply hope that you feel what I do in that situation and you understand as I do what it means to me.

With that in mind, then, let's go immediately into this affirmative case and see exactly what we have heard. Now, the members of the affirmative team today tell us that they are debating restraints of trade. Now I maintain that, in terms of the negative indictments which we will make in today's debate when we consider those affirmative needs, [it] is highly questionable whether or not we are debating antitrust legislation as the affirmative team conceives a restraint of trade. Now why do I make this point? Well, Justice Brandeis pointed out in the case *United States* v. *Chicago Board of Trade* the following information: "The legality of an agreement of regulation cannot be determined by so simple a test as whether it restrains trade and reduces competition. Every agreement concerning trade, every regulation of trade, restrains; to bind, to restrain, is of their very essence." And what does Justice Brandeis go on to point out in this particular case? He goes on to point out that it is not merely enough to cite a restraint of trade; it must be deemed to be unreasonable. What is the definition of an unreasonable restraint of trade? A restraint which is by its intent designed to restrain trade.

Now we maintain that the affirmative team has not been fair with you in today's debate because they have merely talked about restraints of trade, thereby asserting that they are unreasonable. What we maintain they have to do is to show the intent of the labor organization in every one of these cases to significantly restrain trade before they can talk about such unreasonable restraints. I maintain they have not done that in the evidence which they have presented to us.

Well, they did tell us that their major premise in today's debate is that labor organizations can restrain trade in such ways which business organizations cannot do. And they said there were two areas that they wanted to talk about here. The first one was production, and the second one was distribution. Well, looking at that first area of production, what did we hear? We heard that, well, actually we have a tremendous problem in terms of featherbedding and makework practices; and then we had certain specific areas cited.

Now I'm going to read a quotation from one of the areas which the affirmative team talked about, and when you first hear this quotation, you're going to think that it's affirmative; but I think

I can show that it's negative without too much trouble. Quoting from Daniel P. Lomas in *U.S. News and World Report,* February 20, 1959. By the way, Mr. Lomas is president of the Association of Railroads. He said that "Makework union rules requiring payment for services not rendered were costing the industry more than 500 million dollars a year." Now I think that's very interesting, because what does it point out? We know that under the existing Labor-Management Relations Act an employer cannot be compelled to pay for services not rendered. Hence, we would maintain that a great deal of the need which the affirmative team has been talking about in today's debate probably can be taken care of under the present system.

Secondly, we would point out that, if it has not been taken care of under the present system, it seems to me that we've got that existing legislation. We're not even taking advantage of the legislation that we have. So we ask the members of the affirmative team, what is the criterion for introducing additional legislation at the present time? As a matter a fact, the president of one of those railroads that Mr. Lomas represents in his capacity is not really sure that he agrees with Mr. Lomas in terms of the extent of the need. Mr. Henry W. Von Willer, President of the Erie Railroad, said: "In my opinion, the so-called featherbedding of railroad wages has been exaggerated by railroad executives. There has actually been very little so-called featherbedding." So we would maintain two things in this particular area: number one, the problem is not significant; number two, where we may have certain problems, it probably can be corrected under the present system.

Well, then, we've heard that actually when we got to other industries such as the construction industry, we've got problems here. I think we can best evaluate the totality of the affirmative need by turning to some expert advice in this area. In the book, *The Impact of Collective Bargaining on Management,* by Messrs. Slichter, Healy and Livernash of 1960, what do we find? "Unions undertake to encourage technological change fairly frequently. This policy usually is followed when the union is worried about the ability of an industry or a plant to hold its own in competition." He goes on to point out that examples of this—that is, receptivity to technological change—are found fairly frequently in the plastering industry and many other construction industries, in the railroad shops, in the trucking industry, and in the printing industry. Certainly, then, in Mr. Livernash's report this does not seem to be a significant problem as submitted by the members of the affirmative team. We would suggest that they analyze the totality of the problem before they pick out isolated examples.

Well, then we go down to the next area, and they've told us that really we've got a problem here in terms of restrictions on the entertainment business. And we were told by the members of the affirmative team that they went to see "Carnival" last week and they found that the wages in this area were actually—or the cost, the prices—were actually prohibitive and that really they had a great deal of trouble here, and they suspected that there was a great deal of harm in light of the analysis that they had made. Well, we also would submit that we would have liked to have seen "Carnival"—and there seemed to be a great deal of restraint of trade in that particular case, too. But it was not due to the construction hands; it was simply that the play was completely sold out and we couldn't get in. So I wonder, where is the restraint of trade? Exactly what are they talking about in this particular area? We see no particular problem here.

Before we leave this area, though, I think we ought to consider the repairs which the affirmative team might possibly advocate in this particular debate. Now why do I say that? Because there was supposedly a provision which was going to be written into the Taft–Hartley Act back in 1947 that would have prevented the specific practices which the affrmative team talks about. Now why were these provisions not put in? Senator Taft, who helped write this bill, said before the Senate Committee on Labor and Public Welfare, 1953: "We hesitated to put further provisions against featherbedding into the Taft–Hartley Act because of the difficulties of implementing these provisions. If the employer decides what is featherbedding then the problem of safety may be involved. Suppose a union says that there should be two mine inspectors for safety provisions, whereas the employer says that only one is needed. This is a very crucial problem just from the standpoint of safety." He goes on to point out that there are thousands of arrangements that are going to have to be determined by any court or by anybody, which Senator Taft feels are not going to be qualified to make these determinations. We really wonder how they are going to operate under the affirmative proposal. This is the reason why that specific provision was left out of the Taft–Hartley Act.

And finally we would say that—in terms of the restrictions on technological innovation—this can be done only when it concerns a legitimate union bargaining activity which is connected with wages, hours, and working conditions. To point this out, we would turn to the case of *Austin* v. *Painters Council* before the NLRB. And here I think is another point to keep in mind. Remember, we do have two areas of legislation dealing with restraints of trade: number one, labor legislation; number two, antitrust legislation. We maintain that the members of the affirmative team have to show why we have to have that repair under antitrust legislation. They have not done this, rather than considering labor legislation at the same time. But referring to this case, what do we find? "In collective bargaining negotiations between painting contractors and painters' unions, the union demand that the use of pan rollers and pressure rollers be barred was unlawful since it lacked any reasonable connection with hours, wages, health, safety, or the rights of collective bargaining." So we maintain that, once again, labor union activities in this area can be circumscribed by the law.

Well, that's the first need contention. What was the second one? Well, we heard that actually there were restrictions on distribution, and I think we heard here first of all the Adams Dairy Company case. You know, I'm really beginning to wonder, in this particular area, if any affirmative team has a need. I've been debating this resolution all year, and I bet I've heard the Adams Dairy Company case about 80 thousand times. But we've got it again, and let's see what was said about it in this particular instance. We heard that actually the labor organizations were forcing a certain employer, Mr. Adams, to pay higher wages and, therefore, this necessarily fixed the price. Well, they didn't actually say that; they said that they were somehow fixing the price in this particular case. What we would point is, in analyzing that case, that this was a problem of determining commission rates. So, first of all, we're going to maintain that this was not fixing prices; it was simply negotiating over legitimate ends of wage activity. And I think we can point that out by turning to the court in this particular case. What do they say? "A labor organization is immune to the Sherman Act liability unless it conspires with nonlabor groups for purposes not connected with legitimate ends. That the labor contract might have affected the price at which the dealer could sell and deliver milk did not, in and of itself, stamp the contract as illegal per se." Why? Because they were bargaining over wages. They weren't attempting to set the price in these particular cases. Once again we fail to see where there is a legitimate indictment in this area.

And then we heard a case which concerned the Davis Pleating and Button Company of California, and we heard that there was really a problem here. Supposedly there was price-fixing. Well, I'd like to turn to that case, too. Now this is what the plaintiff alleged: that the organization of nonunion firms was actually unsuccessful in this area in that, supposedly, there was an alleged conspiracy between the Sportswear Cotton Garment, Undergarment, and Accessories Workers Union of the AFL. Now this is what the court held in this particular case: number one, that there was no unreasonable restraint of trade on the flow of goods; number two, there was no proof of intent of the union to collude with California Sportswear; and, number three, there was no proof of actual collusion between the union and California Sportswear. Now, once again, remember we talked about that idea of intent. We said that it's actually got to be shown before you have an unreasonable restraint of trade. I maintain that it has not been demonstrated in this case.

The final case that we heard discussed was the Weier case. I happen to have that one, too. I'd like to turn to the court's opinion in that one. What did they say here? "There was total absence of proof that any restraint existed as to the flow of plaintiff's materials in interstate commerce as to its use." So once again, we would maintain there was no restraint of trade in this particular case. The court so held that there was no restraint of trade. Where, after all, is the affirmative need? All right, I think there are a lot of questions that that affirmative team is going to have to answer, particularly in light of the definition of terms in the analysis of the entire case. We urge rejection of that affirmative position.

2nd affirmative: Mike Henke

General Westmoreland, ladies and gentlemen. As Dale has said, I hardly need to say that it gives me a great deal of pleasure— so much that I can hardly talk, I guess—to be up here this afternoon.

I think that my colleague has shown the mistaken emphasis on preserving legitimate union functions that has characterized American labor policy since 1932. I think that he has gone further to point out the legal inconsistency resulting from this mistaken emphasis—a legal inconsistency that has manifested itself in the fact that unions, acting alone, are allowed to do things today that businesses can't do. They're even allowed to do things that unions, acting together with nonunion groups, cannot do either. I think that the fountainhead of this problem lies in Section VI of the Clayton Act, which declares that even combinations of unions are exempt from antitrust legislation when they are, quote, "lawfully carrying out their legitimate objectives," unquote; and which guarantees that unions may not be, quote, "construed to be illegal combinations in restraint of trade," unquote. The affirmative plan would quite simply be to amend Section VI of the Clayton Act— to extend antitrust coverage to labor unions even when they're acting in their own self-interest and alone.

Now the rule of reason would of course be applied in these cases as it is in all antitrust cases, so that, although union activities would be subject to prosecution even when they're acting alone and in their own interest, their activities would actually be proscribed only when those activties were contrary to the public interest. I think you can easily see from this program, then, that we would place primacy on the public interest. But we would still preserve legitimate functions so long as the preservation of those legitimate functions was not detrimental to the best interests of the American public.

With that brief explanation of the affirmative plan of solution, then, allow me to return to the affirmative need issues which my colleague delineated for you in the first affirmative speech and see how they've been met by that first speaker of the opposition.

Well, his first objection, you remember, was to the concept of antitrust which the affirmative team has chosen to defend in this debate. He said it's questionable whether this is antitrust in the case *U.S.* v. *The Chicago Board of Trade.* The precedent was set and the court ruled that a restraint of trade must be an unreasonable restraint—meaning that it must have the primary intent of restraining trade for it to be covered by antitrust. Well now, we're not going to quarrel with this ruling of the court. I would refer you, however, instead, to the case of *Alpha Beta Food Market* v. *Meat Cutters Union,* 1956, U.S. Supreme Court—the precedent in that case: "Where the primary purpose of a provision in a union contract is to restrain trade, that provision already violates both federal and state antitrust laws." In other words, when the direct intent of a union is to restrain trade in the product market, it's already covered by antitrust legislation. So why in the world would the framers of this proposition limit the affirmative team this year to debating something that's already being done? No, I think that the framers of the proposition had something entirely different in mind. I think that they had in mind the extension of antitrust coverage—not only to direct product-market restraints, but also to union labor-market activities which carry over into the product market. I think the framers of the proposition were thinking in terms of protecting the public interest with regard to the activities of labor unions.

Then, with regard to the problems in the area of production, the gentleman said, first of all, he thinks this is a decreasing problem—one that's being met by collective bargaining—a very minor problem and not a need for a change. Lloyd G. Reynolds, in his book *Labor Economics and Labor Relations,* seems to disagree with the gentleman of the opposition. Here are his words: "If the expedients adopted were temporary and were used only until more basic remedies could be devised, one might make out a case for their use. The difficulty is that restrictive work rules and practices are scarcely ever discarded." Well, let's get to some more specific ideas then. The gentleman said, with regard to the railroad industry, the first affirmative example, the services in this industry which were not rendered were costing the industry 500 million dollars. Well, I would refer the gentleman in turn to the interpretation of the Supreme Court—its interpretation of that section of Taft–Hartley which attempts to forbid certain featherbedding activities. And the interpretation of the Court has been that when an individual was actually present for work, whether he worked or not, he was deemed, therefore, to have rendered a service, and thus he could not be prosecuted under the Taft–Hartley Act. Thus, when a fireman rides a diesel locomotive for 500 miles, he is, in the determination of the Court under the Taft–Hartley Act, rendering a service or at least extending a service, and thus cannot be prosecuted under Taft–Hartley. It's still featherbedding. It's still costing us 500 million dollars a year. It can still be proscribed by the adoption of the affirmative proposal. He went on to say there is very little problem in the railroad industry. He thinks the 500-million-dollar figure has been exaggerated. Well, if the 500-million-dollar figure has been exaggerated, let's go to a neutral source—the Interstate Commerce Commission, which in 1958 calculated that railroad workers worked only 57% of the hours for which they were paid. This doesn't sound like a small problem to me; to me, it sounds like a pretty serious problem.

With regard to the construction industry, the second affirmative example, the gentleman quoted Slichter, Healy and Livernash to the affect that the usual union policy toward what?—technological change—is willing acceptance. All right, there are two things that the affirmative would say in comeback to this point. First of all, we're not talking about technological change. Do you remember the quotation that my colleague read you from that first affirmative speech? The quotation from Mr. Fertig in his recent book? Here it is: "In homebuilding and manufacturing the list of expensive makework is endless—20% of the on-site cost of building a home. There is a limit on the number of outlets which an electrician may install. Carpenters may not hang more than a given number of doors. Plenty of money could be saved if threaded pipes could be delivered for installation. Bricklayers who used to lay a thousand bricks a day are not allowed to lay more than 500." Bricklaying being restricted in its production, carpenters hanging too few doors—this is clearly, I think, a restriction of production, a form of makework, but not the restriction of technological change. We'd suggest that the gentleman of the opposition confine his objections to the affirmative need issues as they've been set up. But then we'd go one step further and say that even in the instances of introduction of technological change, although the union's policy may be willing acceptance of the technological change, what happens after they've accepted it? Well, the gentleman's own source, I think, answers this question. Sumner Slichter, in an article entitled "Technological Change: The Policy of Control," 1959: "The policy of accepting a new machine or process and then attempting to control its operation is by far the most important of the several policies of unions toward technological change."

This might be applied to the railroad industry, where unions accepted the diesel locomotive; but they've attempted to control its operation by requiring that a fireman ride it even though the fireman is not needed. We would suggest, then, there still is a need: 20% of the on-site costs of building a home, running to 260 million dollars a year in the American economy when you take 20% of the on-site costs of building homes, according to the 1962 *World Almanac and Book of Facts.*

How about the entertainment industry? Not really a problem here? Well, I'd suggest rather humorously that it was certainly a problem to the Baylor debate budget to pay $6.90 for three tickets to see that play. But I would suggest even furthermore that I don't think the gentlemen have ever come to grips with the basic idea here: that five men are required backstage on Broadway for a job that only takes one—the pushing of a button to raise and lower a curtain—and certain other problems that exist within this area. Rather than attempting to slough it off, I'd suggest that the gentleman come to grips with this specific problem.

Well, we went on a little bit further, and he said there are certain problems resulting from the fact that legitimate union activities may be harmed in certain areas. Yes, we're not going to deny this for a minute, ladies and gentlemen. This is the entire philosophy of the affirmative case: that we shouldn't worry about legitimate union activities anymore. At least we shouldn't worry about them when it's a question of them or the public interest. We should give primacy to the question of public interest and then worry about legitimate objectives after that.

How about that second area of distribution—discrimination, dictation, and driving firms out of business? What have they said? With regard to the Adams case, he gave you a lot of explanation, but then he came up with this significant point: they were simply arguing over wages. It was a legitimate activity. All right, two things here. In the first place, they weren't simply arguing over wages. As was pointed out from the official transcript of the cases, of the case, the *Commerce Clearing House Labor Law Reports,* 1960: "The union's sole purpose was to increase Adams' distribution cost, thereby forcing him from the competitive market." A legitimate labor objective? It doesn't sound like it in this case. But furthermore, in going back to the point that I made earlier, what difference does it make if it was a legitimate labor objective? Why should we be so concerned with legitimate labor objectives that we forget about the public interest? Why shouldn't we put the public interest first? Why should merely the fact that the union was agitating for higher wages give it per-se exemption from the antitrust laws?

Let's go a little bit further—the case of *Davis Pleating and Button Company v. The California Sportswear Association.* They said we haven't proved intent. This goes back to the point I made at the outset of this speech. We don't think that you have to prove intent to apply the principle of antitrust. And this is the philosophy of the affirmative team.

Third case—driving firms out of the market: *Weier v. Chicago.* Dale says "Aha, we've got you here," because there wasn't any interstate commerce. My colleague and I realize that. And that's the reason my colleague took such great pains to point out, when he presented that case in the first affirmative speech, that what we're really concerned about in this area is the precedent that the Weier case set—the precedent it set for other areas where there was interstate commerce involved, the precedent which allowed 10 thousand small businesses to be driven out of business in the two-year period from 1959, the Weier precedent, to 1961 when the report was published. I think this is the area of need.

Then the gentleman says, well, he doesn't really believe that we can set standards under this plan. He doesn't really think that we can decide what should and what shouldn't be outlawed. He's back to featherbedding now, and I omitted this point earlier. But the idea was that featherbedding restrictions were eliminated from Taft–Hartley because you couldn't set standards. Certainly you can't set standards for featherbedding on a legislative, definitive basis—the sort of basis that you have to have to set up legislation like Taft–Hartley. But you can set standards when you do it case by case—when you apply the rule of reason, the antitrust approach, and look at each individual case on its own merits.

We think that we have a need for a change in the areas of production and distribution. And we think we have a plan, the application of antitrust to labor unions, which will meet that need. Thank you.

2nd negative: Sarah Benson

I'd like to go right to that affirmative plan and consider it in relationship to each of the need areas which we heard. First of all, remember we're told that unions can restrict production through makework practices. Well now, remember, at the opening of this debate the affirmative team told us there was a legal inconsistency between what labor unions can do and what business could do; therefore, we need antitrust applied to labor organizations. Well, I'm going to submit that, first of all, the affirmative need area here is not compatible with the philosophy of antitrust legislation. Now remember, we've never been told that business can't restrict production. I point out to you that business certainly does restrict production. We know that steel mills only operate 9 or 10 months out of the year. Certainly there is no legal inconsistency here. This doesn't fit in with the philosophy of the affirmative team. It doesn't fit in with the philosophy of antitrust legislation.

Number two, I'm going to point out that in terms of this affirmative plan that either the plan overextends the needs in terms of restrictions on productivity, or else the plan does not meet the needs. We've got a dilemma here. Why do I say this? Now if we're really concerned about restrictions on production, then what the affirmative team is going to have to do is to outlaw the strike, because every strike restricts production for the length of time during which the strike occurs. Now if the affirmative team doesn't want to do this, this means that the plan does not meet the need because restrictions on production can go on during the time of the strike. And if this is the alternative which the affirmative team gives us, then I suggest to you that restrictions on production are not per se undesirable. The affirmative team is going to let them go on sometime, not on others. I'd like to know what criteria we use to determine when restrictions on production are all right—when restrictions on production can be permitted.

Number three, I want to point out that under the affirmative plan in this area the affirmative team is assuming that some third party can do a better job of setting initial production quotas than can union and management in collective bargaining. First of all, I thought it was rather interesting when we heard the affirmative plan, we never heard who was going to tell us whether or not we have a makework rule present. Extremely interesting. We had no criteria here. And I think once again Senator Taft illustrated the difficulty very well, questioning before the Senate Committee on Labor and Public Welfare, 1953. What did he say? "The difficulty we had was in determining who was going to decide whether a demand was a reasonable demand or not. We hesitated to give the National Labor Relations Board power to go into every industry and decide how many men were needed and how many men were not needed." Now Senator Taft brings up this issue of musicians. He said: "What if the union says we need five men in this band to do a good job? The person who wants to hire them says 'no you don't; you only need three.'" Now who is going to decide this? What are the criteria going to be? I don't think this was answered in the affirmative plan. I certainly think it's an important issue.

Well, number four, I'm going to submit that the affirmative plan merely calls for the extension of existing labor legislation in this area, not for antitrust legislation at all. Now why do I say this? All the affirmative team has submitted to you is that we need an extension of the existing antifeatherbedding provision of the Taft–Hartley Act. What does Taft–Hartley say? It says that management does not have to pay for work which is not performed or not to be performed. To implement this affirmative

plan, all we'd have to do is add three words to that provision—
that is, "work not needed"—and then we'd have no problem. It
doesn't seem to me there's any kind of an inherent difficulty here.

But, number five, in objecting to this affirmative plan, we're
going to submit that it's not desirable to make this extension of
the Taft–Hartley Act. Why? Because I think that the affirmative
team forgot to discuss a very important issue with you, and that
is: why in the world does the union ever institute makework practices in the first place? What in the world is the purpose of this
kind of activity? Well, we're going to submit that the only purpose of this kind of activity is to prevent unemployment and that,
consequently, we have a value judgment on the part of the affirmative team that productivity is more important than is employment
—and I don't think that value judgment has been substantiated.
Now, to establish this, let's once again turn back to that book by
Slichter, Healy and Livernash in 1960. What do they tell us?
"Makework rules are intended to create employment opportunities
for the groups imposing them, but they may have the opposite
effect. Perhaps the safest generalization is that makework rules
stimulate technological change. Processes will be altered so that
output will no longer be restricted." I think this points out a very
important thing. Remember we said this need area wasn't significant. And why isn't it significant? Because makework rules are
a check against the union activity; because if management finds
it's not profitable to use union men who are having restrictive
production quotas, obviously they're going to replace these men
to get more efficient methods. We say that this checks unions
against their own excesses. Number one, then, not a significant
problem. Number two, the alternative is unemployment in these
industries, and I think it's very important to look at the specific
areas we were given.

Remember we heard about the entertainment industry. We
heard about musicians. We heard about railroads. And again,
what did the affirmative team forget to say here? They forgot to
say that each of these is an unstable industry, certainly an area
where we have a great deal of problems in terms of job security.
It seems to me, once again, we're back to that value judgment on
the part of the affirmative, that in some way it's more important

to have productivity here than it is to have employment. And again, I don't think this has been substantiated.

All right, now I want to consider the affirmative plan in terms of the second need area which we had—and that was that unions can discriminate against employers. I call your attention to the fact, first of all, that we've only had one example in this area—and that was that now infamous Adams Dairy case. We're going to submit to you, first of all, that this type of activity on the part of the milk-wagon industry is certainly necessary. And I think once again we can turn back to testimony before the Senate Committee on Labor and Public Welfare, 1953. And here we find Senator Paul Douglas making the following point: "In the old days where the city distributors dealt with each dairyman individually, the result was that they would play one dairyman off against the other. And the dairymen were consequently in very bad shape. So they combined together in their federations, which are really marketing unions, and drove as good a bargain as they could with the city distributors. Obviously they needed organization for their protection." I think this points out, first of all—certainly it's no surprise to anybody, and particularly Mr. Douglas —this kind of activity occurs. Number two, Senator Douglas submits that this activity is necessary to preserve competition in this industry. We submit certainly there is no unreasonable restraint of trade here.

Number two, I think it's rather interesting to note in this area that what we're dealing with is the problem of minimum commission rates, really wages; and I think the last affirmative speaker agreed with that. In the first place, what was the affect on the price in the Adams Dairy case? Well, we find that the price of a quart of milk went up three cents. And I'm going to ask the affirmative team by what judgment is a three-cent increase in the price of milk an unreasonable restraint of trade? What about those poor steel workers who want ten cents an hour? Seems to me there's certainly going to be some problems in workability here.

Number three, we're going to ask the affirmative team in this area again—what criteria do you use to determine when wage-fixing becomes price-fixing? We're going to ask again in this area —what indeed should the wages have been in this area? What

should the commission rates have been in the Adams Dairy case?
I think, in terms of workability, we've got to see that plan related
back to the affirmative needs. I don't think that was ever done.

All right, let's go on to this third area. Here we were told that
unions could control the internal operations of industry. And
what was the first case which we heard? Well, it was that California Sportswear case. And what did the members of the affirmative team say? They said that the union can make agreements
with the employer not to do business with other employers. I submit to you, first of all, this is a "hot cargo" agreement—a violation
of Section 8-E of the Landrum–Griffin Act, which tells us that
unions cannot make agreements with employers to cease doing
business with other persons.

Number two, we're going to submit that the only exemptions
allowed under the "hot cargo" provisions are exactly in this case
area which they presented—and that is the garment industry. So
I think we have to ask, thirdly, why was this exemption granted.
Well, I think the exemption was granted because, once again, the
practice in this industry is necessary to the preservation of competition. Let's turn again to testimony before the Senate Committee on Labor and Public Welfare, 1953. What do we find? As
a result of industrywide bargaining, we find that competition
which resulted from the undercutting of the wage scales has practically stopped, and that greater efficiency in factory operations
and progressive merchandizing methods have become the important factors in determining the success of a clothing business. I
wish to stress that competition is probably stronger among the
manufacturers than it has ever been. The profits of the industry are
certainly no greater than they have been in the past; however,
competition is now on a socially desirable level. It is not based
upon lowering wages, but rather upon efficiency and merchandising skills. Once again, then, certainly no restraint of trade here;
as a matter a fact, the practice—just like in that milk case—necessary to the preservation of competition in the industry.

Well, as far as that Davis case goes and as far as the Weier case
goes, you know, I wonder exactly what this affirmative team
could do. Remember they told us that antitrust legislation dealt
not only with restraints of trade but with unreasonable restraints

of trade. We read you those court cases. What did they say? In the Davis case the court held there was no unreasonable restraint of trade. Affirmative plans couldn't work here. In the Weier case they said there was no unreasonable restraint of trade. Now the affirmative comes back and says, "Yes, that may be true, but certainly we've shown you the precedent exists." All right, affirmative team, now you've got a theory; now let's see some empirical examples which support this theory. Let's see some cases where there actually is harm. I submit we've got this advantage to that plan. I submit we haven't seen any cases that the affirmative plan could even apply to. I'm going to ask you to reject that resolution.

1st negative rebuttal: Dale Williams

I began my first negative constructive by saying that I felt the affirmative team had a certain obligation that they had to fulfill in today's debate. And I said that that obligation rested around the idea of proving that the labor organization intended to restrain trade, thereby proving an unreasonable restraint of trade.

Now I quoted from the Chicago Board of Trade case in which Justice Brandeis handed down this particular decision. Now what was the answer that we got? Well, first of all, we got the idea that supposedly this doctrine is no longer viable because we can turn to another case, the *Alpha Beta Food Market Case* v. *Amalgamated Meat Cutters*—and I also have this case—and what happened in this particular instance? This case took place May 24, 1956. Here we find that the court held that a union contract prohibiting the sale of meat in self-service markets which was not cut, prepared and packaged, intended to restrain trade in this particular case. Now this is exactly what I am pointing out. In this very case which the members of the affirmative team cite, once again the intent doctrine came into play here. Now remember, the members of the affirmative team told us that really we've got an unequal situation here. On the one hand, we've got labor organizations which supposedly get away with restraints of trade. On the other hand, we've got business organizations that would be prosecuted. Well, I'd like to take that premise, show that in the area of intent, which we consider to be extremely important, this is simply not the case.

I'd like to turn to the book, *An Evaluation of Antitrust Policy*, by Theodore J. Kreps, of Stanford University—and what does he maintain? In a 1955 antitrust case involving the Standard Oil Company, the Standard Oil Company was accused, and in fact found guilty, of fixing prices and engaging in price discrimination throughout the economy. Yet what did the Supreme Court hold in this 1955 case? That the good-faith proviso was an absolute and complete defense to the charge of price discrimination. In other words, the Standard Oil Company in this particular case, once again, did not intend to restrain trade; this was not their purpose. It was merely a binding arrangement, and I submit that that point does not stand. In further substantiation of this, we could turn to Robert A. Dix, Assistant Attorney General of the Antitrust Division, where once again he says that intent must be demonstrated to prove unreasonable restraints of trade.

Well, with that thought in mind, then, let's go back to the specifics of the affirmative need. And here I pointed out that really, I wondered how significant this affirmative need was. I said, look, we can turn to the railroad industry; we can find in this area that where we do have many of these practices, they're already outlawed; and I said Mr. Lomas, President of the American Association of Railroads, tells us that this 500-million-dollar figure indeed applies to services not rendered. What did the members of the affirmative team say? They said, well, supposedly this is covered in some case that they talked about. All I can say is that if you turn to the Taft-Hartley Act, you find that there is no compulsion for an employer to pay for services not performed. Now Mr. Lomas says these were services not rendered. I can't see a great deal of semantic difference between those two points. I don't think that particular problem has been answered.

But then we come to the question of whether or not this is really significant—whether or not we have an important problem here. We heard from the members of the affirmative team they were going to turn to an unbiased source. Well, let's do the same thing: The United States Bureau of Labor Statistics, 1961. They tell us that "well over half a million railroad jobs have disappeared since the war, while productivity rose 65%." I submit that the problem is decreasing in this area. We're getting an increase in productivity. We're certainly geting rid of these unneeded workers in this area. We maintain that the status quo is desirable in that it does this on a flexible restricted manner. Hence, we maintain that there is no particular problem in this area either.

All right, we go down to the question of distribution. Once again we're back to that Adams Dairy Company case—and only that case, because the members of the affirmative team refused to discuss any other cases with us. Now what did they say? They said in the Adams Dairy Company case, really, we weren't concerned here with wage-setting; we were concerned with direct price-fixing. Now they read some quotation from the transcript of this case. I maintain, number one, they may have read from the transcript of the case, but they probably read from the plaintiff; and they certainly didn't read from the findings of the Justices in this case themselves, because, once again, what does the court say? "Where a labor organization and certain milk producers entered into a bargaining contract which increased the commission rates paid to milk-wagon drivers, this was not an illegitimate labor-union activity." Why? Because in the court's finding it was primarily concerned with bargaining over wages, which is a legitimate contract in the—or legitimate, ah, activity—in this particular area.

We go down to the other cases. I submit there's been no significance of affirmative need here. The Weier case: We pointed out there was not restraint of trade on interstate commerce. The only answer we got here was, well, maybe you're right, but probably there might have been on intrastate commerce. I never heard it substantiated that there was a restraint of trade on intrastate commerce. And I might add I never heard that this federal law which the affirmative team advocates is even going to be able to apply to intrastate commerce. So, really, I wonder what is the significance of this?

With regard to the Davis Pleating and Button case, what did we say here? The court found no unreasonable restraint of trade. We said, secondly, it probably is covered under Landrum-Griffin. Once again, we see no significant need. We urge rejection of the affirmative position.

1st affirmative: Cal Kent

Harry Adams, in his book *The Education of Women,* tells us that "Words from a pretty mouth are hard refuted." And my task is doubled because there are so many of them that I am going to have to deal with in this period. But be that as it may, let's take a look at some of these objections, and let's take a look at the major issues that we actually have in today's debate. First of all, they tell us this: well, we don't think that you're complying with the principle of antitrust. Because why? The steel mills aren't forced to operate all the time. Well, this doesn't have any relevance to our case at all. I think we pointed out to you that we were within the philosophy because the court had clearly decided in the case of *U.S.* v. *Brims* that makework and featherbedding were restraints of trade. And this point they never dealt with. Why? Because they raised prices and pinched productivity. And antitrust, as they themselves admit, is intended to do away with this particular problem. So I think we are complying with the antitrust principle.

Then she came up and constructed her own straw dummy in the case of strikes. She said, "Well, what about this particular strike problem? Are you going to outlaw all strikes?" Well, first of all, our case was not specifically concerned with strikes. This was never really tied into our case. Secondly, have we not already realized the principle in Taft–Hartley that public interest in strikes should be primary? This, I think, is the point that we have to recognize. I think that this principle carried through antitrust as being the best vehicle should be extended to the other union activities which result in this particular area. If a strike should happen to occur which goes against the public interest, we'll get rid of it under our particular proposal.

Then the next idea she came up with is, well, you've really given us no criteria for makework. And what did Mike point out? The very last thing he left the stand with was simply this: You can't do it, we agree with Mr. Taft, if you take a flat legislative prescription and say every instance of makework is illegal. But if you take the case-by-case approach, which is the essence of antitrust, you can set these standards, and this point has not been mentioned.

Let's go on to the next idea. We had two points here. She says, well, all we really need to do is extend labor legislation by adding three words, and we can get rid of all makework. Then the next thing she tells us is we don't want to get rid of all makework because some of it's justified. First of all, this stand is inconsistent. She tells us on one hand, let's get rid of it by adding three words. Next she says, let's not get rid of it because some of it's justified. The point is this: If there becomes an instance in which makework is justified under the case-by-case approach, it's going to be declared reasonable under antitrust. The problem is not going to exist. We're going to resolve the inconsistency. Then she came up with the idea and said, well, it's sometimes necessary to prevent unemployment in these industries. Let's turn to her very source on this point, Summer Slichter, once again, and see what he has to say. "In the building industries, railroads, and among musicians and stage hands—our three need areas, and, um, let me see— makework rules do not eliminate the intermittency of unemployment or the unemployment caused by it." In other words, makework rules do not do what she said that they were supposed to be doing in this area—and that is, preserving jobs.

Then the last idea she presented us with is, sometimes these industries are unstable. I think, as their own source points out, they are even unstable, true, because of makework practices.

What about our specific need? Well, she came back with this idea against the Adams Dairy case: She says this type of activity sometimes may be needed. And yet, what have we been contending? We've been contending that Adams Dairy used a legitimate function to what?—and we read you the court's opinion, not the plaintiff, as they allege, which said their sole purpose was to do what?—hurt the competitive position of Adams Dairy. They merely hid behind the guise of wages, hours, and conditions of employment to do this.

Then the next idea she came out with—in the Davis Pleating and Button case—was to tell us in this specific instance that, first of all, we might have had a "hot cargo" arrangement. Well, I'd like to point out that, once again, she is becoming inconsistent upon this point. Why? Because Taft–Hartley, or this type of provision, would outlaw all "hot cargo" agreements or all instances of this particular practice. Now what would happen under the affirmative plan? You'd use the rule of reason. If it was decided to be necessary, as her colleague said sometimes they are, then they can exist when they're unnecessary. When the public interest is hurt by them, we can get rid of them under our particular program. The point still stands in this particular area.

What about the Weier case? She said, well, here you don't really have any restriction in trade, and she also said this about the Davis Pleating and Button case. And I think, if you go to the transcripts of this case, you find the reason that the court ruled that there was no restraint of trade in these particular areas was why?—and it's in the sentence right before the quote she read you: because they couldn't prove a combination. Therefore, you couldn't prosecute them under this particular problem. This is the thing I think we need to talk about in today's debate.

What about the Weier thing? We pointed out the precedent established in this case had caused 10 thousand instances of this particular problem, and so far this has not been contended. Certainly I think we've shown you more than one isolated example of need.

Then she said this: well, we're really debating—this is her colleague's speech—we think that intent is important. And then he came up and reproved what Mike proved in the Alpha Beta Food's case—that when unions' primary intent today is to restrain trade, they're already covered. Therefore, if we upheld it, we wouldn't be upholding anything different. What we said is, let's move into another area—and that is when their primary intent is not to restrain trade. But they do restrain trade unjustifiably to the detriment of the public interest; and this basic philosophy has yet to have been denied, even mentioned, by either one of the members of the opposition.

She then, he then came up and said this: well, what about these people who cannot be compelled to pay for work within the industry? And what did Mike do? He pointed out to you that the Supreme Court has said: if you show up for work, then you are performing a service whether you do anything or not. And what about it? You have to be paid. This is the Supreme Court's interpretation. This is why Taft–Hartley is not effective within this area.

What about more production? We could have more if we didn't have the problem. What about fewer jobs in the railroads? This may be because we have less lying.

2nd negative: Sarah Benson

I'm rather sorry that the last speaker paid so much attention to my lips that he didn't pay a great deal of attention to the things which I said. Let's go right back to those objections to the plan.

Remember, first of all, first of all we said that the need area in terms of restricting production is not compatible with the philosophy of antitrust legislation. We were told it was irrelevant. I'm not quite sure how irrelevant it is. Remember, it was the premise of the affirmative team that there's a legal inconsistency, a double standard between what labor can do and what management can do. We've said management can restrict productivity. There's certainly no justification for antitrust legislation here. We think that argument is extremely relevant if the affirmative team is going to contend that we have a legal inconsistency between what labor can do and what management can do.

Remember, number two—in terms of this need area—we presented a dilemma in terms of the strike. Well, you know, I thought that in this rebuttal I'd be able to say which end of the dilemma the affirmative team wanted. Well, they told us, first of all, that they weren't concerned with the strike; it was irrelevant. And then they said, well, we won't take care of the strike under our plan if there's any damage to the public interest. Well, I'm not quite sure which end they want to take—whether they're going to outlaw it or not. Frankly, I thought the answer was pretty unclear. What I would say is this: If they are not take caring, taking care of, care of all strikes under their provisions, then restrictions of production can go on during the strike. If this is true, if all strikes are not regulated, then restrictions on production are not per se undesirable. Now why are they permitted during the strike, but when unemployment is the issue they're not going to be permitted? I don't think that value judgment has been substantiated.

Well, we had a third, what I thought was an important, objection that I don't remember hearing being answered. Remember, we said the affirmative assumes a third party can do a better job of setting initial production quotas, and of telling us when we have makework practices. We asked who is qualified to go into industry and to make these determinations. Now I'm perfectly willing to admit that courts may be experts on law. I'm not quite sure that they're experts on music. I'm not quite sure they're capable of making the determination whether three musicians are needed in this band, whether five musicians are needed in this band. And remember we heard an awful lot about the American Federation of Musicians. I think we're going to have to hear something about these criteria.

And then we said, fourthly, that the affirmative plan here calls for the extension of existing labor legislation, not for antitrust legislation at all. Well, here we were told that really we were being inconsistent—that first we offer minor repairs and then, secondly, we say, well, really we don't want to do this. What was the point here? The point here is that if we want to take care of this problem, we're not dealing with an inherent problem because the addition of three words to the Taft–Hartley Act would take care of the problem. But what did we say next? We said it would be possible to do this if this is what the affirmative team is worried about. But we said we don't think it's desirable to do so. Why did we say this? Because we said that here we're dealing with unstable industries. We're dealing with entertainment; we're dealing with musicians; we're dealing with the railroad industries. I think we pointed out to you these are atypical examples of industry, industries where there is a great deal of problem over job security. It seems to me there certainly is a problem.

Now we were told by the last affirmative speaker that, as a matter a fact here, these restrictive practices haven't eliminated unemployment at all. I think this substantiates the other point which we made that makework practices check against the excesses of union demands. Remember Mr. Slichter said these practices encourage technological change. That's exactly why he says the need area is so insignificant. Most unions can't benefit from these practices. That's exactly why we don't have a widespread problem.

As far as the railroad cases go, we pointed out that here what the trouble was was that unions were asking for money for work which hadn't been performed. We said this is a violation of the antifeatherbedding provisions. That's exactly what Taft–Hartley outlaws. If we've got a problem, let's take care of it under the provisions of the status quo.

Well, then we go over to the second area concerning the Adams Dairy Company where unions can discriminate against employers. Once again, we've only got one case to support this conclusion. I think we raised some important objections which weren't answered. We've said the result of this case was a three-cent increase on the quart of milk. We've said, why in the world is this unreasonable? We said, what are you going to do about the steel workers who want ten cents an hour? I don't remember hearing an answer to this. I think, in terms of workability, it certainly is important here. Then we're told that what the union wanted to do here was to destroy the Adams Company and put it out of business. Well, I have to say to that, just a minute! This means, then, that the union wanted to destroy their own employer, not only put him out of business but put themselves out of a job. Seems to me more logical to assume they were after minimum commission rates after that increase in wages. We suggest because one firm is driven from the market doesn't mean we have an unreasonable restraint of trade.

In terms of this third need area, what did we do? We said that if we're talking about unions making agreements for employers not to do business with other people, then we're talking about a "hot cargo" agreement—illegal under Section 8-E under the Landrum–Griffin Act—a significant admission agreed to by the last affirmative speaker. We were told that when the public interest is important, we're going to go in and prosecute. I'd like to know where they're going to prosecute. In the Weier case there was no unreasonable restraint of trade. In the Davis case there was no unreasonable restraint of trade. And that's all this affirma-

tive team is going to prosecute. They've got a theory, but they've
got no cases to prosecute. I'd like to know where that need area
is. Again we ask you to reject this proposition.

2nd affirmative: Mike Henke

Ladies and gentlemen. It is my hope that in the next five minutes I can convince the lady and gentleman of the opposition
that I have been paying attention to more than the lips of that
lady—that I have indeed listened to her words. In fact, I hope to
crystalize the affirmative arguments in your minds in order that
you may have clearly in mind at the end of this debate just what
the affirmative team has been trying to say.

First of all, I think perhaps I should review that basic affirmative premise which I don't think has ever been challenged by this
negative team throughout the debate—the idea that was presented back in the first affirmative speech; that the time has come
to give primacy to the public interest in our dealings with labor
unions and to relegate the preservation of legitimate union objectives to second place behind the public interest. As Douglas
B. Brown of the Massachusetts Institute of Technology pointed
out in an address delivered before the American Bar Association
in 1955, "The broad philosophy of the Sherman Act, however,
should and must deal with monopoly power, whether it be manifested in combinations of employers or in combinations of unions.
In either instance, it is the free economy of the nation, not merely
relations between employers and employees, which is threatened
or adversely affected." Now, the negative team has repeatedly
come up here with objections that this was a legitimate function.
They were arguing about wages. We must preserve legitimate
functions. But never have they given you any reason why we
must preserve legitimate functions at all cost. Never have they
given you any reason why we should cling to this traditional attitude toward antitrust and its application to labor unions. And
I think this is the important thing for you to keep in mind
throughout this rebuttal.

Now let's go to some specific points. First, with regard to the
need issue—the area of production, makework; the examples:
railroads, construction, and entertainment. They have contained,

they've maintained repeatedly that the need is insignificant; and in fact, when we come to the rebuttals, this is about the only objection that still remains on the floor. The need is insignificant. Well, in the railroad industry it's costing us 500 million dollars a year. In the construction industry it's costing us 260 million dollars a year. In a recently enforced contract in New York City, electricians won a 35-hour week in spite of the fact that there is now a shortage of electricians in New York City. The cost is estimated by *U.S. News* to be 125 million dollars in the next two years. I'd say this is a pretty significant need, and it's a need that can be met by the adoption of the affirmative proposal.

Second, the area of distribution: Here we've had a little more static with the affirmative cases. *Adams* v. *St. Louis*. Well, it seems that the main contention now comes down to be, in this last rebuttal, that, well, a three-cent rise on the price of milk is not really unreasonable. It doesn't sound like much, does it? What happens when you multiply three cents by a million, which is about the volume of milk that's sold in St. Louis in a year? It comes out to be about thirty thousand dollars. That sounds like a pretty substantial sum for one city, for one union, for one restraint of trade. It sounds unreasonable to me.

She said, with regard to the Davis case and the Weier case, you didn't have unreasonable restraints. They've never dealt with my colleague's idea that the reason the court ruled there was no unreasonable restraint is because it couldn't be proved that there was collusion. And it couldn't be proved that the union wasn't acting in its own self-interest. We would maintain, then, that in these cases the union should not be exempted from prosecution merely because they were acting alone, or merely because they were acting in their own self-interest—that we should consider, first of all, the public interest.

How about the objections to plan? Well, first of all, they said management can restrict productivity; therefore, your legal inconsistency must fall by the wayside. No, lady of the opposition, our legal inconsistency was that unions can do things alone that they can't do when they're acting together with management. And we would suggest that this legal inconsistency still stands. We'd further suggest that unions today have primary emphasis placed upon preserving their legitimate objectives, whereas this is not the case with business organizations, as illustrated by the recent steel controversy. When U.S. Steel wanted to raise the price of a ton of steel by six dollars, obviously a legitimate business activity, there were hoots and cries from all over the economy, and personal intervention by the President of the United States. We don't see this sort of thing when a union attempts to engage in a legitimate function.

Let's go a little bit further. She said our plan either overextends our need or else doesn't meet our need—pointing to the example of strikes. Two points of refutation here, as my colleague said: First, this is not our need. We're not concerned with strikes. We'd suggest they don't set up straw dummies and knock them down, but that they deal with the areas that the affirmative delineated. Second, we said that we have already recognized the policy of protecting the public interests in the Taft–Hartley 80-day injunction. And we suggest that we extend this recognition to the other areas of featherbedding and product-market restraints.

Then this idea that with makework you can't tell what's going to be done. You can't set standards. We've repeatedly said you can on a case-by-case basis. Milton Adelman and Irving Kavorsky, in the *Labor Law Journal* for April, 1959, says: "As regards to the objection that no standards can be established, there is growing literature dealing with both procedural and substantive matters in arbitration which can and will develop into an industrial common law. This important method of settling featherbedding questions cannot be neglected." The affirmative, she says, calls for the extent; she says that all we need, actually, is the extension of labor law. Redefine Taft–Hartley. Get rid of featherbedding. Then she says, "No, we don't want to do this because some featherbedding is justified." The point that we were trying to make, the inconsistency that exists is just this: that if they say that all featherbedding, if they say that some featherbedding is good, then they can't outlaw it by Taft–Hartley because Taft–Hartley gets rid of all featherbedding. Let's face up to it realistically. Some is good and some is bad. For example, spray guns are prohibited on the west coast because they're detrimental to our health and safety. This makework practice should be allowed. But some makework practices are unreasonable. We should apply antitrust to determine in each individual case what's best. We suggest the adoption of that affirmative proposal. Thank you.

AN AFFIRMATIVE BRIEF

RESOLVED: THAT A
FEDERAL WORLD GOVERNMENT
SHOULD BE ESTABLISHED

INTRODUCTION

I. *Immediate cause of discussion.* The question of an international organization with federal powers has arisen recently as a result of world tension and the threat of a third world war.

    A. Controversy as to the ability of the United Nations to maintain peace has furthered talk of world union.

        1. The actions of many nations lead us to believe they have little desire to cooperate within the United Nations.

        2. The inability of the major powers to establish a basis of agreement on questions of atomic control or an international police force within the structure of the U.N. raises serious doubt as to its functional value.

    B. The inability of Russia and the Western powers to resolve their day-to-day conflicts has brought an armament race and renewed fears of a third world war.

1. Unofficial Russian occupation of Czechoslovakia, through underground agents, has increased tension between the United States and Russia.
2. The inability of the United States and Russia to agree on policies for the control of Korea or Germany is a further sign of mutual noncooperation.

C. The vast destruction wrought by the second world war has led to many economic and social maladjustments which demand unified action and effort for their solution. This condition has furthered the talk of federation.
1. In Europe, Churchill and many other prominent men have publicly campaigned for an economic and military union of Western Europe.
2. The leaders of most of Asia met at New Delhi to discuss the problems of the continent in an attempt at unified effort for security.

II. *The history and origin* of the movement for a federal world government.
A. In the struggle against Catholic domination in 1313, Dante proposed ending European strife through the establishment of a universal empire.
B. Emeric Cruce, in his volume *The New Cyness* (1623), argued a possible need for a central world authority to enforce peace.
C. Duc de Sully's "Grand Design of Henry IV" planned a Christian Republic for Europe. This was to operate through a central authority which could negotiate, make, and enforce decrees.
D. William Penn, in 1688, proposed as the only means of ensuring peace, an immediate organization of the European parliaments to legislate "rules of justice for sovereign princes."
E. In 1713, the Abbé de Saint-Pierre's *"Project de paix perpetuelle"* was actually only an elaborate draft for a world constitution. This, he hoped, would interest peacemakers at Utrecht.
F. The first proposal of a true federation of states of all the peoples of the world was made by Immanuel Kant.

G. The proposed League of Nations, although not a plan for world federation, was a large step toward international cooperation.

H. At the time of the League of Nations debate, the Lepart plan for world federation was presented to the French League for the Society of Nations.

I. Belgian's Paul Otlet suggested, almost simultaneously, a democratic people's world parliament.

J. The present United Nations is not a federal world government, but it *is* the largest step yet taken toward world cooperation.

K. Today there is a movement for federal world government.

III. *Definition.* The definition of a federal world government is flexible in that no specific details of the functions and limitations of the government can be given on the individual level without making the debate question hopelessly involved. However, certain basic principles can be set up for the operaation of a federal world government. (Sources for definition of federal powers found in Bouvier's *Law Dictionary.*)

A. The federal world government would have the collective power to vote and enforce limitation or abolition of armaments by national governments.

　1. Certain military forces necessary for the maintenance of internal peace would be allowed the several nations.

　2. On the question of control of atomic energy or any other weapon with peaceful uses, the world government would have the power of inspection, subject to the limitations of majority rule.

B. The federal world government would have the power, upon majority vote, to require belligerents to submit their disputes to an international court, whose decision would be binding and enforceable.

　1. In cases of violation of a court decision, the police force of the world government would be used if affirmed by a two-thirds vote of the members.

2. The international court would be a body separate from all other units of the world government and would have certain of its own powers.
    a. The court would have the power of making recommendations in the fields outside aggression or war.
    b. The court would have the power of calling a temporary truce between belligerents while engaged in arbitrating the dispute.
    c. The court would have the power of enforcing its decisions upon the individuals of nations should they be found guilty of aggression or international crimes such as those outlined at Nuremberg.
C. The federal world government would have the power to set up other councils and branches in such fields as immigration, international trade, world health, and taxes. These councils would not have power vested in them, and could receive their specific power only by an amendment to the federal world-government constitution. While such fields as are listed above are certainly vital to the long-range success of any government, they are not so important as the immediate cessation of wars. Also it might be added that such problems as trade can be more readily resolved after effective peace instruments have been established.
    1. The power of amendment would be by two-thirds vote of all member nations.
    2. There would be specific provision for the investigation of an International Trade Council similar to the one at present in the United Nations.
    (*Draft Charter for the International Trade Council,* Department of State Bulletin, Publication 2027, Commercial Policy Series 106.)
IV. *Admitted, waived, and irrelevant matter: none.*
 V. *The following major issues present themselves:*
    A. Is the United Nations inherently inadequate to cope with the dangers to world peace?

    B. Is a federal world government capable of preserving peace?

    C. Would a federal world government be the most desirable plan for world peace?

VI. *Points in partition.*

    A. The present system of international affairs under the United Nations is not satisfactory.

    B. A federal world government would avoid the inherent weaknesses of the United Nations confederation.

    C. The plan of federal world government is the most desirable framework for international relations.

DISCUSSION

I. The present system of international affairs is not satisfactory, for

    A. The United Nations is failing to keep the peace, for

        1. It is not resolving present international armed conflicts, for

            a. "The very existence of the Greek state is today threatened by the terrorist activities of several thousand armed men, led by Communists, who defy the government's authority at a number of points, particularly along the northern boundaries." Speech by Harry S. Truman before the Congress of the United States, March 12, 1947, *The Turkish Aid Program,* Department of State publication 3014, Economic Cooperation Series 1, p. 13.) And

            b. In Palestine the lack of effective action that exists today has been brought about by the Anglo-American fear that the Arabs might turn to Russia if they were not allowed to continue supreme in the Middle East. (T. Das, *Human Rights and the United Nations, Annals of the American Academy,* July, 1947, p. 59.) And

            c. In China the differences between the forces of the National government and the Communists appear to be incapable of solution as long as the present basic differences of ideals and goals exist. "Involved are differences as basic as those between the North and the South over slavery."

(David Rowe, "American Policy Toward China," *Annals of the American Academy,* January, 1948, p. 140.)

2. It does not guarantee the political integrity of nations, for

   a. In the case of Czechoslovakia: "After a weekend of sustained governmental crisis, Gottwald acted. Police of Communist Nosek's interior ministry, armed with tommy guns and bayoneted rifles surrounded most government offices and the Prague radio station. Equally ominous was the act of General Ludvik Suvboda, Minister of National Defense . . . his advice to the troops read: 'The army must seek a stronger brotherhood with the Soviet Union.' "

      (*Time,* March 1, 1948, p. 18.) And

   b. In the case of Finland: "Finland was forced against its will to sign a mutual aid treaty with Soviet Russia. The treaty tucked Finland even more snugly into the Soviet orbit."

      (*Time,* April 19, 1948, p. 30.) And

   c. In the case of Italy: "Both the United States and and Russia have actively attempted to influence the Italian election; the former by sending food, coal, and by enlisting the support of the various factions; the latter by a campaign of propaganda demanding social reforms through the agents of the Italian Communist party."

      (*Time,* April 19, 1948, pp. 27, 28, 29.) And

   d. In the case of Korea: "For about two years the United States government has been trying to reach agreement with the Soviet government about the independence of Korea. Korean people, not former enemies, but a people liberated from forty years of Japanese oppression, are still not free. They have been deprived of the right of free elections and have suffered great economic losses as a result of the failure to agree on terms for Korea."

(Excerpt from the address by the Secretary of State delivered before the General Assembly of the United Nations, September 17, 1947, *Korea's Independence,* Department of State publication 2933, Far Eastern Series 18, p. 15.)

B. A fundamental code of international law which is capable of punishing aggressors is impossible in a confederation of sovereign states, for

1. Majority decisions cannot be enforced because of the veto power, for

a. "Decisions of the Security Council on all other matters shall be made by an affirmative vote of seven members including the concurring votes of the permanent members."

(*United Nations Charter,* Article 27, Section 3.)

2. The method of reaching decisions under the United Nations makes any code of international law impossible, for

a. Each decision is made according to the political alignments and power blocks of the day, for

(1) ". . . the behavior of the United Nations stems from the stresses between the Western world and Soviet Russia. The occurrence of this trend confirms that the United Nations is an instrument of its members. In spite of its corporate personality . . . the United Nations is basically not an agency with a will of its own."

(E. N. van Kleffens, "The United Nations and Some Main Trends of Our Times," *Annals of the American Academy,* July 1947, p. 74.)

3. The World Court fails to meet the fundamental premise of law—the power to enforce decisions, for

a. "The jurisdiction of the Court comprises all cases that the parties refer to it and all measures specially provided for in the Charter of the United Nations or in treaties or conventions in force. The states parties to the present Statute may at any time declare that they recognize as compulsory the jurisdiction of the Court." (The *Charter of the International Court*. Article 36, Section 1 and 2.) And

    b. If a nation fails to abide by the decision of the World Court, appeal to the Security Council for enforcement is still blocked by the veto.

C. It perpetuates war by forcing the nations into competitive armaments, for

    1. The structure of the United Nations puts the burden of security on the individual nations, for

        a. The United Nations has failed to establish a workable system of atomic control, thus perpetuating an atomic armament race, for

            (1) "I shall content myself with the comments as to the imperative necessity for speed. I beg you to remember that to delay may be to die. I beg you to believe that the United States seeks no special advantage . . . there must be no more delay in the setting up of an atomic control program. Already the atomic armament race has begun."

                (Address by Bernard Baruch, United States Representative to the Atomic Energy Commission, December 5, 1946, *Report by the President to the Congress,* Department of State publication 2735, report series 7, pp. 179–180.)

        b. The United Nations has failed to establish an international police force, thus forcing individual nations into an armament race, for

            (1) "The work expected of the military staff committee on the building up of the United Nations police force was unfortunately obstructed during the whole of last year and nothing was accomplished."

(Alexander Cadogan, "Disarmament and Security," *Annals of the American Academy*, July, 1947, pp. 88–89.)

2. The United Nations has allowed the growth of a "cold war" between the United States and Russia, for
   a. The "cold war" is a part of the vicious circle of fear, distrust, and insecurity that perpetuates competitive armaments, for
      (1) The declarations of a "cold war" have been so numerous that there is little point in a formal listing of them here. One of the chief outgrowths of this has been the proposal of universal military training in the United States.

II. A federal world government would avoid the inherent weaknesses of the United Nations confederation. (In this section we shall content ourselves with the logic behind federal world government. Since the proposition of world government has not been proposed to the world by any nation, it is impossible to state definitely that all of the nations will accept it. However, federal world government does offer the solution to the problems which all the nations face today. Therefore, logically, it should be adopted.) For

A. The institution of federal world government would bring a solution to the present poltical and military threats to world peace, for
   1. It would be capable of resolving present armed conflicts such as those in Greece, Palestine, and China, for
      a. Federal world government would establish an investigating committee, and
      b. An enforced truce would be effected, and
      c. Enforcement of the decisions of either the World Court or the Assembly would be necessary, and
      d. The prestige of a world organization with force behind it would in itself tend to prevent the outbreak of armed conflicts.
   2. It would guarantee the political integrity of all nations. (Unlike armed conflict, political coercion is not easy

to see. It is difficult, therefore, to set down procedures; instead, a general system of principles is necessary.) For

 a. Every nation should have the right of free election without fear of coercion from neighboring states, and

 b. No nation shall be forced into agreements against its will by a single nation by either economic, military, or political pressure.

B. The institution of federal world government would bring enforceable law into all fields of international affairs, for

 1. There would be no veto power in either the Assembly or the World Court, and

 2. Majority decisions would tend to produce a greater long-range consistency in reaching international decisions, for

  a. In the present system, under the United Nations, a change of policy of a single major nation can completely alter the course of the United Nations action, and

  b. Under a world government a change of attitude on the part of many nations is necessary to alter the course of action, thus tending to produce long-range consistency.

C. The establishment of a federal world government would tend to lessen those strains which lead to war, for

 1. Under a system of federal world government the burden of security preparation would be taken off the individual nation, for

  a. The federal world government would establish control of atomic energy as recommended by the United Nations Atomic Energy Commission, and

  b. The federal world government would set up an international police force sufficiently powerful to enforce decisions on any nation.

 2. The federal world government would alleviate the "cold war" between the United States and Russia, for

a. It would bring the conflict out into the open and allow frank appraisal of the factors in the tension, and

b. World-government control of atomic energy would guarantee to all nations that they need not arm for individual security.

III. The plan of federal world government is the most desirable framework for international relations, for

A. All other attempts at maintaining permanent peace in the past have failed, for

1. Attempts to create permanent peace by conquest have failed in every instance, for

a. The peace of Rome lasted for three hundred revolution-racked years and finally disintegrated, and

b. Ghenghis Khan's attempt to wipe out all opposition by conquering the world ended in the total destruction of his plans and the continuance of war, and

c. Adolph Hitler's failure to subdue conquered nations or the world is another example of conquest failing to bring permanent peace.

2. Attempts to bring permanent peace by power alliances has failed in every instance, for

a. The Holy Alliance of Austria, Russia, and Prussia failed to maintain peace either between the members of the alliance or in Europe. (Hall and Davis, *The Course of Europe Since Waterloo*, p. 27.) And

b. The Quadruple Alliance of England, Prussia, Russia, and Austria, which, upon the entrance of France, became the Quintuple Alliance to guarantee territorial integrity for Europe, failed to keep the peace. (*Ibid.*, p. 29.) And

c. Alliances before the First World War, such as the Franco-British and Franco-Italian alliances, failed to prevent the growing armament race which led to the Second World War. (*Ibid.*, Chap. 27.)

3. Attempts to bring permanent peace by confederate organizations have always failed, for

a. The confederation of the Congress of Vienna failed

to maintain either the status quo or the peace of Europe. (*Ibid.,* p. 29.) And

    b. The League of Nations failed to maintain security for the nations and prevent armament races, and thus by its inaction brought on the Second World War. (*Ibid.,* p. 658.) And

    c. The United Nations, as was pointed out above, is failing today to bring about peace.

B. The federal type of government has always been used to resolve intergroup conflicts and has thus far had the best record in this field, for

    1. In the consolidation of the German states the power of any one of the small states to veto action of the confederation of Germany brought strife and ultimately federation as the solution to the problem. The German state has had relative internal peace since then. (*Ibid.,* p. 187.) And

    2. In the Italian states strife and war were rampant until the unification of the Italian duchies into the federation of Italy. (*Ibid.,* pp. 180–182.) And

    3. In the United States the many faults of the Articles of Confederation were remedied and the situation was improved by the adoption of federal powers in the national government. (Commager and Morrison, *The Growth of the American Republic,* Vol. 1, pp. 350–370.)

C. World federation would solve international problems constructively, for

    1. Resources, energy, and time formerly devoted to war will be channeled into the paths of peace, and

    2. The federal world government can be kept democratic by a system of checks and balances similar to those of the United States, for

        a. The limited field of the federal government's jurisdiction in questions of aggression, armament control, and international relief would simplify the problem of limiting the powers of the federal government, and

b. The existence of widely differing groups would provide the element of active opposition to any steps toward dictatorship.

3. The present frictions between nations could be overcome to bring those nations together in a world government, for

a. The overwhelming desire of the peoples of the world for peace would be a powerful factor in forcing the national governments to consider world government, for

(1) Public-opinion surveys show the following percentages of people to be in favor of world government:

U.S.	56%
Holland	44%
Sweden	47%

and in addition in Canada and England over 50% of the people have shown their willingness and desire to turn over the atomic bomb to a world government.

(Gallup Poll, December 23, 1947.)

b. The increased economic dependency of devastated nations upon international trade would be a further stimulus to the acceptance of a trade-stimulating world government, for

(1) "The Soviet Union considers it imperative to the welfare of the peoples of the world that free world trade be immediately resumed and that reconstruction of devastated areas be carried on without delay. At the same time the general disarmament of the world is essential in order to reduce military budgets without which it is impossible to lighten the burdens of taxation borne by the people, who will be unable to carry this load for long without complaint."

(Speech by V. M. Molotov at the United Nations General Assembly, Nov.–Dec., 1946, Publication of the Embassy of the Soviet Union, pp. 4, 10, 15.)

CONCLUSION

Because

1. The present system of international affairs under the United Nations is not satisfactory;
2. A federal world government would avoid the inherent weaknesses of the United Nations confederation;
3. The plan of federal world government is the most desirable framework for international relations;

therefore, a federal world government should be established.

A SPEECH

MAKE OUR COMMITTEES
REPRESENTATIVE *

Senator Paul Douglas (D., Ill.)

MR. DOUGLAS. . . . I find two main faults with the present
method of selection and composition of the policy committee and
the steering committee. First, the members are appointed by the
leader; they are selected by the caucus. Second, if we analyze
their composition we find that they do not adequately represent
or even make any approach toward proportional representation
of the industrial areas of the country or, indeed, of the Pacific
coast. A part of this trouble is brought about by the seniority rule
which we have adopted. However, whatever the reasons, the results are very unfortunate. If Senators will pardon me, I should
like to give them figures on this question which I had assembled
a long time ago and which I tried to bring up to date this morning after I received a copy of the Senator's prepared remarks. Let
us take the policy committee, which consists of nine members. It
consists of one member from Texas, two from Montana, one from
Missouri, one from Oklahoma, one from Georgia, one from Ala-

* 86th Congress, First Session. *Congressional Record*, March 9, 1959, pp.
3195–3199.

bama, one from Arizona, and one from Rhode Island. There are nine members from eight States. I find that the population of those States amounts to approximately 22 million—22.5 million, to be precise—and that they represent only 80 electoral votes; that in terms of the total votes cast in those States for President in 1956, there were only 6,762,000.

Now let us take the main industrial States which are not represented on the policy committee. These are States which have Democratic Senators but which are not represented on the policy committee. They have no representation whatever on the policy committee: Maine, Massachusetts, Connecticut, New Jersey, Pennsylvania, West Virginia, Ohio, Michigan, Indiana, Illinois, Wisconsin, Minnesota, California, Oregon, and Washington. If we look at that list and look at the figures, we find that these States have a total population of 68 million, and 255 electoral votes; that in the last presidential election they cast 35,118,000 votes. . . .

If one examines the list—and this holds good for the steering committee also—he will find that the New England States are completely excluded, except for Rhode Island; that the Middle Atlantic States are excluded; that what the census calls the East North Central States are excluded even if we include West Virginia, which is becoming a Middle Western State rather than a Southern State; and that the Pacific Coast States are excluded.

The representation is composed chiefly of Senators from the South and from the small Mountain States. We love these fellows very much; but I point out that the economic interests and beliefs of these sections of the country differ. The States which are excluded are primarily manufacturing States. To the degree that they are agricultural States, they are corn-producing States.

The States which are included are the cotton and the tobacco-producing States and the mining States.

I suppose our greatest cleavage comes over the question of what is loosely known as civil rights. The policy committee, and, indeed, the steering committee are composed primarily of Senators from States where the attitude toward what is called civil rights is unfavorable, or from Mountain States where the issue is not a present one and is not an immediate one in the localities, whereas, the States which are not represented are those which have a considerable Negro population and which therefore feel this as a national issue more acutely than do the others. So the industrial States are on the outside, looking in. . . .

Now let me consider the membership of the steering committee. It has 13 members. One comes from Texas; one comes from Montana; one comes from Virginia; one comes from Arkansas; one comes from Louisiana; one comes from Florida; one comes from South Carolina; one comes from Delaware; one comes from Nevada; one comes from New Mexico; one comes from Rhode Island; one comes from Minnesota. Six members come from the South; three come from the Mountain States; five come from States with a population of less than 1 million. But I observe that the big States are not represented; there is no member from Massachusetts or from Connecticut or from New Jersey or from Pennsylvania or from West Virginia or from Ohio or from Indiana or from Michigan or from Illinois or from Wisconsin or from California. In other words, when the kissing takes place, somehow the Senators from those States are never under the mistletoe. (Laughter.)

Now, let me go to the next point, namely, the distribution of chairmanships in the 16 standing committees, which can be found in the Congressional Record.

Of the 16 standing committees, Members of the Senate from the South hold the chairmanships of 10. They include the most important ones, namely, the Foreign Relations Committee, the Finance Committee, the Agriculture and Forestry Committee, the Banking and Currency Committee, the Armed Services Committee.

Senators from the Mountain States hold four chairmanships.

A Senator from the Pacific coast holds one chairmanship.

A Senator from Missouri, which is part South, part North, part East, and part West, holds one chairmanship.

But once again, no one from Massachusetts, Connecticut, New Jersey, Pennsylvania, Ohio, West Virginia, Indiana, Illinois, Michigan, Wisconsin, Minnesota, or California.

Now, I know that this situation grows out of the seniority system, but I want to suggest that the pure and unadulterated seniority system is getting our party into trouble. The States which run the Democratic Party in the Senate are not the States which can carry a presidential election. The presidential elections are decided in the States which are on the outside looking in, so far as the organization of the Senate is concerned. And, indeed, it has been the election of Senators from these large industrial States which has given us the balance of power—not merely the balance of power, but the preponderance of the power in the Senate itself as well as in the House.

We carried the House, and largely carried the Senate, because those of us who come from the industrial States advanced, generally, a declaration in favor of civil rights, a declaration in favor of liberal tax policy, a declaration to protect consumers of gas and oil, a declaration for liberal labor legislation, and so forth.

The voters, believing what we have advocated will happen, elect us to the Senate and to the House, and, in times past, have elected a President. Then we come to Washington and find that the machinery of the Senate, under the seniority system, is controlled by those who represent localities where the predominant opinion is very different from ours.

Very frankly, we go through a process of frustration. Not only do we go through a process of frustration, but the folks back home somehow feel they have been shortchanged.

I am perfectly frank to say I do not know how long the Democratic Party can continue with this situation. We know it exists. I submit we should do something about it. One way we can do something about it is to make our governing bodies, whether they be the conference, the policy committee, or the steering committee, truly representative.

I am not afraid of getting together with our good friends from the South. I am not afraid of getting together with them in conference. I am not afraid of getting together with them in committee. I have great respect for them as individuals. I have great respect for their skill. I believe that they are patriotic Americans. I think we can probably get a better agreement if we meet face to face than if one group has the seats of power and the other group is on the outside looking in. . . .

INDEX